CW01511106

1100
(5)136

ILLUSION SHOW

David Bamberg in 1965.

ILLUSION SHOW
A Life in Magic

DAVID BAMBERG

Introduction by Robert Parrish
Foreword by Robert Bamberg

**FROM THE ARCHIVES OF
THE AMERICAN MUSEUM OF MAGIC**

David Meyer ✳ Magic Books
Glenwood, Illinois

ISBN 0-916638-48-0 [Hardcover]

Library of Congress Cataloging-in-Publication Data

Bamberg, David, 1904-1974.
   Illusion show : a life in magic / David Bamberg : edited by Robert
Parrish.
     p. cm.
   "From the Archives of the American Museum of Magic."
   Bibliography: p.
   Includes index.
   ISBN 0-916638-36-7
   1. Bamberg, David, 1904-1974. 2. Magicians--Biography.
I. Parrish, Robert. II. American Museum of Magic. Archives.
III. Title.
GV1545.B33A3 1988
793.8'092'4--dc19
[B]   88-4247
                                                  CIP

Meyerbooks, *Publisher*
P. O. Box 427
Glenwood, Illinois 60425

TABLE OF CONTENTS

ILLUSTRATIONS

INTRODUCTION

The full-evening illusion shows which toured the world before and between the World Wars were a remarkable theatrical phenomenon. Technically, illusion shows are magical performances featuring spectacular theatrical effects involving the seeming appearance, disappearance, transformation, levitation and, quite often, the dismemberment of human beings. Illusion shows, like circuses, provide a universal form of blissfully simple but emotionally satisfying entertainment. They border on the edge of human capability, seeming to transcend the possible.

The big magic shows, with their tons of equipment and extensive menageries, were headed by exceptional showmen who made, and often lost, fortunes and who in numerous cases played for decades with essentially the same show—long runs exceeding those of any Broadway attraction.

David Tobias Bamberg was a major figure in this theatrical era and in the history of his theatrical specialty. No other great illusionist could match his conjuring background. He represented the sixth (or possibly the seventh) generation of the Bamberg dynasty of magicians, a Dutch family that spanned the full development of modern conjuring in the Western world. His father, Theodore Bamberg, who worked under the stage name Okito, headlined in European variety and was recognized as one of the most artistic performers in his field. As a boy, David traveled with his father on the Howard Thurston show and became acquainted with Houdini and other leading American magicians of the first quarter of the century. He also worked with Zancig, the most famous stage mind reader of the day. While still a teenager, he found himself at loose ends in London, where much of his time was spent at the Maskelyne family's magic theatre, St. George's Hall. There he watched some of the greatest and most original magicians of England and Europe and observed the remarkable stage illusions and magical sketches they presented. Quite naturally, he never doubted that he would be a professional magician, heading a full-evening show of amazing illusions.

David incorporated many of these ingredients from his youthful experience into his own show and added elements that were new to the illusion show tradition. These included lavish production, dramatic continuity, and wit. A magic trick is essentially a joke, a pun upon appearances. In his later shows, David exploited this aspect of magic, keeping the audience in constant laughter as well as amazement.

In 1937, when David brought his show briefly to the United States, John Mulholland, an authority on the history of magic and editor of the leading American magic journal, *The Sphinx,* wrote: "Fu Manchu (David Bamberg) has been giving his show in New York. Jack Gwynne, as an illusionist, Dai Vernon, as a sleight of hand performer, and Dr. (Milton) Bridges, as a particularly well informed amateur, have each said that it is the most beautiful show of magic that they had ever seen. These three names are mentioned merely as representing the opinion of various groups of magicians. Everyone who has seen the show raves about how good it is. To me, the whole show was the realization of the dream of what a magic show should be. . . . For the first time in my life, I have seen magicians so impressed that they talk only about the beauty and skill of the presentation, instead of the mechanics of the tricks. In case you ever hear of anyone who doubts that magic is an art, send him to see David Bamberg."

David Bamberg is also remarkable for having left a written account of the now vanished way of life of the itinerant showman. Few magicians—few showmen, for that matter—have left such a record. A number are represented by published autobiographies, although seldom of their actual authorship. Clay Hamilton Shevlin's bibliography, *Historian's Guide to Conjuring,* lists seventeen autobiographical works in the English language, five of which are by (or written for) major conjurers of the present century: David Devant, Horace Goldin, Carl Hertz, Jasper Maskelyne, and Howard Thurston. For all their interest to the student of magic, these books are not very revealing about their subjects and are primarily anecdotal.

The autobiography of David Bamberg differs from this literature. It is written by a man who was gifted with a sense of himself as well as a dedication to his craft. He recognized the double nature of the performer. "Like all budding actors," he wrote, "my secret goal was to be myself and yet somebody else, and so be loved and admired." His book provides a remarkably human account of a life devoted to illusion.

In many theatrical memoirs, once the early struggles have been recounted, the theatrical personage takes over. After the first great success, very little of interest takes place. This was not true in the life of David Bamberg. Success only complicated his life, and the rigors of touring with a road show in South and Central America remained various and inexhaustible.

David's account of his life resisted getting into print for over two decades. He finished his first draft on February 28, 1965. Actually, the draft consisted of two books: the autobiography and a technical treatise on the magic of the Bambergs. The latter was purchased by Dr. Robert Albo, whose unrivaled collection of magical apparatus includes many pieces crafted by Okito. With the aid of the English magician and author, Eric Lewis, this material was reworked, resulting in the 1973 publication, *Oriental Magic of the Bambergs* by Robert Albo, Eric Lewis, and David Bamberg.

The manuscript of the autobiography was sent to David's son, Robert Bamberg, to John Mulholland, to Robert Lund, journalist and curator of the American Museum of Magic in Marshall, Michigan, and very likely to others whom David hoped might assist in readying the work for publication and in finding a publisher. When Dr. Albo decided in 1968 to publish a Bamberg book, Lund was asked to send him the draft, which in 1972 was given to Eric Lewis to assist in his work on the Albo publication. A xerox copy of the original manuscript was provided for the Lund archives.

One of the reasons the autobiography has not found a commercial publisher is, of course, that David Bamberg is unknown to the English speaking world except in magical circles. His show, with brief exceptions, was never seen outside of Spain, Portugal, and Latin America, a vast field, as he has pointed out, comprising twenty-two nations all speaking the same language with the exception of Portugal and Brazil. He chose to write his book, however, in English.

His theatrical visibility was not improved through choice of a stage name that could not be used in countries where the proprietary rights of Sax Rohmer, author and creator of the Mysterious Dr. Fu Manchu, prevailed. Rohmer, incidentally, was a member of the Magicians' Club of London.

There is also a problem concerning the audience for whom the book is intended. At its inception, David apparently had a popular audience in mind. The first chapters are shaped to capture interest and entertain. Then something happens. The focus changes. The style relaxes.

What seems to have happened is that David found he was not interested in writing a popular romance. He wanted to write an account of his life for those who could understand it. This audience was essentially that of fellow conjurers and students of conjuring history. With this audience, the names of performers past and present would be recognized, tricks would be known by their trade names, and technical aspects of the craft could be discussed openly. To those who do not share this curious knowledge, such references are puzzling or meaningless.

Another problem that must be acknowledged lies in the author's prose style. It is flowing, conversational, and speaks in an authentic voice. It is also rather primitive from the standpoint of the college composition class, characterized by a series of independent clauses linked by conjunctions. Yet the rhythm is perfect. These words are written by a man who not only writes as he speaks, but who is a master of oral presentation. The personality which delighted theatre audiences captivates the reader as well. This is an accomplishment with which a prudent editor hesitates to tamper.

In spite of his basic candor, discretion inhibited David from dealing with the romantic, even gothic, dimensions of his life story. He found in Bob Lund a receptive correspondent to whom he could communicate about a life experience which he knew to be remarkable. A passage in a letter to Lund quoted in the notes to this book begins, "It is strange that you should ask me about Khelmis. No one ever did. . . . There have been seven women, all of different nationalities, that have greatly influenced my life and I theirs. Khelmis, half Andalusian and half Egyptian, was number four." He shaped her from rude beginnings into the central figure of his show. She was difficult and fearless. In Madrid she left him for more dangerous and, perhaps, glamorous adventures. Years later she turned up in his audience in Buenos Aires. They met again. She had become a sophisticated European woman. They no longer had anything in common. It was possibly the most dramatic episode in his life and he sketched it so briefly in the final chapter of his autobiography that it almost escapes notice.

David had serious reservations about what he had written. In a a letter to me dated April 10, 1966 he said, "I think there will be a spot of trouble as far as editing goes...it's not too good a job. It may be all right for magicians as a story of my adventures but it is a long way from a book...for the general public. I can't edit it myself. In fact, I really can't write properly. That is, not up to an author's standards. My syntax, punctuation, spelling, etc. are disastrous. I have no illusions. I know this. The only thing I have in my favor is style and the ability to tell a good story. Perhaps that is the most important thing of all. However, my book would never be up to the standard of the book you edited for my father." At the same time, as he wrote to Robert Lund, he had no desire to have something ghost written. He wanted to speak in his own voice, and he did. I think the result is the most engaging and illuminating document of its kind produced by a professional magician in the twentieth century.

My first involvement in Bamberg matters began when I met David's father, the celebrated Okito, in 1947. During his residence in Chicago, we became well acquainted and I wrote a book for him, *Okito on Magic,* which was published in 1952. In 1960 while in Europe, I visited Okito's son Donald, an insurance executive in The Hague, and his daughter Dorothy Meier, the wife of a Zurich physician. Both received me with cordial surprise. They had not seen their father since the beginning of World War II but were in correspondence with him. "Is he still so precise?" they both asked. I said he was probably the most orderly man I had ever known and that this undoubtedly contributed to his perfection as an artist, to which they agreed. Dorothy asked whether I knew David. I did not. "He is the genius in the family," she said.

At Theo Bamberg's death in 1963, only a month before his eighty-eighth birthday, I was named a co-executor of his estate. In this capacity I engaged in some correspondence with David and learned with interest that he was writing a book.

"You were the one who put the bee in my bonnet to start a book," he wrote to Bob Lund. He also made it clear that the manuscript was destined for Lund's museum.

In April of 1966, the book was in the hands of John Mulholland (who later told me he didn't know quite *what* to do with it) and David was concluding a three month run in the Lyceum Theatre, his last engagement with a full-evening show: "That makes 29 seasons in Buenos Aires," he wrote.

"Hold (onto) your hat," he continued in his letter to me. "I'm opening a Magic Center in Buenos Aires. I have made arrangements with a partner (a local businessman who is the owner of the largest hardware store in town) and we will open this store in a few weeks. It will be a combined store for the sale of magic, novelties and jokes, a school of magic and a small theatre dedicated exclusively to magical productions. I have had no experience in this sort of thing but as there is practically no competition to speak of in this city I have every hope that the business will be successful. The trouble is that all the tricks we sell will have to be manufactured here as the import duties are frightfully high. So the store will have a small workshop in the back for the sole purpose of making and producing tricks of a more or less medium quality. I have not the mechanical ability of my father who was a great craftsman, but for the manufacture of fairly good grade magical stuff I think I can manage. So let's see what happens."

This shop became the center of his life. In April of 1968, he wrote to Lund: "No, Bob, I haven't given up the theatre entirely. I do a season now and then but I don't have the energy for the old grind. Those two shows a day take it out of you, especially when you have a fast running show like mine. I just don't have the pep anymore. After all, I had over forty years of it. That's enough for anyone.

"And in this venture (the Centro Magico) I am still in magic and show business. I have the store, the school, the shop and the theatre. It's not a large theatre but it is complete. Has twelve colored spots, a nice stage and every convenience for magicians. Stereophonic sound, a bar, a ladies' corner, tables and chairs. The walls are covered with life size paintings of famous magicians in action. It is, I believe, the only magic theatre in Latin America. It is exclusively for magicians. The local clubs are already coming over and using it as their meeting place. All visiting magicians are welcome to make it their home here in Buenos Aires and can have their mail addressed here if they wish." The magicians portrayed in the wall paintings by Horacio Ramon Romero (who adopted the name, Yukito) were Robert-Houdin, de Kolta, Kellar, Thurston, Goldin, Dante, Houdini, Okito, Chang, and Fu Manchu.

In March of 1972 he wrote to Lund: "I had a ten-day stint in the hospital. The cigarettes finally caught up with me and I had a spell of oxygen. The only thing I needed was an astronaut suit. I've shaken the habit (I hope) and I feel much better.

"Thanks for the tip about the British magazine. I had no idea I was famous. It's a strange thing but since I left the theatre the publicity has been pouring in. I must have had thousands of dollars in articles...TV, newspapers, radio, etc. I don't ask for it but they come and hand it to me. I blush to say I am kind of a legend here in Latin America. But it gets me down when some old white haired bastard staggers in and tells me he remembers seeing my show when he was a kid. And the fables that have been invented, you just wouldn't believe. They tell me these things with a straight face, but don't actually lie, they believe it."

During these years, David was recognized by Argentine television with three major productions in which he was interviewed and leading magicians performed in his honor.

Alberto Vergonjeanne E. Hijo, known professionally as Vernet, in an article in the December 1974 issue of the magic journal, *The New Tops,* described David's typical day, beginning with a walk to the cafe at the intersection of Rio Bamba and Bartolome Mitre streets. There he sat facing north in a position from which he could see his shop and read an English newspaper or magazine while sipping his coffee and milk. Once inside Fu Manchu's Magic Center, he sat alone at a green-clothed table, leaning on his elbows, waiting for someone to come in.

While playing a date in Buenos Aires, Neil Foster, a leading American sleight of hand artist and editor of *The New Tops,* visited David in his shop in July of 1974. Although they had corresponded for many years, this was their first meeting. "When I told him my name, he was so surprised that we embraced as long lost brothers," Foster wrote. "From that moment on he seemed to sparkle as we reminisced and laughed...." Before Foster left Argentina, he was honored at a special banquet of the several magic clubs of Buenos Aires, arranged by David.

David Bamberg died on August 19, 1974 at the age of seventy. In a ceremony widely used among magical organizations, Fu Manchu's magic wand was broken at a memorial service attended by members of the Argentine Society of Magicians.

The magical influence of the Bambergs continues. In 1937 when the Fu Manchu show first played Cuba, a young boy named Cesareo Pelaez was taken to see the magic at the Teatro de la Caridad in Santa Clara. He recalled the experience as "like being in love." The spell never wore off. In the late 1940s he saw the show again in Santa Clara and in Havana and met David. Later Cesareo came to the United States to work as an educator. Already a skilled conjurer, he developed a circle of friends, including artists, actors and business people, and shared with them his concept of building a spectacular magic show in the Bamberg tradition. Forming a corporation, they bought and refurbished a theatre in Beverly, Massachusetts and opened on February 20, 1977 for weekend performances of "Le Grand David and his own Spectacular Magic Company."

Le Grand David is David Bull, who learned his magic from Cesareo. David and Cesareo (as Marco the Magi) share the stage with Seth Bartlett, the son of a partner in the enterprise, who began his career as Seth the Sensational at the age of four. Backed by a troupe of sixty performers and production assistants, they have developed a spectacular revue that springs from Cesareo's memories of the Fu Manchu show, an opulent blend of musical comedy, vaudeville, pantomime, and illusion show. In their first ten years the group has entertained half a million people in over 1,000 performances. At each show, Marco spreads his arms beneath two painted dragons, saying, "I first saw this curtain when I was five years old and my father took me to see Fu Manchu."

Publication of David Bamberg's autobiographical manuscript in this form is made possible through the permission of Professor Robert D. Bamberg, David's son, who edited the first draft. Subsequent editorial assistance has been rendered by David Meyer and Irene Richardson. I have taken final editorial responsibility and provided notes in the hope of making the text comprehensible to readers without a background in stage magic and its history.

With one exception, no major surgery has been performed on the text. The exception is Chapter 4, which is condensed from an imaginary dialogue between David's mother and grandfather.

Thanks are due to Robert Lund for making available his file of letters from David Bamberg and providing photographs, posters and other documentary materials. Cesareo Pelaez generously provided photographs of the Fu Manchu show in performance and other rare photographs. James B. Alfredson, Edwin A. Dawes, Neil Foster, Eric Lewis, John McKinven, Jay Marshall, Enrique Jimenez Martinez, and Robert Olson have been helpful in tracking down elusive information.

This publication recognizes the special contribution of the American Museum of Magic in preserving magical documents and memorabilia. It is to be hoped that many subsequent publications may develop from the Museum's extraordinary resources.

Robert Parrish

FOREWORD

A Letter from Robert Bamberg

Dear Mr. Parrish:

Thank you very much for sending me the Introduction you wrote for my father's book. It was fun to read and called forth many memories.

I agree with you that David Bamberg was a natural writer, despite frequent protestations that he lacked education or a knowledge of grammar. He wrote as he spoke and his pleasure with language was infectious. Although you note how humorous he could be in his show what many people do not know was that he improvised continually on stage by playing with words and ideas. I remember spending most of my time backstage in 1948 when I visited him in northern Brazil and how he kept the company in stitches during the whole course of the performance so that the laughter from behind the scenes seemed sometimes louder than the audience's. The members of the company told me that he was always hilarious and that one of the pleasures of working with the Fu Manchu show was listening to him improvise. He limited his improvisations to language and not to the illusions themselves, although he was very flexible in shifting illusions about. He accepted criticism in all areas with ease and good humor. I don't believe he gave himself sufficient credit for this verbal facility because of the need to compare himself to his father, who of course was a perfectionist who never spoke during his own performances.

One should not believe his protestations of lack of general literacy. True, he never got beyond grammer school but he was a good reader of fiction and during the months in 1964 and 1965 when he was writing over 800 pages of manuscript, some of which you are now publishing, he read widely and voraciously. He and his father loved the Sherlock Holmes stories, but he also wrote to me about his admiration for Robert Penn

Warren's *All the King's Men,* Katherine Anne Porter's *Ship of Fools,* and William L. Gresham's *Nightmare Alley,* which he thought was the best thing of its kind that he had read. He did not like Mary McCarthy, Ian Fleming, or anyone who smacked to him of pomposity. As he was writing his own book, he wrote to me in 1965: "I spend more time with Strunk, Alan Warner, the Thesaurus, and the dictionary than at the typewriter. But I love it and I wish I had learned to be a writer in my youth. I think I'd have made a good one." He was proud of his writing ability and wrote the scripts for his show, movie scenarios, radio programs, and what not.

When he began this book, he vacillated between writing a novel and an autobiography of his life as a magician. When he asked me to help out with the book, he broke down the possibilities as follows: "(1) a novel using fictitious characters altho' sticking to historical facts; (2) a combined biography and autobiography with no holds barred; (3) ditto but toned down and re-touched; (4) forget the whole goddamned thing; (5) the Okito and Fu saga; (6) the whole seven generations saga with a lot of fiction for the first four generations; (7) make it an eight generation thing—although your bit would be non-magical but highly interesting just the same. It would give the end-product of seven generations of semi-lunatics." (I know that some have wondered why I myself did not become a magician, too, but I believe that some of my interest in words and language stemmed from the pleasure I used to take in reading my father's letters and essentially "hearing" his voice as I read his vivid descriptions of events and moods.)

Through the 1940s and 50s he worked on the scripts for at least six motion pictures, three television productions, various radio programs, and at least six theatrical "spectaculars." I am not sure how many he wrote, but he certainly kept busy writing. Soon after his father's death, he began to write, in his letters to me, about his family, and to express his feelings of mixed professional admiration and personal dissatisfaction with his father. In 1963 he brought up the question of my writing a history of the Bamberg family, but then agreed with me that information about them was too sparse. (David Bamberg had but one letter from his grandfather, written in Dutch and describing his own show.) In June 1964, he decided to write a series of lectures or small books on magic which would include "showmanship, stagecraft, big illusions, small magic, sleight of hand, card tricks, my magical plays, pictures, and sketches. Some of the material is unique and there are a lot of professional secrets that are almost too good to divulge. But when my father died and took with him a number of really great magical secrets I realized that it would be stupid not to pass things on." He asked me to help him do it and appealed to the fact that I could then adopt the mantle of the eighth generation.

There is one part of this scheme which I haven't decided on yet but could lead to something bigger. That is the life story of a magician. This would or could be in novel form and would explain no secrets but make an interesting story for anyone. This could be published as a book without getting the Ethics-boys on our necks. Any reference to an illusion or trick in this book would be covered by a separate volume explaining the technique and sold only to magicians.

The idea of the novel form appealed to him because, as he put it, "I am one of those guys who cannot tell the whole truth. I have to embroider it...maybe it's the showman in me...and I could say things about Man Chu Fu that I couldn't say about Fu Manchu." There were things about himself and his family that he didn't want to say except indirectly, and his letters to me in 1964 and 1965 have a confessional quality about them that is quite moving. This was especially so twenty years ago because I was in the midst of attempting to reconstruct my own youth and my feelings toward my father, feelings not too far removed from what he felt toward his own father.

So what do we do, Mate? Do we make it strong and tell the truth or gloss over the facts so as not to hurt people?

By fall of 1964 he was writing at a rapid pace, tearing up material, trying to express what he himself was having trouble understanding. When he began sending me the manuscript, I realized that it would be a mistake to tamper with the style and I felt that the materials about magic itself were extraordinarily interesting but (to quote from my letter to him): "the work reads literally like 'a life in magic.' You hardly distinguished between your profession, magic, and your personal life." He had by then decided not to attempt a novel but to gloss over some unpleasant matters. He had lost interest in the Bamberg Dynasty ("Entre nous, I think they were a dull lot") and joked about the pretensions to nobility, court appearances in Holland, and "all the medals." In his many letters of that period he reverted more and more to stories about his own youth, his rivalry with Okito, and his frequent disdain towards his father's behavior. Although he claimed that the book was a "confession,"—"I should have written it lying on a couch"—it was clear to me that it was a somewhat coded one. Just one minor instance, for example, is a reference to his father in a letter to me: "Okito was a hundred times worse than I picture him. He was a selfish, sarcastic, trouble making man. Ask your mother." As to the book as a whole:

> My book is not completely honest. There are a lot of half truths in it. If I told the exact truth about everything I would be accused of being a nasty back-biting son of a bitch. You spotted the real truth in the book...the magic...which is all true and even underplayed.

> Believe me when I say that this goddamned book is the hardest thing I ever undertook to do.... Maybe I better throw the whole thing in the ashcan and the hell with it. But I know I won't and I'll go on with it because I have that streak in me to finish everything I set out to do.

He mentioned sending it to Orson Welles or John Mulholland to write a preface, hinted at the difficulties which he would face publishing a manuscript of 800 pages, and talked abut the future of magic. After an exchange of fifty or so letters in 1964-65, we almost stopped corresponding although we remained on cordial terms. He had written his "confessions" and had helped in making sense out of my own "confessions." In some ways it was the closest I ever came to my father.

My mother, Hilda Seagle Bamberg, was born on March 6, 1896 in Alsace-Lorraine, and died on April 10, 1984 in New York City. She was an extraordinary woman whom my father always held in the highest respect. I am happy that neither of my parents ever really criticized the other to me despite the differences which led to their separation in 1935.

Writing this letter to you has brought back a flood of memories and pleasant recollections, and I am grateful to you for the interest you have taken in my father.

Sincerely yours,

Robert Bamberg

Kent, Ohio
January 27, 1987

ILLUSION SHOW

CHAPTER 1

In that easy going year of 1908, Tobias "Theo" Bamberg, professionally known as Okito, the Chinese magician, his wife Lillian, his four year old son David, and an assistant Erich Rach, without passports, formalities, income taxes or other headaches embarked on the S. S. Caronia at Southhampton and after an uneventful voyage arrived in the old New York of horsecars and gray-helmeted Irish cops.

Okito's six month tour of the Orpheum Circuit started in St. Paul, Minnesota, and the public of the new world were just as pleased with his pantomimic style of magic as the old world had been.

Two weeks later Okito opened at the Majestic Theatre (now the Shubert) in Chicago. Lily loved the big American hotels (so different from the cheerless artiste's digs in the English provinces) where she could safely leave David during the evening show. It was not good to have the little chap hanging about the theatre until the early hours of the morning and becoming a precocious "pro's" kid like the rest of them.

The hotel was a ten story building with a large fountain in the center of the foyer where the guests could loll around in easy chairs and pass the time of day. From any of the floors above, one could look over the iron railing and see the fountain with the loafers around it.

This particular morning there had been a spot of trouble. Erich Rach, Okito's young German assistant, had given David a big rubber ball for his birthday. In a wild moment, David had thrown the ball from the fifth floor into the fountain, thoroughly drenching the unhappy squatters.

This episode did little to endear David to the management of the hotel who took a rather dim view of the affair and politely

1

suggested other quarters where snotty little sods would be welcome.

Lily, with her usual charm, soothed the ruffled feelings of the management and promised that the ball would be removed from her son's store of secret weapons. However, the incident had its use as it indelibly impressed David's existence in the mind of the desk clerk.

That same night at about nine-thirty, the hotel caught fire. In the ensuing panic the desk clerk remembered the brat asleep on the fifth floor.

A fireman on a seemingly endless ladder smashed the window of David's room to find the indignant young gentleman sitting up in bed. There was a moment of lively discussion while the fireman yanked on David's trousers backwards, but David lost the argument and was hustled out through the window into the freezing night. It was so cold that the water from the hoses froze on the window frames, forming long icicles. The trip down the ladder was hair-raising and was followed by a wild ride to the stage door of the theatre where he was safely delivered into the outstretched arms of his mother who was wearing her bright green Chinese robe while the tears running down her face were ruining her make-up.

From that night on Lily refused to leave David alone and his presence in the theatre was justified by putting him into the act. He was taught to crouch in a leather harness under his father's robe and at a signal jump down to appear from an empty cloth. His one other duty was to hang a number of collapsible oriental dolls on hooks on a rack after his father had produced them from an empty canister filled with water. This, with the banging of some cymbals at the end of the act, was the full extent of David's artistic responsibilities.

If Okito had gained a new assistant in Chicago he lost another. One of the thick main electric cables of the Majestic Theatre had fused and melted and there was talk of having to put in a whole new cable until Erich, a trained electrician, cut away the burned parts and spliced the cable so neatly that the join was invisible. The chief electrician was so impressed that he offered Erich a steady job at twice the salary he was getting from Okito. Erich had been with Okito for many years and we hated to see him go and Okito never found anyone to replace him. Erich Rach later became chief electrician at the Chicago Opera House and ended up in the Radio City Music Hall in New York in charge of the marvelous and complicated lighting effects for their famous stage shows.

The rest of the tour was uneventful except for a funny episode that happened in St. Louis, Missouri. Okito did a fast production of four ducks in a metal bowl from an empty cloth.

One evening Lily was startled to see Okito skip his silk routine and go into a kind of whirling dervish dance and, grabbing the cloth from a table, produce the ducks in a tremendous hurry. After the show she found out what had happened. The release for the bowl was a net sewed around a metal ring two inches in diameter. This ring was held by tapes to the body harness. One of the ducks had gotten his head and neck through the ring in search of something edible.

This had been the cause of the dance routine and Lily nearly died when Theo explained and her laughter did nothing to soothe him. Worse was to come when the stage manager congratulated Okito on his new comedy number and advised him to keep it in the act. Okito was not amused and the next day the ring was changed for one smaller than any duck's neck.

And so the six months flew by and Okito was offered bookings on other circuits, although the policy was two or three shows a day. He had played all the "big time" one-a-day houses. He tried it for a short while but the work was very hard and he was not used to it.

With the money he had made in Europe and the American tour, Okito had a nice nest egg and he decided to return to New York and quit show business and try his luck in other ventures.

CHAPTER 2

Certain events stand out clearly in my childhood memories but there are long lapses of forgetfulness. I remember a sub-street level boarding house where we lived when we arrived in New York. It had large round windows, like the port holes of a ship, facing the street and one could see the legs of people walking by. I remember the day in 1909 when my Uncle Emile and his wife, Luisa, arrived from Holland with his lovely present of a mechanical train set. I believe that he was doing an act with his younger brother Edward, as the Nelusco Brothers.

Okito, in partnership with a man named Joe Klein, had opened a magic shop at 1193 Broadway, at the corner of 28th Street. The Bamberg Magic & Novelty Company was the sole representative for Carl and John Willmann, owners of the largest magical factory in Europe, at Hamburg. Besides the Willmann line Okito constructed exclusive magical apparatus of superior quality. Among his many satisfied customers were Harry Kellar, Frederick Eugene Powell, Bernard M.L. Ernst, Samuel Leo Horowitz and many other leading magicians of the U.S.A.

My father often took me to the magicians' clubs and banquets and I remember doing my first trick in public at the Ladies Night of the Society of American Magicians on October 9, 1909 where I did a card trick.

Then there was the unforgettable night in the old back-room theatre of Martinka's Magic Shop on Sixth Avenue. The trick I did employed a self-contained magical box beautifully constructed by my father. I asked for an assistant from the audience and the President of the S.A.M., Harry Houdini, volunteered. I venture to say that very few magicians ever had such a famous assistant.

4

With business going well Okito thought that he would have no further use for his act and he sold it, along with the name Okito, to William J. Nixon, a Brooklyn contractor. Part of the deal with Bill Nixon was to take over the flat he had rebuilt in First Street, Brooklyn. It was a weird bachelor's apartment with a sliding wall panel in the living room for a mysterious appearance to startle his guests. It also had a gimmicked chandelier over the dining room table that sprinkled water over the festive victims.

We lived for over a year in the First Street flat. My mother was very happy to be in one place for any length of time and I was sent to kindergarten. Nixon was doing the Chinese act under the name of Neek Suen with indifferent success for which he blamed Okito saying that the tricks were not suited to his personality. He had a point there as no magician can take over another man's show and make a success of it. Every successful magic show is geared to the personality of its creator.

In 1911, we moved to the upper flat of a two-story house on the corner of Beverley Road and Flatbush Avenue in Brooklyn. This building at 2131 Beverley Road had the imposing title of the Beverley Arms. Here memories begin to take on a more definite shape.

Business at the magic store wasn't any too good as Okito insisted on constructing a limited number of exclusive and expensive tricks for a small clientele much to Joe Klein's disgust, who wanted to mass produce small magical tricks in the American style. In order to increase his income Theo began giving private entertainments. In one of those engagements in a hotel he met an enthusiastic amateur magician, Walter Reuben, who persuaded Theo to return to vaudeville again, and backed him for the production of an entirely new Chinese magic act in which they both were to appear.

The act was called The Hanking Mysteries as Theo couldn't use the name of Okito without Nixon's permission. Reuben, whom we called Pop Robbin, was a hulking six footer who looked as Chinese as Rock Hudson.

The act was shown in a local hall very near to Erasmus Hall High School in Brooklyn and only lasted one night. Mrs. Reuben, a husky brunette, got stuck inside a Chinese tea-chest illusion and when Theo dramatically opened the door for the impressive production of an oriental beauty he found himself staring at the plump rear end of the lady. Some devilish impulse caused him to slap her bottom resoundingly and the outraged

5

woman burst the sides of the tea-chest getting out. The audience thought it was a great comedy bit but the Reubens thought otherwise and the show ended then and there.

After this debacle, Theo seemed to lose all interest in show business and was at loose ends, with fits of black depression. He had a vague urge to quit show business but he couldn't live without it, nor could he live with it. He blamed the poor business at the magic store on his partner, but the truth was that Theo was a very poor businessman. As a last effort to save the store, Klein talked Theo into taking a trip to Germany to scout around and see if he could find a line of cheap, quick-selling articles.

Theo spent a few weeks in Europe, visited his home in Amsterdam and saw his father for the last time. When he returned to New York he brought Willmann's hollow celluloid magic wand for the disappearance of a silk in a paper cone. This was a fast-selling article, and with some other novelties he had picked up, business improved.

But Theo's great love was the theatre and he rebelled at the unjust fact that it isn't always the greatest artiste who has the most success. People would say: "He is not a good magician but he is a great showman." Just what did they mean by a "showman?" It was that certain indefinable trait that Okito had never been fully able to understand.

On the one hand, there were the audacious, publicity minded men of whom Houdini was undoubtedly the king: men with forceful personalities, but, to be honest, not skillful magicians. Kellar, Thurston, Nicola, Carter, Raymond and Goldin all fell into this class. Not one of them, in the true sense of the word, was a great artiste. The shows they presented were high powered, flashy, and based on the greatest illusions ever invented and all these men made fortunes in magic.

Then there were the trained technicians, mostly shy, retiring men: Buatier de Kolta, Servais LeRoy, Percy Selbit, Oswald Williams, Paul Valadon, Owen Clark, Louis Nikola, J.N. Maskelyne and Okito. These men were the greatest magician-inventors in the history of magic, but most of them were financial failures compared to a Thurston or a Houdini.

One afternoon I came home from school to find my mother white with shock. "Your father's committed suicide!" she cried through her sobs. I was too young to understand but I felt that blind panic that a child can feel when he senses a crisis in the family. A neighbor took me to one side and said, "Your mother

6

is very upset, David. Your father has had an accident and you must be a good boy."

I have a vague, kaleidoscopic recollection of doctors, nurses, stomach pumps and white, drawn faces. What stands out most in my mind was my effort to help my mother by opening a can of peaches and cutting my thumb rather badly which made my mother carry on worse than ever.

I pieced the story together from what I heard of neighborhood gossip. My father was very keen on color photography and had been developing stereoscopic color plates, by the Richard process, in the bathroom. In the absolute darkness he had mistaken a glass of developing fluid for a glass of water and drank it.

In retrospect, this explanation doesn't convince me as I know he was far too methodical a man to make a mistake of this kind. Years later when I brought up the subject he flew into a rage and that indicated to me that the attempt had been deliberate; otherwise he would have had a plausible explanation.

During his convalescence I felt closer to him than ever before. He would sit up in bed, propped by a couple of pillows, and with the aid of a candle he taught me to do hand shadows on the bedroom wall. He had beautiful hands with a natural masculine grace and I would try to imitate him. "No, Dafe," he would say. "It's not goot. It all depends on the angle. More to the left. Yah! Yah! Dat's it." And his pale, intelligent face would light up with pleasure. I think I loved him more then than any other time in my life.

He would watch me as I set up my toy theatre and imagined myself as a great magician doing big stage illusions. In this contrived world of my own it was a short step into the fantasy world of magic. Like all budding actors, my secret goal was to be myself and yet somebody else, and so be loved and admired.

When he wasn't too tired he would tell me stories. They were always tales of magic and magicians who became real to me as Pop was a good actor and he painted living pictures that will always remain in my mind.

7

CHAPTER 3

Lillian Maud Poole and her elder brother, Charles, were the children of Charles William Poole, impresario of the Hippodrome Theatre, Winchester, Hampshire, England. It was here in the last years of the nineteenth century and the beginning of the twentieth that the famous Poole's Myriorama shows were presented for six months of the year. The other six months the shows traveled around the south of England; finishing with a London season at the Albert Hall, where they played in opposition to Maskelyne and Cooke at the Montgomery Hall.

It might be said that Poole's Myriorama was the granddaddy of today's cinerama. Poole's shows were based on a series of spectacular sketches which included "Peary at the Pole," "Clive's Conquest of India," "Gordon at Khartoum," and other vignettes of the pageantry of the British Empire.

Faced with the problem of innumerable scenic changes, Poole, who was a very capable stage director, solved the difficulty by use of huge rolled up backdrops which unwound on vertical poles and when combined with a magic lantern projector gave a dissolving-view effect. When Poole produced "War and Peace" he used this method to dissolve the "Road to Moscow" from summer to winter. Charles B. Cochran, the famous producer-impresario, was most impressed and said that the falling snow reminded him of one of those lovely glass paper-weights.

Old C.W. (as Poole was called behind his back) was also keen on magic effects and stage illusions. At various times he had presented Thaume, the living half woman whose body appeared to be cut off at the waist and rested on a swing. One of the best illusions presented at the Hippodrome by C.W. was the invention of a Liverpool civil engineer, one Henry Dircks, who knew nothing of magic but in 1870 invented an illusionary effect based on large sheets of glass, inclined at an angle, and placed on the stage between the actors and the spectators giving the illusion of living persons or ghosts floating in the air. A few years later a man named Pepper improved on the idea and presented it with great success as "Pepper's Ghost."

One of the most successful acts of Poole's, was the Serpentine Dance later to be known as the Fata Morgana. In this beautiful optical effect Lily wore a heavily pleated white silk dress with very wide and long sleeves, the ends of which were attached to round wooden sticks held in her hands. By waving the sleeves in all directions and gracefully twisting her body, the flowing silk created the impression of flowing water. The only illumination used was a magic lantern with two colour wheels that could be turned in either direction. The interplay of colour and design on the flowing silk was remarkably beautiful, and as Lily danced she also sang ballads in a sweet soprano voice. In 1902 this tall, striking, twenty-three-year-old redhead was one of the main attractions of the show.

At that time anything Japanese was the rage. Gilbert and Sullivan's "Mikado" and Sydney Jones' "Jewel of Asia" were at the height of their popularity, so C.W. decided that he needed something Japanese on the show. A London theatrical agent had offered him a Japanese conjurer who had been very successful in London with his trick of catching live goldfish in the air. This was just the thing C.W. was looking for and he engaged this oriental wonder worker, whose name was Okito, for two weeks.

C.W. was rather set back when Okito arrived in Winchester to discover that the Japanese was Dutch and his name was Tobias Bamberg and he had rearranged the word Tokio to form Okito. With a splendid wardrobe of genuine Japanese kimonos and a Samurai wig made by the famous Berlin wigmaker Anton, Okito had passed for a real Japanese.

C.W.'s misgivings were short-lived as Okito's debut was sensational. In a twenty-minute act, with only one blackfaced boy assistant, besides doing the Aerial Fishing trick, he also vanished a solid wooden wand wrapped in tissue paper which was torn into pieces and transformed into a bouquet of flowers. Silks vanished from his fingertips to appear perfectly dry from a glass of wine. From an empty cloth, a large bowl of water, another of fire, and a third bowl of ducks appeared. The water was poured into an empty canister from which a number of brightly dressed Japanese dolls appeared. A flower garden was produced from a paper cone. Several canaries were put into a paper bag which was inflated and burst, the birds reappearing in a cage hanging in the air. For a closing number he did shadowgraphs with his hands.

Okito's personality, his pantomimic showmanship combined with his graceful movements and the speed and cleanness of his work, made him an outstanding success. Off stage, his polite foreign ways, his charm and above all his broken English made him very popular with the people on the show. Being hard of hearing and with limited English, he sometimes gave rather outré answers to questions and this caused great amusement which endeared him to everyone.

He had a burning fervor for his work and was continually improving and inventing new effects. One of his few distractions was to stand between the wings during Miss Poole's Serpentine number. The rest of the company pulled his leg about it and even though he knew that Lily was engaged to be married on the 12th of May, he continued his vigil in the wings.

On the morning of Lily's wedding day C.W. was astounded by a new turn, not on the programme: The Great Vanishing Act. Okito had vanished silently into the night with all his props. This was a clear case of breach of contract and old C.W. would see to it that the blighter would blasted well pay through the nose once he got his hands on him.

Imagine C.W.'s horror when he discovered that Lily had also vanished—and on her wedding day. His blackest suspicions were confirmed when he received a telegram from Bristol informing him that his daughter was Mrs. Tobias Bamberg and asking for his paternal blessing.

She didn't get it.

In London the season of 1903 was unique in the "golden age" of magic. No less than seven world-famous magicians were appearing at the London Music Halls simultaneously. The marvelous American "King of Koins" Nelson Downs, was at the Empire. At the Hippodrome the combined illusionist and quick-change artiste, The Great Lafayette, was presenting his thrilling "Lions Bride" illusion. At the Oxford Palace the genial Belgian inventor-magician Servais LeRoy was levitating a woman in the air. Paul Valadon, a clever German manipulator was at the Egyptian Hall. At the Tivoli was a young and very original card manipulator who was to become America's leading illusionist, Howard Thurston. At the Palace, Horace Goldin, the

Royal Illusionist, was presenting lightning magic of sixty tricks in sixty minutes. And at the Alhambra was the Japanese wonder worker, Okito, with a new redheaded assistant who made him the envy of all the other magicians.

And so it was that Lily Poole stepped into the strange and mysterious world of magic.

After his London contracts Okito took his bride to Amsterdam to meet the family.

The Okito act in 1908. *Left to right:* **Unidentified assistant (possibly Erich Rach), Theo and Lillian Bamberg, and (*seated*) David.**

CHAPTER 4

Lily's first impression as they drove up to the old rambling house at Amstelveld 17 in old Amsterdam was of surprise at seeing the coat-of-arms of the Royal House of Orange over the door and to one side a discreet bronze plaque which read "Academie voor Magische Kunst" which Theo translated as "Academy of Magical Art," as he explained that his father was the official court conjurer to the royal family of Holland.

The Bambergs were an upper middle-class unorthodox Jewish family. "Papa" Bamberg, as he was affectionately known all over Holland, was a disciplinarian with his children; but to Lily he was a warm-hearted, kindly man who went out of his way to make her welcome. His wife, Julia, was a stout, easygoing soul who had very little to say, perhaps because she rarely got a word in edgewise in a household of six grown sons and a daughter, Eva, all of whom shouted excitedly at the same time.

Theo, the oldest of the brothers was, like his father, a full-fledged professional magician. Brother Emile was a good-natured young man who assisted his father and was a clever manipulator who gave magical soirees as a semi-professional. His first love, however, was music and he had graduated from the Holland Conservatory as a pianist. Edward, the youngest of the boys, also assisted his father and later became a professional magician in the United States under the name of Ed Rickard. The only one of the remaining brothers to show any interest in the theatre was Jack, a fairly good tenor who had decided on an operatic career. When he discovered that Lily was a soprano, he insisted on operatic duets at all hours of the day and night. The two remaining brothers, Neddy and Simon, were interested in diamond cutting and polishing and worked together with their cousins on the Diamond Exchange in

Amsterdam and Antwerp.

Life at the Bamberg home was far from dull, due in part to the rather gruesome sense of humor of the boys, as in the case of the celluloid collar which Theo had brought from England as a novelty and given to his favorite brother, Emile, who wore it proudly and gloated over the others until one of them put a lighted match to it while it was still around Emile's neck. The boys would go to no end of trouble for a laugh and one evening literally turned Jack's bedroom upside down by pulling up the furniture (upside down) to the ceiling with the aid of ropes and pulleys. When Jack came home, late as usual with one-over-the-eight under his belt, and staggered into his bedroom, he nearly passed out with fright.

At the table, Papa and boys spoke mostly of magic in rapid-fire Dutch which hardly made the meals interesting for a young bride. The old lady spoke very little English and Lily's conversation with her consisted mostly of sympathetic smiles, head-shakings and pats on the hand.

The Bamberg family of magicians, of which Theo represented the sixth generation, can be traced back to the early eighteenth century. An almanac of 1831 printed in Utrecht contains a wood-cut of Eliaser Bamberg performing in a public square in Leyden, the city in which he was born in 1760. Below the picture is a poem in old Dutch which, freely translated, says:

Nothing can obscure the view quicker than a fast magician—
Hocus-Pocus—and with that the man of tricks is ready.
Unbelievable is the speed with which this art takes place.
And the proverb remains:
"He is blind who sees and sees not."
Many are clever in magic:
Such as Pinetti and Opré—
And still you can hear them call van Gussem by the name of St. Andre.
Bamberg's fame sounds yet in these days:
Father gave the art to his son.
At the market is shown the first of the Bambergs of this name and art.
But whatever you may admire,
It is only magic—nothing more.
Witchcraft it never was,
And bewitchment is what you see.

Both Pinetti and Opré, mentioned in the poem, were associated with Eliaser. Pinetti (Joseph Pinetti Willedall de Merci, 1750-1800) was the most celebrated conjurer of the latter half of the eighteenth century and one of the first to recognize the value of advertising for the theatre. His arrival in Berlin, dressed as a nobleman of the highest rank, his breast covered with chivalric orders and his magnificent coach drawn by four superb white horses, was the talk of the town. Frederick the Great was so annoyed that he commanded Pinetti to leave the city in twenty-four hours. He said that Berlin was not large enough to hold two reigning sovereigns—the King of Prussia and the King of Conjurers.

Eliaser did Pinetti's trick of having chosen cards rise from a silver box supported on the neck of a bottle. On the other hand, Pinetti copied Eliaser's mysterious transformation of frogs into fish in a bowl of clear water, then vanishing the fish and pouring the water into a glass pitcher.

Opré was a master mechanic and constructor of ingenious automata. He built Pinetti's famous "Le Bouquet Philosophique," a small orange tree beneath a glass bell which was sprinkled with magic liquid, causing the leaves to unfold and the flowers to blossom until, finally, the fruit appeared.

In his later years, Eliaser acquired a large collection of Opré automata. One of them was a wooden doll dressed as an acrobat and known as the "Vaulting Figure." Taken by the hand, it could be walked to the center of the stage, where its arms were raised to connect with a slack rope. The figure was then given a push, and after swinging back and forth a few times, proceeded to execute the most marvelous acrobatic stunts, pulling itself up to handstands, turning somersaults and imitating the entire repertoire of the most accomplished human gymnast.

After Eliaser's death in 1833, the figure was passed on to his son, David Leendert Bamberg (1786-1869), then to David's son Tobias Bamberg (1812-1870), who presented the little acrobat with Opré himself operating it from offstage at a wooden keyboard in the wings controlling the thirty-two threads that passed to the figure through the hollow rope. At the conclusion, Tobias always brought the inventor, then a very old man, onstage for bows and credit. In the end, the worn out figure was consigned to the Bamberg attic, where my father played with it as a boy.

Although Eliaser was the first known performer of magic in the Bamberg dynasty, there is evidence of a still earlier generation. In an old book, *Vader Simon Witgeest,* it is stated that Jasper

Bamberg, "alchemist and necromancer," who was born in the early eighteenth century, was Eliaser's father or adopted him. An incomplete sketch of Jasper's life indicates that he attended a discourse given by Cagliostro in The Hague in 1778. Jasper listened avidly to Cagliostro's theories of the philosopher's stone and spent the greater part of his life seeking a method to change the baser metals into gold. He also pretended to raise the ghosts of the dead by having clouds of smoke rise from a metal urn and causing images of the dead to appear in the smoke, probably utilizing the magic lantern described by Kircher in the middle of the seventeenth century.

Eliaser was thirty-three years of age when France declared war on Holland, Spain and England. He became a gunner on a Dutch man-of-war and in a powder explosion on board his leg was so injured that it had to be amputated. He was discharged from the navy and earned a living doing sleight of hand tricks in public squares and at fairs. One day it occurred to him to hollow out the upper part of his crude wooden leg and use it as a secret receptacle to assist in the vanishment of small objects. He finally became so adept with this secret "servante" that his fame spread over the country and he became known as "Le Diable Boiteux," the crippled devil.

When he was a child of nine, Eliaser's eldest son, David, became his father's assistant. As a very young man, he invented the trick of the color-changing clay pipes and he was the first of the family to perform the trick with the eggs and the bag. He devised his own method, using a large bag from which he produced fifteen eggs and finally a hen. He was a great favorite of Prince Fredric, brother of King William the Second.

In 1834, David Leendert was breveted "court mechanician" to William the Second. David's son, Tobias, received this honor in 1857, as did my grandfather, David Tobias, in 1870.

David Tobias (1843-1913) did not initially want to be a magician. As a young man he was an actor, a mimic, and an elocutionist. Then one day he fell under the spell of Compars Herrmann (1816-1887), the elder brother of Alexander Herrmann (1844-1896), who became famous in the United States as Herrmann the Great. His performance consisted mostly of wonderful sleight of hand and a refined misdirection which my grandfather felt never to have been surpassed.

In 1866, when he was twenty-three years, my grandfather gave his first performance as a conjurer in Rotterdam. Four years later he was commanded to appear at the Royal Palace.

In September of 1886, another such invitation was received from the adjutant of the King, saying, "His Majesty the King commands me to invite Mr. David Tob Bamberg, court performer, to appear before the Royal Family consisting of the King, William III, her Majesty the Queen, Emma, and her Royal Highness Princess Wilhelmina, for which you will be paid the sum of one hundred florins in full. Performance must not exceed one hour."

To this performance, my grandfather took his eldest son, Toby (Tobias Leendert Bamberg, 1875-1963), then eleven years old. The occasion was Princess Wilhelmina's birthday and Toby was allowed to do a few tricks, for which he was complimented by the King.

When Toby was about seventeen years old he had an accident which nearly ended the Bamberg family tradition of the eldest son becoming a magician. He was skating on a frozen canal near his home in Amsterdam when the ice gave way. They had a dreadful time fishing him out and during his long immersion the cold water had gotten into his ears and he lost his hearing completely.

Disheartened, he decided to give up magic and learn wig making as a trade. But he was a born magician. When he regained partial hearing, he devised a pantomimic style without patter, as he could not pitch his voice. He thought that a Japanese act would enhance his silent style and would also be a very exotic novelty. His first appearance with this act was in Berlin in 1893. His father had taught him the conjuring techniques of Robert-Houdin, Compars Herrmann, and Professor Hofzinser of Vienna. He was skilled as a carpenter, mechanic, box-maker, and painter. Now he discovered pantomime, the great universal language and the most difficult of the dramatic arts. He combined it with the art of magic. He became Okito.

When Okito married Lily Poole in 1903, she began calling him Theo instead of Toby. "In England, Toby is a popular name for dogs. I certainly wouldn't want my husband to be whistled at," she said. So my father not only acquired an Oriental stage name, but also a respectably English first name, Theodore.

CHAPTER 5

"Roddle" was the Dutch word for gossip in the Bamberg household. Lily spent her days "roddling" with the old lady in the kitchen. From Julia's broken English she learned of Theo's tragic first marriage. His twenty-year-old wife, Jeanette, was a French girl who did a "strong jaw" act that terminated with her spinning rapidly, high up in the air, supported only by a thong clenched in her teeth.

In 1901, at the Circo Parrish in Madrid, Jeanette, who was four months pregnant, fell from the dome of the theatre while in the high spin and was instantly killed. Theo cut short his engagement and left Spain, vowing never to return, although he kept in constant correspondence with his old friend Leonard Parrish, the impresario of the Circus in the Plaza del Rey, which, in later years became known as the Circo Price. Lily never mentioned the subject, and in the long years that followed, Theo never knew that she was aware of his secret.

The old lady's Dutch cooking, so different from the English cuisine, fascinated her. In Amsterdam, live fish were brought to the door in tanks and the selected ones caught with a net and deposited in a squat barrel of water in the kitchen. A large frying pan was heated and great blobs of butter tossed in. The fish were cut into pieces while still alive and thrown into the pan where they often jumped about. It was a rather macabre scene, but never in her life had Lily tasted such fish.

Julia's "gerunte" (green) soup was hailed by the family and served at least twice a week. Here is the recipe of this great soup for a small family. Into a fairly large pot, three pints of water were put on to boil. Julia then cut up a head of celery and three leeks into small pieces. (A diced carrot was optional.) When the water was boiling, in went the vegetables, which were allowed to boil for five minutes. Then a demi-tasse of rice and beef stock was added (three beef cubes can be used) and this allowed to boil under a low heat for twenty minutes.

While the soup was boiling, the old lady grated a small onion into a pound of finely ground chuck or sirloin beef in a bowl. She added the juice of one garlic clove, one teaspoon of salt, one of fine oregano, half a teaspoon of ground pepper, a pinch of English mustard, one egg and two tablespoons of fine bread crumbs. This she kneaded with her hands to a light consistency and then proceeded to roll the mixture into small meatballs about ¾ inch in diameter.

When the twenty minutes were up, she added the meatballs quickly, one by one, and brought it up to the boil. Then, reducing the heat, she allowed it to simmer for ten minutes. Presto! One of the great magical soups of all time.

So what Lily learned of Dutch cooking and with her future experiences with German, French and Viennese cuisine, she, in time, became a marvelous cook. And believe me when I say that there is plenty of magic in that.

It was at this time that Theo came to a decision that was to affect his whole career. He wanted to enlarge his act and had just made the plans for his Mat Trick. He also wanted to do the production of a big bowl of water and the appearance of a child from an empty cloth. But the narrow Japanese kimono was unsuited to this type of body-loading magic and he was forced to change to the more ample Chinese robe. This meant changing his act from Japanese to Chinese. He discarded the Samurai wig and made two Chinese wigs with long black hair imported from Java. His was a half bald wig with a long braided queue that was worn in China until the revolution of 1912. For Lily he made a wig with two long braids that were rolled into circles on either side of her head and studded with small white blossoms.

His chief problem, which caused him quite some worry, was the name Okito. He already had a good reputation under that name and to change it for a Chinese one was to start all over again. So he decided to keep it and was forever after the only Chinese magician with a Japanese name. His make up was perfect and from a few feet away no one could tell that he wasn't an Oriental. In the Netherlands, of course, he was known to be Dutch; but for the rest of the world he was a Chinese.

He perfected and built the Mat Trick and the water bowl production. He also built a novel fire bowl which appeared burning on a marble pedestal. This act was rehearsed in the living room of the house, and when Theo was satisfied, he wrote to his agent in Paris for bookings and was engaged for a tour of variety theatres in France, Italy, Switzerland, Austria-Hungary, Russia, Sweden, Norway, and Denmark, with England as the final goal.

A week before they were to leave for Paris, a letter came from Charles Bertram.

"Theo," said Papa waving the letter in his hand, "Bertram tells me that Maskelyne is doing his Entranced Fakir at the Egyptian Hall."

"I suppose it's some kind of an improved Aga," said Theo.

"Bertram says not. There is no supporting rod used. He says that Maskelyne walks downstage leaving Cooke suspended some ten feet in the air in full light and without any visible means of support."

"Bertram is mad. He's pulling your leg."

"Charles doesn't make jokes like that. Would you agree to a quick trip to London? Have you time?"

"You're sure it's not LeRoy's Asrah?"

"I tell you that Bertram says this is a new principle and Cooke is not covered with a cloth. He says this illusion is the talk of London. Here, read it for yourself."

"If we leave on Friday we can be back by Monday morning," mused Theo. "Agreed! We shall go."

The Egyptian Hall, known as "England's Home of Mystery," was a small theatre seating about two hundred people. An air of mystery was achieved not only by the lighting but also through the mysterious music in the air, produced without a visible orchestra. Suspended from the ceiling were drums, a harp, horns and other instruments which played an accompaniment to the performance without the aid of visible musicians.

Bertram, Papa and Theo sat in this enchanted atmosphere at the Saturday evening show. Five magicians appeared on the programme before the Entranced Fakir was presented.

Finally, on a fully lighted stage, John Nevil Maskelyne in a magical sketch, hypnotized his partner, Cooke, who played the part of the fakir, and placed him in a sarcophagus supported by two trestles. Slowly, Cooke floated upward from the sarcophagus until he was floating over Maskelyne's head. The sarcophagus was removed and a metal hoop was passed over Cooke to dispel any idea of wires or mechanical support. Maskelyne walked forward to the footlights and passed the hoop to the audience for examination, leaving Cooke suspended on a fully lighted

19

stage and well away from the backdrop.

The sarcophagus was brought on again and, with magic passes, Cooke slowly descended into it. At the end he was lifted out and brought out of his hypnotic trance.

Papa and Theo were speechless and Bertram chortled with joy at their bafflement. Finally, as they were leaving the theatre, the old man spoke.

"Theo, my boy, I was always under the impression that no illusion could mystify me, and of all the illusions I have seen in my time I could make out a theory of my own regarding the techniques—even those of Robert-Houdin, although I came away highly impressed. But, my boy, what I saw this evening is beyond my comprehension. It is a masterpiece. I have no idea how it could possibly have been done."

He did not learn the true secret until 1913, the year before he died, when Okito explained it to him from first-hand knowledge of the Kellar-Thurston version.

Birthplace of David Bamberg, 24 Sitwell Street, Derby, England.

CHAPTER 6

Okito's new Chinese act was very successful and he was head-lining the best variety programmes in Europe. Early in the tour Lily became pregnant but continued assisting until her eighth month, disguised by her wide Chinese robe. In St. Petersburg, she feared the child would be born in Russia and insisted on returning to England. Okito postponed his contracts in Russia for a later date and with a short stopover in Copenhagen, Denmark, skipped to England arriving early in February of 1904. Two weeks later, on February 19, a baby boy was assisted into this world at 24 Sitwell Street in Derby by a doctor who was also an enthusiastic amateur magician. Okito was playing the Grand Theatre and Professor Carl (James Wakefield), a magician, was the godfather.

Named after his grandfather, David Tobias Bamberg showed no great magical ability apart from an enormous pair of lungs.

A few months later they returned to Amsterdam where little David was presented to the family and immediately became one of Papa's obsessions. He stayed with the family for his first year but later was taken on the road for those exciting years that Okito and Lily played all the leading capitals of Europe, including a return to Russia to play the postponed dates.

Theo met and became friendly with many magicians all over the continent, and in Antwerp he made the acquaintance of the shy and retiring Servais LeRoy, an ingenious magician-inventor, whose advanced ideas of stage illusions, using novel principles, influenced Okito's future stage career to a great extent. Their friendship endured a lifetime and Okito was always a staunch admirer of this modest man.

LeRoy told Theo of his dream of opening a magical factory, which he did in 1910 in Hatton Gardens in London. There he built his improved Asrah illusion, the Duck Pan, the Devil's Cage, the Magical Farmyard and together with such inventive minds as Zelka, Bretma, Percy Naldrett and Max Sterling invented and built illusions for top illusionists such as De Biere, Chung Ling Soo, Carmo, Carl Rosini, Chefalo, Rameses and Culpitt.

LeRoy was the first to realize the importance of rubber and elastic in the construction of certain magical effects, and at one time he was jokingly referred to as the "Rubber Magician."

Okito also met Charles Morritt, another clever inventor, who played for three years in St. George's Hall. Morritt was the first magician to introduce hypnotism in his act and he created a sensation at London's Alhambra theatre by putting a man in a trance for a week. Sir Francis Laking, medical advisor to King Edward VII, admitted that the subject was really in a trance and tried to have Parliament stop Morritt from doing this feat, but the Home Secretary informed the Members that he had no legal power to do so.

Morritt built the largest illusion ever seen on any stage, which he called Tally-Ho. From an empty cabinet the size of a small house, he produced huntsmen on horses, girls in hunting outfits and a pack of hounds. He was also part inventor of the Mystery "Oh," the most baffling illusion of all time. Houdini bought or borrowed many of Morritt's illusions, but he told Okito that they were far too clumsy and heavy.

Morritt's most famous illusion was the Morritt Cage based on an original principle which allowed a person to disappear inside a cage.

Okito, during his engagement at the London Palladium, had one of those unpredictable disasters that often embitters a magician's life, but sometimes lead the way to improvements.

For his Chinese water bowl production Okito used a white crockery wash basin, which was brought loaded onto the stage during the act by an assistant and placed on the stage floor between the wings, ready for body loading.

One night the assistant set it down too heavily and the bowl cracked neatly in half but the rubber and canvas cover that was stretched and bound over the top held it together and not a drop of water leaked out.

Okito loaded the bowl under his robe without noticing anything amiss and went on with the trick, but at the moment he removed the cover the two halves fell apart and a flood of water rushed down into the floodlight and caused a rip-roaring short circuit which exploded the high-wattage light bulbs, scaring the audience (and Okito) half to death. There was almost a panic as people started running from the theatre, but fortunately calmer heads prevailed.

After this debacle, Okito had a metal bowl spun which he enameled white, and in later years he added the foot and the improved release to perfect it to such a degree that it became the greatest of all bowl productions.

One incident that always remained in Lily's mind took place on a train on their way to Christiania in Norway in July of 1906. Although it was after eleven o'clock at night, the midnight sun was shining brightly, low on the horizon. Sharing the compartment with them was a tall, swarthy man who spoke quite good English and introduced himself as Julius Zancig and was accompanied by his wife, Agnes, a short hunchbacked woman with piercing black eyes. Theo had heard of the sensational success this Danish couple had in London with their act "Two Minds With But a Single Thought," which was an elaboration of a second-sight act of Robert-Houdin.

Childless herself, Agnes took a great fancy to little David and asked Theo if he intended to have the little fellow follow in his footsteps. "If not," said Agnes, "I'll take him with me and make a mind reader of him." Everyone laughed at her little joke and no one suspected that her remark was prophetic.

The tour ended in February of 1907 and they returned to London where Okito received a long letter from his father informing him that a tour of Dutch India had been arranged for both of them and said he would leave on the S.S. Berlin that sailed on Wednesday night for Holland from Harwich.

On a dark, bitterly cold February night in 1907, a hansom cab rumbled through the storm-swept streets of London on its way to Liverpool Street Station. Occasional bursts of freezing sleet knifed through the ill-fitting side curtains, wetting the worn suitcases and the three miserable occupants.

"Bloody English vetter," snarled Theo with an accusing glare at Lily, who being English was obviously to blame. "Godverdomme!" he cried in his high-pitched voice as a sheet of ice-cold rain caught him on the side of the jaw and dribbled down his ulster.

Lily pulled little David toward her. "I have to do pee-pee," said David.

"We'll be at the station in a moment dear. Be a good boy."

"Vot? Vot he says? Vot he wants now?"

"Nothing, Theo nothing." Lily thanked the Lord that he was hard of hearing, for that would have been his cue to go into a melodramatic scene.

Theo glared for a moment and turned to rage silently at the wet cobblestones through the flap. A lighted bookshop caught his eye. I mustn't forget to buy a copy of *The Strand* at the station, he thought; there might be a new Holmes story.

It always pleased him when people said how greatly he resembled Frederic Derr Steele's illustrations of the master detective with the hooknosed ascetic face and the two ridges over the eyebrows. Like his hero, Sherlock Holmes, Theo did possess some deductive powers and was a keen observer.

His thoughts were cut off by a porter running alongside the cab. "Boat train to Harwich, sir?"

"First class," said Theo as he stepped down to the platform. "Ven the bags are in the compartment get me a copy of *The Strand*. I'll check the trunks," he said to Lily as he rushed off.

When the bags were on the rack Lily tipped the porter and took David to the waiting room. Later, at the bookstall, she found to her dismay that *The Strand* was sold out. Good Lord, she thought, I'll never hear the end of it. Now I'll be blamed for. . . .

"Mrs. Okito! What a surprise." Lily turned to see a smiling, wiry blonde, was puzzled for a moment, and then suddenly remembered that the girl was an acrobat, Nora something, who had played on the bill with them at the Oxford Empire. They chatted for a moment and Lily was disappointed to learn that Nora was going second class to Harwich. As Nora trotted off to find her partner, Lily had a sudden feeling of envy for the girl's assured manner and wished that she had. . . suddenly she realized that David was gone!

A dozen thoughts shot through her mind as she stood there half paralyzed with shock. The platform was crowded and she tried to look everywhere at once. She never clearly remembered what had happened—people staring at her curiously—a uniformed man who was asking what was the matter—Theo's angry face—doors slamming—whistles blowing—the train pulling out and gathering speed.

A good five minutes after the train had gone and the platform had cleared, they found David inside the bookstall, sitting on the floor looking at picture books.

The ride back to the digs in the hansom was terrible. Theo was furious at having missed a train for the first time in his life.

24

He worried about the bags although the stationmaster had wired to Harwich to hold them. Lily was sure the landlady at the digs wouldn't let them have the room again after the unspeakable thing Theo had done. He had suddenly gone berserk at the constant fare of steak and kidney pudding and had rushed out into the street and thrown the meal, plate and all, in front of a passing dray. The plate had been part of the poor woman's wedding set and there had been a bloody awful row about it. He not only had to pay for the china; he was also told to get out. There was also no doubt that David was in for a good whipping and Lily for a night of Theo's rage.

When they got to the digs, to Lily's surprise and relief, the normally stone-faced landlady burst into laughter after hearing what had happened and made a remark about "The nipper being a chip off the old block and doin' his own disappearin' act." She let them have the room as she didn't have the heart to see Lily and the nipper search for lodgings on a foul night.

The moment the door of their room closed, Theo went into a harangue that included women, kids, England, steak and kidney pudding, the climate, and the delights of having to sleep in one's underwear without even a toothbrush—so on and on and on until he got fed up with it and lapsed into the silent-martyr act, with an occasional fulminating stare. Surprisingly, David was spared his hiding and miraculously Theo had forgotten all about *The Strand*. Finally he dozed off.

David, who had begun to fear that the end of the world was not far off, gained confidence.

"Mummy."

"Shh. Be a good boy and go to sleep."

"What's a Lily, Mummy?"

"A lily is a white flower. Now go to sleep."

"What's a David?"

"David is just a name. It means 'beloved one.' "

"Am I beloved, Mummy?"

"Not tonight, David. Go to sleep."

Later that night Lily was awakened by repeated knocking on the door.

"Just a moment," she called as she hurriedly slipped on her skirt and blouse. She ran her fingers through her thick auburn hair and made a few feminine pats here and there, then opened the door to find the landlady standing there with an awed expression and bursting with excitement.

"'Ere, 'ave a look at this," said the woman thrusting the

morning's paper into Lily's hand.

Lily caught the headline—TERRIBLE SEA DISAS-
TER—S.S. BERLIN LOST IN VIOLENT CHANNEL
STORM—NO SURVIVORS. Lily skipped trembling through
the story..."Thursday, Feb. 21st: The S.S. Berlin which left Harwich last night for the Hook of Holland...sunk in the channel...reasons unknown...assumed that heavy storm caused
a defect in steering gear...150 passengers and crew including
Captain Precious lost...S.S. Hellevoetlius and S.S. President
Van Heel searching for survivors."

Lily looked dazedly at the landlady and mumbled her thanks
as she closed the door. She shook Theo awake and without a
word handed him the paper. He read it through twice and then
looked at David with awe.

David didn't know what it was all about but from the sudden change in his social life he knew he was in solid with the
old man again.

Lily remembered something she had read about Moira and
became a fatalist.

(Moira is a kind of inexplicable Greek fatalism which seems
mere blind accident. Moira is essentially amoral and beyond
human logic.)

In Amsterdam, the sinking of the S.S. Berlin caused great
consternation. Then Papa received a wire from Theo informing him that they were safe and would be home on Saturday.

Their arrival was celebrated with a party and David was the
center of attraction. He took it in stride and made the most of it.

Lily and David stayed with Julia in Holland while Papa and
Theo made the Indonesian tour that lasted six months and
embraced Java, Sumatra, the Straight Settlements, Singapore,
Bali, Borneo, Ceylon and part of British India. On April 13,
1907 they appeared before His Highness, the Prince of Solo,
the most influential prince of Java.

Upon their return to Holland Theo left with Lily and David
to fulfill his contract at the Folies Bergere in Paris. While there
Theo was approached by the American impresario, Martin Beck,
accompanied by his agent Richard Pittrot, and the upshot of
the conversations was a twenty-six week contract for the
Orpheum Circuit in the leading cities of the United States
of America.

CHAPTER 7

Harry Kellar had been one of Theo's most satisfied customers and he influenced Thurston to engage Theo in the double capacity of building new illusions and tricks for the Thurston show and doing his shadowgraph act as a special attraction. And so it was that these two men who had become friends in Paris and British India were brought together by Kellar to collaborate on one of the finest magical productions in the United States.

It is axiomatic that no magician can do another magician's show in total. Every magician has his own individuality and, as a rule, one starts with a small act and works his way up to the full night's show. Thurston already had quite a large show of his own when the Kellar show was handed to him, yet he couldn't adapt himself strictly to the Kellar personality. There were certain tricks which Thurston either couldn't or didn't want to do. This is understandable when one takes into consideration the vastly different personalities of the two men.

Kellar was the serious type of performer with little or no personal charm, a methodical man and a stickler for details. On one occasion he noticed that the inside of a wooden production box was unpainted. When he called the dealer's attention to the fact, the man said, "What does it matter? No one sees it." Kellar's retort was, "You're wrong. *I* see it."

Thurston was exactly the opposite. He had a charming, polished manner and was a dreamer in contrast to the hard-headed business man that Kellar was. Thurston was careless and paid slight attention to detail. A piece of scenery could be hung badly and he would take no notice; most of his illusions were badly in need of a coat of paint, but he let it slide. To keep the show going, he depended on George White, a kindly, honest, faithful and warm-hearted man who had been with him from the early days when Thurston did his card act and George had been his assistant.

Kellar was in a savage mood about the way things were going and on one occasion said to Theo, "You see this match? I wouldn't waste it to burn the whole damned Thurston show." This was strong talk for Kellar, but he was in such a bad temper that he was on the point of forcing Thurston to remove the Kellar name from the lithographs which announced "Kellar presents Thurston." Theo soothed Kellar's feelings and an open break was averted.

Kellar once said to Theo, "You are a man after my own heart. Why didn't I give the show to you instead of Howard?" This was very flattering but Theo knew that he was not the man for that type of illusion show, and Thurston had all the necessary qualities. He was native-born American with a fine command of the English language having graduated from the Dwight L. Moody School with the idea of becoming a medical-missionary; he was polished and handsome and he had an outstanding personality, a good speaking voice and wore his evening clothes as if born in them.

The years proved that Howard was the right man. The show eventually became an American institution and Thurston made a fortune.

Theo acted as a brake on Thurston's impracticable impulses. It was a hard job that required tact, as Thurston had a strong will, but Theo's common sense and inventive genius was what Thurston needed most. This is not to say that the Thurston show would not have been such an outstanding success if Theo had never been with it, but I do believe that he had a great share, in the early days, in guiding Howard and helping to create that great show.

Thurston was my idol: he could do no wrong. When the show played near New York, in Boston or Philadelphia, I was allowed to troop along, and despite my father's warnings not to "pester" Howard, I would visit his dressing room whenever possible. He always received me kindly and usually had a few minutes time for me. He taught me my first card sleights, the pass and color-change which I did with small cards, and he would sit and watch me with genuine interest and helpful suggestions. In time, I grew to love him like a father.

I knew the show by heart, every movement, every word, every gesture. His influence on me was overpowering and years later, when I had my own show in Latin America, I would turn on the "Thurston charm" and it paid off in countries where they love a "simpatico."

At this point, I must take issue with Guy Jarrett. I respect his ability, his craftsmanship and his rare common sense in the illusions he built for Thurston, but I deplore his bitterly acid attacks on Thurston as a person. In his book, Jarrett paints Thurston as an egotistical, bumbling fool, and this is very harsh judgment indeed. Thurston may have made many mistakes, but as I said, he was a dreamer. His outlook was broad, no one can deny his sensational success, and one would never think of this polished gentleman as a "mental stumble bum."

Another man who went out of his way to be very kind to me in those days was Jack Jones, Thurston's manager, and when Jack had his disagreement with Thurston and left the show, I felt that I had lost a great friend. I never saw or heard of Jack again.

In 1912, while playing the Auditorium Theatre in Baltimore, Thurston had me do a card trick for the children during a matinee. Dressed in a sailor suit, I was sitting with the other kids in the hall when Thurston stopped in the middle of the show and pointed to me and said, "Children, this is a little friend of mine, the son of Theo Bamberg who showed us those very clever shadow pictures. This little boy is Master David Bamberg and his father, grandfather and great-grandfathers have been famous magicians in Holland, and he represents the seventh generation. David promised me that he would show the boys and girls a little trick right up here on this big stage."

Thurston then borrowed a hat from a spectator and had another boy come up on the stage to help

I showed the boy five cards fanned out (Deland's Phantom Card Trick) and said, "Please choose three of these cards and don't forget them." The choice was made and all the cards thrown in the hat. "How many do three from five leave?" All the kids in the theatre howled out "Two!"

I was now full of confidence and glanced up at Thurston as if to say, "This is where we get them."

Gleefully lifting two cards from the hat, I asked the boy if either of them were among the chosen ones. He replied, "No."

"Then the three remaining cards must be those selected?" And handing the hat to the boy I continued, "I will show you that two from five leaves nothing. Look in the hat." The three cards had vanished.

29

At the resulting applause, Thurston was the most pleased person in the theatre. Then he did one of those gracious and courteous things so characteristic of him. He gave me a dollar bill saying, ''Do not spend this dollar. Keep it and it will multiply. You have talent, my boy, and some day you will get to the top.''

It was on this tour that Thurston presented me many times to the audience as his future successor. It may have been a theatrical gesture without meaning, but as a child I believed it and this influenced my life to such an extent that I never went through the cowboy-fireman-aviator phase that other boys went through. I never had the slightest doubt that one day I would be an illusionist. Not just a mere magician, mind you, but an illusionist with my full evening's show. Thurston, far more than my father, inspired me to be a magician. In fact my father tried to discourage me from going into magic, often telling me that with my handshadows I could make a good living without the headaches of a big show.

As the years go by, one tends to look back with nostalgic sentimentality on the old days. On TV one sees old silent movies which were considered sensational in those days and are downright embarrassing today. This may apply in a way to my memories of the Thurston show, but it must be emphasized that this show was perfectly geared to his time. There was nothing subtle in the Thurston show. It was the old pistol-shooting, march-playing, slap-bang, jumping-in-and-out-boxes, old-time magic show that was thrilling and exhilarating. (Goldin's act, during his prime, was also a perfect example of what I mean. One big illusion followed another with lightning speed and the props were thrown to the assistants at the end of a trick. The audience had no time to think or catch their breath. It was a kaleidoscopic whirlwind of magic, color and loud music.)

It is said that the Thurston show was at one time the most valuable property in show business. Mr. Dariel Fitzkee in his book, *Showmanship for Magicians,* quotes a nationally prominent theatre executive as saying, ''If your principal can so present a magic show that it once more appeals to the masses, he will be greater than Thurston or Herrmann or Houdini, and,'' he added, ''he'll make a fortune.''

Such is the power of a great illusion show.

CHAPTER 8

At the risk of repeating the accounts of others, I invite you to see the Thurston show as I saw it as a boy.

"The Wonder Show of the Universe" opened on a dimly lighted stage in a setting of dark red plush. In the center of the stage close to the backdrop was a large book entitled "Magicians. Past and Present." No attempt was made to present this as an illusion. Two assistants turned the pages, one by one, showing life-sized pictures of Heller, Herrmann, Harry Kellar and finally the last page, which was just a frame with Thurston standing there clad in evening dress.

At the applause of the audience, he came forward and was handed a large foulard and from it produced a bowl of fire, another of water, and some large feather flower bouquets and a number of doves.

He then went into his "Original Card Passes" based on the back hand palm and finished with the rising cards. He did not use the card reel, preferring the thread across the stage method worked by George between the wings.

Instead of forcing the cards, Thurston had them freely selected by people calling out from the audience. The only forced card was the joker, which a stooge in the gallery shouted for in a loud rasping voice which always got a laugh.

During the selection of the cards, George, off stage, removed prepared duplicates from a satin-cloth bag with twenty-six pockets in it. In each of these pockets were two cards, the black aces, the black deuces, the black threes and so on.

The selected cards, four in number including the joker, were clipped together on one of the long sides with a small bulldog clip. A needle-sharp pin on one side of the clip allowed the load to be hung on an assistant's back.

The thread at this time was high up over the heads of Thurston and his assistants, allowing freedom of movement. The loaded assistant walked on stage bearing a small tray with a glass goblet and a white handkerchief on it. Thurston displayed the goblet and polished it with the handkerchief, which he did not return to the tray but threw over the assistant's shoulder, thereby copping the card load off his back very neatly. It was a natural steal and imperceptible. The palmed cards were added to the deck that Thurston had placed momentarily on the tray. The tiny clip stayed on the assistant's back and was later collected by George.

The first two cards were engaged in the lowered thread by means of little tabs pasted to the backs and they rose from the goblet to Thurston's outstretched hand.

Thurston then removed the deck from the goblet and the assistant carried the goblet off stage on the tray.

The third card rose from the deck held in Thurston's left hand to his extended right hand held over the deck. The card was then tossed onto the stage.

The last card, the joker, was allowed to rise into the air and then slowly descend until it almost touched the floor. He asked someone to say "rise" and a stooge in the gallery would shout "rice!" Thurston would look up into the gallery and say, "I said *rise*, not rice." The stooge shouted "Up!" and the card flew up into the air to be caught on its way down by Thurston who took his bow.

His next trick consisted of apparently pulling off a duck's and a rooster's heads, then placing them in a box to the left of the stage. In another box, to the right, he put the bodies. A third box in the center was shown empty. A spectator selected one of the boxes and from it the fowl appeared, but with the rooster having the duck's head and vice versa.

The Barrel of Diogenes followed. Both ends of an empty barrel were covered with white paper held by metal hoops. A light was inserted through a bung hole in the top of the barrel and slowly a distorted shadow appeared and took shape on the papered end facing the audience. Suddenly the paper burst and Diogenes with his lantern and staff crept forth and hobbled off stage. Technically, this was rather a poor illusion.

Then came the pièce de résistance, the levitation of Princess Karnac. This was the Kellar version which Thurston had inherited. In the first years he adhered to Kellar's original presentation by having a kneeling Oriental to one side of the stage reciting a prayer. Thurston's changes in this presentation in the following years was the cause of much justified criticism by his fellow magicians. The illusion was an exact copy of the original Maskelyne levitation which, although it appeared to be a miracle from the audience's view, had its limitations and Thurston was so confident of the invisibility of the wires that supported the cradle that he invited committees on the stage and even had a stooge stand backstage, close to the backdrop. Sometimes he even had the boldness to allow one of the committee to walk with him all around the suspended girl and rather obviously cut off the person's view at the critical spot where the wires plainly stood out against the footlights. With all this he proved nothing and completely ruined the mysterious presentation that had been so successful over the years. This was Kellar's main gripe.

The next trick was a large wooden ball with a hole bored through it that rose and descended on a metal rod stuck into a large wooden base. After the levitation this trick was anticlimatic and should not have been used at that spot. Even as a child I could feel the letdown this trick caused but Thurston was my idol and could do no wrong, so I applauded loudly.

The mood of the audience was lifted again with the hilarious presentation of the Spirit Cabinet. The mysterious floating stools, tambourines and bells and the antics of the terrified stooges always got screams of laughter. In those days Thurston had not yet combined the floating ball with the spirit cabinet. That came many years later and is a story in itself.

Then came the Lady and the Lion illusion. Two large curtained cabinets were shown empty. A girl entered the one to the left and the curtains were drawn shut on both cabinets. A shot was fired and the curtains fell. In place of the girl there was a large cage with a live lion inside, and in the other cabinet the girl sat on a swing hanging from the roof in the cage.

The first act of the show closed with A Bit of Fun in which Thurston vanished a red silk and produced it from a spectator's coat collar followed by a live, kicking rabbit. Then, cajoling the victim onto the stage, he proceeded to extract baby clothes and a silk stocking from the man's coat collar and finally, turning the man's profile to the audience, he was seen to have a great hunch on his back. After some chasing around, a duck's head appeared from the victim's coat collar and pecked at his neck. The scene ended with the frantic man running through the aisle of the theatre with the duck still pecking the back of his head. Thurston's handling of the duck load was a fine piece of magic.

The second act opened with Theo Bamberg, "Europe's Greatest Shadowist," who performed a ten-minute act of hand-shadows.

The Mystery of the Automobile, which followed, was one of those raincoat and whisker dramas so dear to Howard's heart. Thurston with a lady at his side, both wearing the long dustcoats, scarfs and goggles so popular at that time, drove an Abbott-Detroit automobile onto the stage. Thurston left the lady alone for a moment while he entered a wayside inn for refreshments.

Two thugs steathily appeared and grappled with the woman, who screamed. Thurston then rushed out of the inn and wrestled with the villains. A cop arrived and the cut-throats surrendered. Their masks were torn off and one of the thugs turned out to be the lady and the other criminal was Thurston. The sketch was weak and the changes poor, but Thurson insisted that it had publicity value. Eventually, Theo convinced Thurston to change this sketch for one of Lafayette's quick-change acts, the combined transformation and vanish of "John Phillip Sousa." Theo admired tremendously the great Italian quick-change artist, Fregoli, a man fifty years ahead of his time who, when he died, took his secrets with him so that very little is known of his basic technique. They rehearsed some of Frigoli's sketches but Thurston never did them. The obvious reason was that a quick-change artist must be a great mimic and actor and Thurston was neither. His charm lay in just being Howard Thurston.

The third act opened with a production of pigeons called Pigeon Pie, followed by a comedy routine using a baby pig and a feeding bottle.

Then a borrowed lady's hat was shot from a cannon to appear on the head of a passing girl assistant. The biggest laugh in this number occurred when the assistant who was bringing up the borrowed hat—one of those enormous affairs that they wore in those days with birds-nests, flowers, ribbons and feathers on it— tripped over the floodlights, flat on the hat and squashing it flat as a pancake. Then followed Thurston's ineffectual efforts to straighten it out again, finally, in frustration, rolling it into a sausage and stuffing it into a cannon.

Then came the trick I always waited for avidly: The Eggs from the Hat (a la Devant). Thurston used a little boy and girl as assistants and, needless to say, I was the boy and sometimes, in order not to be forestalled, I was already on the run-down before he had got the words out of his mouth. At one matinee Thurston accidently cracked an egg when placing it on the others that I held with my folded arms and it started to run out and stain my shirt. As I tried to grab it a dozen eggs dropped from my arms to smash on the stage. It got a yell from the audience but Thurston was not amused. After the show we had a little heart-to-heart talk about it and he was so kind over the mishap that I loved him more than ever and never dropped another egg unless he gave me the signal to do so.

The appearance of a girl in a glass lined trunk was next.

The Prisoner of Canton, a copy of Maskelyne's New Page illusion, consisted of strapping a boy to a board which was placed upright in a shallow cabinet. The door of the cabinet was closed for an instant and then opened to show the boy upside down and still strapped to the board. In the original English version, due to the fact that St. George's Hall was specially arranged for this sort of illusion, the cabinet could be shown all around and unmistakably empty. But Thurston could not do this and thereby weakened the effect considerably.

Chung Ling Soo's piercing-arrow trick followed.

The Inexhaustible Coconut was half a coconut shell which Thurston held in his right hand and from which an endless flow of water filled three large metal tanks. Later, this was combined with the Japanese Water Fountains.

The Lady and the Boy illusion was a trunk-like box with a raised platform resting on the top. On this platform there was a metal framework which allowed a curtain to be raised and lowered. In the air, hanging on chains directly over the framework, was a cabinet. The lady and the boy stood on the platform and the curtain was raised for a few seconds. A shot was fired and the curtain fell. Simultaneously, the doors of the trunk and the suspended cabinet flew open. The lady was in the trunk and the boy was in the cabinet.

The show closed with the Triple Mystery. Two light boxes were shown empty and nested, a shot fired and a girl appeared from them. The girl was then put into a sarcophagus which was hoisted into the air and another shot was fired at the suspended sarcophagus which fell apart in the shape of a cross. The girl was gone. A trunk that had been hanging from the dome of the theatre all during the show was lowered onto the stage. It was opened and with the aid of two poles that slid through the brackets a second trunk was removed and placed on a low platform. This second trunk was opened to show a third trunk inside which was removed with the poles and brought downstage almost to the footlights. When this small trunk was opened, the missing girl jumped out. (In later years, Thurston used Goldin's Cannon illusion to "shoot" the girl into the trunks.) Curtain.

After the show Thurston lined up the assistants and crew to talk over the mistakes that had been made. This was most annoying to everyone who wanted to get the hell out of the theatre, but they had to go through with it. I always raced backstage to be in time to hear this daily harangue and the snide side comments.

One evening, some joker with a misguided sense of humor sprinkled sneezing powder from the grid while Fernanda was floating in the air during the levitation. Her sneezing rocked the cradle so violently that she nearly fell off. Someone informed Thurston what had been the cause and after the show he gave them a dressing down that I have never seen equalled. That was the first time I ever saw Thurston really angry. I knew who had done it and so did my father and I think that he should have told Thurston, as a bastard who would do a thing like that had no right to be in the theatre. Had Fernanda fallen from that height, she could have been badly injured. Twenty of the sixty sustaining wires had snapped and it's a wonder they all didn't go.

Once in a while Howard's cussedness and Theo's irascibility clashed head on over the construction of an illusion. The Mystery "Oh!" was a typical example. Theo naturally was in favor of the original Maskelyne version which had baffled him, along with the whole of London, when he saw it peformed at St. George's Hall. He insisted on the original presentation and the subtle principle it employed, but Thurston wanted a modified version suitable for any stage.

The effect of this masterpiece of stagecraft was so surprising that Maskelyne christened it "Oh!"—which was the usual exclamation of anyone who saw it performed.

In the exact center of a fully lighted stage a thin platform rested on four short legs. Four metal tubes at each corner of the platform supported a thin metal framework of angle iron like an open roof.

A committee of eight to fifteen persons was invited onto the stage and seated on either side near the footlights.

A young girl dressed as an odalisque was introduced and a handkerchief was borrowed and tied around her upper right arm. She now stepped onto the platform and sat down in a reclining position facing the audience. A heavy leather strap was fastened to the girl's right wrist and a strong cord which was attached to it ran over a pulley on the upper left side of the metal framework and thence to one of the committeemen who could raise the girl's arm up and down at will.

Four blue silk curtains with rings attached were hung on hooks in the angle-iron framework. From a slit in the lower right side of the front curtain the girl could extend her left hand.

A plywood board was now brought on stage by the assistants and dropped into the angle-iron framework forming a wooden roof.

Another committeeman was invited to hold the girl's hand which extended from the slit in the curtain and the other committeeman was told to pull the cord that ran to the girl's right wrist, gently up and down.

A third committeeman was asked to climb a small ladder and sit on the plywood roof of the apparatus. A fourth was asked to lie on the floor under the platform and the remaining men were asked to hold hands and form a circle around the illusion. Therefore there was no possible way for the girl to escape without being seen.

"Go!" cried the magician and the girl pulled her hand inside the cabinet. A moment later the cord in the committeeman's hand went slack and simultaneously the four curtains dropped to the stage. The girl was gone! The curtains were rolled into a small ball and thrown to one side, while the astounded committeemen were at liberty to examine the skeleton framework of the illusion.

It's no wonder that the audience gasped..."Oh!"

The magician clapped his hands and the girl, with the handkerchief still tied to her arm, came running toward the stage from the back of the theatre.

Naturally Thurston was in love with this illusion and wanted Theo to build it, but Theo pointed out that this miracle had been specially designed for Maskelyne's own stage and there was a great technical difficulty that made it unsuitable for traveling.

Thurston acknowledged the difficulty but suggested that a second platform built like the Azrah table could be constructed under the original thin platform; a double-decker you might call it.

This was like waving a red cape in front of a bull for Okito and there was a heated argument about it with Okito proclaiming he would not "bugger-up" the illusion for anybody. He pointed out, rightly, that such an ungainly and highly suspicious prop would not fool a discerning audience and that the clarity and the beautiful simplicity of the illusion would be lost.

Finally Thurston had his way and Theo started construction. The boys on the show dubbed the prop "Uh!" instead of "Oh!"

As Theo had predicted, it was just another of those things without rhyme or reason; but because so much trouble and expense had gone into it, they kept it on the show for a season or so.

Another of Thurston's pet theories that never failed to irritate Theo was Thurston's belief that a good small trick would make a great stage illusion.

Theo had just perfected his first model of Matter Through Matter in which a small star-trap was placed over the center of a wide silk band so that various objects could be pushed through the star-trap without harming the silk.

Thurston thought that the principle involved was too ingenious to be wasted on a small trick unsuitable for the stage and immediately had visions of shoving a girl through a sheet of canvas. Theo's nostrils began to twitch, which was a danger signal, but an unheeding Howard went blithely on until Theo blew his top. Again they went through one of their life-and-death struggles.

But Thurston was the boss and had his way as usual. As a last resort Theo suggested Walking Through a Mirror, but Thurston said that Kellar had already done it and, besides, he had heard over the magicians' grapevine, that Houdini was making plans for Walking Through a Brick Wall, and his mind was made up. So get busy.

The Impermeable Girl illusion turned out to be a bulky unwieldy prop with no audience impact. Unfortunately (or fortunately, from Theo's point of view) the crate containing the illusion was smashed to bits in a railroad accident and it was never revived. Thurston, some years later, had a spot of cold comfort when Houdini's Walking Through a Brick Wall turned out to be almost as big a stinker as the Impermeable Girl.

But the successful illusions far outweighed the mistakes. Theo supervised the construction of some really fine stage illusions and corrected the mistakes and improved some of the old ones as the show constantly became bigger and better.

The laughs in the Thurston show far surpassed most of the other stage offerings of the time in number, volume and spontaneity. Thurston had no trouble getting people to come up on the stage to act as his voluntary assistants. Reporters liked Thurston because he was never obtrusive in his publicity seeking and because he was a person well worth knowing in any capacity.

As Thurston played the same territory year after year, it was essential to present at least three or four new illusions each season. This was a man size task and sometimes Thurston did a bit of borrowing without asking permission, as in the case of Leon's Fire and Water illusion, and sometimes this habit led to trouble, such as the disagreeable episode at Tomashevsky's Theatre in New York.

On the night in question Houdini, Okito and I were watching the show from a lower front box. Thurston had just announced his Fire and Water illusion when the great Leon (Leon Levy) stood up in the audience and in a loud voice accused Thurston of being "a thief, a pirate and a liar." There was a confused titter from some of the audience who thought it was part of the show.

Leon, of course, was right about the inventor of this routine in which a girl is placed in a cabinet walled with wire-mesh and covered with a white sheet. A second skeleton cabinet had a glass tank of water suspended from the roof by chains. Curtains were closed around this cabinet. A shot was fired and the girl inside the wire-mesh cabinet started to burn with a bright red fire until she was consumed and the curtains fell from the second cabinet showing the girl locked inside the glass tank of water. The only difference between the two versions was in the construction of the tricked staircase which was the means by which the girl passed from one cabinet to the other. The Thurston steps were far superior to the crude steps that Leon used.

But Leon picked the wrong time and place to have it out with Thurston as the audience, who knew nothing of backstage cloak-and-dagger intrigue, was on Thurston's side and the situation began to get out of hand.

Thurston decided to justify himself by calling on Houdini as a witness in his favor, but Harry wasn't having any of it and slunk in the rear of the box, refusing to get mixed up in the quarrel.

Hard-of-hearing Theo, who didn't understand what was going on, kept asking me, "Vot iss it? Vot he says?" but I was too scared to give a sensible answer.

When Thurston saw that Houdini wanted no part in the row, he changed tactics immediately and said to the audience,

"Europe's greatest magician and inventor of magical illusions is sitting in that box with Harry Houdini, and I call on Mr. Bamberg to attest as to who is the originator of this Fire and Water illusion. Theo! Is it not true that these effects are mine?''

Theo, who had no idea of what was going on said, ''Yes,'' thereby making an enemy for life when Leon was removed from the theatre by the ushers.

When Theo found out exactly what had happened, he was indignant with Thurston and after the show rebuked him for having dragged him into the dispute; but the harm was done and Leon refused to accept any apology. He spread the word around that Okito did not come from a long line of heel-clicking foreigners but rather from a long line of foreign heels who never clicked. Theo was not amused.

During the summer months, Thurston laid off and returned to his home in Beechhurst, Long Island, not far from the huge barn-like shop in Whitestone Landing where the show was repaired and repainted and where new illusions were built. I spent my summers there doing odd jobs and running out for beer and cigarettes. Once in a while, to my great delight, I was invited to lunch by Mrs. Thurston and played with her daughter, Jane.

In the shop, the first thing they did was to give the levitation a good going-over. This was packed into about eight or nine trunks, which included the drapes. It must have weighed nearly two tons and it usually took three men about four hours to set it on the opening day. (Of course this included stalling and going out for beer.) It took half an hour to set it before each performance and it was struck and packed in the trunks immediately after the act.

One summer Thurston wanted to combine the levitation with the Asrah version which allowed the girl to vanish at the end. Theo argued that after the girl's descent onto the couch, after the levitation, to remove the couch and bring on another table, cover the girl with a white sheet and levitate her again, was both inartistic and anti-climatic. (Years later, Kalanag, a German illusionist, used three distinct methods of levitating a girl in a single presentation, which meant absolutely nothing to the audience with the exception of the last method which floated the girl over his head without using the complicated Maskelyne system.)

Theo suggested, as an alternative, a simple sofa illusion that would allow the girl to vanish without the floating effect, but Thurston was adamant and they built the Asrah table. In later years it turned out to be a good thing for me that Thurston refused the sofa illusion as Okito had Willmann build it for him and it became one of the strongest features of his act. Later it was passed on to me and I used it for over thirty years.

Over half a century has gone by since those hot summer days filled with fried eggs, flies and sticky candy, but I vividly recall the wonderful illusions and tricks that were created in the old barn to maintain the show in its high place.

Thurston was fortunate in having the choicest theatrical territory in the United States: a rough square from New England to Minnesota, south to Kansas and Missouri and then east to Washington. It took about nine months to play this territory in weekly stands. Thurston never played the Far West or the South and his only serious rival in those days was Blackstone.

Many years later Thurston tried to corner the magic market by having a magician named Tampa do a reduced version of his show in the southern states and Dante do another in the West, but nothing ever came of it and Dante left for South America and Europe and returned to the United States only after Thurston had died. What became of Tampa I never knew.

As a final curtain to those happy carefree days, I would like to quote part of an article written by Arthur Leroy in *The Sphinx* magazine: "We were driving through Whitestone and suddenly Carl (Rosini) told me to stop. The sun was beginning to set, and the January dusk was almost upon us. 'Look about you!' said Carl. 'Not so long ago Howard Thurston owned all the land within sight. Here he had his home and his workshop. Horace Goldin lived down the line. His workshop was here too. I lived across from Thurston and it was here that I built Tavma, and oh, so many illusions. Across from Thurston was Alexander Herrmann's mansion. Many years before we arrived, Herrmann and Billy Robinson (later Chung Ling Soo) worked in the shop and built such things as the Divorce Machine, Chinese Immigration and the Decapitation. . . . Do you see that pile of junk over there in that vacant lot?'

"The sun was sinking low now. There was a chill in the air. I shivered; I felt like one who was gazing upon the beloved dead. In the center of a vacant lot strewn with garbage lay a twisted, corroded mass of metal wreckage. Carl pointed bemused, 'That pile of rubble, that bunch of junk was once the greatest mystery ever conceived by the mind of man. Once upon a time it played the legitimate theatres of the country. Every evening and two matinees a week it thrilled and amazed audiences for years and years. That garbage, that twisted nothingness was the Kellar-Maskelyne Levitation. That was the original American equipment, billed as the Levitation of Princess Karnac. Thurston made it the most dramatic mystery ever witnessed.'

"The sun was down now and the chill air made me shiver a little more than I should have as I looked out at the remains of Karnac. . . . I thought I heard a long stilled voice.

" 'Rise, Fernanda, I command you rise! Rise, as you rose in the Temple of Krisna one thousand years ago!'

"The orchestra filled the quiet of the dusk as it played the Meditation from Thais. Two figures attired as Hindu Holy Men knelt, and Fernanda rose slowly, like a dream creature into space.

" 'There she lies, asleep in space, suspended by nothing but the power of thought. There she can remain in peace for two hours, two weeks, two years. The slightest sound, the slightest whisper can disturb her sleep.'

"The audience was hushed, overawed, as so many audiences had been by the beauty and grace of the perfect mystery—Karnac.

"The sun was gone, and twilight enveloped the area, this tiny area where Herrmann, Chung Ling Soo, Thurston, Okito, Horace Goldin, Paul Valadon, Carl Rosini, had dreamed such wonderful dreams, conceived such beautiful fantasies, produced such marvelous mysteries—illusion-land, U.S.A.''

CHAPTER 9

In 1911, my sister, Dorothy, was born in the flat at the Beverly Arms. Theo was with Thurston in Grand Rapids, Michigan at the time, so she was called the Grand Rapids Baby and Thurston was her godfather.

The local Nickelodeon, the Auditorium, just across the street from us, was run by a good-hearted Greek named Boulibasis. Here Lily sang ballads to illustrated slides accompanied on piano by Joe Dobrovulhska, a young man of Polish parents. A few doors away from this movie house on Flatbush Avenue there was a stationery store run by an old German couple, whose son, S.L. Rothafel, took over the Auditorium and had the effrontery to raise the price from a nickel to a dime, justified by putting in a three-piece orchestra, a thing unheard of in those nickelodeon days. His boldness was well rewarded inasmuch as he eventually sold the Auditorium and crashed Broadway with his combined vaudeville and picture palace known as the Roxy.

In 1913, we moved again to the house owned by Joe Dobrovulhska's parents, just a few blocks away, where we had the entire upper story. But this didn't last long as little Dorothy emptied an ashtray with a lighted cigarette butt into a basket of flowers that my father was making for Thurston. The old wooden house almost burned down and we had to get out and consider ourselves lucky that the house was insured.

Theo quickly found a third story flat at 245 East 25th Street in Flatbush.

Theo fixed up one of the five rooms as a workshop and a large adjoining room was divided off as a magic den where Theo displayed his latest tricks in glass showcases. The door to this den was always locked but, inspired by Thurston and for the benefit of future Latin-American theatre managers, I found the

43

way into this magical paradise.

The only thing that separated my bedroom from the forbidden sanctum sanctorum was a combined book- and-showcase raised about eight inches from the floor.

Any student of magic knows that a nice plump girl with plenty of "oomph" can get through an eight-inch trap door. So why did they go to all that trouble of locking the door when I could slither my skinny "un-oomphed" frame under the showcase and find myself in this Utopia of thumb tips and egg bags?

The key to the showcase of the very latest in miracles was unskillfully hidden in a Chinese vase, so that Goldston's Locked Mysteries were heartlessly unlocked. I soaked up all the *The Sphinx*—magic magazines, the Lang Neil's, Hoffmann's and all the rest of the books, including those in German and French, which I couldn't understand, but which were full of inspiring illustrations.

I remember one drawing of a beetle-browed magician doing the rising ball on the rod trick with one eye cocked on a young woman with tremendous bosoms. I know now that he was worried about that eight-inch trap.

I also did a spot of exploring into the hidden mysteries and no one ever knew that a phantom magician had been performing Okito's pet tricks in the dead of the night. I believe my mother suspected something, but as she knew I'd be skinned alive if my father found out, she said nothing. For my part I hung my hopes on the fact that Pop was deaf and slept like a rock.

That most admirable piece of furniture, the showcase, also served another purpose. When my father had clients and was in the middle of a "bull fight" (conference among magicians), I was glued to the other side of the showcase and imbibed many an earful of magic and blue gags. There were "bull fights" with Thurston, Kellar, Houdini, Carl Rosini, Mme. Herrmann, Ching Ling Foo, Dr. Hooker, Carter and many others. I learned the technique of the duck vanish and the traveling salesman simultaneously.

A few of the Thurston raincoat and whisker dramas were plotted in the den and nobody knew I was in from scratch and needed no Yogi to teach me breath control. When Thurston produced one of these epics, I was taken along for being a good boy to see the show. Afterwards, when I gave an entirely unsolicited explanation of this miracle, both Thurston and Pop did a collective pratfall. I just bowled them over with my magical insight. Thurston once said to father, "This child is a genius. One day he will be a great magician. He has a most uncanny sense of perception." Little did he know that my grapevine was the old showcase.

My father was not a deep believer in the cultural influence of a razor strop, so I took some risky chances in the workshop, which was *verboten* when my father was out. Although I hankered to build impressive illusions, I didn't dare fool around in there too much. A nicked chisel would have meant instantaneous obliteration. I once burred a dowel with a hammer and for the next week expected Scotland Yard on my neck.

My father did beautiful work in that shop. Always a marvelous craftsman, he made the most attractive and original apparatus. He loved his creations so much that he hated to sell them. He used the finest materials and gave loving care to each detail. Thurston's sloppiness used to drive him crazy and they almost had mayhem on hand at times.

Okito taught me the proper use of tools, which is essential for every illusionist to know for it is most important to be able to repair your own props. As far as constructing new illusions is concerned, it's always better that the secrets stay in the family. Magicians will agree with me when I say that a well-made piece of apparatus by a responsible dealer is always a bargain at any price, since it lasts for years and pays for itself over and over again. Some of Okito's tricks are still in use after fifty years of service and still work perfectly.

Houdini's brother, Hardeen, with his wife and two sons, lived near us at 550 East 21st Street and Harry and Bessie visited them frequently and often stayed for weekends. My father sent me there quite often to deliver repaired props or a new trick that Okito had made for Houdini.

Houdini had no children of his own and took quite a fancy to me. One day I was bold enough to show him my card work and mentioned, slyly, that Thurston was my teacher. That did it. He said he would show me things that Thurston could never do and proceeded to do a series of juggling card tricks that took my breath away. Spreading the cards on his arm he threw them into the air and caught them as they came down. He had a brilliant routine which he finished up by dropping the cards in a stream from his right hand and catching them with the same hand just as they reached the floor. This flashy card jugglery fired my imagination and I spent hours practicing something which I never used on the stage in my life.

Houdini was always very kind to me. One red letter day in my life was the Sunday afternoon he took me to the Brighton Beach Theatre to see Ching Ling Foo; and on that afternoon Houdini almost had a spat with my father because he insisted on giving me chewing gum which was a habit my father abhorred.

Houdini had a dominating character and it was part of his personality and drive to always try to be greater and bigger than anyone else. A typical sidelight on Houdini's character is shown in the photo published in the *The Sphinx* of March 1941. The photo shows Houdini standing alongside Nelson Downs. Houdini is resting his arm on Down's shoulder to enable him to stand on his toes so as to appear as tall as Downs.

Houdini was a man who could seemingly do no wrong. The night he opened with his first full evening's show at the Globe Theatre in New York, his opening trick was the vanishing and re-appearing lamp, a mechanical trick in which the lamps collapse in one table and expand from another.

The trick failed and the audience snickered. This was rubbing salt in the wound for a man like Harry. He stopped the music and, stepping to the run-down, said, "The cause of the failure of this trick is due to the poor workmanship of Herr Conradi-Horster of Berlin."

In spite of Houdini's experience, showmanship and personality, the show was a flop. It just wasn't his metier. Alongside his sensational escapes, his tricks and illusions were flat. The background of suspense and danger was lacking and he just wasn't being Houdini.

Thurston, on the other hand, never tried an escape in his life. He just presented illusions. Yet both men were great successes...but to each his own.

However, Houdini's lectures on anti-spiritualism were sensational. He was on firmer ground here. Here was the defiant Houdini, the crusader, the superman who defended the sucker from the wiles of the fraudulent medium. Even after his death, his prearranged spirit message to Bessie was highly publicized and his fame augmented until today he is a legend.

I had seen Houdini do his famous trick of swallowing dozens of needles and pulling them threaded from his mouth. I had not the slightest idea how this could be done, and in those days it was next to impossible to discover the secret of a trick, even for a magician's son. Commercialism had not yet set in for magic and the dealers wouldn't sell certain tricks to outsiders and in some cases, as in Martinka's, the customers were sworn to secrecy. This is one of the prime reasons why magicians had such prestige in those times.

I untactfully mentioned to my father my desire to know how the needle trick was done and was rewarded with a stony glare.

"You vill do me the great fafor," he said sternly, "of confining your undoubted talents to your homvurk and stop vurrying about how Mr. Houdini does his tricks. Besides, I don't hold with that type of trick; it is highly dangerous and if Harry vishes to risk his neck, that's his affair. So let us hear no more of it."

Soon after this lecture came the fateful Sunday afternoon that I still remember as if it were yesterday. I was given a quarter by my father to take a gadget to Houdini's house at 278 West 113th Street in New York. Twenty cents for the streetcar and subway fare, there and back, and a nickel for an ice cream cone. When I got to the house I found Houdini alone as Bessie had gone out. He must have been bored to distraction because he invited me to stay for a while.

He was wearing an old sloppy pair of pants and was stripped to the waist and I was awestruck by his marvelous physique. He noticed my admiration and gave me a good talking to about the value of exercise and the advantages to be accrued from plenty of swimming and chinning and of the harmful effects of smoking. He told me that his great strength not only helped him in his escapes but it was useful for taking care of wise guys who came onto the stage. His resemblance to old illustrations of Cagliostro was striking. He had that same proud, arrogant, fearless expression. Houdini was disliked by most of his fellow magicians; it might have been envy, I don't know. To me, he was a kind man. However, he never allowed me backstage as Thurston did. I always had to wait in his dressing room or catch the act from the front.

But on this Sunday afternoon, after he got through with his no smoking lecture, he asked me if I wanted some gum and started feeling around the pockets of his sloppy pants and found none.

"Open that drawer," he said, pointing to the desk, "and get a packet."

I opened the drawer and my heart slammed against my ribs, for there, neatly arranged in a row, were the prepared needle loads. One look was enough...I knew! I found the gum and quickly closed the drawer. He talked for a while but I don't remember anything he said as I had a guilty conscience and I was afraid he would divine my thoughts. So I fled at the first opportunity, which must have caused him great surprise as he usually couldn't get rid of me.

When I got home I was like a cat on hot bricks as I wheedled a dime from my mother and early the next morning bought a package of needles and some thread in Woolworth's. I locked myself in the bathroom and made up a load just as I had seen it, alternating the points and winding the thread around each needle and then making a large knot at the end. I put the finished load in my mouth and it felt like a hamburger. I wondered how Houdini could talk with that load in his mouth, until I discovered that I could hide it on the left side between the gums and the cheek.

Now came the dangerous part. Houdini would place a bunch of needles on his tongue and, throwing his head back, apparently swallow them and then drink some water. I found that the needles would adhere to each other with saliva, and in the movement of tossing the head back, it was not difficult to deposit them on the other side of my mouth between the gums and the cheek.

Finally I did the whole trick and nearly swallowed the lot in my fright when my mother banged on the bathroom door and inquired suspiciously what I was doing in there for so long. My quietness had disturbed her. She was used to noise.

Of course, I couldn't keep my big mouth shut and I told my playmates that my bosom pal, Houdini, had taught me the famous East Indian needle-swallowing trick. I was called a liar and a four-flusher on the spot and was challenged to do it. As I couldn't back down after such a drastic statement, I said I would and I did.

The word got around and some woman complained to my mother that I was teaching her son bad habits by doing sword swallowing, so the foul deed was brought to light. After a tearful scene, my mother promised not to tell my father or Houdini if I gave her my word I would never do that trick again. I gratefully agreed and didn't do the trick until many years later when I had my own act.

At school, however, I was the white-haired boy. When I gave a show in the school auditorium at P.S. 89—my handshadows on the slide-projection sheet—everyone agreed that my future lay in the theatre.

CHAPTER 10

The year 1914 was the end of the easy-going, peaceful world that we knew. In May of that year Theo got the news that Papa had passed away in Amsterdam. The three brothers, Theo, Emile and Edward brought their mother and brother, Jack, to New York; but the old lady was very unhappy in this strange land and returned in less than a year to Holland, where she died in 1917.

In August the world war started and all imports from Germany were cut, which was the final blow for the Bamberg Magic and Novelty Company which had been ailing for some time. Theo and Joe Klein dissolved the partnership.

Nineteen-fourteen was the beginning of the end of those lazy carefree days in the tree-lined streets of Flatbush; the baseball games in the back lot; the free-lunch counters; rushing the can for the neighbors at a nickel a throw; the job at the A & P that paid five cents for every delivery we made on a push wagon; selling *Saturday Evening Post* subscriptions to the neighbors. (Mr. Collins of the Curtis Publishing Co., a keen amateur magician, had personally given me this route.)

Our movie heroes were Wally Reid and Charlie Ray. Out on Elm Avenue was the Vitagraph Studios, and Mr. French, one of the directors and also an amateur magician, was a friend of Theo's and often let me go out to the lot and pick up a few cents as an extra in scenes in which the leading people were John Bunny, a fat comedian whose foil was a skinny comedienne, and Flora Finch. The handsome Maurice Costello and the dashing Antonio Moreno were the glamour boys of the period and Theda Bara was the leading vamp. One of our great idols was William S. Hart, the first of the fighting cowboys, who visited us at home on occasion, accompanied by Eddie Polo.

Hart was as much a cowboy as Okito was Chinese. Hart was Dutch and Eddie Polo was a Rumanian.

When Mr. French came to the house for magic lessons, he often tried to get Theo to invest in the Vitagraph Company, but Pop wasn't interested. He had little faith in this newfangled business, and even when he was invited to sit in on a conference with Marcus Loew and William Fox, who were interested in investing in this new business, it was still no go. Theo just couldn't see it. Vitagraph was protected, but the independent studios were having a bad time with the Patents Company and there was talk of getting out of New York and making pictures on the coast in some place called Hollywood in California. Chaplin had quit the Fred Karno show and was making big money with one and two reel shorts; but Theo said that magic was not for the movies and he may have had a point there as a few years later Houdini lost a lot of money in his film ventures.

How clearly a Sunday in August in 1914 stands out in my memory. I was playing Kit-cat with the kids on the block when a newsboy came running by shouting "Extra! Great Britain declares war on Germany." At once we took sides, and being a born Englishman, I was naturally the leader of the Allied-minded band. Our private war was confined mostly to fist shaking from a distance. To my dismay it was discovered that Bamberg was a city in Bavaria, which was a frightful blow to my prestige and worse was yet to come when Brooklyn circles were convinced that a Dutchman was a German. For a time I felt like the spy who came in from the cold, but it was a faraway war and like all kids we got fed up with it and turned our attention to Jack Johnson.

However, there was one boy who remained my mortal enemy, Herman Schmidt, a husky blonde lad of German parents. He had a mania for drawing pictures of the Kaiser, the double-headed eagle, the German flag, and at night would scribble in chalk on the wall of our house "Deutschland uber alles," which I could not reciprocate because he lived in a frame house on Roger's Avenue with a garden in front and a high wooden fence. But on my way to school I did get a certain satisfaction by spitting on the crab apple tree in his front yard.

Imagine then my tremendous surprise one morning when there was a knocking on the front door and I opened it to find myself staring at the face of my arch enemy.

"Hello," he said bashfully handing me a jar of crab apple jelly (poisoned, no doubt). "My mother sent this over for you."

For once in my life I was at a loss for words.

There was an embarrassing silence for a few moments and then he continued, "Well, it's like this. My father is a house painter and in a vacant flat he's repainting over on Nostrand Avenue he found a box of magic tricks on a shelf in a closet. He brought it home for me but there are no directions and I thought that because you know all about magic and all, maybe you could explain to me how to do these things."

Magic! The Kaiser and the war were forgotten as we flew off to his house. Herman's magic set was a beautiful outfit made in France with a wire-haired boy magician pictured on the lid of the box. The tricks were well selected and included the little soldier in a cape that vanished and re-appeared at will, a small set of linking rings, a miniature die box, the die through the hat trick, a little wooden wand with ivory tips, grandmother's necklace and some card tricks. Most of the tricks I knew and I started with those. My father put me wise about the ones I didn't, so my prestige was safe as far as Herman was concerned.

(The big magic shows were never geared for children; they were an intellectual challenge to adults. In the matinees, special tricks were performed for children and some of the heavy stuff was cut out. A child is not impressed by magic. In his child's world magic is a natural thing, and the older he gets, the more his doubts grow about magic and magicians in general.)

I taught Herman to do the tricks and his interest in magic became an obsession that lasted all his life. (One day I even took him along with me to visit Houdini and Hardeen. He was speechless and I became his idol.)

In turn he taught me his hobby of making wireless sets with decoherers made from glass tubes and iron filings, using galena crystals for "cat-whisker" receivers. I became just as crazy about wireless as he was about magic. Herman became my greatest friend and this friendship lasted as long as he lived.

We lived for four years in the East 25th Street flat. The house alongside ours was identical and only a narrow alley separated them. I was usually awakened in the morning by "The Rustles of Spring," played by an eccentric woman whose living room window faced my bedroom. Sometimes I would put a roll in our player-piano and grind out "The Awakening of the Lions" or "The Wedding of the Winds" as loud as I could and she would retaliate, I thought, by giving me a load of Bach that drove me from the house.

51

Lily played the piano well and her choice stock of old English music hall ditties delighted our guests. Lily's ribald version of "Chase me, Charley" was a riot and she was very popular.

Mother never lost her precise British accent and this was the cause of aisle-rolling hilarity in a neighborhood that spoke the worst English in the world, including the Bronx.

When Lily would have words with a typical Brooklyn housewife, the discussion was in two entirely different languages. She would shudder when she heard me say, "I seen a guy on de roof uva joint on twennytoid street," and would politely beg me to translate the statement into English.

Theo, between Thurston tours, constructed his latest inventions in the shop. For Madame Herrmann he built a forerunner of the now-popular Squared Circle trick. A three-sided screen on a table was lined with black velvet—the open side of the screen towards the audience. A brass flower pot stood in the center of the table and on it rested a metal cone covered with black velvet that melted into the screen and was invisible from a few feet. Another bright red cone was placed on the pot (over the black cone) and when both were removed together, a large rose bush appeared. The weak spot of this trick was that any overhead lighting showed up the black cone. Years later someone thought of placing a cut out facing on the screen which effectively killed the shadow and perfected the trick.

Another fine trick which he constructed at that time consisted of six wooden cubes of different colors. One color was selected and the spectator could decide the position of the cube when they were stacked one on the other. A small folding screen was closed around the cubes for an instant and when opened the selected block had vanished, to be found in a previously borrowed hat. He also perfected his wonderful card frame in which a card torn to pieces was restored, piece by piece, and finally jumped out of the frame.

When Theo's magician friends came to dinner, I was always allowed to stay up later than usual so I could listen to their stories.

One evening Oscar Teale told a vivid story of that mystery man of magic, Harry Sears, who had produced a magical extravaganza, the Blue Pearl, in London in 1911. Sears disappeared one day when leaving his home for the theatre and has never been heard from since.

Professor Frederick Eugene Powell, with his typical mustache and goatee of the Herrmann era, told us tales of his tours through Mexico and Cuba. I was fascinated by his account of his adventures in Mexico City, when Madero and Don Porfirio Diaz were struggling for power.

The next day at school I opened my geography book to the colored plates of Latin American flags and was bewitched by such fanciful names as Brazil, Peru, the Argentine Republic, Mexico, El Salvador, Ecuador, Colombia, Paraguay, Chile, Venezuela, the Port of Spain and so on. I tried to find out if there were any magicians in those far off mysterious lands, but the only one I ever heard of was the mysterious Mexican who had first shown the back hand palm in Otto Maurer's magic shop in the Bowery. My father told me that the only one of whom he knew was the famous L'homme Masque, a Peruvian nobleman, Jose Antoner Gago y Zavala, whom he saw perform as a boy. L'homme Masque performed in Europe, mostly in private functions for the aristocracy. He apologized for the black mask that he wore, saying, "I wear it for private reasons." He was a wonderful sleight-of-hand performer and made a great impression on Papa Bamberg and the boy Theo.

In 1916, Maurice Kains, a young and enthusiastic amateur magician, rented our spare room and his great delight was to watch Theo at work in the shop. He learned well and in later years he created a new artistic style of his own in Los Angeles. In 1917, he was drafted and after the war he became a cameraman for some of the major motion picture studios in Hollywood, specializing in color photography.

He joined me in my love for Latin America. Every day when the *Journal* would arrive, we would laugh our heads off at the comic strip "Krazy Kat" which had a New Mexican background. Besides the Kat, who had a Yiddish accent, there was a brick-heaving mouse known as Ignatz Mouse. Offisa Pup tried to keep the peace but the Kat was in love with the mouse and his greatest joy was to receive a brick in the back of his neck which was a sure sign of the mouse's affection. The foreign words "mesa" and "corral" were always good for a laugh and I called Maurice Los Kains and he called me El Dave. We used to make up our own Spanish words by adding an "o" to English ones. It was el bedo or el chairo or el streeto. Little did I dream that one day I would be doing a full night's show in Spanish. It was then that I found that the "la" interested me more than the "el."

After the sinking of the Lusitania, America's attitude towards Germany changed. Only a few months before, when Okito was breaking in a new vaudeville act in Baltimore, Captain

Koenig, who had been the first to cross the Atlantic in a submarine, was feted in the theatre and his box draped with American and German flags; but now things were changing and Uncle Sam was rolling up his sleeves.

Herman changed his name from Schmidt to Smith and was the most pro-Allied of us all. He organized my kid shows in the cellar at two cents a throw with the proceeds going to the Red Cross. One memorable afternoon we had a world-shaking box office of $1.10 and we were in the big time.

The act that Theo was breaking in was called ''Theo Bamberg & Co.'' Lily was the Co. The act opened with mother seated at the piano singing ''In Old Madrid.'' Theo would walk on dressed in a riding habit. After a distressingly corny routine of jokes and crisscross patter, he would go into a very nice routine of cigar and silk manipulations, followed by handshadows. Lily then sang ''A Little Bit of Heaven'' while Theo prepared for his finale of Chinese magic, terminating with the Mat Trick.

They played all the New England states and Canada with this act and I was taken along. We played the Gus Sun time, the Poli circuit, Loew's, Interstate time and the New York Proctor Houses. When we played the Riviera and the Riverside in New York City, I had all the kids and neighbors on the block come to see the show and applaud like mad. During this tour we played with the magicians Ziska and King. I still remember Ziska's superb handling of the egg bag, especially the howl that went up when the real egg dropped to the floor and smashed. One of the funniest acts we played with was Frank Van Hoven and his block of ice trick which stopped the show cold. (No pun intended.)

Theo and Lillian Bamberg in their 1915 patter act described on page 54.

St. George's Hall, London. Home of "Maskelyne's Mysteries."

CHAPTER 11

In the summer of 1917, Thurston had an attraction in Luna Park, Coney Island, romantically called The Kiss Waltz which was a number of round, cage-like cars, whirling around on twisting track that caused many a loving couple, under the delusion that they were waltzing, to throw up their hot dogs. Naturally, I had to go down for an inspection and Herman went with me. One of Thurston's assistants was in charge and he invited us to ride free, as long as we acted as if we were having a whale of a time. So we spent an hour on this whirligig until we were almost stupefied. From there we staggered out to study the technique of "Slip-the-Jit" Harry Casino, the weight guesser, who was later to play a part in my checkered career. It was a typical Coney Island Sunday afternoon with the brassy music of the Calliopes, the smell of salt-water-taffy and sea air and the mingled cries of the ballyhoos and screaming kids. Wedged in between the Candy Butcher and the Tunnel of Love was a little theatre with a huge banner over it that read, "The Zancigs! Two Minds With But a Single Thought," and in smaller letters below "Prof. Christiansen—Knows All...Sees All."

Our money was running low and Herman was for blowing it all on the Shoot-the-Chutes, but I persuaded him to invest our capital in seeing a great artiste that I had heard so much about but never seen. So we bought two tickets and shoved ourselves as far down front as we could get.

Prof. Christiansen worked first. A number of white postcard-sized cards were distributed and questions were written on them. A member of the audience was asked to collect the cards, shuffle them well, and throw them haphazardly on a small table on a raised platform that served as a stage. I watched closely and there was no switch.

Christiansen was blindfolded and led to the table and with a most simple and effective one-ahead system, he answered the questions. After eight or nine questions were answered he feigned fatigue and went into his pitch about answering the rest of the questions in private readings in the back of the tent.

By this time Herman was bored stiff and wanted out, but I managed to hold him down by sheer willpower.

Then Julius Zancig stepped up on the platform and made his opening speech. Here was a man who had been the rage of England, the protégé of Lord Northcliffe, headliner of a command performance for the Royal Family of England, and who had made, in his time, a substantial fortune, but was now working in a cheap side-show, doing so many shows that at the end of the day he probably looked like he had been pulled through a taffy machine.

Zancig introduced his "medium," Henry (Paul Rosini), and did a fast, amazing mind reading act divining articles, colors, names, mathematical problems and finishing with a convincing book test.

During the act Herman asked in a low voice how it was done. I didn't know so I told him the chair backs were wired with telephones. I had to keep up my reputation as a know-it-all mastermind.

Zancig must have heard us muttering and came over and asked me what my name was. I said "David Bamberg Okito." He looked surprised and a moment later Henry said my name, much to Herman's surprise. Zancig whispered to me to stay after the show and went on to conclude the act.

After the tent cleared Herman and I went to the back of the small stage and Zancig greeted me effusively and asked me if I remembered his late wife, Agnes, who had taken such a fancy to me on the train in Norway. I shot a side glance at Herman to see if he was getting all this and was properly impressed. Zancig went on to say that the act was breaking up because Henry was drafted and he needed a new medium and would I like to do that kind of work.

Can you imagine a thirteen-year-old kid saying no to such a proposition. I said "yes" good and loud, with another glance at Herman who was properly slack-jawed.

Then a cold hand clutched my heart. Would my father give me permission? I asked Zancig to come over to our house the next day and talk it over with my father. I gave him the address.

All the way home on the open air street car Herman was

goggle-eyed and speechless. Even then I had to have an audience.

When I burst into Pop's shop to announce that I was to be a great mindreader, he received this startling bit of news coldly. He reminded me that I had lost many weeks of schooling while with his act and the Thurston show and when, pray, would I learn to read and write? I saw my career going down the drain.

That evening, at dinner, he talked it over with my mother and for the first time I heard the story of the two leading London newspapers going for each other, one denying and the other affirming the power of thought transmission. Lord Northcliffe, owner of the *Daily Mail,* Sir Oliver Lodge and various scientists and men of letters were in favor of Zancig against critics like Anatole France and others. This was sugar for Zancig who cashed in on the spectacular publicity.

Then poor, deformed Agnes died and Zancig went to pieces. They had built up the act from a very simple beginning and during the years had brought it to a state of perfection bordering on the miraculous. Zancig searched for but never found the kindred spirit that is the basis of this work. He was now married to a Brooklyn school teacher, Ada, a shy and retiring lady who was a confirmed spiritualist. She learned the mechanics of the code but performed the act with her head down and answered in a hardly audible voice. She knew the act was a fake and it made her feel guilty and ashamed to look at the audience. She only did the act to please Zancig. Later Zancig taught the code to the brilliant young Henry, who was to one day make a reputation for himself as Paul Rosini.

That same evening Harry and Bessie Houdini showed up for coffee, and when Pop asked Harry his opinion of the deal, Houdini wasn't very keen on it. He thought kids should go through school. My parents were already cold towards the idea and Houdini's opinion seemed to put the lid on it.

When Zancig showed up the next afternoon things didn't look too good. But Zancig was a fast talker and he convinced my parents that the act would not interfere with my schooling. He said that if I learned the rudiments of the code quickly, I could break in the act at Luna Park with Henry as a prompter doing a spot of ventriloquism now and then to get me out of my tight spots. Then, after the summer vacations were over, he intended to rent a house on West 87th Street in New York and use the lower floor as a studio for private readings. We could have the upper two stories rent free. He intended playing private engagements with the act and I was to get a percentage, with a guaranteed minimum of $100 a week. He had also rented a store on Lexington Avenue where he intended doing the act in the evening as a come-on to sell horoscopes and occult books. The rent-free $100 minimum bit did it for Pop and Mother was steamrollered into saying yes.

(When the deal had been settled, Houdini suggested the stage-name Syko for me, just as years before he had suggested the name of Buster for the youngest of the Six Keatons tumbling act.)

I was given the code under the vow of strictest secrecy and told to memorize it. Luckily I had, still have, a retentive memory and I crammed day and night to memorize a code that had no system, no phonetics, no mnemonics and no anything. It had been slowly built up over the years, adding a bit here and a thought there, and this unbelievable hodgepodge was given to me to learn by heart in a month.

Within three weeks I was doing a simplified version of the act in Luna Park and the day Herman came down and saw the act, he nearly had a stroke. He sat there with his mouth open and frantically looked for telephones in the chair backs. After the act he applauded his head off with that vicarious pleasure in my success that was so typical of him and lasted all his life.

In the fall of 1917 we left Flatbush forever and moved to a brownstone house at 109 West 87th Street, between Amsterdam and Columbus Avenue. I had my own room on the top floor next to Pop's workshop and although I saw very little of the $100 deal (my share coming roughly to about a buck a week), I still managed to construct wireless equipment, and in my wall closet I had a Nikola Tesla-looking laboratory.

My rapport with Zancig increased and the act was getting to be a fast, sure-fire thing, almost as good as the old act with Agnes. Zancig was highly pleased and between us we perfected the code for transmitting drawings, which was something new in mind reading acts.

We used the one-ahead system for this and Zancig would cue the next drawing while asking the spectator if the previous drawing was correct. Then he would lift his thick spectacles in order to concentrate on the slate he had in his hand and with his extreme farsightedness would spot a drawing half across the room and cue it to me. His misdirection was unique and he also possessed colossal nerve. If the drawing was too difficult to code, he would hold the slate in his left hand with the drawing face down to the floor and choosing another slate with a simpler drawing, would place it on top on the one he was holding with the drawing face up. When I had finished drawing the simple figure he would hold up both slates for the audience to verify the simple drawing, thereby giving me a good squint of the complicated drawing on the back slate. A while later he would "discover" he had this slate in his hand and dramatically say just one word, "Right," and I would duplicate the drawing and the audience was flabbergasted. Okito was delighted when we pulled that swindle since anything so bold made him happy, and when Zancig would go into his Mr. Magoo routine, my father would hug himself with glee.

Another barefaced swindle was a series of memorized numbers like 30589. Zancig would borrow a newspaper and opening to the financial page say, "Right," and I would rattle off the memorized numbers Then he would thrust the paper under the owner's nose and pointing vaguely to the center of the page would ask "Correct?" The poor sucker would always say yes and no one could ever prove anything.

The funniest swindle we had, which almost killed Okito every time we did it, was the hunh-hunh voice gag which we swiped from "Slip-the-Jit" Harry's weight-guessing swindle. It was used only for uncommon names that were too hard to cue. Zancig would give me the "hunh-hunh" signal, and I would mumble, "The gentleman's name is Vrowman Sfrunntz," and Zancig would triumphantly bellow, "Correct. Kermit Roosevelt." It's a miracle we weren't scragged for that one, but no one ever noticed and the applause was deafening.

The easiest test of all was the book test but it was the one that baffled them the most. All I had to do was to find the page and line that was cued to me and read the corresponding line from a duplicate book. To make it look hard I would clutch my brow and turn pale with mental strain, and in the deathly silence I would repeat the line in a weak and hesitating voice. The audience would fall for it and I would secretly gloat. I was on my way to becoming an obnoxious little ham.

We worked at the finest clubs and private homes in New York, and it is surprising that many intellectuals in America believed it to be genuine telepathy. It seemed to be such an obvious code with Zancig muttering in his Dansk-English, "Go come now here will you?" But no one seemed to notice it; although at one private party, John Barrymore, who had one drink over the eight, suddenly came out of his stupor and hollered, "The act's a fake. He's telling the kid in Swedish!" He wasn't far wrong.

Whenever we played a highbrow stag party, I always got the bum's rush and five cents for subway fare home right after the act was over. I was curious why they were so anxious to get rid of me, until one night I did a raincoat and whisker drama of my own and hid in the locker room of a rich club. After a while I sneaked out just in time to see a voluptuous blonde, wearing only a prop smile, emerge from a huge cake. I was just fourteen at the time and that started something. When I told Herman about it, I was called a flat-footed liar and it was a thing I couldn't prove. Nobody ever believed me.

I even tried to fool magicians when I could. A clever young amateur magician, John Mulholland, who was in later years to become one of the great names of magic in America, was intimate with my father. I found out that Pop highly valued John's hunting case watch which he had inherited from his father. Inside the case was a picture of John's mother. On a later occasion I spotted John at our show and to Zancig's surprise, I started to describe John's watch and mentioned the picture inside. Zancig knew that there was some chicanery somewhere but Mulholland was flabbergasted.

John got me back very neatly. We were selling Liberty Bonds in Union Square. Charlie Chaplin, Mary Pickford and Douglas Fairbanks, Sr. sold the bonds and I read the number by telepathy with a little help from Zancig, who was in the crowd screaming his head off to make the telepathic vibrations clearer. Suddenly, among those hundreds of faces, I spotted Mulholland's Cheshire cat grin. He held up four fingers which was the next number I was to call out. He had twigged the code and he very nearly threw me off that day.

Some inexplicable things happened, too. One evening at a shindig Zancig cued me "coin" and I said, "A Roman coin." Zancig looked surprised and asked me to repeat it. After the act he said, "How did you know that it was a Roman coin?"

I thought he was kidding and I said, "You cued me."

"I did nothing of the kind," he said, "I, myself didn't know what kind of coin it was until you said Roman."

"You must have cued it was Roman or else how could I have known?"

Zancig gazed at me pensively and started to speak, but thought better of it and, shrugging, he turned away.

This happened once or twice more in the following months, until the day I gave the initials on a watch which Zancig hadn't cued.

"Maybe it's an association of ideas," I said, "like coin-Roman—ribbon-blue—things like that," I finished off, lamely, as the idea wasn't any too clear in my own mind.

"That wouldn't account for the initials on the watch. All I cued you was watch-gold because the initials were in Hebrew which I can't read. But the owner said you were correct. Explain that."

"I don't know," I said. "Maybe we're mind readers."

"You make a joke of it," said Zancig, "but this sort of thing happened many times to me with Agnes, never with Ada nor Henry."

I still have no explanation of how this could have happened.

One of our engagements took us to Atlantic City where we played in the Latzcellar of the Alamac Hotel on the boardwalk.

Harry Latz, the manager, was a tall, lanky young man, full of original ideas and with the drive and personality to put them into effect. He was a keen amateur magician and his imaginative ideas for presenting magical effects greatly influenced my outlook on stage presentation.

Once he went so far as to dream up a "Prehistoric" night in the Latzcellar in which all the waiters wore skins and furs and carried clubs. We did the act with Zancig dressed as a caveman and I as a gorilla, introduced as the mind reading ape.

It was here in Atlantic City that we gave a private show for Sir Arthur and Lady Conan Doyle. Sir Arthur, creator of Sherlock Holmes, was a firm believer in spiritualism and the occult and was greatly impressed with the act, declaring it to be genuine mind reading but adding, shrewdly, that at moments of great mental strain Zancig might have resorted to "spoken words and signs."

Okito's idol in his youth had been Sherlock Holmes and when he met Sir Arthur he was overwhelmed. He showed Sir Arthur some close-up magic that would have baffled the great detective himself.

Harry Latz had one of the original Kellar Talking Buddhas in his office and, as the principle of electrical induction was practically unknown to the average person in those days, he got some good publicity with this trick for his hotel.

One day Houdini and Conan Doyle were in Harry's office and Sir Arthur was completely taken in by this mysterious Buddha that whispered messages from the great beyond. This was about the time that Sir Arthur was working on his novel of spiritualism *The Land of Mist*.

Sir Arthur's and Houdini's friendship ended when Sir Arthur, through the aid of a spirit medium, produced Houdini's mother's voice, using perfect English, whereas Mrs. Weiss only spoke a few words of English with a thick Hungarian accent.

Among the guests of the Alamac Hotel was an English sculptor named Frank Lascelles who was making a bust of Harry's mother. He never missed one of our shows and sat there fascinated and enthralled. Harry had tipped Zancig about certain details of Lascelles' work as director of some of the famous Pageants of the British Empire and his adept handling of the Great Indian Durbar for King George V. When Zancig pretended to see all these great events in a crystal ball, Lascelles became a firm believer in occultism.

Back in New York again life went on as before. Theo had joined the act with his magic and Zancig continued his private readings on the first floor.

Whenever I had a chance, I would spend my time in the closet where I kept my wireless outfit. One day in a magazine named *The Electrical Experimenter* published by Hugo Gernsback, I found a description of a device called a helix which could easily be made by winding a thick copper wire into a coil. I made one and fitted it to my crude apparatus and was struck dumb when I heard voices in my earphones. I phoned Herman about it and he said that the helix must have acted as an induction coil and I had overheard a telephone conversation.

I had to elaborate and spread the story in school about my mysterious voices coming through the air. The story spread around the neighborhood.

One day two sour-faced men appeared at the house and showed their Secret Service credentials. They questioned me about those mysterious voices. At first I was scared stiff and denied the whole thing, but it didn't take long to get the story from me and they went up to my room to have a good look at my homemade outfit. They asked me if there was anything in that closet I needed except the wireless outfit. I removed my few treasures and they proceeded to drive two thick screw-eyes into the door frame and, padlocking it, sealed the lock with lead seals and with strict instructions that it was not to be opened until further instructions from the police.

At the time I didn't know what was going on, but later I found out that I had heard what was probably the first tests of transmitting speech by wireless telegraphy developed by the U.S. Navy.

Always the actor, I had to make a big production of this, and invited a few of my classmates up to see the sealed door and regaled them with outrageous stories of international spy rings in which I played a leading part.

On a visit to Herman I tried to feed him this wild story but he just looked at me calmly and said, "Banana oil. It happened to all of us. They shut me down too. It's a war measure for security reasons."

On one of these overnight stays, after Herman's folks had gone to bed, he got out his latest treasure, a book which had just come out named *The Insidious Dr. Fu Manchu* and together we read and shivered over the machinations of the Chinese Devil Doctor. This was really something up my alley and we began to horse around. At one point when I was making hollow sounds and saying in a sepulchral voice, "Fuuuuu...Manchuuuuu," and waving my hands like a maniac, the sliding door that led from the parlor to the dining room opened by itself. We nearly dropped dead. A heavily loaded dray passing the house would cause it to tremble and the blasted door would slide open by itself; but we didn't think of this at the moment as there are moments when the process of thinking is frozen, and we got the hell out as fast as we could.

After that, Fu Manchu was a scare word for us and got to be a running gag. I would call Herman up in the dead of the night and in a guttural tone would cheerfully offer to cut his throat and once in a while I would receive letters smeared with tomato catsup and signed "Fu Manchu."

In the summer of 1918 Carl Rosini and his charming wife, Peggy, were constant visitors. Carl spent hours with Theo in the workshop and Carl's original idea of the Triple Bowl production was perfected by Theo and later known as the Multiple Production, perhaps the best of all production mysteries.

It was during this association that the release for the large Chinese water bowl was perfected doing away with the complicated and insecure original method which was never leakproof.

Theo also built a highly improved version of the Duck Vanish trick which was the rage of the moment with both LeRoy and Nixon claiming to have invented it. Actually it was LeRoy's original idea but Theo's model was superior to either of theirs. In 1935 I eliminated the one weak spot of this famous trick so that I had the joy of baffling Okito with his own trick.

Finally the atmosphere began to change at the house on West 87th Street. One day a couple of women came for a private

DAVID BAMBERG

reading. Afterwards, when Zancig asked for his fee they refused to pay, called him a crook and said they were policewomen. Picking up the phone they asked for Spring 3-100 and told the desk sergeant to send over a couple of cops to make an arrest and hanging up, quickly left the house. In a short while two cops showed up, but Zancig swore that no fortune telling went on in the house and all he did was give private exhibitions of mentalism. Calling me in, we went into the act and, after he slipped them a ten spot, they left the house, puzzled that anyone would pay for a private exhibition of this kind.

This unsavory episode was very depressing and I began to get a glimmering of what a cheap racket it was. My mother was disgusted with the whole affair and constantly nagged my father to move out.

To be quite honest about Zancig I would say he had something of the psychiatrist in his make-up and was a very humane man with a lot of experience of life.

Perhaps I rationalize in retrospect when I say that he did a lot of good with his crystal ball. He tried to solve his customers' problems with the disinterested viewpoint of the outsider, and often he would suggest the solution of a problem that they had been blind to. Some of the greatest names in the business world came to him for advice and many swore by him.

In magic circles Zancig was branded as a swindler, but he never cheated people for large sums of money as some spirit mediums did. He charged a nominal fee and often a client in desperate financial straits would leave Zancig's studio with a few dollars in his pocket to help him along.

Everything seemed to happen at once. After the Armistice, which Pop and I celebrated in Chinatown, came the great plague of Spanish Influenza. Both Dorothy and I caught it and the house was quarantined and the customers stayed away in droves. One day, Thurston, who had just undergone a newfangled operation for having his jowls lifted, came to the house to display his new found beauty, but when he was told that we had the "flu," he did the fastest vanishing act of his career.

Our only constant visitor to the house was the English sculptor, Lascelles, who inveigled his way into my mother's confidence by painting a lurid picture of the disgraceful future that awaited me if I continued in this kind of work. He bewailed the fact that such a "brilliant child" should not go through Eton and Oxford to enable him to become a young gentleman with the necessary education and training to confront a cold and

64

hostile world. And poor English Lily fell for his line—hook and sinker. He painted a beautiful picture of his manor in Oxford-shire and offered to take me to England after I graduated from public school.

The showdown with Zancig came a few weeks later at a very exclusive party in honor of Charles Schwab, the multimillion-aire steel magnate, where we were engaged to do the act. Mr. Schwab took out a hundred-dollar bill and said that if I could tell him the serial number on it I could have it. This was noth-ing new as I had been given dollar-bills and even five-dollar bills many times as a present after reading the serial number, but one hundred dollars, gosh—I'd never even *seen* a hundred-dollar bill.

But Mr. Schwab was sunk the moment he took that bill from his wallet as Zancig had gone into his ''short-sighted act'' by lifting his glasses and peering at a card in his hand but actually reading the serial number on Mr. Schwab's bill.

I clutched my youthful brow and slowly read off the num-bers. Schwab handed the bill to Zancig to give to me, but Zan-cig put it in his pocket.

After the show I mentioned something about a split and Zan-cig handed me a dollar and said, ''That's your commission.'' I did a slow burn and then blew my stack and said too much, too loud. In fact, I overdid it and was frightfully rude to Zan-cig who had always been kind to me.

When we got home there was another row and the whole deal was called off.

In the confusion of the next few days everything went hay-wire. The indignant sculptor Lascelles appeared and it was decided that I would go to England with him to become a gen-tleman. I still can't figure out where my father's head was at that time to permit me to go with a stranger. What I didn't know was that he was planning to go to South America with Carl Rosini. Our family was splitting up.

My father had become an American citizen in May 1916, and that automatically made me an American, but I was refused a passport as a minor so they got me a British passport.

I graduated from public school ''by the skin of my teeth'' and a few days later left with Lascelles for Canada. In Quebec we boarded a freighter that took a limited number of passen-gers for Queenstown, Ireland. The weather was foul and the fact that the boat had a system of wire nets strung around it for protection against the floating mines which were still around from the war, did nothing to cheer us up. Eventually we arrived at a small village called Sibford Gower in northern Oxfordshire where Lascelles was lord of the ancient stone manor.

Poster of David as the Great Syko, 1920. (See page 97.)

CHAPTER 12

Immediately after our arrival Lascelles left for London to arrange his affairs and left me with a servant and a Canadian housekeeper in this old manor house with lead-lined windows. It had everything I had read about in books: old suits of armor, a huge fireplace with ancient weapons crossed on the wall above it, a musty old library with hundreds of dreary books, even an old hand-pumped organ on which, I was told, Ivor Novello had composed his popular war-time song "Keep the Home Fires Burning." The doors were thick English oak and the whole place had a gloomy medieval atmosphere—so different from the rush and bright lights of Broadway.

I learned to mount a horse and trotted about the sweet-smelling English countryside with its charming atmosphere and its simple, kindhearted villagers.

Lascelles wrote from London that he would be away for two months. I suspected that he had been a C.O. and was in London justifying his absence during the war.

Time hung heavy on my hands as there was nothing much to do. Daily I visited some neighbors, a young girl named Doreen and her mother, Lady Jane, who were much amused by my Brooklyn accent.

The village had no cinema and radio was a thing of the future. On Sundays one was obliged to attend the local parish church where the vicar gave interminable sermons that drove me to distraction.

Sometimes I would ride over to Oxford and imagine myself dressed in a long black cape and mortar board.

One morning while leafing through some London newspapers I saw an article written by Will Goldston on magic. He had been the author of those Locked-Mystery books in my father's library and was the proprietor of a magic shop in Leicester Square in London. I wrote a letter to Goldston, telling him who I was and begging him, please, send me his catalogue.

The very next day it arrived and my heart pounded as I saw all the old familiar tricks illustrated. I had no money but I did have the nerve to ask Goldston to send me some tricks on credit with the promise to pay from the proceeds of the shows I could give in the local schoolhouse and parish, and I enclosed a list of the tricks that came to £3/ 12/6. Goldston kindly obliged and with the miraculously efficient English postal system at its best, a large box arrived by the next post.

I tore off the wrapping and there they were in all their splendour...the bright red billiard balls, the lifelike rapping hand, the rabbit pan, the Chinese rice bowls, the die through the hat, silks, pulls, a wand...everything for a complete evening's show.

Suddenly I was confronted with a soul-shaking problem. I didn't know how to perform most of these tricks. This was indeed a paradox. I had been practically weaned on magic, had witnessed some of the world's greatest magicians at first hand, had toured with and assisted Thurston, had been a professional mind reader for over two years, and now I found myself at a loss to perform the simplest tricks in the book. I had seen most of them done by amateur magicians and had read and re-read the hyperbolic descriptions in the catalogues so many times that I honestly thought I could do them with just a few minutes practice. I soon discovered my mistake and using the instructions that came with each trick, I slowly and painfully managed to work them into a passable routine.

I believe that I was already developing a sense of originality in presentation which accounted for my long delay before I ventured to give my first show at the schoolhouse. But practice I did, all through the day and into the night for a month, until I could do the act backwards.

There was keen interest in the village and all the 2/6 (about 50 cents) seats had been sold and only the cheaper shilling seats were left, which I hoped would be sold at the last moment.

Finally the great night arrived and while I was preparing the show the audience started to trickle in—slowly at first—then in a rush until the small hall was full.

Imagine my chagrin at the moment of preparing the rice bowls to find that I had unaccountably left the celluloid disk at home. There was no time now to go back to the manor to look for it and regretfully I cut out this excellent trick and went on preparing the others.

My careful rehearsal paid off. Everything went like clockwork. All my tricks were cheerfully applauded and, flushed with success, I finally came to my breathtaking finale, the production of a white rabbit from the Welsh Rabbit Pan. Into the empty pan I blithely broke eggs, tossed in flour and salt and airily poured in a stream of alcohol; then flicking in a lighted match, I was rewarded with a flash of fire at least triple any blaze I had in my rehearsals. It resembled the launching of a small moon rocket. I was visibly shaken as I didn't know what had happened. I jammed on the cover to extinguish this bonfire and immediately removed it to produce a scared and half-suffocated rabbit. I took my bows to a satisfied audience and the show was over.

When I got home I found out what had happened. I hadn't forgotten to take along the celluloid disk. By a coincidence it was exactly the diameter of the interior of the fake for the rabbit pan and had stuck in the bottom. Because it was transparent, I hadn't seen it. This had been the cause of the fierce blaze that had almost hasenpfeffered the poor rabbit. From that time on, I separated fire effects from livestock.

A few days later I gave another show in the parish at a neighboring hamlet and made enough money to send Goldston what I owed him with a couple of quid left over.

A week or so later I received a wire from Lascelles to come up to London at once. I arrived in London the next morning and he was at the station to meet me. He told me that he had arranged for my entrance at Dulwich College and I had to take some kind of an examination.

When we arrived at the college I was taken to a small stuffy room where a stone-faced master questioned me about my previous schooling. I explained what my education was in New York. He seemed nonplused and said that in England the students were slightly more advanced. I hadn't told him that I had been an inattentive pupil with show business on my mind.

He then gave me a sheaf of papers with questions printed on them and told me I had an hour and left me alone. I couldn't answer one single question. In fact I didn't understand most of them. Was it possible that kids in England of my age were already steeped in Latin and Greek? I was so ashamed that I sneaked out without saying good-bye and returned to the hotel where Lascelles was staying.

He said the only thing would be private instruction with a

tutor for a while until I was ready for another test. Then he sprang it on me. He said that in the meanwhile, to pay for my tutelage, it might be a good idea to do the Zancig mind reading act in London clubs. That sounded all right to me and we returned to Sibford Gower.

I got out the code book I had taken with me and he started to memorize the code. After a month or so we had a primitive kind of an act but enough to get started with.

Looking back I should have known that he could never take Zancig's place, but it wasn't obvious to me until we had our first date in a private club in Brighton. It was something awful, and it's a wonder we weren't thrown out on our necks. Lascelles was so nervous that he cued everything wrong. What actually happened of course was that he found it impossible to say, "Go now please say I" in a company of fellow Englishmen. He lacked Zancig's misdirection and craftiness. It was a disgusting exhibition and even I had to laugh at times. The people who owned the club refused to pay and cancelled the act.

Everything had gone sour and relations were strained. I had my Uncle Charlie's address in Newton Abbot, Devonshire and I wrote and asked him if I could come down to see him and he replied that he would be delighted.

Uncle Charlie, his wife Emma and their two daughters, Ivy and Sadie, lived in a rambling two-storied house in Newton Abbot quite near the cinema that he owned. He made me very welcome. I told him the story of what had happened and he advised me to get in touch with my father as soon as possible, but I didn't know where Okito was, except that he was in South America somewhere with Rosini. So it was decided that until I had news of him I was to stay with Uncle Charlie. I was in constant contact with with my mother who was having a pretty hard time of it in New York. She hadn't the money to send me my fare home.

A few days later Uncle Charlie had to go to London to book pictures for his cinemas and he took me along with him. We had a high old time. I had my first airplane ride in an old Handley-Page left-over from the war. For a quid they took you up for a fifteen-minute tour over London. I knew that Herman would never believe this.

That same night we went to His Majesty's Theatre to see Oscar Ashe in "Chu-Chin-Chow." I had never seen such a magnificent stage production with such wonderful music and scenic effects. They even had black camels on the stage. The show had broken all theatrical records with its five-year run and I was lucky to have seen it as it greatly influenced my future concept of the theatre for the use of magical effects in stage production.

When we returned to Newton Abbot, Uncle Charlie offered me a temporary job as a operator in one of his movie houses. For eighteen shillings a week I cheerfully cranked my brains out in the booth.

If I remember correctly, it was Douglas Fairbank's "Thief of Baghdad" that was to be my downfall as a movie operator and bring me back into the world of magic again. There was a close-up of a snarling gorilla that fascinated me and as my tastes in pin-ups was rather outré, I snipped a length of it from the reel and hung it on the wall of the booth.

A few weeks later we ran "Auction of Souls" starring Milton Sills. There was one scene where Sills knocked on the door of an Arabian mosque and the camera cut to a close-up of the slave who opened it. With feverish zest I cut out the slave and cemented in the gorilla. From an audience standpoint the result was a trifle bizarre as no one understood the role of the gorilla-butler, but Hollywood got the blame as usual and I left it in and forgot to remove the dirty work.

When the picture opened in Cardiff and they got over the shock, they wired London about it. London traced the dastardly deed to Newton Abbot and Uncle Charlie convinced me with a little sleight-of-foot that gag men were unappreciated in Devonshire.

It was at this time that I realized that any further schooling for me was out and that I would have to make up my mind what I wanted to be. The prospects of a movie operator were not too bright and although Uncle Charlie was most kind and treated me as one of the family, I knew there was no future for me in his business. The only thing I knew was magic and mind reading. I was over fifteen years old and it was time to put on long pants. After the experience of the two shows I had given in Oxfordshire, I thought I could do a small act in London for private engagements, and if this didn't work out, I could always get a job as a magician's assistant.

I knew that Uncle Charlie would never allow me to go alone to London so I told him I had received a letter from my mother, in which she said I should come home and my passage money was at the American Consulate in London. He swallowed the story and gave me a couple of pounds and his blessing; so I did a

Dick Whittington and went to London to seek my fame and fortune as a magician.

Left to right: **Harry Houdini and his wife, Beatrice, Ching Ling Foo and his daughter, Chee Toy, and Theo Bamberg (circa 1914).**

CHAPTER 13

For the first time in my life I was really on my own. I felt that I didn't have a friend in the world as I unpacked my bag in the dismal diggings in Soho that was to be my home for the next few months.

Mother had written me that I had a baby brother, Donald, and knowing how bad things were, I didn't want to worry her, so I wrote glowing letters of my great success in England.

I tried all the agents and couldn't get a single date for my act. I did manage to get one private engagement at a children's party, but it fell flat as a pancake. It wasn't like the parish show where everyone knew me as the young master of the manor. I answered all the ads in *The Stage,* a theatrical weekly, for jobs as assistant to magic shows but not one single letter was answered.

To keep going I took a job as an electrician's assistant that paid a few bob a week and on the side I wrote letters in what I fondly believed to be German to Siemens-Schukert for some London importers who were anxious to open up trade with Germany again. By some miracle the cryptographers at Siemens deciphered my lousy Dutch-German and usually sent the right material. This meant another few shillings a week, and with fish and chips being the price they were, I made out all right.

Herman would write once in a while but he never imagined the despondency I felt when his cheerful chatter reminded me of the old carefree days in Flatbush. I didn't realize it at the time but I was becoming a hard boiled little bastard with a chip on my shoulder. I learned a lot about life in the thief and whore-ridden streets of Soho. The shock of seeing gin-sodden sots being thrown out of pubs to sleep it off sprawled in the gutter made me take such a dislike to booze that I didn't take a drink for years and then only an occasional beer or wine.

73

In contrast to this seamy side of life I spent many of my evenings in that dreamland that was St. George's Hall. I introduced myself to Mr. Facer who was manager of the Hall in those days and informed him that I was the son of Okito and grandson of C.W. Poole so he kindly allowed me to occupy a back seat to see the show.

This was my world and I gulped down enormous doses of magic and reveled in the originality and the *savoir-faire* of English magicians.

I devoured the work of Nevil and Captain Clive Maskelyne, De Biere, Oswald Williams, Selbit, Louis Nikola, Owen Clark, Lingah Singh and many others.

I was privileged to watch Jardine Ellis with his wonderful manipulations and Oswald Williams presenting his charming conception, "A Box of Tricks." This was an oversize half-crown box of tricks sold for children and contained the Ball Box, the Die and Hat, the Pillars of Solomon, the Obedient Ball and the Coin Slide, but with a novel twist to each of these well-known tricks that completely fooled any possessor of that outfit. This was a most delightful interlude and it could be used today with great success.

Williams' Washing Day was a comedy routine in which a white shirt was shrunk to doll size in a washtub, then run through a mangle to come out six feet long, then burned with a trick electric iron until finally, in disgust it was vanished only to appear hanging on a clothesline. I have often thought that this would be a very fine routine for a borrowed handkerchief.

Williams' Jewel with the £1,000 dress was a beautiful illusion in which he placed a large "diamond" in the center of a velvet covered board in a gilt frame. The diamond visibly expanded until it grew into a woman wearing a dress studded with thousands of imitation diamonds.

Williams was rather keen on illusions where one object changed into another, such as "Where My Caravan Has Rested" in which the girl seated in a caravan handed him a rose which he threw at the caravan, causing it to change into a bower of roses, while he sang "Roses of Picardy."

Williams both on stage and in private life was a sarcastic man who gave the impression that he was far more intelligent than his audience. When Mr. Facer introduced me to him he stared coldly through me, mumbled something and gave me his back. So much for my fleeting acquaintance with this very original magician with his fine inventive mind.

Another fine performer at the Hall was Allan Shaw and his coin manipulations. Nevil Maskelyne did his plate spinning act and his son, Captain Clive, the typical stiff upper lip British military officer, with his clipped English presented "The Spirits...are Here" with appropriate lip smacking after the word "spirits." This was a fine version of the old Cassadega Propaganda illusion of spiritual manifestations in a light shallow cabinet which rested on a sheet of glass placed over the backs of two chairs. A most convincing illusion and one that Kellar used for years in his show. The basic principle of this illusion was later used by Owen Clark for his Cannon Ball production and by Thurston in his Bangkok Bungalow illusion.

It was quite a shock for me when Maskelyne presented his New Page illusion. I had seen it dozens of times on the Thurston show where it was called The Prisoner of Canton. This was one illusion that I knew the secret of and my amazement can be imagined when Maskelyne showed the cabinet completely empty by turning it around with the doors open before placing the boy strapped to the board inside. It was then that I began to have an inkling of how right my father was in this admiration of the original Maskelyne technique in stage illusions. I had to see the New Page three times before I "got" it.

Another illusion that impressed me was Owen Clark's Flunkey's Dilemma, in which a dummy divided into three sections was placed on shelves in a shallow cabinet and transformed into a living person.

It was at the hall that I first saw the Dizzy Limit illusion, a modernized and simplified version of Maskelyne's Out of Sight illusion. A girl disappears from a falling net and only her clothes flutter down onto the stage. Years later I used this principle for the vanish of a "gorilla" and later, using the same basic principle, changed it for the Cage illusion, called The Cheating Cheetah.

Gus Fowler, the Watch King, did a watch manipulating act, produced alarm clocks and finished up by producing a huge grandfather clock.

Arnold DeBiere got a lot out of his Thumb Tie trick but I found his illusions rather poor and, in the case of the Turtle illusion, downright clumsy.

Some of the magicians who played the Hall attained an incredible perfection. I was told that Billy O'Conner, Fred Culpitt, Chris Charlton and Henry Hilton performed their acts, word for word, move for move, for over thirty years.

One excellent illusion of John Nevil Maskelyne's was the Living Picture in which a dozen large wooden cubes rearranged themselves in a shallow cabinet to form a selected work of art chosen by a spectator. When the doors of the cabinet were again closed and immediately opened, the painting was transformed into a living tableau.

John Nevil Maskelyne became a professional magician by accident. He was originally a watchmaker (as was Robert-Houdin) in his native town of Cheltenham, Gloucestershire. One day the famous Davenport Brothers, from America, gave a performance at the Town Hall with their bogus spiritualistic seances.

Maskelyne, then twenty-six, was appointed one of the committee of inspection due to his reputation as an amateur conjurer.

The accidental falling of a piece of cloth used to exclude light from one of the windows of the hall enabled Maskelyne to see Ira Davenport throw some of the musical instruments from the mysterious cabinet and re-secure himself with the ropes that bound his wrists.

Maskelyne later duplicated all the feats of the Davenports together with his friend George Cooke. His exposures were so popular that he gave up his watchmaker's business and went to London where he later hired the Egyptian Hall for three months, never dreaming that he would be there for over thirty years.

It was here that the famous Box Trick was first presented. Maskelyne and Dr. Lynn both claimed to have invented it. The case was taken to law and after three trials and appeals it ended in the House of Lords. Again, it was dismissed and Maskelyne lost the suit.

Later P.T. Barnum, the American impresario, paid Dr. Lynn £500 for a model of this illusion and took it to the U.S. where in later years it passed on to Houdini who made a sensation with it.

Although it is not generally known, Henry Bate, who owned a photographic studio in Brighton, was the real inventor of many magical illusions shown in the Hall. He built the Mascot Moth for Devant. He also built the Chocolate Soldier illusion, the Magic Kettle, and the Vanishing Motorcycle and Rider for Goldin, called "Bigg." He also had a hand in the Artist's Dream, the Birth of Flora, the Enchanted Hive, the Fairy Grotto, the Haunted Window and the Diogenes illusion.

I became quite good friends with Carlton, the Human Hairpin, a comedy magician who wore black tights, a false forehead and high-heeled shoes to add to his height. He was at one time one of the most popular acts of the English variety halls. His Die Box routine brought the house down. He was extremely thin and one of his gags was, "Mother, I can see the wires,"—"Hush, child, those are not wires...they are his legs."

Carlton drank terribly and many a time I would find him in a stupor on the floor of his dressing room. I would scrape him up, give him cold water and coffee and he would stagger out and in some miraculous way do his act, take a bow, stagger off-stage and collapse. It was a great pity, as he was the funniest comedian-magician I have every known and when sober, a lot of fun. Good old "Billiky-Bolicky."

I was very inspired by the technique of the magicians at the Hall. After seeing an illusion performed a dozen times I became well versed in the subtle misdirection that is so important in magic.

I had come to England to complete my education. That's exactly what I was doing in St. George's Hall. If an aspiring magician wanted to complete his magical education, where could he find a better place to learn?

One of the first things I had done when I arrived in London was to pay a visit to Will Goldston, whose magic shop, Alladin House, was on the first floor of a small building at 14 Green Street, Leicester Square. He received me very kindly and I artfully asked his permission to have my mail sent to his address. He agreed and this gave me an excuse to come by every other day or so and hover over his magic counter, drink in all the apparatus on display and occasionally meet some of the well-known conjurers who visited him.

One day he invited me to a meeting that evening to be held at Goldston's Magician's Club and asked me if I would care to perform a trick for the members. With the irresponsibility of youth I agreed and it wasn't until I got to my digs, and looked at my props, that I realized what a rash promise I had made. What trick could I do for all those professionals and well-versed amateurs who would be there? All these little stock tricks of my act were inadequate. I became desperate, even going as far as thinking of bandaging my hand with the pretext of a bad cut, when suddenly I got it...the needle trick! True, I had promised my mother not to do it, but that was ages ago when I was a kid and now I was a professional. So I bought some needles and thread and after one or two rehearsals I had it right and was prepared to knock 'em off their seats.

I arrived early with nice clean hands and my hair slicked down and at once made myself at home exchanging easy persiflage with my compeers, broadly hinting at the great surprise I had in store for the boys that night, when suddenly in walked Harry Houdini.

My brain froze as I sat there with an idiot's grin on my face. Houdini spotted me at once and came over to give me a hug and a warm handshake, which boosted my stock a few notches in the esteem of the magicians present, but did nothing to assuage the turmoil in my head.

I really had a bad few minutes as I dejectedly sat there and tried to figure a way out when Moira, that blind Greek fate, came to my aid.

Through my mental haze I began to hear a commotion and looked up to see The Great Raymond, a famous American magician, standing near the entrance and a furious Houdini ordering him out. Raymond walked forward but was intercepted by Goldston who tried to arbitrate but was shoved aside. The two famous magicians came to blows but were again separated by Goldston and some of the members. Raymond indignantly left in a huff.

In the ensuing embarrassing lull I asked someone what had happened and was told that the feud between Houdini and Raymond was a long-standing one. Raymond alleged that early in his career, when he had just started on his escape act, Houdini had sent over a stooge who dropped lead buckshot in the keyhole of the handcuffs he was given to examine and when Raymond tried to escape, the pellets had jammed the mechanism of the lock and the cuffs had to be sawed off with a hacksaw. Raymond had found out who was behind this jape and had sworn to "get" Houdini at the first chance.

In the subdued excitement that followed this row I was completely forgotten and Billy O'Connor diplomatically saved the meeting by jumping up onto the platform and performing his sensational rapid fire act of cutting a shuffled deck to any card called for, which relieved the tense situation and he was given a thunderous ovation.

Fortunately for me, the meeting broke up early and as we were leaving I hooked onto Billy and he invited me to have a spot of tea. I mentioned how I admired and envied his superb card work and he most generously presented me with the tricked deck he had used that night and taught me the rudiments, and we became fast friends.

At the digs I practiced his routine for days but was never able to come anywhere near his dexterity and I finally abandoned it. It has always been a quirk of mine that if I can't do a trick as well as the next fellow, I put it out of my programme. This may sound conceited but I cannot abide a poor imitation either in my own work or anyone else's. I believe this decision is justified when, for example, one sees what a disgusting mess the imitators have made of Channing Pollock's masterful dove manipulation.

About this time I contracted a severe case of Sherlockismus. I had read all the Sherlock Holmes short stories as a boy and later I had met Sir Arthur, so it was not surprising that I should read everything I could get my hands on. I was fortunate enough to pick up a few of the second hand *Strand* magazines of ancient vintage in the street bookstalls in Whitechapel.

Many an evening I spent haunting the East India Docks and Limehouse inspired by the great detective's adventures. I would go to Madame Tussaud's Wax Works to see all the famous criminals of England and from there it was but a step to Baker Street where I vainly tried to find number 221-B where the master had lived.

I imagined myself to be the great magical-detective, a dream that was realized twenty five years later when I made my motion picture series.

Another diversion of mine to while away the long evenings was to watch the street entertainers do their acts for the long lines of people queued up to see the big London revues and music halls. Some of these acts were quite good and lasted a few minutes and then they would pass the hat. It was a depressing spectacle. Most of these disillusioned artistes would collect a few pence and then head for the nearest pub where gin was sold at tuppence a noggin. I saw stark poverty in the London slums just after the war that made the east side New York tenements seem opulent. It had such a shocking effect on me that I have dreaded poverty all my life. I swore then that I would get out of it somehow.

CHAPTER 14

Some magician friends invited me to a get-together a few miles from London and I had to go to Euston Station to take the train. As usual I got down far too early and was hanging arund the platform when I suddenly saw my father standing on another platform. I rushed around and was waving my arms to attract his attention when he suddenly saw me and smiled. As I approached him it dawned on my bemused mind that it was not my father at all; it was Carl Rosini. To this day I can't understand how I could have been so confused.

Carl hugged me and was delighted to see me. He told me my father would be in England within a fortnight. He told me of the act that Okito had built and presented with great success in the Casino Theatre in Buenos Aires and that he was using the name of Okito again, which Nixon had given back to him.

The next day Goldston handed me a letter from my mother in which she said that Theo had arranged to meet her in London with the kids and she would be there within a month.

I was sore because my father had not written to me since I left New York and I decided to adopt the role of frigid politeness, but when we met at the station a couple of weeks later everything was forgotten and I fell on his neck, which only goes to show that magic is thicker than water.

We accused each other of not writing but he was so obviously glad to see me that I made a mental vow never to separate from him again.

The change in him was remarkable and he was full of self-confidence. He told me the story of what had happened in Buenos Aires. He had gone to South American on speculation with Rosini doing his shadowgraph act. Rosini had been successful in the Casino with the act Okito had built for him. One day Carl had a heart-to-heart talk with my father and had pulled him out of the rut he had been in for so many years. Carl convinced Theo to return to the old Okito type of act that had been so successful in the past. Theo took his advice and planned a half-hour act that included all the outstanding effects that had been so successful in the U.S. during the war years and were all new for England and the Continent. So he designed and built a beautifully balanced act that included the Duck Vanish, the Floating Ball, the Mat Trick, the Multiple Production, the improved Giant Water Bowl and some good sleight-of-hand tricks such as the Silks and Soup Plate and the Burnt and Restored Ribbons. He had a fine collection of genuine Chinese robes and his scenery had been painted by Coll, the famous scenographer of the Colon Theatre in Buenos Aires.

He had been booked to open at the Chelsea Empire and I immediately offered to assist him but was deeply disappointed when he told me that his act consisted of only three people. He had brought his assistant, a girl and a young man, from South America as he had not time to break in new people. His London debut was most important, but if I wanted the off-stage job of taking care of the ducks and sweeping the ground cloth and props, I was his man. So I accepted. What the hell—you have to start somewhere.

The next days were hectic. We chased around London and spent some time at Liberty's where he bought some beautiful costumes and yards of the famous Liberty silk which magicians prized so highly for magic.

My job was to get to the theatre early in the morning and inspect every trick and prop in the show to see that nothing was damaged or broken. If I found anything wrong I was not to touch it but report it to him at once. There was always plenty of time to make a good repair job before the evening show. He was a man who hated what he called "the last minute rush" and could not abide those magicians who arrived at the theatre a few minutes before curtain time.

He taught me the proper handling of live stock and especially the ducks:

> Behold the Duck.
> It does not cluck.
> A cluck it lacks.
> It quacks.
> It is especially fond
> of a puddle or a pond.
> When it dives or sups
> It's bottom's up.

The mess that the ducks left on the stage was the main objection that theatre managers had against magicians but Okito broke this taboo.

We had a light three-sided screen made of wooden frames and covered with wire netting which was placed against the wall of the yard or patio with the portable cage the ducks traveled in beside it.

At ten o'clock every morning I had to fill a large tub with water and let the ducks free. There was no need to bathe them as they smelled the water and rushed into it, cleaning themselves thoroughly.

In the meantime I removed the gate and swept out the soiled sawdust and replaced it with a fresh layer and put back the gate-screen. The clean ducks were shooed back into it and left there until an hour before the show without food or water. Then they were put into the cage and taken up to the stage white as the driven snow. I now filled a trough, only wide enough for the ducks' heads to enter, with fresh water. On the other side in a shallow pan was a heaping mound of corn kernels. A small quantity of pebbles or broken stones were thrown into the sawdust as this apparently helps their digestion. After the show they were returned to the screen-cage where they had their big meal. No one was allowed to feed them but me, and as they appeared on stage with empty stomachs, we never had any trouble with dirty stages and soiled props.

The props themselves were designed to protect the ducks from harm. Instead of oilcloth bags Okito used open cord network so that they could breathe. Okito's ducks were the healthiest lot imaginable, got disgustingly fat and usually died of old age.

Once in London a duck died from some natural cause but as the S.P.C.A. was very strict and prone to long discussion, Okito decided to get rid of the duck himself. He wrapped it into a neatly tied brown paper package and tried to leave it on a seat in the Underground, but someone raced after him and returned the package with a my-daily-good-deed expression, and was thanked by a disfigurement of the lips that was supposed to be a grateful smile. Then Okito furtively tried to throw the package away but it seemed that all London had a perverse eye on him and finally, in disgust, he handed it to me and told me to get rid of it. With a far less guilty conscience I simply threw it into an ash can and to hell with it.

The act itself was really a very beautiful thing and ran like clockwork. There was no doubt that Okito was a great artiste and he was in his element with that show. After the opening at the Chelsea Empire he was immediately booked for all the Syndicate Houses of London.

A couple of weeks after he opened he sent me to Southampton to meet my mother and the kids who had come over on the S.S. Majestic. We had a tearful and joyful reunion. When we arrived in London Pop was at the station to meet us and once more the family was together again. We lived in a theatrical hotel in Wardour Street where most of the theatre people lived together with the drunks and the tarts.

Just at this time The Great Raymond was having quite a success in England and had a shop in Brixton where he was building some illusions. He asked Okito to keep an eye on the place while he went on a trip to America, promising to return within a month.

Okito was working the London Halls at the time, supervising the shop during the morning. One day his girl assistant vanished without notice along with a trumpet player and Okito was in a desperate fix. Marie Dean, Raymond's chief girl assistant, volunteered to help him out and with practically no rehearsal did the part as if she had done it all her life.

For personal reasons Marie had been discontented with Raymond for some time and decided to stay with Okito as his main assistant. There was a hell of a row when Raymond returned to England and found he had lost Marie, but as assistant swiping was considered part of the game, nothing came of it except a few harsh words. Their friendship did cool, however.

One afternoon when my father and I were standing outside the digs, a short stout man on the other side of the street excitedly waved his hand and shouted to my father to come over. It was Horace Goldin and he was beside himself with joy. He had a paper-wrapped package under his arm and with a satisfied grin tore off the wrappings to display a cigar box. "No more headaches, my dear fellow," he said. "This box is made of sheet metal. Look!" And right there in the middle of the street he did the trick of changing a cigar box to a tray with a bottle of whiskey and tumblers on it. Goldin loved that cigar box trick but his old one, which had been made of wood, was always getting out of order. He looked at Theo triumphantly and folded the tray into the cigar box again.

"This is made of sheet iron," he repeated, "and it's strong enough to support an elephant." And so saying, he placed the box on the sidewalk and stood on it and it collapsed.

83

His expression was so rueful that I burst into laughter. He gazed at me coldly, but Okito soothed his ruffled feelings, took the box up to his room and tried to straighten it out while Goldin looked glumly on.

It was a good chance for me to observe this highly original magician who often used the current events in the news as a basis for an illusion.

During the Dreyfus affair he had produced an illusion which he called Dreyfus Escapes from Devil's Island, a quick-change effect done with a cage to represent Dreyfus' cell in Cayenne.

He built an illusion around the famous Potato Jones affair, and when the ascot Gold Cup was stolen, he created an illusion descriptive of the theft that same night at the Palace Theatre.

He was a most sensational magician and his show was thrilling to see. He worked at high speed and threw the props to his assistants to gain time. Speed was revolutionary fifty years ago.

Allan Shaw, the dexterous coin manipulator, also lived in Wardour Street and was one of those quiet easy-going Americans who had the habit of leaning up against the wall outside his digs and constantly manipulating a coin in his right hand trouser's pocket. One afternoon, a tart, who was passing, stopped to watch with amazement a grown man who was doing something mysterious with his hand in his pants pocket. Finally she could stand it no longer and approaching Shaw she coyly said, "Wot's the matter, dearie? Can't you afford a lidy?" Shaw blushed to the roots of his hair and dove into his digs.

Suddenly Okito was booked for a three months' tour of South Africa and was to leave on the Union Castle the following week. When Okito told me that the Consolidated African Tours would only pay three fares and I was not to go, I was dismayed. I almost begged him on my bended knees to take me along but he refused and a few days later they sailed, leaving me in London.

Bitterly I decided to somehow get back to the U.S. I went to a school for wireless telegraphy with the idea of joining the Navy and seeing the world but found out they wouldn't have me as I was an American citizen and could not be an Englishman until I was twenty-one. I still cannot figure it out as I had a British passport.

After that I didn't even bother to look for a job but just wasted my time bumming around London. I haunted the Hall as usual and sometimes would go out to the pub around the corner from the Wood Green Empire and sit around with the stagehands. They all had different versions of the death of Chung Ling Soo, who was killed on the stage a few years before, doing the bullet catching trick. Some thought it was suicide, others thought it was an accident and there were one or two who said it was murder. The official inquiry had proved it to be accidental death but all the stagehands agreed that there had been an obvious nervous tension in Soo's manner the days preceding the tragedy. This spectacular event so impressed me as a youth that I used the Chung Ling Soo tragedy as part of the plot in my first motion picture, ''The Specter Bride,'' and in this same film used the Houdini Water Torture Cell combined with the alleged story of the buckshot in the handcuffs, which Raymond told me was true and had been the cause of the fight in the Magician's Club.

Talking about Chung Ling Soo's show, the stagehands told me that the illusion they liked the best was his Dream of Wealth. Soo would produce, with bare hands, handfuls of coins from the air, then £5 notes followed by £10 notes. Reaching into a clear glass box, which appeared to be quite empty, he would produce several bundles of bank notes. These were all placed back in the box, two hooks were lowered from the flies and attached to the box which was raised high into the air. A gun was fired and the glass box vanished. In its place was a giant replica of a Bank of England note which filled the entire stage.

CHAPTER 15

When Okito returned from South Africa, I got my job back again and decided not to spend a penny of the small salary I earned.

I soon became friends with Carl Petersen, the former heavyweight champion of Denmark, who had toured with Okito in South Africa doing a dancing act with his sister under the name of the Brissons. He taught me boxing and one day, with a friendly flip, he flattened my nose and my desire to be a world's champion. Later Carl went to Hollywood where he starred in various films. His son Freddy married Rosalind Russell.

Although I didn't realize it then, I was getting a good solid magical groundwork. Okito was constantly inventing or improving tricks and illusions and his time-saving methods of construction were a good lesson for me. He could not abide poor workmanship as most homemade apparatus for him was "gerclotched." If I rarely did a simple repair job he would look at it and say, "Very nicely oopvercalifartered," which would burn me up.

He could have been a bit more lenient but maybe he was right. Consider the case of the floating ball.

The mysterious golden floating ball was the piéce de résistance of Okito's act and was widely acclaimed, but Okito was not satisfied with the ball he was using and was trying to perfect the trick even more.

The history of the floating ball goes back to 1913 when Thurston was playing in Omaha, Nebraska and was invited with Theo to the home of David P. Abbott, author of that fine book, *Behind the Scenes with the Mediums,* an expose of fake spiritualism that was the talk of the magical profession.

Mr. Abbott entertained his guests with a demonstration of

tricked spiritual phenomena that left them perplexed. The methods used by mediums were far more subtle than the ones used by the average magician since anything that even faintly smacked of trickery could have been fatal.

The only effect that Abbott demonstrated that could be compared to the magician's trick was a small golden ball about six inches in diameter that rose from a small pedestal and floated around the room and finally came to rest on the pedestal. This trick was performed in a dimly lighted room so appropriate for spiritualistic effects and the movements that Abbott had evolved were extremely simple—yet the effect was uncanny.

Thurston wasn't too keen on the trick as it required delicate manipulation and he felt that it would slow up the show. He ignoted it, although many years later, when the trick had gained popularity, he used a large metal ball on a dimly lighted stage in combination with his Spirit Cabinet.

Okito, on the other hand, was intrigued and saw great possibilities in this charming, dream-like illusion, and Abbott generously made him a present of the ball which was made of thick papier-mache and was rather heavy.

Theo worked on the trick in his spare time and came to the conclusion that if it was to be of any use for the stage it would have to be a bigger and extremely light affair which gave the appearance of a solid metal cannon ball. There were large hollow metal spheres used for floats on the market but they have a thick rim to hold the two halves together and this was a dead give-away that the ball was hollow.

Okito's first ball was spun from thin brass and the two halves neatly soldered and burnished. This ball was much lighter than the Abbott ball but had one great disadvantage: if the ball fell and was dented it was impossible to get the dent out. So metal was out.

His next ball was papier-mache half the thickness of the original model and covered with gold leaf and burnished. Using a very long black silk thread he evolved a series of complicated but deceptive moves that required a very delicate sense of touch. The first time Okito performed the trick in public was on Martinka's little stage for an audience of magicians who were most impressed. Unfortunately, after the trick was over, as Theo walked offstage, he tangled in the thread and the ball followed him off. Due to this mishap his fellow magicians became shy of the effect and it was exclusively Theo's baby.

My father had a habit, common to many magicians, that he

called "snuffling around," which consisted of exploring shop windows on the chance that they held something that could be used for a magical effect.

One afternoon while we were strolling down a London side street, he stopped to snuffle at an ironmonger's shop window. He spotted a half sphere of some white material with hundreds of tiny holes in it like a sieve. He darted into the shop to inquire what it was used for and was told that it was a celluloid sponge holder for the bath. They handed him one and it weighed next to nothing. It had a celluloid rim which ended in a hook for hanging on the edge of the tub, but that could be removed. He bought three and we rushed home.

He was very excited with his find and the first thing he did was to carefully cut away the rim and the handle, but by removing this the remaining half sphere had no substance and squirmed like jelly and was devilishly difficult to handle. Cutting off the rim of a second sieve, he was dismayed to find that when held together they did not form a perfect sphere and he had to construct a thin cardboard rim that fitted inside the two halves to make it look like a ball.

In those days we didn't have the efficient cements that exist today and he glued the rim into one of the halves with hot carpenter's glue, which, when it dried, became brittle and the rim fell off.

With his characteristic patience (in magic) he covered the rim with thin white silk which he stuck to itself with flexible fish glue. Next he sewed a thin edge of silk to the rims of the spheres and finally glued all together. That did it. When the ball was dry he had a perfect sphere.

Then he cut the bottom out of a cigarette tin and from that hammered out a thin round plate which had the same curve as the ball. In this he drilled two sets of tiny holes about 3/16 of an inch apart, passing thin piano wire through the holes to make two tiny bridges which he soldered from the underside to keep them firm.

He glued this metal shell to the ball; but knowing that it wouldn't hold, he cut up small squares of thin white silk and pasted them one by one, slightly overlapping each other, until the ball was completely covered. He ruefully admitted that he should have made the metal shell first and drilled small holes all around the edge and sewn it to one of the perforated half spheres before joining them, but it was too much work to take the ball apart. Finally, he shellacked the ball and let it dry.

Then he made his first trial and the floating ball was born at this moment. He tied a very fine machine twist #00, used by tailors for the lapels of evening clothes, to a small hook eye in the ceiling of his bedroom and threaded the ball on it. Then he opened the door to my mother's room, which gave him a few more feet, and tied off the end of the thread to his collar button.

The feathery light ball responded beautifully as he did moves and manipulations that had been utterly impossible to do previously. The ball seemed to float from his fingertips and the slightest pressure on the thread was enough to make it glide in any direction he cared. His delight was childlike and he was in high good humor. "Dafe, my boy," he said to me with a grin, "the artifice is over, now begins the art."

Together we went to the burnisher to have the ball gold-leafed and polished, and begged the man to be careful. The artisan did his best, but at the first touch of the burnishing wheel, the whole side of the ball caved in.

Never had I seen Pop so disappointed. He said nothing, but in a cold rage he took the ball from the workman and crushed it into pieces and threw them to the floor and walked out of the shop. The contrite workman wrapped the remains in a piece of paper and handed them to me. As I walked slowly home I really felt sorry for the old boy. All that tedious work and all his high hopes gone for nothing.

But I knew his moods and the tantrums of his indomitable spirit when his ingenuity was challenged by a problem so I put the remaining sieve in a place where he was forced to see it during the day.

Just as I thought, a couple days later he said to me, "Dafe. Do you remember the street where we bought the half shells?" I replied that I did. "Then get me a half a dozen," he said giving me the money.

I had a bit of difficulty finding the street and finally came in from the opposite end. Looking for the shop on both sides of the street, I passed a tailor's shop and in the window was Howard Thurston.

It had been a hot summer and a dummy in the window of this shop was in the direct heat of the afternoon sun. The wax head had melted slightly giving it a very sad expression. The cheeks had melted over the collar into heavy jowls, just like Thurston had before his operation. It was a startling caricature of him and for me, always on the lookout for omens, it was a good sign.

89

Right next to the tailor was a sweet shop and alongside it was the ironmonger who only had four sieves left. I bought them and returned to the digs just as my father was leaving the house and in one of those unthinking aberrations of mine, I said in an offhand way, "You'll never guess who I met."

"Who?" said Pop.

"Howard Thurston," said I.

He looked at me with amazement, "Howard? Howard here in London? Vot is he doing in England? You know vere he iss?" He was so excited and was pulling on my coat sleeve which so flustered me that, with a hollow feeling in my belly, I led him to the tailor shop. I knew I had gone too far and that the gag would backfire, so staying well out of arm's reach, I pointed to the tailor's window and said, "There."

His reaction was extraordinary. He stared at the dummy in disbelief and suddenly his face seemed to fall apart and all the pent-up tension of the last few days was loosed in a wild whoop of laughter. The tears ran down his face and I was so relieved that I joined his contagious laughter. When the tailor stepped out to see what all the row was about, he was startled to see a man and a boy holding each other up and laughing their heads off.

This had been powerful medicine and as an exhausted Okito was wiping his eyes with his handkerchief and turning to go, his eye caught something in the window of the sweet shop.

"Jesus Crits," he muttered and vanished through the door. I looked in the window but saw nothing but plates of sweets and chocolates and in a daze followed him into the shop.

As I came in he was being handed a chocolate wrapped in gold foil which he removed and throwing the chocolate to one side, much to the surprise of clerk, proceeded to examine the foil. It was a heavy white paper with a brilliant gold backing. Pop looked at me and I got it at once and again we burst into uncontrollable laughter. The open-mouthed clerk was convinced he was dealing with two maniacs. His deepest suspicions were verified when Okito cajoled him into selling a few sheets of the gilt paper, which he reluctantly did, probably thinking that to humor a lunatic is better than being torn to shreds.

I knew that my wax Thurston had been a good omen when the gold paper turned out to be the proper solution for building the ball. Tearing the paper into one inch squares and pasting them carefully with an overlap on the new ball he had made, the illusion was perfect. He had a ball that weighed an ounce or so but looked like a solid golden ball.

He rehearsed in the theatre in the morning using a white thread to perfect his routine, and when he felt he had it right, he broke it in at the old Elephant and Castle Theatre. From the first night it was a sensation. This artistic trick became the talk of Europe and in many places he was booked on the strength of that trick alone.

Pop used to call himself "The guy who nefer takes chances," and every piece of apparatus he built was given what he called "The Bamberg Test," which usually consisted of pretty rough treatment and doing everything possible to cause the trick to fail. If it withstood his drastic handling, it was ready for the stage.

He took a great pride in his work and was a great man for small details. For example: a slit had to be cut in the back of a Chinese costume for back loads or duck releases. Anyone else would have picoted the edges like buttonholes, but not Okito. He procured a roll of extremely thin pure rubber tape and a small piece of this was placed between the gown and the lining and pressed with a hot iron, which welded the cloth together. He used this same system for the edges of curtains that had to be rolled and it served the double purpose of preventing fraying and did away with the added thickness of a hem.

His "thumb-test" for silk and cloth was the horror of all the London shops. He would grasp the material between his two thumbs and holding them close together would twist them down causing the material to split. They loved him for that, especially when he didn't buy anything.

Boy-like, at that time, I made a lot of drawings of all the tricks and illusions I had ever seen and a few original ideas of my own. Some of them were pretty bad and simply a lot of half-baked ideas that looked good on paper. One look and two words from the old man were sufficient to destroy most of these world-shattering illusions but a few of them weren't too bad and I used them in later years with good results.

Only once was I vindicated, and this helped me to gain confidence in myself.

Okito had an appearing vase made of spun metal sections that telescoped into a inch-thick table. When it was extended the vase was about two feet high and with its graceful curves appeared to be a solid urn. A metal rod that fitted snugly into the center pole of the table held it rigid.

Okito wanted to improve the effect and constructed an ingenious mechanical lamp shade that expanded with springs and catches to form a hexagonal shade. It was beautifully made but the shape was wrong and aesthetically I didn't care for it and said so. The old man nearly bit my head off.

"Ha!" said he. "The world's greatest magician knows it better and will solve this mystery. I would be extremely in your debt if you would explain your artistic solution to this problem." Then he sat back. I said I didn't have a solution but I still didn't like that ungraceful shade and I was rewarded with a baleful eye and a Dutch sneer.

This so annoyed me that I spent the next few days trying to figure it out and, by Jove, I got it. It was very simple, perhaps because I didn't have the ability to make it complicated. I suggested changing the solid center rod for a threaded brass rod and within that having another rod which could be pulled out like a camera tripod and to which an accordion-pleated lamp shade with contrasting colored celluloid strips could be attached. I made a drawing of it.

Okito studied my plans for a moment and with a muttered "Bah!" brushed them off the table. Another of my great ideas had gone down the drain.

But a day or so later he said to me, "Your idea is not bad, not bad at all. But you don't grasp the basic principles of mechanics. Will you please tell me how to thread a thin brass tube and expect it to last more than one show? Now, if you use a steel tube and thread it from the inside. . ." He went on into a long technical explanation. But he wound up by scrapping his lamp shade and using my idea. He improved it considerably but the fact remains that he *did* use my basic idea and this pleased me no end.

Another time I wounded him to the quick by daring to criticize his great love: the duck vanish.

"The duck vanish," I stated with the expert's opinion, "has a weak spot." The old man stared at me for a moment in stupefaction and then came the warning—white patches on the sides of his nose.

"Ha!" he said, ominously. "Now we find that those two shlemiels, LeRoy and Okito, have been wasting their time. The world's greatest magician has suddenly discovered that the duck vanish is a rotten trick."

"I didn't say it was rotten. I only said it has a weak point."

"Pray be so kind," he purred, "as to shed a little light on my ignorance in magical technique."

I was no match for his sarcasm but I doggedly went on. "Look," I said, "you show every board of the box on both sides when you take it apart, but the board with the concealed load is only shown on one side and quickly placed on the cage. Wouldn't it be a great improvement to be able to show that board on both sides as well?''

''Congratulations! And no doubt you have figured out the solution.''

''No. I haven't the faintest idea how it could be done, but it's worth thinking about.''

''Then I beg of you not to waste my time,'' he snarled. ''You may sit in front of the fireplace spinning fine theories, but I am a practical man and a busy one, so don't bother me.''

That was Inspector Lestrade's line. Pop had lifted it right out of Sherlock Holmes but I was too tactful to mention it.

He ranted about this for weeks until I got fed up with it and wished I had kept my mouth shut. For many years after, in his letters to me, there would be a sly dig about the duck vanish. In Mexico in 1935, I built the darned thing and in 1940 when he saw it for the first time he was completely baffled by his own trick.

Okito got bookings for the continent and again I was left in London with the promise that if things went well he would send for us later.

I had saved up enough money for a cheap fare to America but I needed fifty dollars for landing money, which I borrowed, and a few weeks later sailed for New York on the S.S. Mauretania for better or for worse.

CHAPTER 16

Herman was at the dock waiting for me the day I arrived. He had grown in two years into a strapping, handsome young man half a head taller than me but with the same boyish laughter and healthy outlook on life that was so characteristic of him. He was still an enthusiastic magic and radio ham and had gotten a job with All America Cables as an operator on the South American lines. Always a great audience, he was enthralled with my highly embroidered versions of my adventures in England.

I had left all my magic with a friend of mine in London, a man named Fred Barton, of Golder's Green, who was an enthusiastic amateur magician. So I lugged my one suitcase around until I found a room on West 46th Street, almost opposite from the old National Vaudeville Artists' Club. This cubicle cost me three dollars a week.

Herman told me that Thurston was playing at the Fulton Theatre in Brooklyn and I decided to go out that evening and see the show. Herman accompanied me as far as the theatre but had to get home early and continued on to Flatbush.

As I sat in the audience and watched the house lights dim and the orchestra strike up the old overture, the clock ran backwards. Nothing had changed. I was back in the world that was meant for me and the old thrill came back when the curtain rose on the book of magic and my idol stepped out and took his opening bow. He was older and greyer but still had that commanding personality that I knew so well. I thought of the goddamn dummy in London and smiled to myself.

As the show went on I slowly began to realize that something had happened. A great change had, in fact, taken place.

It may have been that the magic I saw in England influenced me but it seemed that the sparkle was gone. Thurston was his usual polished self but he appeared to be tired and lacked enthusiasm. The show was shoddy and uncared for and the assistants poorly dressed. The few new illusions he presented were none too good. For the first time I saw him do the floating ball which he tapped with a ring to prove it to be metal but only proved it to be hollow. He did the ball in very dim light whereas Okito used a fully lighted stage and even had spotlights directed on the ball.

The show dragged on until the final curtain. While the audience filed out, I remained seated, with a heavy heart, wishing that I had never come to see the show and losing my childhood's greatest illusion. Finally I got up and walked slowly around to the stage entrance and asked to see Thurston.

He received me with his usual warmth and charm and was most interested in my father's success and plied me with questions. We talked for over an hour and he was particularly interested in Owen Clark's Flunkey's Dilemma and Oswald Williams' Jewel illusion (described in Chapter 13).

I had intended asking for a job as his assistant but I didn't say anything and when it was time for me to go, he took my hand and said, "Stay with magic, David. Never give it up and one day you will be my successor." Yet he didn't mention anything about a job. That was the last time I ever saw Howard Thurston, but the memory of that wonderful man has remained with me all my life. It was he, more than anyone else, who inspired me to go on and eventually create what became the biggest magical production in Latin America.

I didn't know it then but it was the beginning of the end of the Thurston show. A few years later, just before he died, he handed the entire company over to his brother Harry; and although the William Morris Agency pumped over a thousand dollars a week into the show to keep it going, it finally expired and with its passing there ended a great American dream.

I was now at the ripe age of seventeen and if I wanted to get that big show I would have to get a move on. Remembering how elegantly the magicians were dressed in St. George's Hall, I bought second-hand tails for twelve bucks in a hock shop on Eighth Avenue. It was slightly green with age and far too big and I looked like an accordion in it. The lapels hung down so I glued them back into place, but the glue soaked through the satin and left two stains. Therefore I cut two carnations from an old handkerchief and glued them over the stains, thereby setting the style of two carnations instead of one.

Tacking a bed sheet to the wall of my room, I would practice my handshadows by candlelight which gives an excellent, non-feathery shadow. Then I would don my evening dress and go into a card routine.

By this time I only had about thirty dollars left and as I knew this wouldn't last very long, I hit on the ingenious device of not eating.

My day would begin with a trip to a little basement restaurant for a bowl of vegetable soup. That cost a dime but bread and butter were free so my daily expenses for food came to about a quarter. One day the guy at the counter asked, ''Don't you ever eat anything but soup?'' I told him I was under medical care and on a diet so he never argued anymore and when I arrived the soup was waiting.

Then I would do the rounds of the agents, without any results. In the early evening I would drift into the N.V.A. Club and by having someone sign the guest book, hang around playing chess and talking magic with Servais LeRoy and Professor Waters. Sometimes Dunninger would drift by with a long mane and a black hat that was a first cousin to my evening dress. He always carried a violin case and I never found out why. He looked like a starving poet.

I managed to get a job in the toy department of Macy's but it didn't last long as I was fired for coming in late. Even to this day I love to sleep until noon in the firm conviction that anything anyone has to say at eight in the morning can be said at eight at night to a more receptive ear.

On Clown Night at the N.V.A. I was right in the thick of the corny gags they pulled there, and I called a lot of big shots in vaudeville by their first names—for all the good it did me. I was the original invisible man. I made myself especially invisible to Harry Chesterfield, manager of the N.V.A. who could have thrown me out for doing a Lafayette (impersonator) routine with the guest book.

I wanted to do an act different from the others so I invented and made my own props. I had a wonderful collection of useless junk such as old pieces of plywood, tin cans and glue. None of these great inventions ever reached the finishing stage but I could never throw anything away and the rubbish accumulated until my room looked like the old curiosity shop. This habit of saving everything has stuck to me all my life and I still have the soul of a garbage collector.

Weeks went by and my money was running low. I sometimes

managed to scrounge a sandwich from some affluent ham in the Automat, and on Sundays I'd drop in "by accident" at somebody's house around mealtime and they had no alternative but to suffer the man who came to dinner. I would stuff myself to the ears and then drag my weary bones to the joint on 46th Street.

After some weeks of this high living I was practically a skeleton, with a pale face and two enormous eyes showing a Frankenstein gleam. I had forgotten the blonde and only thought of the cake.

One day while I was sitting in the outer office of an agent named Finnegan, looking like a character trying to haunt a house, the private door flew open and a burning ham rushed out mumbling something about bloodsuckers and, with a slam of the outer door, vanished.

I thought that this was not the moment to see Finnegan and stood up to go when the great man himself, a lovely shade of magenta, yelled at me from his office door to come in. I was in no condition for a wrestling match with anyone but I went in anyway.

"You want me?" I asked.

"Yeah," he screamed, "that sunnavabitch just let me down and I need an act for tomorrow at Huntington. Three days and forty bucks, less commission. Who the hell are you and what do you do?"

"I'm a magician," I proudly said, "The Great Syko."

"No good," he groaned. "Too many magicians. Can't use ya."

For a moment I was stunned, then I had a great inspiration.

"I am also a shadowist," I said.

"Whazzat?"

"Shadowgraphs on a white sheet done with my hands. Animals, birds, famous people. A great novelty."

"I don't know," he said after a long pause. "It sounds dead to me. But I'll take a chance and if you want it, the split week is yourn."

I signed the contract and with my heart in my mouth I flew back to the joint and told the Italian proprietor of my good fortune. He seemed greatly pleased and I suppose secretly glad to get rid of me. I told him I needed train fare and conned three dollars out of the good-hearted guy. Not content with this I asked him for another favor—would he lend me the bed sheet? This nearly flattened him until I explained that I needed it for my shadow act. He agreed.

I dived down to the restaurant and when he saw me coming the guy started to ladle out the soup.

"Take it away," I yelped. "The diet is over. Bring me a porterhouse with all the trimmings and no bread and butter!" I think I even ate the bone.

I took the first train out at six in the morning and found that Huntington was in Long Island, so the very short ride cost only a few cents. When I got to the theatre nobody was there so I had to wait until the janitor showed up at eight-thirty. The dressing room list from the previous bill was still on the board and taking no chances of being thrown out I took the smallest dressing room on the top floor.

About eleven o'clock the stagehands and electricians showed up. The crew nearly died when I brought out that bed sheet. It had seemed so big in my room but looked like a postage stamp on this big stage. They suggested using the picture sheet and masking it off.

I tried out various spots that the gaffer had but they all gave a feathery shadow. I mentioned that my father had used an arc lamp and the gaffer said they had an old one in the projection booth and had it brought down and cleaned. It worked fine and I was set.

At orchestra rehearsal, when the maestro asked me for my music and cue sheet, I had neither so I told him to play several waltzes and the drummer should use his own judgement for sound effects.

The first show was at five in the afternoon. In order not to be late I donned my evening dress at noon and went through the act over and over again in the dressing room.

I spotted number one, with the hook in easy reach. After a million years five o'clock came around and I was between the wings, waiting, as the newsreel finished.

The house lights went up and I walked out during the overture and got a hell of a laugh and had to go back. The audience thought it was part of the act. The second time I came out I got a belly laugh and couldn't understand why. I did my card routine and got a fair hand, then I went into the shadowgraphs which really got a good solid hand, and the hook stayed where it was.

I rubber-legged it up to my dressing room and I almost passed out. I wanted to vomit but nothing came up. I had been so nervous that I had not even thought of going out for bite to eat.

Since that steak dinner the day before I hadn't even had a cup of coffee.

Before I had a chance to change into my street clothes there was a loud knock at the door and I opened it to see a severe-looking man who introduced himself as the house manager. My heart sank and I thought "This is it. The old merry-go-round all over again." I invited him in.

"You've got a very cute little act," he said, "but you spoil it with all that corny comedy."

"What comedy?"

"That clown outfit you're wearing," he said. "What the hell is it supposed to be? You look like a ghost in a tent."

I informed him with great dignity that I wasn't a clown. I was a magician and dressed as such. Then I told him the whole story about it being my first date and how I planned to improve the act as I went on.

He took it all in for a while and then made me a deal which was one of the kindest things that anyone had ever done for me. He said he would advance me the money to go to New York the following day and buy a ready-made tuxedo. He arranged to have a sheet made up for me and sold me the arc lamp cheap. Naturally my forty bucks wouldn't cover all that but he said he was putting in a good word for me at the New York office and he guaranteed me a few weeks' work. The head office would deduct twenty dollars a week until everything was paid and that would insure him against my magician's instincts getting the better of me. He also suggested that I cut the name Syko and think up a more suitable stage name. We talked it over and finally came up with David King.

The next day I bought the tuxedo and it certainly was an improvement. I was spotted number four and the act went over quite well.

After three days I returned to New York and paid off the Italian and returned the bed sheet and gave him a bottle of Chianti which made him happy.

I went to see the surprised Finnegan who looked at me as though I were a sort of Al Jolson. I had to listen as he told me that he knew when he first saw me that I had a great act and he had arranged a tour for me through Montana, Wyoming, Nebraska and Canada at $100 a week. I was ushered out personally by the great man with bows and smiles. Show business.

And so as David King I had me a high old time in the beautiful West and returned to New York with nearly $500 in my jeans. I had never had so much money in my life. At last I was a millionaire.

Howard Thurston.

CHAPTER 17

As a man of means I went to Atlantic City and found Zancig playing at Rendezvous Park, an amusement center styled after Luna Park. I didn't know how he would greet me after my rudeness to him and the violent split up in New York. However, he was genuinely glad to see me and was most impressed with the British accent I had acquired. He said it would be good for the business and would I care to join the act again? Why not? I hadn't forgotten the code and in a few days it was just like old times again. I got sixty dollars a week and thirty percent of all club dates.

Coincidentally, "Slip-the-Jit" Harry Casino had his pitch in front of Zancig's theatre. Harry was one of the real old-time carny men and I loved to watch him work. We became fast friends.

His pitch consisted of a chair attached to a large scale which hung from three iron poles like a tripod. He was supposed to guess the weight of anyone within three pounds and was permitted to feel the arms and legs of the men but only the upper arms of the ladies. If he guessed their weight wrong they didn't pay and sometimes he would purposely lose as a come-on for the others.

The gimmick was that the three-pound leeway he allowed himself was really seven pounds; the actual weight of the person and three pounds on either side; and as the chair swung back a judicious touch of his fingertips to steady it was good for a pound or so either way.

On Saturday nights and Sundays he would have a line waiting and wouldn't even bother to guess the weight of the fat ones but would cry in a shrill voice, "The gennelman weighs a hunnerd and fromtifrum pounds," and triumphantly point to the scale and say "On the nose—a hunnerd and eighty-six pounds." This was the original "hunh-hunh" bit that Zancig and I had swiped for the act. Harry's one bugaboo were the fat women. Since he couldn't feel their thighs, he was sometimes off twenty pounds.

Rendezvous Park was a financial flop and business went from bad to worse. Poor old Zancig didn't take in enough to pay the rent of the theatre, was forced to close down, and left for Asbury Park.

In a choice spot on the Boardwalk a certain Prof. Seward, an astrologer, was coining money with his entertaining zodiacal lectures as a pitch for selling his dollar astrology book. Seward was a shrewd man and gave a semi-humorous lecture with just enough corn in it to sell thousands of his books to people who came in from all over the United States. He also sold Dream Books, Talismans, Occult Works, Crystal Balls and all the rest of the out-of-this-world paraphernalia from his headquarters in Chicago.

With every book he sold, the reader had the right to a free question. My British accent came to my aid again when Seward hired me as the mysterious Prof. Zaza, dressed in a red cape and a fez, who could tell everyone's future but his own.

The free question was a come-on and a more complete palm reading cost a dollar. On Saturdays and Sundays, when the sucker trains came in from Philadelphia, I would read as many as a hundred mitts a day at fifty-cents per mitt for my share. I coined money and managed to save over a thousand dollars. I gave a stock reading and learned to "fish" in a short while, which was the art of getting them to give me information without realizing it. But it was monotonous work and I got fed up with everyone's gripes and bleats and broken hearts. Even if one could predict the truth, they wouldn't want to hear it. All they wanted was good news. I tried to kid myself for a time that I was doing some good when I would tell some poor working woman with a half a dozen kids "that a great change" was coming into her miserable life but deep down I thought it was a revolting racket. I finally quit and hoped that I would never have to do it again.

So with my new-found opulence, I returned to New York and walked smack into the great Sawing a Woman bubble.

In the long history of magic perhaps no other illusion has had the tremendous impact on the theatre-going public as Sawing a Woman in Two.

It is claimed that the first version of sawing a person into halves was performed by Torrini, the French magician, in 1809 before Pope Pius VII in Rome. Later, the American circus clowns, the Hanlon Brothers, performed their version in Paris in 1878. In this comedy version one clown sawed the other in two and then separated the platform until the head was eighteen feet away from the box containing the feet and legs.

There can be no doubt that Percy Selbit revived it in London in the early 20s. In his version a girl's neck, wrists and ankles were tied with long ropes by a committee on the stage. The ropes were passed through holes drilled in the sides and back of an upright shallow wooden box, 12" deep by 20" wide, and the girl was placed into the box and the ropes pulled taut and knotted on the outside. The door of the box was closed and padlocked and the box was tipped over and rested on a scaffold. The box was then divided into eight small compartments by thrusting three sheets of glass and two steel blades through various slots. Finally the box was sawed in two. After this the glass plates and blades were removed and the lid opened to show the girl unharmed.

Goldin used the original Selbit method for a time in 1920, but due to a fearful row with the husband of the acrobatic woman who was the "victim" in the illusion, Goldin fired them both. In revenge the husband sold the secret of the trick to a cinema company who exposed the full working details in a short film. This forced Goldin to think of another method and he came up with the pull-apart boxes showing the head and feet of the girl in full view.

Selbit and Goldin made a rush for the United States in order to be the first to present this new sensation but the wily Goldin slapped a court order on Selbit in New York and his Sawing illusion was seized and destroyed. That started the great battle of the Divided Woman.

(Goldin loved lawsuits and was forever suing and stopping other magicians from doing certain illusions. He even had the gall to try and patent a trap in the stage, but this was turned down by the Patent Office. He sued Fasola and stopped him from doing the illusion in which a girl is shot from a cannon into a suspended trunk. This illusion was actually invented by Walter Jeans of Leeds and sold to Goldin who patented it.)

In order to forestall Selbit, Goldin, together with the Orpheum Circuit, sent out various units to the key cities. The line-up included Goldin, LeRoy, Bert Kalmar (the song writer of "Three Little Words" fame), and Harry Jansen (not yet Dante).

Even Thurston put it in his show with Goldin's permision, having patched up their long-standing feud through the diplomacy of Carl Rosini. From a purely professional standpoint, Selbit's version was more baffling, but Goldin's more spectacular. Goldin finally won the battle although he made very little money on the deal. It was a spite war and the only ones to make any money were the big shots who controlled vaudeville. They made a fortune.

When I met the long-faced and disgusted Selbit in New York he was on the point of throwing the whole thing up and going back to England. Every big city in the United States was blocked except the west coast. The Pantages Circuit offered him Seattle, Portland, San Francisco and Los Angeles—playing the leading Canadian cities on the way out to break the jump. Selbit gloomily accepted and hired me to take charge of the technical end of the illusion, since a lot of work was required to repair the box between shows. I also assisted him on stage. I had accepted gladly as I wanted to get out to the West coast.

We opened in Ottawa and from there to Toronto where we played on the same bill with Carl Rosini, who was doing his regular act with Bill Meyenburg (Frazee) as his assistant.

In Winnipeg, I met a young man named Len Vintus who had a dream of founding an International Brotherhood of Magicians, with local clubs in all the larger cities, to be called "Rings." I did not think such a bold scheme would be feasible but Vintus insisted and today his dream is the largest magical organization on earth, with members in all parts of the world.

When we got to Vancouver, Selbit was informed that Goldin had jumped the gun on us and LeRoy was in San Francisco. Selbit put the act in charge of an English magician named Hamilton and left for the East.

When we opened in San Francisco we weren't the headliners anymore. The main attraction was Jack Dempsey, then heavyweight champion of the world, doing a sparring act with some pugs and dialogue with Chuck Reisner.

When we finally arrived at Los Angeles LeRoy had come and gone and our act folded.

On the same bill with us all the way from the East had been a young dancing comedian named George E. Stone and we used to hang around together. He told me not to worry but to try and crash the movies as he was going to do. He played a lot of extra and bit parts until he finally got a break playing in "Cimarron."

I knew quite a few movie people from the old days in Brooklyn and decided to try the movies myself.

I met Floyd Thayer who had a wood turning factory in South San Pedro Street. He was manufacturing some excellent magical apparatus, mostly made of fine turned woods. I gave him the idea for an illusion which he later brought out as "Thayer's Re-Incarnation."

One day he took me to visit Harry Kellar, who was most amiable. I spent a very interesting day at his home. He was greatly interested in my father's new act, which I explained in detail.

"What a pity," he said, "that Theo never spoke on the stage. He would have been my logical successor."

He took me down to the basement of his home and showed me a model of a new levitation he had in mind. The cradle of his new idea had four prongs which supported the girl and one at a time they lowered and raised to allow the hoop to pass completely over her without having to make the turn at the foot and be brought back. It was a most complicated affair and I do not believe it was ever presented.

Another model of the levitation that Kellar constructed after his retirement was passed on to Blackstone. It was a beautiful thing and was later improved by Blackstone and his brother Pete Bouton. It could work on any stage, which the old levitation couldn't.

I visited Mr. Kellar once or twice more and we had long chats about magic in England. A few months later he died.

Another interesting personality I met in Los Angeles was David M. Roth whose mail order memory system had made him famous. (Can you still remember Mr. Addison Sims of Seattle?) He was very interested in mind reading codes and we combined a code based on his memory system. A few months later, in Philadelphia, I suggested this type of code to Harry Usher and he in turn worked out a simpler code based on our mnemonic idea. He used it for years with his wife, Frances, in their mind reading act.

Together with George Stone and another guy named Harry Miles, we tried crashing the movies. A friend of my father's, a former magician by the name of Carter De Haven (Gloria's father) was making two-reel comedies with his wife, and I played as an extra in one or two of them. In one of them I was thrown out of a train window, but when the picture was released all that was seen was the back of my head and a split second profile.

I played as an extra in an Erich von Stroheim epic and one of Douglas Fairbanks' pictures, but it was only bread and butter money and my funds were dwindling fast.

In order to save money I shared a room in a boarding house with Harry Miles who was an old hand at the "extra" game in Hollywood and knew all the girls in the casting offices. He didn't have a cent but he was always meticulously dressed and even went so far as to iron the occasional wrinkled dollar bills that he got to make them appear fresh from the bank.

Whenever the phone rang he made a wild dash to get there first—just in case it was the casting office calling. One day I came home to find Harry in a dither and he begged me to lend him my tuxedo as he had a call for a bit part in a movie.

The next day he over-generously paid me five dollars for the use of my tux and said that he had sent it to the cleaners and it would be returned the next day.

I was a bit suspicious at this open-handedness and did a bit of detective work and found out that the call from the studio had been for *me*!

When Harry had answered the phone and heard that they were offering David King twenty-five dollars for a bit part, he gulped and said that he would be there first thing in the morning. He was told to bring his tuxedo. Twenty-five smackers was nothing to be sneezed at in those days.

Harry showed up immaculate as ever in my tux and was told to stand in a doorway and step forward smiling. This was to be a close-up shot that every ham hungers for. In the rehearsal it went fine, but when the actual filming began his smile was wiped away when he was slapped in the puss with a huge cream pie. They never told an extra in those days what was to happen because the recipient of this delicacy, if he knew beforehand, would wear a strained expression and they wanted it au-naturel.

That pie was for me but by divine justice Harry got it.

I could see that these dramatic roles would never make a star so instead of sticking it out like the others did until they got their break, I got fed up. I called on Alexander Pantages, who sat on the window ledge of his office eating nuts and offered him my shadowgraph act combined with Sawing a Woman. He said he'd give me a tryout in San Diego. I had a box made up quickly, hired a couple of assistants and played the date. It went all right and they offered me a tour starting in Salt Lake City and ending up in Chicago. In Chicago I sent the two assistants back to Los Angeles and went to New York alone.

CHAPTER 18

When I arrived in New York there was a fat letter from Pop who was in Bombay, India. The "sawing" craze had extended all over Europe and Okito decided to take it to the Far East. Under the direction of Maurice Bandman, of the Bandman Tour, they had formed a company which included Okito's act, Fred Attila presenting the Selbit sawing, some other acts, and had opened in Cairo, Egypt and from there gone to India.

Business was good but in a small town called Mao, in spite of the handbills both in English and Hindustani warning the people to boil all drinking water, some of the artistes disregarded this advice and seven people in the company died of cholera and the tour which was to have embraced China and Japan ended then and there.

I also got news of Selbit who had introduced a new illusion in London called Through the Eye of a Needle, in which a steel plate with a small two inch hole in the center was placed between two upright barrels. A girl had a rope tied and sealed around her waist and this was passed through the small hole in the metal plate and then through another hole in the side of the lower barrel. The girl was covered with the upper barrel and the rope pulled giving the effect of pulling the girl from one barrel to the other through the two inch hole. This illusion had no audience appeal and he tried another, The Wrestling Cheese, a silly thing in which a huge wooden slab with a spinning gyroscope concealed in it, refused to lie down when wrestled with by professional wrestlers. This was really a stinker.

In his desperate attempts to create another "sawing" he tried everything, including a very flashy illusion called Broadcasting a Woman, using the dimmer principle of Pepper's Ghost. In later years this illusion was changed to the Television illusion.

Dante did a version of it. I also used this principle for my Atom Machine in the "Flight to the Moon" show, which I produced in Mexico in 1935.

There wasn't much to do in New York as summer was starting and the season was dead for vaudeville, so I went to Atlantic City to see what could be done to keep the wolf from the door.

Rendezvous Park had been repainted and a couple of new attractions added and I went to see the manager whom I knew slightly from the previous year. He got me a job as brakeman on the roller coaster at $20 a week.

In this cock-eyed world you never know what's going to happen next and sometimes a fortune can be made from an accident. It was at Rendezvous Park that summer that a young fellow who worked at an ice cream stand let a lump of ice cream he had scooped out for a nickel cone accidentally drop into a pan of half-melted chocolate. He knew the boss would raise hell so he quickly fished it out and hid it in the ice box; but the boss found it and instead of hell being raised, he had a brilliant idea and Eskimo Pie was born. It just goes to show you.

The starvation wages I was getting on the roller coaster weren't enough to make ends meet so I got the extra job of washing the windows of the stores on the boardwalk at seven in the morning, including the window of my ex-boss, Prof. Seward. But I wouldn't touch that mitt reading again.

There was a clever young man who used to cut out silhouettes on the Boardwalk at a quarter a throw. He was also a very good card manipulator and we became friends. His name was Dai Vernon, the man who is today considered to be the best all-around sleight of hand artist in the business.

After the window washings I would go down to the beach and sit in a quiet corner near the Steel Pier and divide my time between the ocean and the sun. My paleness had gone and I was putting on a deep tan and ate like a horse. Once in a while a would-be Houdini was nailed into a packing case and thrown into the Atlantic from one of the piers. It was mostly the crudest kind of imitation and the funny part of the whole thing was that in their advertising and spiels they talked so much about Houdini that they might as well have been working for him.

It was on the beach that I met Dorothy, a sultry brunette chorine on vacation from a New York show. She was a lot of fun and had contagious laugh and before long we were going steady.

One morning she told me that she would soon have to be getting back to New York for rehearsals and I was abruptly aware that I didn't want her to go. My mind was threshing around for some solution to convince her to stay when I suddenly thought of the mind reading act. There was good money for this kind of act in the New York clubs during the winter season and I painted a lurid picture that convinced her. She said she'd take a chance.

I knew I couldn't do the Zancig code as the same thing would happen to me that had happened to Lascelles so I decided to do the new mnemonic code which was easy to learn and did not require much memory.

Dorothy was great from the start but I was terrible. The trouble was, I couldn't forget the old Zancig code. In rehearsals I wasn't so bad, but when we had our first date, which was a short stint in a nightclub on the Boardwalk featuring Evelyn Nesbit, I was not so hot.

"Slip-the-Jit" Harry was in his old place at Rendezvous Park and business all around was worse than the previous year. He suggested that we leave Atlantic City and make a tour of the carnivals and state fairs.

We toured through Ohio, Kentucky, Tennessee and the Carolinas. Carny life was hard but interesting. I soon learned that almost everything was gaffed. Besides the act, I sometimes worked the Swing Ball and the Three Disk Game. Harry taught me the Shells and Pea game and Three Card Monte using the real gambler's throw.

As a card manipulator I was particularly interested in the work of professional gamblers, but I never saw a really top-flight man do his stuff. Most of the birds I saw were pretty bad and pulled the crudest kind of deals.

One of them, who looked like an old-time Mississippi steamboat gambler, used no sleights or subtle methods at all. He played the Turkish baths, and after the bath and massage, when the sucker was feeling good and sitting around draped in bed sheets like a Roman toga, he would bring out a deck of cards and a few fifths of rye.

For the first few hands the game was legit, but after a few slugs the sucker would get careless and half the time he didn't know what cards he was holding. The deal was raw, with the crudest false shuffles and cuts.

There was a jolly-good-fellow atmosphere about the whole thing and the gambler didn't overdo it and usually the victim was happy to be plucked. I never saw strippers or cold decks used as I sat there and marveled at how stupid people can be.

When the sucker woke up, the gambler was already in the next town and on his way to a Turkish Bath. He must have been the cleanest man in the world.

In Spartanburg, South Carolina, I got a letter from Zancig telling me that he was doing fine in Philadelphia and to come on up.

I said good-bye to Harry and with Dorothy went to Philadelphia where I found Zancig in a place called the World's Museum on Chestnut Street. This was really a dump, for it was nothing but a side-show with freaks and moth-eaten acts. An announcer would lead a small crowd from booth to booth and give them a loud-mouthed, long winded ballyhoo on the ossified man, the three-legged man, the blue man, the dog-faced man, Zippo and other delightful personalities.

Finally he came to Zancig who did the act with Ada and finished with the usual horoscope and private reading pitch.

Dorothy looked at me and I nearly died. However, Zancig told me that he had rented a nice place on N Street in Washington which was being decorated. He felt confident that we could make fat pickings with the act at the embassies and homes of wealthy politicians. So after a dismal two weeks at the museum, we left for Washington.

Zancig was right. We did play some fine places but never reached the White House to perform for President Harding.

Dorothy sold a lot of horoscopes in the government buildings and offices and the politicos fell for Zancig's crystal ball just like the big shots in New York had.

Strangely enough, Zancig began to take up spiritualism seriously. When Ada had first started playing around with the ouija board and table rappings, he would snicker and give me the eye but, little by little, he began to believe in it and finally we had nightly seances that lasted until the early hours of the morning.

We visited the leading spiritualists in Washington. I couldn't believe that Zancig, of all people, could fall for this obvious trickery. Personally, I never saw anything that convinced me of supernatural forces at work. One can never prove simple clairvoyance, and I felt like an ass sitting there in the dark with all this monkey business going on.

After a few months of this I felt the urge to get back into show business again. I said good-bye to Zancig and that was the last time I ever saw him. We corresponded over the years and one day in Buenos Aires I got a letter from Ada Zancig from Ocean City, California, telling me that on July 29, 1929, the poor old boy had passed on. In this very touching letter she said that as he lay dying, his mind wandered and he imagined he saw me at the foot of the bed giving a show.

Many harsh things have been said of Zancig and his way of life, but who am I to judge? I only care to remember the old days. Believe me when I say that he was a good man at heart.

I knew many of the old time mentalists and mind readers. There were Mercedes and the Svengalis with their musical mind reading acts. There also was a rage for answering questions from the stage in vaudeville theatres. Norman Frescott, Mystic Clayton and the Great Alexander were the first of big-time operators who coined money this way. Later dozens of pikers flooded the market, over-did it, and were finally banned by law, with some of them going to prison for swindling. Readings were broadcast until the airwaves were seared with seers, and again they over-did it, until the whole thing ended in the ash can.

One of the few men with brains enough to keep it clean and mysterious was Joe Dunninger. Although some of his methods were extremely crude, he was still at the top as a first-class showman.

Dorothy and I went to New York and played a few dates, but one day she told me that she had got her old job back as a chorus girl with the revue, so gradually we saw less and less of each other until she finally faded out of my life.

I went back to my old shadow and card act and played a date here and there. I also took a job selling rubber sponges, which were a novelty then. It was a house to house deal and I got used to having doors slammed in face by irate housewives. One day I remembered that a friend of my father's, a Doctor Hooker, an English chemist and a very clever amateur magician, had a laboratory on Remsen Street in Brooklyn. I thought he might be a client for my type of rubber sponge for lab use so I paid him a visit.

He received me most cordially, inquired about my father, and was pleased to hear of his success. I broached the subject of the sponges and he examined one and bought all I had in my suit-case. I don't thing he really needed them, but he was a wealthy man and wished to do me a good turn. He invited me to tea and showed me his marvelous laboratory and some of his original magical apparatus.

I spent a most pleasant afternoon and when I was about to go he mentioned that some years previously he had bought a complete Chinese act from my father. He told me it was of no use to him as he would never do the act, and he asked me if it would be of any use to me.

This was a great windfall and I told him so. He took me into his magic den and from a closet removed the props still wrapped in the paper they had come in. The act consisted of a large duck tub, a canister and pedestal for duck productions, a Chinese water bowl complete with release and harness, the double Duck Pan with net release, and a few other tricks. In another box there were two Chinese costumes and a mandarin hat.

After my profuse thanks, which seemed to embarrass him, I said that I would have to carry the props away one at a time. I made many subway trips carrying as much as I could to my shoe-box sized room on West 46th Street.

Once my wild jubilation had calmed I began to regard these props with a more speculative eye. To this day I don't know if it was caution or cowardice that restrained me from rushing headlong in trying to do an act like my father's. I have already mentioned the audacity of certain individuals which often reaches brazenness. I was only eighteen at the time, but even then my artistic sense warned me that the act would be a poor imitation of Okito's.

The water bowl production was an old model with the complicated release for the cover that required fumbling and stalling. The few times I had seen it performed always reminded me of a man squatting on a chamber pot. This bowl could not be converted for the instant release that made it such a breathtaking effect in Okito's hands.

The rest of the material was more or less the same, all beautifully constructed but slow and old fashioned. I regretfully came to the conclusion that my Chinese act was a thing of the future.

Okito's youngest brother Edward lived in Westchester with his wife, Hattie, and was doing a vaudeville melange under the name of The Rickards. It was a combination of magic, juggling by Hattie, and shadowgraphs, and worked fairly steadily. Their only opposition was Max Holden who did a similar act with his wife under the name of Holden and Graham.

I visited Uncle Ed and told him of my windfall and he suggested that I come to live with them and occupy the spare room in his flat. I agreed and a week later I had all my stuff in

Westchester. When Uncle Ed saw the collection he sat on the floor of my room and almost went into hysterics laughing. I couldn't see the joke but his laughter finally killed any idea I might have had to use it. I stored it away in the closet and forgot about it.

Uncle Ed was keen on the idea of reviving the Fly illusion which he had worked with his father in Holland. This old illusion, the origin of which I'm not certain, was popular in the latter part of the nineteenth century and the beginning of the twentieth. Maskelyne was among many of the illusionists who had performed it.

The effect involved an outsized fly that ran around a lettered and numbered mirror supported on an easel. It spelled out cards, numbers and articles thought of by the spectators. When this illlusion was first produced, magnetism was almost unknown to the general public; it had no practical use and was considered a scientific novelty.

From the times of early Egyptian thaumaturgists who used steam for opening the doors of a shrine when a fire was lit on an alter (described by Hero of Alexandria in his *Pneumatics*) until today, magicians have always been in the vanguard of using new scientific principles for magical illusions.

Using magnetism, Robert-Houdin, in his Light and Heavy Chest, quelled a threatened uprising in Algiers, and when he "proved" that the power of the French magicians was greater than that of the Marabouts. He was given the Legion of Honor by a grateful government for his performance.

The trick was simple. It was just a small wooden chest with a heavy iron plate concealed in the bottom. Under the stage were some old-fashioned wet batteries which caused the chest to cling to the stage when the power was turned on.

In France Robert-Houdin presented the trick as the chest that grew light and heavy upon command. But with exquisite psychology he changed it in Africa to prove his "powers" of robbing the strongest man of his strength and leaving him so weak that he was incapable of lifting the chest that he had so easily lifted with one finger a few moments before.

The obviously tricky giant cork fly that my grandfather had used was unsuitable for modern New York, but Uncle Ed had obtained a photograph of a gigantic Brazilian beetle that completely covered a man's outstretched hand. He made a facsimile of this insect in cork and, with thin spiral antennae made of brass wire and legs made of rubber bands, he created a lifelike creature. With this prop as a basis, he decided to build the illusion. I agreed to work as his assistant and manipulate the magnet and also teach him the code for the mind reading act. The title of the act was "Syko—The Beetle with a Superhuman Brain."

Edward had none of Theo's gift for careful planning and building and rushed into things without thinking. This habit caused us plenty of headaches in the next few weeks.

Our first headache was the etching of the letters and numbers on the back of the thick mirror we used. Even when we used gloves, the nitric acid we used ate through and burned our fingers, and the letters were uneven. Other headaches followed. Even though it was carefully packed in a padded crate, any jolt would crack the mirror. Another obvious drawback in using a mirror, and one we should have thought of beforehand, was that the mirror would reflect the modern spotlights in the faces of the audience, blinding them. After a couple of broken mirrors, with my fingers stained like a chain smoker's, and just at the point of Edward's giving up the whole thing, I hit upon the solution.

My idea consisted of a thin plywood backing which could be painted flat white and the letters painted in matte-black on it. All around the edges were to be thin plywood slats to make a frame to hold a thin sheet of plate glass slightly smaller than the frame. The whole thing would be much thinner than the $\frac{1}{4}$ inch mirror we had been using, giving the magnet greater force, and it would be far lighter and easier to handle.

As usual in the Bamberg family, the idea was greeted with a snarl. "Where will you get a perfectly flat sheet of glass without bumps and ridges, and where was plywood made that was perfectly flat and wouldn't warp?" There are the words—you can set it to music.

After enough time had passed for him to believe that the idea was his, Uncle Ed became quite enthusiastic. There is no doubt that once his mind was made up, he was a hustler. He chased around town until he found a beautiful sheet of Finnish plywood and a very thin glass used for expensive mirrors. A professional sign painter did the lettering, and when the model was finished, it worked like a charm. Above all it could stand fairly rough treatment.

The trick frame in which the glass rested and the wooden easel to hold the frame were not too difficult to build at home; and in order to get even lighting on the glass, we constructed a sheet metal trough fitted with four electric lights in the top of the frame. We were exceptionally happy about this added improvement.

A powerful magnet connected to two six-volt automobile batteries allowed the beetle to fly around the glass resting on the knife-edged iron rail buried in its belly.

In order to protect the secret and to fool the acts on the bill (and above all the stagehands and electricians), we made a wooden box that fitted over the batteries, which had a lot of false dials and buttons on it that we would solemnly fiddle around with before the act when anyone was looking our way.

We rehearsed and tried it out a hundred times at home and it worked like a charm. A delighted Uncle Ed spread the good word in vaudeville centers and waited for a break.

One evening, in the winter of 1922, Uncle Ed came home and shut the street door with a bang which was the signal that something had happened. He had the Bamberg eagle look as he marched into the dining room and, like all good actors, held us in suspense for a long moment. We held our breaths.

"I spent the afternoon," he said slowly, "on the fifth floor of the Palace Theatre Building."

The fifth floor—where the moguls that controlled the big-time held court. We still held our breath.

"I had a chat," he continued offhandedly, "with Frances Rockefeller King," F.R.K., the Queen, one of the big shots in the world of private engagements.

"We are to give a try-out of the act at a dinner show in which all the big shots will be present." Nonchalantly he went on, "Albee, Wegefarth, Martin Beck and a few others."

We exhaled with a rush. What a break! We were in!

We slaved for a week getting everything in shape. Polishing and cleaning, getting the batteries charged, rehearsal and more rehearsal and finally the big night was at hand.

The stage where we worked was small but ample and we had plenty of time to set the act because George M. Cohan did a twenty-minute monologue that had 'em in the aisles.

With the audience in high good humor the emcee made a short announcement and the curtain slowly opened for the first time on Syko, the mysterious beetle with a human brain.

The whole goddamn act only lasted a minute. Owing to the noise, or excitement or nerves, we got our signals mixed up.

When Uncle Ed lowered the glass to rest against the lower part of the easel he had to say "right," which was my signal to jump down from behind the frame, close the flaps, and crouch on the floor behind the glass.

Edward would then lift the frame on its hinges and show it clear through, then drop it back to its original position. The combined slam of the frame and a whispered "right" was my signal to pop up, open the flaps and jump up behind the frame, using the lower flap as a seat.

I don't know what happened but either he didn't slam the frame or I didn't hear the second "right" and Uncle Ed, too nervous to wait for my confirming "right" when I was safely ensconced behind the frame, lifted the blasted glass to display to the crowned heads of American show-business, a young punk, dressed in black tights staring at them in dismay.

There was a tremendous belly laugh and then...Curtain!

For the next few weeks family relations were strained.

A few weeks later we knew something was up when the door slammed again. Uncle Ed marched in with the Bamberg falcon look and we held our breaths.

"I spent the afternoon on the fourth floor of the Palace Theatre Building," he said with pursed lips.

We let out our breath. The fourth-floor was the small, split-week time, but there was plenty of it.

"We open in the Grand Street Theatre for three days starting Monday, and I fervently hope that no s.o.b. nephew gets any ideas."

Woe was me!

The Grand Street Theatre in the Jewish quarter was noted for the toughest audience in the world. It is said that even Sarah Bernhardt was booed there. I breathed in and out quickly.

We opened, but some perverse demon seemed to have taken control of the bloody illusion. In rehearsals, just before the act, the blasted bug would fly merrily around the glass, but once the act started it did nothing but fall off into the net which was hanging below the frame.

I was convinced that some genie from the netherworld had it in for me. It worked fairly well in the first show, and beautifully, without falling off once during the supper show when the house was poor; but for the evening show, when the house was packed, the bug just wouldn't stay on the glass for more than a few seconds before taking a nose dive into the net.

I was accused of mishandling the magnet, which I stoutly denied. Edward would try it himself just before the act and it worked like a charm, but the moment the curtain went up, it did nothing but fall on its cork pratt.

I was within a stone's throw of the padded cell when we discovered what the trouble was; it was the blasted light strip. In rehearsals we never lit the lamps and everything was okay. But the moment before curtain, we would light the frame, the house curtain would rise and a rush of warm humid air from the hall caused a thin film of condensation on the glass that acted as a brake. The friction stopped the beetle in its tracks, the magnet went on and the beetle went off.

Once we knew this we cleaned the glass with alcohol and lit the lamps a good ten minutes before the curtain rose, allowing the glass to heat evenly. The beetle rarely fell off again.

Once this kink was ironed out the act improved and we got plenty of work at good money. Uncle Ed engaged an actor named Doc Hawley, who had a very impressive manner, to introduce the act. Uncle Ed, dressed in jodhpurs and a pith helmet, played the mind reading explorer from the Brazilian jungles.

We played all over the country without missing a day, except for the time I got a terrible sunburn at the Old Spanish Fort in New Orleans, and when I gorged myself on crab chowder in Mobile, Alabama and was laid up for two days with a heaving belly.

We wound up this long tour at Proctor's 125th Street Theatre, and on the bill with us was an act called Paul Poole's Melody Maids, four pretty little girls playing the violin while Paul did magic.

One of the girls was a tiny, pert little thing who was the best musician of the lot, besides being a serious, well-educated girl whom one so rarely meets in vaudeville. Between shows I would take her out for coffee and doughnuts and she'd listen to my tall tales with quiet attention. If she thought what was said was a lot of hot air, she was too well-bred to say so. After the Proctor date was over I urged her to keep in touch with me and she promised to write and she kept her word.

CHAPTER 19

We worked very hard and it was a tough grind. Vaudeville had degenerated to four and five shows a day. In some places they even charged admission for the rehearsals.

The whole set-up was graft ridden. The head booking office would pay an act a couple of hundred dollars a week and then sell it to their own houses for double or triple. One of these bills would consist of one highly paid legitimate act with a fill in of fake acts, like the so-called ''sister-teams'' that worked for peanuts kicking back $400 on a $500 salary. In the long run this sort of thing hurt vaudeville terribly.

We were all scared to death of the big-shots and no one did anything about it. The first attempt to buck this system had been the ill-starred ''White Rats'' strike and years later there was the infamous blacklist when the Shuberts tried to buck the system by opening their own circuit to vaudeville acts and hundreds gladly went over to them, only to have the bubble burst in their faces. When the venture failed, they were on the blacklist and many of them never played vaudeville again.

The old staunch rule of show business, ''Leave 'em hungry for more,'' was changed to, ''Make 'em give till it hurts,'' and the audiences began to stay away in droves. Then talking pictures came along and the whole thing folded.

Uncle Ed refused to kick in. He was only getting $250 a week for the act and he fired Hawley to cut expenses, but there wasn't enough work to keep going and the act split up. I was on my own again.

While looking for work with my own act I had many an afternoon with nothing to do. I would go up to Frank Ducrot's magic store, which was still called the Hornmann Magic Company. It was there that I met some very fine magicians, both professional and amateur. I became friends with Al Baker and Sam Horowitz. I learned a lot from them, especially Sam who had just perfected the use of the short card in some brilliant routines that had all the boys wondering. With his characteristic kindness, he taught me his routines. Al Baker was no less kind in teaching me some exclusive close-up magic.

It was at Ducrot's that I met Doc Wilson, editor of *The Sphinx* magazine, Dorny (Werner Dornfield) who had just completed a tour with the Elsie Janis show, Fred Keating and many others.

I visited Dr. Hooker and told him the truth about the material he had given me and offered to return it. He told me to sell it and buy tricks that were suitable for my act. So I made a deal with Ducrot for the act in exchange for other tricks. He drove a hard deal and for the Chinese canister and pedestal I got the equivalent of five dollars in merchandise.

My pretty little melody maid, Hilda Seagle, was back in New York and we were going steady now. One day I was invited out to her home on the East Side to meet her father, who ran a dry goods store and lived there with his three daughters and his son. I don't think I made much of an impression on Hilda's father. He looked me up and down without saying anything and I heartily wished that Zancig had taught me to be a real mind reader.

I haunted Hilda until she finally broke down and we were married secretly at City Hall on November 2, 1923. As I had spent my last two bucks on the marriage license, our honeymoon consisted of her going home to sleep at her father's place while I trekked back to my depressing room.

We had hoped to keep our marriage a secret until better times came along, but we didn't count on enterprising firms who got Hilda's address from the registry office at City Hall and flooded her mail with circulars and offers to the "New and Happy Bride." With all this publicity it didn't take the old man very long to discover that he had a son-in-law. He was none too happy about this as he had better plans for his little girl—but what could he do?

It was Hilda's steadying influence that stopped me from chasing around like a lunatic and got my mind on my work. One sure thing is that my luck turned and things began to get better.

Broadcasting was just starting in those days and for the first time magic was the topic for a ten minute talk on "Magic and Magicians" that I gave over Radio WGY. Harry Latz heard the broadcast and got in touch with me. He had sold the hotel in Atlantic City and had opened a skyscraper hotel on West 72nd Street, the Alamac, with a nightclub on the top floor called the Congo Room. It had an African background and a Negro ''savage'' dressed in a leopard skin to greet the guests as they stepped from the elevator.

Harry was still keen on magic. He wanted me to do the Sawing illusion in his nightclub, dressed as an African explorer, and nightly sawing a cannibal in half. He offered me a good salary and in a few days I had built the illusion and for the first time an illusionist played a nightclub.

Harry had Paul Specht's band playing jazz and I got the bug, so Johnny O'Donell, one of the sax players, tried to make a musician of me by selling me a C-melody saxophone. Bootleg booze and gangsters were riding high and although Harry tried to keep booze out of the Congo Room, the clients brought it along in pocket flasks. Bootleggers were selling bathtub gin to the boys in the orchestra, and when Harry protested, they slashed the beautiful red leather seats of the chairs and sofas of the club.

Hilda and I had a room on West 96th Street, and to the delight of the neighbors, I practiced my sax every morning. After I finished Hilda would get busy on the violin. It's a wonder we weren't thrown out on our necks.

After the sawing engagement Harry gave me a steady job as spotlight man in the Congo Room and this kept me going until something else showed up.

The news from Europe was heartening. After the ill-fated Asian tour, Okito had returned to England and from there was booked direct to the Winter Garten Theatre in Berlin. His success was sensational and he was the talk of Berlin. This was just what he needed and he plunged into an orgy of spending for improving the show. More Chinese costumes were added to his already imposing wardrobe. He branched out into large stage illusions and created an act that was comparable to the splendour of the late Chung Ling Soo.

A tour of the leading German cities followed with increasing success and then, suddenly, the bubble burst. The great inflation started. The mark dropped to inconceivable millions to the dollar. A new salary was arranged every morning, but after the evening show the money was almost worthless. The desperate artistes bought anything they could lay their hands on—cameras, jewels, watches. One artiste even went so far in a desperate moment as to buy a cow, which he kept in the basement of the theatre.

In monetary terms, Okito was wiped out, but he had a gold mine in the act. He left Germany and went to Vienna where he opened at the Ronnacher Theatre. His success in Vienna was even greater than in Berlin and he immediately sent for Lily and the children to come over. But the inflation monster was spreading its rapacious maw over all Europe and the Austrian crown began to wobble. The Russian ruble was the worst of all. With the exception of England and the Scandinavian countries, nothing was sure. And then suddenly Germany established the Renton-mark to be followed by the gold mark. Okito was offered a thousand gold marks a day for the Scala in Berlin. This made Okito the highest paid magician in Europe. He wrote me a glowing letter of the wonderful condition of variety in Europe.

Moira was at it again, and one morning I was standing with Hilda on the corner of 96th Street and Amsterdam Avenue when two speeding cars came hurtling up from Riverside Drive. A gangster machine gun battle had started. I grabbed Hilda and threw us down on the sidewalk a few seconds before the drugstore window behind us was smashed to pieces by gunfire.

When we stood up and were brushing off our clothes I decided to get the hell out. I went upstairs to our room and got the saxophone and sold it to Al Baker. I said good-bye to Harry Latz and dear old Herman, and with the money we had saved from the Congo Room deal and a kindly gift of money from Hilda's family, we sailed for England on the 14th of July, 1924.

CHAPTER 20

That first night in London at the hotel with the rubbery coffee, the crockery wash basin and pitcher of cold water, the atmosphere in general brought back bleak memories. Hilda loved it and thought it was great fun and wondered why I was miserable. But I bucked up considerably when we went down to the charming English countryside in Devon for a visit with Uncle Charlie.

A week later we left for Munich where Okito was playing at the Deutsches Theatre. I proudly presented my bride to the old man who made a great fuss over her.

Okito was headlining a bill of ten acts and closed the first half. When I saw his act that night I was thrilled to the core. It was a dream of what a pure magic act should be and I kept looking at Hilda to see what effect it had on her. She couldn't believe it. I was elated and dispirited at the same time. This was my life, this was the thing I was born to do—but how? I felt that I didn't have half the artistic talent of my father, and even if I did, where would I get the money to produce such a gorgeous production, not to mention the mechanical and technical ability involved? With the impatience of my twenty years I didn't stop to think that it had taken him over thirty laborious years to get where he was. I wanted it handed to me on a silver platter.

For two solid weeks I watched his act every night and twice on Saturdays and Sundays. I reveled in it; I bathed in it; and poor little Hilda was forced to watch it with me.

With his reputation I knew that a word from him was enough to get me bookings in Germany. He agreed to do what he could but warned me that it would take some time as acts were booked for a month's engagement in each city and sometimes as much as a year in advance. He showed me contracts for twelve theatres that completed his year. He suggested that while I waited for my first date I should spend a few weeks in Vienna with my mother and the kids, so with high hopes Hilda and I left for Austria.

Mother was at the train station to meet us with Dorothy, a skinny knocked-kneed kid with gas pipe legs, and Donald, a whirlwind in a sailor suit. With them was a bald, mustached, thickset gentleman whom she introduced as Herr Ottokar Fisher, president of the Wiener Magische Club.

Mother had a small flat in a rather poor section of the city in the 10th Bezirk, near the Margaretner Orpheum Theatre where the nights ended with wild revelry and a few stabbings now and then. Fortunately Lily and Hilda liked each other and all in all they were happy days.

As the son of the renowned zauberkunstler Okito, I had carte-blanche everywhere and was made an honorary member of the Wiener Magic Club where my card routines based on Horowitz' short-card technique created a sensation. One member, an Italian youth named Grazia a Dei begged me for the routine, which I taught him, and later he went to Italy where he did an act based on it and made a lot of money.

The standard of the amateur magicians in Vienna was very high, which I discovered was due to the initiation system they used for all aspiring members. When an amateur thought he was adept enough to be a member he made a written application. When five or six applications were at hand the club would rent a small hall for the afternoon and all the applicants did their acts. Watching them was a committee of seven judges, and if the amateur had a majority of four votes, he was admitted. If he had less than four votes he was given another chance six months later. If he failed on his second try he could never get another. This kept magic at a very high level in Vienna and is a system that could be used elsewhere with great advantage for the good of magic.

I became fast friends with Fischer. He regaled me with the history of magic and magicians of central Europe from the pre-Hofzinser times to the present. Fischer had been a professional magician for years in the old Kratky-Baschik magic theatre in the Prater and he took me to this historic show place where they were presenting the original Tanagra illusion, the most perfect optical illusion ever conceived.

The stage setting for this remarkable illusion was a study with a large desk in the center. On the desk was an inkwell and some books and from the inkwell tiny people not over six inches tall climbed out and played in a Viennese operetta. The whole thing was delicate and enchanting with those tiny folk running around the desk top, climbing over the books and finally going back into the inkwell as the show ended.

Fischer took me backstage and showed me the working of this masterpiece which is based on a circular concave mirror at least three feet in diameter. If this show could be reproduced today as I saw it in Vienna it would baffle the television engineers.

One of my joys was to "roddle" with Fischer in the back room and workshop of his magic store in the Favorittenstrasse. Here, for the first time, I saw his Blue Phantom, Water from the Fingertips, the Japanese Fan Card, the Cords of Fantasia, and the thimble routine he had worked out for a small act my mother wished to do, ending with the production of a giant thimble a foot high. Together we worked on a model for his packing box escape described in Volume VI of the Tarbell course.

It was a rare treat to visit his home in the Columbusgasse and admire the original Prof. Hofzinser apparatus, most of which was made of solid silver. Especially interesting were the tricked cards that the master used, one of them being a four of spades which, when held in front of a candle, appeared to be the five.

Fischer had great affection for me and called me "his magical son." One day, in a burst of generosity, he offered me the complete Hofzinser collection as a gift, but I refused his kind gesture as I knew that this was the pride of his life and, secondly, because I was sure it would get damaged or lost being carried around. I believe the collection is in the United States now. However, I did accept one small metal vase for the change of an egg, and Fischer taught me the original presentation for Hofzinser's card in the lemon, which I later used for my Bill in the Orange routine. Fischer also helped me with my act and gave me many fine tricks and some beautiful shadowgraph fakes made of thin brass.

At the Vienna Magic Club I saw, for the first time, small table tricks made of plastic and performed by Karl Edler. The magical klatches at the club lasted until the early hours of the morning and the last to leave were the "fearless foursome": Fischer, Franz Holl, manager of the bank of Austria, Herr Oberstatsbahnrat Leutkens, one of the big wheels in the Austrian State Railways and myself. Our password was "Salamunta."

Rarely have I known a magical enthusiast like Fischer, a linguist who spoke seven languages and whose love for magic was his life. This affable and courteous gentleman was so jealous of the secrets of magic that he often refused to sell certain tricks to prospective customers and politely edged them toward the door and out of his shop.

Without a doubt he was the world's worse businessman, but he was happy in his world of fantasy until the shadow of the Nazis obscured that wonderful country and he died of a broken heart, a destitute and embittered man.

While waiting for news from Okito I played the Margaretner Orpheum in Vienna, close to where we lived, and in the Austrian towns of Graz, Linz and Innsbruck.

Finally I had word from my father's agent in Vienna, Hugo Neubauer, who booked me for Belgrade and Zagreb in Serbia, Brunn and Prague in Czechoslovakia, and a few other towns in the Balkans.

When I returned to Vienna there was a letter from my father offering me a job as assistant in his act. I was in a quandary because the wages he offered me were far less than what I was earning with my act but, on the other hand, I knew that the experience of working and learning from him was invaluable for my future if I intended to be a magician. Hilda advised me to go, and although it meant leaving her in Vienna, I set forth with a high heart for Hamburg, Germany.

CHAPTER 21

The big variety halls were the training ground for magicians and I learned a lot during those months with Okito.

I was no longer the duck-keeper and carpet-sweeper of the old days in London. I was now first assistant and had charge of all the big props and scenery.

Okito either headlined or split the bill with such big variety stars as Grock, Captain Winston's Mermaids and Sea Lions, Charlie Rivels, the Flying Condonas, Franco Piper, Ratelli the great Italian juggler, and dozens of others. I had the opportunity to watch their acts many times and learn stagecraft at its best.

Okito's show ran like a piece of well-oiled machinery, and everything was checked and foolproof. The whole production could be set up or packed in less than an hour. It was a marvel of compactness and lightweight illusions and props, so different from the massive apparatus of Thurston. Dante once sneeringly referred to it as "Okito's cardboard show," but in view of the dead weight Dante hauled around, I can understand that the remark was triggered by envy. Dante was of the opinion that stage illusions should be rugged and heavy for rough handling. Okito claimed that there should be no rough handling and props should be regarded as precision objects. They both had a point and perhaps they both over-did it. When I had my own show in later years I tried to strike a happy medium between the two with a show that, from an audience standpoint, was as impressive as Dante's although it weighed less than half.

An interesting note about Okito was the widespread popularity of the musical theme he used for the Floating Ball. It was known in Germany as "Okito-Leid" but was actually "The Sheik of Araby" played very slowly. Later he changed this music to "Allah's Holiday" from the operetta "Katinka."

126

We played all the big cities in Germany and I learned to speak fairly good German but with a "Wiener" accent. It may be that my understanding of Dutch, which I learned as a child in Brooklyn, helped me.

Okito would allow no one to touch the small tricks which he prepared himself, such as threading the spools for the ball trick, loading the water bowl, the preparation of the mat load and the silk handkerchiefs for the plate trick. He would trust no one to make the final inspection of the act. But I finally convinced him that I could take over this tedious preparation and soon I learned to satisfy his exacting demands. Years later when I had my own show, people would laugh when I showed up at the theatre in the early afternoon. They asked me if I lived in the dressing room. But it's a habit I can't break and often when I am nervous and out of sorts, I find peace among my props in a quiet dressing room and very rarely did I have a failure on the stage. In over thirty years of doing the floating ball the thread only broke twice and both times due to freak accidents.

Okito enjoyed a triumphal success in Paris at the l'Empire Theatre in the Rue de Wagram and, near the end of his first engagement, presented to the Parisian theatregoers the Faquir Blackman, a shock-haired Sicilian, who became famous all over Europe as a hypnotist of wild animals. It was at the Empire that the impresario M. Dufrenne was found locked in his own safe, murdered by a degenerate sailor from Marseilles.

I visited the site where the old Robert-Houdin Theatre had stood and found a modern building with shops in its place. Cagliostro's old house in the Rue St. Claude still stood. The lower floor was given over to an automobile supply store. The Egyptian Chamber, where Cagliostro performed his clairvoyant seances, was occupied by a furrier, M. Goldstein. Henry Ridgely Evans wrote: "The Hebraic cognomen Goldstein (gold-stone) is suggestive of the Philosopher's Stone, which is credited with turning base metals into gold. Perhaps the gentleman furrier is an incarnation of Cagliostro. The subject is worth considering from a theosophical point of view."

After France we played Belgium, Denmark, Sweden, Poland, Hungary and Czechoslovakia. One morning in Prague, Okito, with a huge grin on his face, handed me a telegram. I read the exciting message that said we were to open at St. George's Hall in London. I knew the Hall couldn't pay his salary and I wondered why he took the date, but it was a case of professional pride.

At last I was to realize my dream of getting backstage in

England's home of mystery. But a fat lot of good it did me. The Hall used a protective system for the magicians who played there. No one was allowed on the stage during another magician's act, and when I finally got down into the famous cellar under the stage I found the traps were enclosed within wooden bins with all the doors locked. In all the time I played the Hall I never discovered a single thing that was of any use to me. A quiet mysterious air hung over the place. Years later, when the Hall was bought by BBC for their Music Hall series, the producer of the broadcast, John Sharman, said that there was something weird about the Hall. He occupied Nevil Maskelyne's former office and claimed that mysterious writing used to appear on the blotting pad. Nevil was found dead in a flat above the Hall and it was claimed that his ghost appeared and vanished through trap doors. However, it must be taken into account that Mr. Sharman was also in show business.

Sometimes I would drift into Jasper Maskelyne's dressing room. Jasper, the third generation, had modernized the style of magic at the Hall but with little success. His cronies were the caustic Selbit and the sarcastic Williams. It was not a congenial atmosphere for an outsider and they barely condescended to admit my existence on earth, so I soon learned to keep away.

On the other hand, Louis Nikola was very friendly. I would rush around to the front to catch his act when ours was over. He had a dry sense of humor and was very entertaining. Most of his tricks were original and his Glad Eye, the production of a large kewpie doll with a sash and a staggering hat, from a previously shown empty London pillar box, was very effective and amusing.

One evening in my father's dressing room, while we were having a snack between shows, I had the temerity to mention that Goldin's new Sawing A Woman had a weak spot: the trick suspicious table. All the sawing illusions had this defect, and although they tried to disguise the thickness of the table, it was fairly obvious to a discerning person that a girl could be partly concealed in one.

Why in hell couldn't I learn to keep my mouth shut?

"Ha!" cried Okito, jubilant to begin the joust. "I seem to remember a few years ago something about an improvement for the duck vanish, but nothing ever came of it and now I find that the genial Horace Goldin has finally joined the ranks of the inept shmucks that the future world's greatest magician has to bear with. I am sure the magical fraternity will be forever beholden to you when you demonstrate your ingeniuos method of sawing a woman in halves without using a table. My dear chap, allow me to be the first to congratulate you."

How the devil could anyone argue with a sarcastic guy like that? It's like that crack of Wilfred Jonson, "I have yet to see a magician dismember himself, but it would no doubt be a popular effect in some quarters."

Despite his great success, my father was glum about the future of magic and did his utmost to discourage me from becoming a magician. It wasn't that he thought I did not have the ability, but I think he wanted me to have a more secure life.

"It's a thankless dog's work," he would say. "You've got to keep on working steadily or in time you lose your capital. Good and honest assistants are hard to find. Take my advice, Dafe, stick with your shadow act and you will make a good living, without headaches all your life like Tom Jersey."

I said that if I had some good tricks and an illusion or two I could make a go of it, but he shook his head.

"With that you think you can compete with the great magicians? Your idea is out of the question. Where would you play? The cream is gone and every variety theatre in Europe has been worked to death by magicians. So what chance do you stand?"

Neither he nor I knew that Moira was listening in on our conversation.

The Great Raymond would come to the Hall between shows and chat with the boys and I got to know him quite well. Although he was at loose ends he still lived in style and sometimes invited me to lunch at some of the best restaurants in London where he was well known and popular.

Raymond was the exact opposite of my father. He was the optimistic, audacious type of man who fascinated me. I remembered in 1920 when Raymond had first come to London with his show and, before opening, had asked Goldston's advice in certain matters. The next day Goldston was holding forth to a bunch of loafers in his shop on Green Street. "The man is mad," he stated indignantly, "and thinks that London is living in the Stone Age. He has the cheek to do the Egg Bag, the Substitution Trunk, Out of Sight, and the Kellar Rope Tie and for this he expects to get a thousand quid a week." But Goldston had overlooked one thing: Raymond's magnetic personality. Raymond opened in London with outstanding success, to everyone's surprise and secret jealousy.

Raymond told me that he was arranging a tour of South America and painted a fantastic picture of those countries where he had been so successful on previous tours. I told him that one of my ambitions was to visit South America and branch out on my own as I had a few ideas that I thought would be successful. He asked me for my permanent address and I told him he could always get in touch with me through Fischer in Vienna.

After the St. George's Hall engagement we returned to the Empire in Paris for the second time and during this season, because of a silly joke, Pop lost an excellent assistant, a Chinese boy named Wong. This was indirectly the cause of the luckiest break in my life.

The story began in Stockholm some months before. One day Okito noticed that the small change that he carried in his vest pocket was diminishing in some mysterious way. As I was the only one, besides Marie, who was allowed in his dressing room, I got cold looks, but nothing was said openly. I was only earning £2 a week and it was a struggle for me to make ends meet, so I was the logical larcenist.

We had a sleight-of-hand expert on the show, but who?

Then it dawned on him that the only other person who ever entered the empty dressing room was Heinrich, a German boy, who loaded the fish pole during the floating ball trick.

It so happened in Stockholm that the dressing rooms were under the stage and early one morning Okito augured a hole through the stage floor right over his dressing room.

When the moment came that evening to do the Ball trick Okito walked on stage and, getting down on his knees, salaamed the audience and bowed down with his head touching the stage. His eye was over the hole and he saw the assistant go through his vest pocket, remove a couple of coins, and then start to load the fish into the pole.

After the show that night, Okito told Heinrich that he wanted to rehearse a new trick and had him salaam on his knees and look through the hole. Okito then banged on the stage floor with a stick, which was my signal to walk into the dressing room and pocket the coins in his vest. After which, with a sinister grin, he pointed to the stage exit and that was the end of Heinrich.

By a stroke of good fortune he picked up a jewel of an assistant, Wong, a boy made for magic—intelligent, honest, polite, fast in his reactions, clean and neat and who spoke perfect English. This was the paragon he lost in Paris.

One afteroon, Okito was cleaning out a private trunk and

throwing out a lot of useless items that one picks up while travel-ing. He came across a pair of brilliant scarlet suspenders which he hung on the wall of his dressing room. Wong came in for some reason and seeing the gaudy suspenders, gazed at them in wonder.

"Would you care to have those suspenders, Wongie?" asked Okito.

The delighted Wong rolled them up and put them in his pocket with profuse thanks.

The following day, while delving deeper into the trunk, Okito discovered a duplicate pair of suspenders and hung them on the wall with the intention of giving them to Wong.

When Wong arrived and saw the suspenders he gave a start of surprise and Okito, noting his puzzlement, decided to play one of his practical jokes.

"My dear Wongie," he said in an injured tone, "I gave you those suspenders, but if you don't want them, say so, and I'll give them to someone else."

"But I did take them home, Mr. Okito. I took them to my lodgings and put them in the drawer of the night table."

"I beg of you, my dear Wongie," said the old man, "not to play games with me. If you want the suspenders then take them and don't let me see them again."

Wong stuffed the suspenders in his pocket and walked out bemused. The old man was hugging himself with joy. He tipped me off to sneak into Wong's dressing room during the act and swipe the suspenders.

The next day Wong appeared with a dazed look.

"Mr. Okito, sir," he said hoarsely, "I know you won't believe me but I swear it's the truth. On the bus home I found the suspenders missing from my pocket and when I got home they were in the night table drawer again."

Wong took the suspenders from his pocket and placed them on the dressing room table. "I don't want them. Give them to someone else." And he left the room.

Pop was in raptures and still chuckling with delight when the grin was wiped off his face by a note from Wong saying that he had to take care of a sick relative and please forgive him for leaving without notice. Okito did very little laughing for the next couple of days while he chased around trying to get an assis-tant. Finally, instead of a male assistant, he engaged a young and luscious girl who was a decided asset to the act.

A couple of weeks later came the bombshell. Okito was booked for Buenos Aires and a tour of South America. This was it! This was what I had been waiting for.

A few days before we closed at the Empire, Pop took me into his dressing room and hemmed and hawed a bit and finally came out with the staggering news that I was not included in the South American tour. My rightful place was with my wife in Vienna. I nearly grovelled in the dust, but his mind was made up and I was to leave him the following week.

I suspect that the beautiful new assistant had something to do with it and I was so mad I could have eaten the ducks alive. The first time he had pulled the South African deal and now this.

I wrote a letter to Raymond in care of his club in London, hoping he was still there, and told him that I was at his orders but had no reply. Okito saw me off from the station on the train to Vienna and little did we know that the next time we were to meet would be in Brazil.

I got back to Vienna with very little money and I was lucky to pick up some odd dates with my act for Yugoslavia, Bulgaria and Rumania. In Bucharest I received a long letter from Raymond, forwarded by Fischer, in which he told me that he had arranged his South American tour and was opening in Lisbon before sailing. He said I could do my shadowgraph act and double as chief assistant. He also asked me if I could bring a mechanic with me, who understood locks and handcuffs and who would be useful for building new apparatus.

I wired that I would accept if Hilda could go along. He wired back "OK" and sent me three fares from Vienna to Lisbon. In the Wiener Magic Club I put up my problem of a mechanic. Herr Epler, a chemist, said he knew of an amateur magician of the Berlin Magic Circle who had been a mechanic at Siemens-Halske in Leipsig. He had a very bad accident in a falling elevator but was now in a condition to work again.

I sent an express letter to the mechanic whose name was Johannes E. Spreer and told him that if he was interested he should meet me in Hamburg where I had to change trains for Portugal.

A few days later Hilda and I left for Hamburg and Spreer agreed to come along. I left him his ticket and told him to get a passport as soon as possible and come on a week later.

Raymond was at the station in Lisbon to meet us and introduced his wife, Litzka, a beautiful woman who played the harp as an interlude in the show and also acted as Raymond's chief girl assistant.

Raymond's debut in Lisbon was set within ten days at the largest theatre in Europe, the Coliseo de Recreos, and besides the rehearsals, we had to repair and paint the props. We slaved day and night and finally got the illusion in working order and repainted. This was where my apprenticeship with my father paid off. I even surprised myself at the efficient manner in which I whipped that big show into shape in such a short time. Raymond was delighted and it was then that I began to have confidence in myself. Spreer arived just a day before the debut.

I played the part of a Chinese assistant and, as agreed, did my act. Hilda and Spreer were assistants and Litzka did most of the big illusions.

Business was fair, but in such a tremendous theatre it always looked empty, although there were enough people to fill an ordinary theatre. There were threats that the great British strike of 1926 was soon to start and Raymond decided not to play the other Portuguese towns and arranged passages on the last boat that left England before the strike, the S.S. Arlanza. We sailed from Lisbon on the 21st of May for Bahia, Brazil.

Moira must have had a knowing smile. I didn't know, and wouldn't have believed, that the great South American continent was to be my happy hunting grounds on and off for the next forty years.

CHAPTER 22

The tropical port of Bahia with its palms and the great hills in the background was an exotic new world for me. The boat docked in the noisy lower part of the city with its markets piled with bananas, pineapples and mangos, in contrast to the dried slabs of codfish black with flies. The garish attire of the preponderantly Negro population, the cries and songs of the fruit vendors balancing huge baskets on their heads, the beggars, the bustle, the pungent odor of rotten fruit and fish was a far cry from anything I had seen before.

To get to the upper residential and business center of Bahia there were huge elevators that ran straight up the side of the cliff. The upper city had none of the dirt and squalor of the sprawling lower section and we were installed in a big rambling hotel with large high-ceilinged rooms and broad bladed, slowly turning, electric fans that were never turned off.

The doors and windows were lattice work and no door had a key as they claimed that stealing in hotels was unknown. They may have been right because we never lost as much as a pin in those hotels.

To my delight breakfast consisted of a big bowl of hot black coffee, tostadas, orange juice, large chunks of papaya, crushed pineapple and mangos. What kind of a world was this? This plentiful fruit diet was to be Hilda's and my salvation as we didn't care for the inevitable dish of feijoada, which in a mixture of black beans, rice and salt pork, usually served twice a day. One excellent dish was batapa, spiced shredded crab baked in the shell, but too gut-curdling to be eaten every day. All the food was liberally sprinkled with farofa which looked and tasted like dried sawdust. But all in all I loved it and basked in the tropical heat as the cold, damp winters of New York and London faded from my mind.

The old dilapidated theatre where we were to open had an exaggerated inclined stage. We had to make wooden chocks with protruding nail points that bit into the stage floor and prevented the illusions from rolling into the orchestra pit. One big illusion called Ava, in which a huge folding cage was concealed in the roof, refused to function due to the incline. Raymond ordered the back legs of the platform sawed off sufficiently to make it level with the stage. I pointed out to Raymond that it would be a shame to cut down the original carved legs and have to make new ones again for other theatres. I suggested making a pair of cheap short legs just for this one date and then throwing them away. There was quite an argument about it and for the first time I saw that stubborn streak that was part of his character. He knew I was right but he was the boss and we had to do what he said. It was Thurston and Okito over again. Spreer cut down the legs and, just as I predicted, in the next theatre we had to have new ones made that cost him a pretty penny.

The Great Raymond opened in Bahia with the following programme:

1: The "Raymond Overture."
2: The Human Wardrobe: A cabinet from which the entire company appeared, including Raymond.
3: Mystic Oranges: A production of oranges that filled two large bowls covered with serviettes, followed by the fruit being tossed to the audience with some good comedy as an excited man in an upper box tried to catch the oranges in his straw hat.
4: The Vase Mystery: Flags of all nations produced from the Ghost Tube. (Raymond being the first to present it in South America, it is known in the Latin American countries as El Tubo Raymond.)
5: The Dentist: An adaptation of the Electric Chair illusion in which Litzka vanished in a cloud of smoke from a cabinet.
6: The Dress Trunk: The appearance of a girl from a previously shown empty trunk which was filled with dresses of all nations. A girl appeared from the trunk wearing a costume selected by the audience.
7: The Egg Bag: Very well done. Raymond really milked this old trick.
8: Card Throwing: Raymond pitched advertising cards into the audience a la Thurston. The excitement grew when he pitched some of them to the back of the top gallery of the theatre.

9: Divorce: The Out of Sight illusion (Maskelyne) in which Hilda, seated on a chair hung high in the air within a wooden scaffold, visibly vanished with the chair as her clothes fell to the stage.

Second Part

10: Shower of Silk: A bare-handed production of dozens of silks.
11: Ava: The production of a huge golden cage in an empty cabinet with Litzka seated inside on a swing dressed like a giant canary.
12: The Enchanted Rings: Two borrowed finger rings were hammered flat and stuffed into a blunderbuss which was fired at a bottle which then was smashed with a hammer to find a dove inside with the two restored rings tied to its neck by a ribbon.
13: The Substitution Trunk: Raymond changed places with Litzka who had been handcuffed and locked in a rope-bound trunk. The change was instantaneous and the high point of the show.
14: Syko: Shadowgraphs.
15: Spookville: The hair-raising adventures of a spectator seated in a tent alongside Raymond who was bound hand and foot to his chair. This was an excellent comedy routine and ended the show with screams of laughter.

For a change of programme, Raymond would substitute the Selbit Sawing illusion which I built for him, the Egyptian Box and Asrah. In construction was the Beetle illusion that I had done with Uncle Ed in New York. We built the frame and easel of beautiful Brazilian hardwoods but suddenly Raymond ordered that we stop work on it and we carted the half-finished illusion all over Brazil.

We played Bahia for fifteen days with rather poor business. The impresario of the theatre blamed the slack attendance on the phenomenal success of a Chinese magician called Li-Ho-Chang who had played Bahia in another theatre weeks before.

Another point in Raymond's disfavor was his lack of Portuguese. He had great difficulty in making the audience understand him. Most of his talking gags were lost on them. One of his gags in the Egg Bag trick was to show the empty pockets of his trousers saying, ''Nothing in my pockets—naturally—I'm married,'' but in Portuguese he said, ''Vacio-matrimonio,'' which translated into ''Empty marriage,'' so the audience didn't crack a smile and the joke, which is a weak one anyway, fell flat.

On the wall of my dressing room was pasted a programme, with a large cut of a fire-breathing Chinese dragon. This was Li-Ho-Chang's, who had unintentionally wrecked our business. His show was called "A Place in Peking," and, in my broken Portuguese, I asked the stagehands about it. They made me understand that he had a wonderful show and played to capacity houses. They tried to explain his show but I couldn't understand most of what they said, although I gathered that it must have been a great production. I was most anxious to see it. I had never heard of him and I knew of almost all the big illusionists in the world.

Instead of going south toward Rio our impresario decided to go north to get away from the Li-Ho-Chang influence. We went to Pernambuco as our first stop and again there were the Li-Ho-Chang bills pasted on the walls of the dressing rooms. Business was worse than in Bahia and our only hope lay in getting to the big cities where people forget quicker than in the small towns. It was arranged to jump from Pernambuco straight to Rio de Janeiro, skipping all the intervening towns.

It was in the north of Brazil that I had the living daylights scared out of me. Brazil is largely unexplored, with nearly all its cities on the Atlantic coast from Belen de Para in the Amazon to Rio Grande do Sul near the Uruguayan frontier.

I had heard stories of the inpenetrable jungle of the Matto Grosso and only a short while previously the British expedition headed by Redfern had been lost. Rescue parties were constantly leaving from Forteleza and Pernambuco to search for them. I had never seen a real jungle close up and thought it might be fun to make a trip a few miles out of town to where the thick Matto Grosso started.

An acquaintance of mine, Ernst D. Owens of the British Bank of South America, arranged for a friend of his to drive me out to see it.

A few miles out of town the so-called road ended and there was the great Amazon jungle ahead of me.

Owen's friend, who was an old hand at this sort of thing, said he would wait in the car, but warned me not to go too far and keep a sharp eye peeled. I suppose my imagination fired by Conan Doyle's *Lost World* led me to believe that I was one of those intrepid conquistadors, ready to grapple with unknown dangers. My dream didn't last long. I strode forward boldly but was suddenly brought up short by a huge spider staring at me not a foot from my face. It was a loathesome yellow thing with black bands and must have spanned at least a foot across. Its gigantic web extended between two trees and this horror squatted in the center without moving. My scalp and the back of my neck tightened and my heart pounded with fear. I broke out in a cold sweat and for the moment I was paralyzed and couldn't move. I don't know how long it was before I backed away slowly and then ran like hell. From a safe distance I heaved a rock at the hideous thing which hit the web and caused the beast to run rapidly up one of the trees. I ran all the way to the waiting car and was nauseated almost to the point of throwing up. Owen's friend said nothing and drove me back to town while I mentally made Redfern a present of the bloody jungle.

We left Pernambuco on a Brazilian coast steamer and finally entered the breathtakingly beautiful bay of Rio de Janeiro. We opened at the old Sao Pedro Theatre to a packed house. We were convinced that the Li-Ho-Chang jinx was over. A few days later business dwindled to a trickle and we had no doubts that we were voodooed.

After Rio we went by train to the bustling, industrial city of Sao Paulo and opened there in the best theatre in town, the Sant'Anna. It was the same story over again, but this time it wasn't Li-Ho-Chang who was to blame. Another Chinese magician had scored in the Santa Helena Theatre just a couple of weeks before. The world seemed full of Chinese magicians.

In a suburb of Sao Paulo called Braz, we played the Politheama Theatre and we were surprised by a visit after the show from Okito and Marie. They were startled to find me in South America as I had told my mother not to say anthing about the Raymond deal. Okito had been the mysterious Chinese magician who had crabbed our season in Sao Paulo. Worse was yet to come when we both played Santos, the coffee port, the following week. The competition did us no good and we were almost stranded there. Santos was Okito's last date in South America and from there he sailed for Algiers, Morocco and Russia.

Just before he sailed we were sitting in a cafe that we called the "Laughing Lion," because some local artist had painted a lion with a leering grin on its face. I asked my father who this Li-Ho-Chang was and he said he had never heard of him. Raymond said he didn't know either but Marie looked at him with a tight smile which I noticed. I guessed that there was something in the wind that nobody wanted to talk about. It was in Santos that we got the news of the death of Harry Houdini. Okito was quite upset about it, but Raymond merely shrugged his shoulders.

Still going south we made a tour of the German-speaking towns of Santa Caterina where business picked up and lasted until we got to Porto Alegre, which was our last stop in Brazil.

Our season in the Solis Theatre in Montevideo, capital of Uruguay, was short and unfruitful. This was the first Spanish-speaking nation I had ever been to and I set to work to learn Spanish as fast as I could. I had a fearful Brazilian accent which was very hard to get rid of, but my teachers, mostly stagehands, were most patient. I soon learned that rope was soga, wood was madera and chains were cadenas and with this as a start, I soon picked up a fairly good four letter vocabulary. I found that the quickest way to learn a language is to get out and speak it and not mind being laughed at. In those days I didn't understand ninety percent of what they said to me, but I could get around quite well on the few basic words that I knew.

Finally in December of 1926 we crossed the River Plate to Buenos Aires and opened at the now torn down Teatro Buenos Aires on the Calle Cangallo.

CHAPTER 23

Buenos Aires was the most cosmopolitan city I had ever seen and very much like Paris with its sidewalk cafes. It had a more decidedly European flavour than anything I had seen up till then.

A huge spread-out metropolis, it is the tenth largest city of the world and capital of the fabulous Argentine Republic, one of the greatest cattle and wheat countries on earth. A rich country which has had no war for over a hundred years, its food was practically given away and its incomparable beef, milk, vegetables and fruit were sold for next to nothing. It was impossible to starve in a country where everyone ate about two pounds of steak a day. Tall glasses of rich milk with cream cost about an American cent, with lady-fingers thrown in free. What the restaurants threw into the garbage can every night would have kept many other countries going. It was really shameful the way food was wasted and, curiously, no poor people ever showed up to cart it away. What the restaurants didn't sell by the end of the day was thrown out. I saw huge loaves of bread, chunks of beef, lamb, goat, and fish thrown into the rubbish cans and I could never get used to it. Often I had the urge to swipe a garbage can! But even if I had, what good would it have done me, as we paid about fifty cents, American, for a hotel with three gigantic meals a day that included steaks, chicken, puchero, soup, salads, desserts, fruit and coffee.

Just opposite our theatre was the Teatro Sarmiento where the renowned Spanish actor, Ernesto Vilches, was giving his unforgettable role of the Chinese mandarin in the play, "Mr. Wu." I caught the show just before we opened, and although I didn't understand most of it, I could appreciate his brilliant characterization. His Chinese-Spanish accent intrigued me. In later years I became a good friend of his, and was helped greatly by his sound advice, and much of my success as an actor I owe to him.

Business was really bad in Buenos Aires and Raymond, understandably, was in a sour mood and vented most of his spleen on Hilda and Spreer, who although they did their best, never seemed to please him.

Raymond's feud with Spreer had started in Bahia when Raymond taught him to chip away the bottom of a champagne bottle with a small hammer. They needed a bottle or two a day for the ring trick, and it was a tricky job which Raymond did rather well. Poor old Spreer tried his darndest but broke a lot of bottles which were rather expensive. Raymond blew up. "I can't understand how a trained mechanic like you can be so clumsy," he said. "I never break a bottle. Never!"

Spreer returned to his dressing room with grim determination and managed to prepare six bottles, breaking another six in the process. In order to avoid Raymond's wrath, he sneaked through the stage door with a sack full of broken glass to dump in a vacant lot just outside the dressing rooms. There under Raymond's dressing room window he found dozens of broken bottles. Tactless Spreer rushed back into the theatre and gave Raymond the horse laugh, thereby making an enemy for life.

Raymond made Spreer's life pretty miserable on the tour. I felt sorry for the guy and felt somewhat to blame as I had brought him to the show. The incident that made Spreer want to quit the show in Buenos Aires occurred on the day that the tin fake, which Raymond used to hold the rolled silk handkerchief load on the back of a chair, fell off. The janitor swept it out as old scrap metal.

Fortunately we discovered the loss in the early afternoon so there was plenty of time to make a new one for the evening. Raymond told Spreer to cut one out of an old piece of tin with shears, but Spreer, a precision mechanic, wouldn't do it. He set to work and made a fine prop with doubled over, rounded edges, nicely curved and polished, which he handed to Raymond and stepped back with pride, waiting for applause to take his modest bow. Raymond took a good look at it and flew into a tantrum. "I told you to cut one from an old tin sign and not waste your time and my money," he raged. He twisted the prop out of shape and threw it into a corner and grabbing a pair of shears, he started hacking a piece of tin and cut his thumb. Spreer was almost in tears and he looked so helpless that my heart went out to the guy. I was just on the point of butting in when Hilda beat me to the draw by tersely remarking that "All magicians have a screw loose." This did not endear her to Raymond, and from then on she was in the vendetta, with me in the middle getting it from both sides.

A few mornings later I was glumly on my way to the market place in Carlos Pelligrini Street just around the corner from the theatre. I still had the fruit mania and thought that a few juicy pears would drown my sorrows. Coming out of the market I saw a new billing being pasted up on the old Teatro Comedia and I realized with a jolt that the chimerical Li-Ho-Chang with his "Palacio de Peking" was to open in two days time. This was all we needed. All we had to do was dig our graves.

I walked over to the lobby to look at the photos and lithos, and as there was no one around, I stepped into the theatre. On the stage was a young man setting up a Chinese gateway. I walked down the aisle toward the stage and saw that he was about thirty-five years old, tall, slender and with decidedly oriental features.

He calmly stopped working and asked me in Spanish what I wanted. I tried to answer him in my broken Spanish when he interrupted and asked me in perfect English if I was an American.

I told him who I was and he greeted me warmly and told me he was a great admirer of Okito, although he had never met him. He asked me if I could help him as he had bought a prop of Okito's from Ducrot's in New York and didn't know how to use it. He opened a trunk and there it was, the same canister and pedestal that I had sold to Frank for five bucks! Li-Ho-Chang said that he had paid fifty dollars for it as it was made by the master. I gulped and realized what a lousy businessman I was.

I taught him to do the trick and asked him to come to see our show but he refused. He had been on the outs with Raymond for many years and he told me the story. He was a Panamanian by birth and his real name was Juan Pablo Jesorum. He was a boy of seventeen when the Great Raymond with his spectacular show came to Panama City for the first time. Young Juan Pablo was quite proficient in English, having picked it up from the workers who had built the Panama Canal. He was hired by Raymond as interpreter, assistant and general handyman.

He traveled with Raymond for four years and with him had made a tour of the world in 1908. Finally, matters backstage and petty friction between members of the company led to a stormy scene and Juan Pablo quit in a huff. Later he decided to do his own show and after a few abortive attempts as the Great Pablo, he finally appeared as a Chinese magician in 1913.

As we had no Saturday afternoon show, Li-Ho-Chang gave me tickets and I could hardly wait for Saturday to come around.

When the great day arrived Spreer and I, well down front, waited for the curtain to go up on this spectacle that had caused us such grief all along the line. I didn't know what to expect but I had visions of a combined Thurston, Okito and Ching Ling Foo rolled into one. With all the money he had made, I knew this must be something extraordinary.

What I did see changed the whole course of my theatrical career, and I will try to give as true and unbiased opinion of the show as I remember it that hot summer's day so many years ago.

A five piece orchestra played an oriental overture and the curtain rose to show a red cyclorama with a few Chinese designs and characters on it, opened to form an arch in the center, a la Italiana showing a black velvet backdrop.

Directly in front of this at stage center was a Chinese gateway. A flash of gunpowder that didn't coincide with a black curtain that rolled up in the gateway caused Li-Ho-Chang very visibly to appear. Spreer and I exchanged glances, but no one seemed to care. There was applause in which we joined.

The show included the Noah's Ark illusion, the escape of a very stunning girl from a small tank of water, the Spookville routine just as Raymond did it, but with the levitation of a large kitchen table at the end, with the committee rushing around the stage with their hands glued to the table top.

He did a number of small tricks, including the Egg Bag and a cleverly done Glass of Milk Through the Hat, then the shooting of a ribbon through a girl. He closed with an effective routine of dancing luminous skeletons in the dark that brought screams from the women in the audience. After this the house lights when on and Li-Ho-Chang, alone on the stage, thanked the audience and announced that the next day there would be three shows and to please bring their friends. With a smattering of applause, the people filed out.

I sat there for a while with Spreer. I was so mixed up I didn't know what to say. The show was a confusing mixture of good and bad which could be boiled down to just one word, mediocre. It was unlike anything I had ever seen and it defied everything that I had been taught about technique. I tried to analyze the show to discover wherein lay the secret to Li-Ho-Chang's indisputable success.

First of all there was the man himself, the exact opposite of Okito. Li-Ho-Chang combined audacity with a marked understanding of his audience and a shrewd business acumen. He had very large hands which he ungracefully waved about with indecisive movements, as if brushing away cobwebs—so very different from the graceful movements of Okito.

Li-Ho-Chang's manipulative skill was nil; in fact, he was so awkward at times that it bordered on the ridiculous. With the exception of the glass of milk through the hat, any attempt he made in manipulation was next to unintentional exposure. In order that the reader may not think that I am being too harsh in my judgement, I can only say that Li-Ho-Chang himself admitted his maladroitness. He even asked me to teach him close-up card work for impressing reporters, but as he lacked manual skill and had a poor memory, he couldn't get it right and was a dismal failure. He used the most primitive and direct approach to all his stage tricks and illusions with no attempt at misdirection. Most of his material was automatic and required little more than button-pushing.

All through the show he wore one Chinese costume, much the worse for wear, with large perspiration stains under the arms. Okito changed his robe after every trick, which was one of the features of his act.

Li-Ho-Chang's scenery was in a deplorable state, with patches of rain stains and dust and a tear or two here and there.

So what the devil was it that made this show such a moneymaker?

The answer was simple. It was the man himself—of prime importance in the theatre and in any other venture.

He was a sincere, generous man of humble origin who understood the problems of the poor Latin Americans. His audience felt he was one of them and not playing down to them, which was the unfortunate impression Raymond gave.

For the stage he had adopted an atrocious Chinese-Spanish which was very funny to the paisanos. He called an egg *la heuva* which is the feminine gender instead of *el heuvo*. This may not seem funny to the Anglo-Saxon mind, but in these countries it is simple sure-fire humor. If a trick failed, he would brush it off with a simple, "El espiritu esta cansado" (the spirit is tired) and to hell with it. The public loved him and called him simpatico (a congenial, nice person) which is of prime importance on the Latin American stage.

He loved to play the small towns and, with great sacrifice and hardship, played in some of the tiny, out of the way, villages where no magician had ever been before. This hard-earned money he would cheerfully give away to some less fortunate artiste when he returned to the bigger towns. His was a complex and wonderful personality.

My whole outlook on magic changed that day. Up till then it had never entered my head that a Chinese magician could do a full evening's talking show. I had been under the delusion that oriental acts must be silent like Ching Ling Foo, Chung Ling Soo and Okito; but Li-Ho-Chang shattered that myth once and for all. The only real advantage that big oriental acts had was that they could play any part of the civilized world, no matter what language was spoken; but the big money lay in the full night's talking show.

It also came to me that there was no need to start with complicated mechanical tricks and expensive illusions. I knew now that with a small investment I could do a show equal to or superior to his. But Li-Ho-Chang had more experience and the deciding factor, personality. I decided then and there to go slow and try to build up a personality suitable to my temperament. The first things I had to fight were my prejudices. I should try to broaden my outlook, and for the time being, forget Okito and the other big shots.

That evening I told Raymond I had seen the Li-Ho-Chang show and gave him my impression. He refused to go and accused Li-Ho-Chang of stealing his whole show! Maybe so, I thought, but don't we all do it? After all, where did Raymond get his tricks? Weren't most illusions bought, borrowed or stolen outright? The trick in itself wasn't the main thing—it was the presentation. There were perhaps a dozen true magician-inventors in the world and all the others used these men's ideas and sometimes improved them. I knew that if I ever started my own show, I would use all of Okito's tricks, besides any other good trick or illusion that I had seen in my day.

As expected, Li-Ho-Chang's competition with us was the coup de grace for an already ailing season.

Hilda and I had moved to a pension in Calle Tucuman run by an ex-wrestler, a Turk by the name of Yousoff. An understanding, big-hearted man he ran this artistes hotel as a sideline and took care of a lot of out-of-luck hams. I owed him over a month's rent and was ashamed to look him in the face, although he never said a word and was always most polite and helpful.

In spite of the bad situation Raymond was in, I asked for an advance on our salaries. Just a few pesos to show Yousoff my goodwill. Raymond told me to meet him at his hotel the following morning.

Raymond lived in a first class hotel. When I arrived he was very cordial and picked up a few sheets of paper covered with figures which he handed me to check over. I hastily glanced through the various items, hotels, advances, expenses and so on. I turned to the last page and found to my delight that the total was forty pounds. Terrific! With that I could easily pay off the Turk and have enough left over to get Hilda and myself some clothes that we needed badly.

I felt sorry for Raymond and told him that if he couldn't spare this amount, I would gladly accept half. He could pay off the rest when it was convenient. He looked at me as if I were demented.

"You don't seem to understand," he said. "I owe you nothing. *You* owe *me* forty pounds."

I did a color change. I rechecked the list: Hilda's and my boat fare from Lisbon to Brazil, hotels and extras that I couldn't check, no pay for layoffs although our salary was monthly. To cut it short, I was in hock. I had been in some tough spots in my life but this was a lulu.

The big item on the list was the fares and I told him that the company always paid travelling expenses; besides, he hadn't paid those fares. It was the Brazilian impresario who had paid all the fares from Lisbon to the frontier of Uruguay. At this Raymond flew into a rage and ordered me out of the hotel.

Back at the pension I talked it over with Hilda and Spreer, who was in a worse hole than I as he had far less salary. After a long talk, we finally decided to make a break.

I went to Li-Ho-Chang's hotel on the Avenida de Mayo and told him the story and asked his advice. He told me the first thing to do was to go to the police and get our "Cedula de Identidad," a most important document that insured us as residents and, according to Argentine law, guaranteed protection and allowance to enter and leave the country as many times as one chose.

In two days we had our "cedulas" and I returned to Li-Ho-Chang and asked him if he could use my shadow act in his show.

"You're quite sure you want to leave Raymond?" he asked.

"Definitely."

"This puts me in a rather bad position," he said. "I've already had enough trouble with Raymond and I don't want to be accused of stealing his assistants."

"I'm sorry you feel that way," I replied, "but whether I go with you or not, I have made up my mind to leave, no matter how tough things may be."

"Well," he said after a long pause, "I'll tell you what. I'm leaving for Bahia Blanca, a town some two hundred miles south of Buenos Aires. Here's a hundred pesos and if you can get away, come down with your act and I'll see what I can do."

That was fair enough and I thanked him and returned to the pension for another conference with Hilda and Spreer. We decided that I would make the first break and leave Hilda at the pension for a week or so until things were arranged with Li-Ho-Chang. Spreer was to stay on until I could get something for him too.

That night I told Raymond I was leaving without saying where. He said I was free to go anytime I pleased, but he was holding my shadow lamp, some of my props, and tricks until I paid him the money I owed.

For the next couple of days Raymond watched me like a hawk so I decided to leave without warning, a thing frowned on in the theatre, but I had no alternative. I figured out a melodramatic raincoat-and-whisker drama that would have done Thurston's heart good.

We planned the escape very carefully, with the aid of an assistant named Jean Fay, a Singhalese boy who was about my height and build. He had only been in the show since we opened in Buenos Aires.

The Buenos Aires fire laws require an underground tunnel that leads from the stage to the street entrance of the theatre. In some theatres the dressing rooms are underground on either side of the tunnel, which acts as a passageway. This was the case in the Teatro Buenos Aires. Raymond had the third dressing room from the stage end of the tunnel and could see everyone who came in and out of the theatre.

On the night of my cloak-and-dagger getaway, Jean, wearing my raincoat and hat and flanked by Hilda and Spreer, noisily walked past Raymond's dressing room and said "good night" all at the same time and kept on going. Raymond leaned out and saw what he thought was Hilda, Spreer and me and said, "See you tomorrow."

Just a moment before they left I had locked the door of my dressing room and crept up to the stage and stepped into the Modern Cabinet, the illusion used for the opening of the show, and shut myself in the double-back compartment.

As Raymond always stalled after the show, we knew that the night watchman would lower and lock the iron shutter of the street end of the tunnel so Raymond would have to come up to the stage and use the run down and center aisle of the theatre to get to the main lobby.

And so it turned out. After about twenty minutes I heard Raymond and Litzka come up and go down the runway to the main entrance. After he was gone I had to wait until the night watchman made his inspection of the stage and turned off the lights. I don't know how long I waited in that stuffy cabinet, but I finally heard his steps on the stage, footsteps going away, and the noise of the big iron shutter of the lobby entrance being pulled down.

I waited a few more minutes just in case. I was alone now and there was no way of getting out of the theatre until the janitors showed up in the morning.

I didn't want to put on the stage lights so I just pushed the switch for the dressing rooms. I dismantled and packed my shadow lamp with the aid of a flashlight and went down into the orchestra pit and got my music. Then in my dressing room I packed all of Hilda's things and mine. I tried to get into Raymond's dressing room as some tricks that Fischer had given me were there, including all my silk handkerchiefs and a fine card sword that Raymond had ordered from Fischer and never paid for. But his door was locked with a thick padlock and I didn't try to open it because he could have accused me of theft.

Finally, when everything was packed, I dragged my trunk to the run down and sat down to wile away the night. I didn't lie down for fear of oversleeping and I passed the longest five hours in my life.

At seven o'clock I heard the shutters go up and I sneaked out to the front of the house. When the janitor was out of the lobby, I dodged out into the street to wait for a small truck I had engaged the day before. About ten minutes later it arrived and I walked back to the theatre making a lot of noise. The janitor was surprised to see me there so early but I fed him a story of some broken props that had to be repaired and, with his aid, carried out my trunk and bags and loaded them on the truck. We were just on the point of leaving when I suddenly remembered the blasted sheet. I wasn't going to leave that behind, as it was 15 by 21 feet and had cost quite a bit of money. I ran to the grid, lowered the sheet and tied off the lines. Then I descended to the stage and untied the tapes from the batten. I didn't even try to fold this huge sheet alone; I just rolled it into a ball and climbed up into the grid again to raise the batten as I didn't want the stagehands to tip off Raymond that something was wrong. I carried the bundle out to the truck with an offhand remark to the janitor about "laundry" and got out fast.

It was too late to catch the morning train to Bahia Blanca and I was afraid that Raymond would send a cop to the station when the night train left at 11 p.m. I figured he would logically suspect that I was going to join Li-Ho-Chang after being so thick with him in Buenos Aires. I arranged with the truck driver to take me out to the first stop that the Patagonian Express made at Temperley, about fifteen miles from Buenos Aires. This was rather expensive but it was worth it. I waited all day and half the night in Temperley until the train came.

It was good that I thought of going ahead to Temperley because Raymond had sent a cop together with his "representante" (manager) to watch for me at Constitucion station.

Spreer told about this a few weeks later after he, too, had made his getaway in Rosario (during Litzka's harp number). He dragged his tool trunk and suitcase through the fire door into a waiting truck and, together with Jean Fay, beelined it for San Nicolas, where they made connections for Buenos Aires.

Spreer told me that no one had noticed Hilda's and my absence until almost curtain time. Raymond had his "representante" phone the pension. When he discovered I had left, he broke open my door and found the birds had flown the coop.

Naturally he was furious and called in the police and made a statement that I had stolen some valuable objects. I had been right the previous night not to try to open his door.

Raymond questioned Spreer and Jean but they played it dumb. Raymond made Spreer his chief assistant and he was the white-haired boy on the show for a while until they started the tour of the provinces, where the salary problem came up again, and as Spreer couldn't take it anymore, he did his own version of the vanishing act.

CHAPTER 24

My tour with Li-Ho-Chang was short and sweet.

He was playing the Municipal Theatre in Bahia Blanca and packing them in. With these big audiences my act went over better than ever and the future looked bright.

However, I got a good chance to see how he operated backstage and I had never seen such a disorganized show in my life. Everything was thrown around, no one knew where anything was, the routine of the show was changed every night because some prop or other was mislaid or missing. No one took any responsibility. Even the costumes were thrown on the floor of the dressing rooms. It was a mess. I asked Li-Ho-Chang to let me take charge and try to get some sort of system and order into the show and that is where I made my mistake as it created ill feeling among the assistants.

It involved Li-Ho-Chang's wife, Olivia, who was a stunning blonde and just to be around her was intoxicating. When she appeared in a bathing suit for the Water Tank escape the jaws of the men in the audience went slack. Her blonde beauty was a novelty in Latin America and she did her share to fill the theatre every night.

With my good intentions for improving the show, the first thing I did was to throw out some delicate shade of silk handkerchiefs for the Jap Box production and substitute bright stage colors. I didn't know those delicate silks had been Olivia's cherished favorites.

After Bahia Blanca we played a few small towns in the south of Buenos province. Some of these places were nothing more than a long cafe with a small stage at one end. Li-Ho-Chang would give a show of small tricks with few illusions. He charged the same prices as in the big theatres with the full show and made money. He had no layoffs and played every town in sight.

I learned a lot about the business end of booking a magic show in these places. He would send his ''representante'' to those towns and hire the theatre or cafe without saying who it was for and get good conditions. In one place he rented the hall for 20 pesos and took in 3,000. He gave me a lot of advice on how to do things in these parts and encouraged me to do a show of my own. I knew he didn't need me or my act and after a few weeks I left the show. He had been a good friend and asked me to keep in touch and left for the southernmost city of the world: Punta Arenas.

I was lucky to get a few weeks in the Teatro Casino, the famous variety theatre where Okito had such success. They booked me immediately when they knew I was his son and I was promised the tour.

Let me describe the South American variety tour. From 1910 until 1935 the headquarters was the Casino headed by Don Carlos Seguin, whose European representative was M. Tolomei in Paris. The best variety acts from all over the world were engaged for a six month's tour, which included Buenos Aires and Rosario in Argentina; Montevideo, Sao Paulo, Santos and Rio de Janeiro in Brazil in combination with the Serrador theatres. Like everywhere else, when talkies came in, variety went out. There never was sufficient local talent in South America to warrant the continued upkeep of the variety houses. In addition, the top-notch foreign acts were too expensive to bring down any more. However, the legitimate theatres were still going fairly well, and they accepted full evening magic shows on the same terms as revue and stock companies; so it was a question of having a full evening's show or working once in a blue moon.

Latin America is a vast continent of twenty-one countries that reaches from Argentina to Mexico. All speak the same language, except for Brazil; but one of the disadvantages in routing South America was the great distances between cities. The Pan American highway didn't exist in those days, and from Chile to Mexico it was all mountainous country with stretches of vast plains, deserts, jungles, lakes and some places the still wild Indian country. There were huge mountain passes considered the most dangerous in the world and all the climatic conditions from sub zero to fierce heat.

In a few places the theatres were modern and comfortable and, once in a while, really beautiful. But in most places they were very bad. In the smaller towns musicians were not to be had and the few who showed up played with all the inspiration of a bilge pump. Stage lighting was unknown and one had to carry complete equipment for both 110 and 220 volts. In Bogota, Colombia, it was 150 volts! In some places the current was direct, others alternating.

That was what lay ahead for me if I insisted on having my own show. Did it bother me? It did not. I'd been half around the world on a shoestring so what could happen to me? I had nothing to lose.

I played everything the Casino people had to offer and finished up at the Maipo Theatre. It was during this engagement that Hilda was hit by an automobile in the Calle Florida and hospitalized. Fortunately no bones were broken and her cuts were superficial, so she was out within a few days. This obliged me to do the act alone for a few days and led Hilda to the sensible conclusion that she was wasting her time with so little to do in the act; so she decided to strengthen the family finances by getting a job as a secretary. She had learned typing and shorthand in New York and spoke far better Spanish than I. It wasn't long before she was secretary to Mr. Jackson, the manager of the Buenos Aires branch of the Burroughs Adding Machine Company. In a short time she became an essential fixture there by employing her considerable ability to demonstrate and teach the salesman how to operate the adding and calculating machines. Spreer held a job as electrician with the Thornquist Company.

In an American magazine I read an advertisement of Dr. Harlan Tarbell's correspondence course in magic and I wrote and inquired for prices. To my surprise, Tarbell very courteously put me on the mailing list free of charge and I received the first thirty lessons complete with some essential fakes in a tin box. This was the beginning of a lifelong friendship with this remarkable man.

The lessons included many small club tricks and clever ideas for routines that were cheap and easy to make, so it didn't take me long to make up two one-hour shows which I worked in clubs and various organizations of the British community. This led to shows in Argentine clubs where I did the act in my broken Spanish and caused as much laughter as did Li-Ho-Chang. However, I included a lot of American gags which were new to the Argentines. I was hailed as a great wit.

A typical programme of my club act included the Egg Bag, the

Vanishing Wand, the Linking Rings, the Paper Tearing, the Card in the Banana, the Needle Trick, the Multiplying Balls, the Ghost Silk and Tarbell's revolutionary cut and restored rope. These shows were of the greatest value to me for the future, since most of these tricks were to play an important fill-in for the big show that was to come later.

A publicity stunt reaped me a lot of free advertising in the Buenos Aires *Herald,* the largest English newspaper in the Argentine. I had written an article about fake spiritualism (shades of Houdini) and was challenged in an open leter by someone who signed himself I.B.M., to spend the night in a celebrated haunted house in the suburb of Belgrano. My viewpoint was upheld by the paper's columnist, a man named Goldflam whose byline was H.G. The resulting correspondence caused a major flap in the British and American communities.

I found out later that the mysterious I.B.M., who had a profound knowledge of magic and magicians, was the Rosario correspondent of the *Herald,* Mr. E. Leslie Briant. He was connected with the Bank of London in South America. We later became fast friends. He was to be my chronicler in *The Sphinx,* in his monthly article "South American Notes." He was a friend of all the local and foreign magicians who visited the Argentine from 1910 on.

A South African comedian named Billy Cardo (William Bosnach) was stranded in Buenos Aires and he offered me the part of the comedy magician in a version of Fred Karno's "Night in a Music Hall," a very funny comedy sketch. Karno had brought it to the United States from England years before with Charles and Sydney Chaplin and Stan Laurel as the chief comedians. Karno's act was one thing, but the show scraped together by Cardo with fifth-rate hams was another. We opened in the Coliseo Theatre as "Frank Ruby's Burlesque Comedy Company"—with me playing the part of Professor Humbug. We lasted one night and the press tore us to pieces. The evening newspaper *Ultima Hoa* elected me as "the most mediocre magician they had ever had the misfortune to witness," and the influential *LaRazon* recommended my "immediate deportation as an undesirable element." In my defense I can only say that the illusions were supposed to be bad as an excuse for the comedians to heckle the artistes. The levitation illusion was done with a wooden board pulled up by four wires and it was ghastly. Fortunately, I worked under another name, and with my mustache, goatee and bald wig nobody recognized me.

In general this seemed to be an unhappy epoch for magicians in these parts, as the episode of the languorous lion will illustrate. The Great George, an American magician, was playing the Teatro Royal in Montevideo and his main attraction was the illusion of the Vanishing Lion.

This king of the beasts was a toothless worn-out wreck who looked like a moth-eaten rug and was confined to his cage in the cellar whence he was taken onto the stage to do his daily stint, and then was rewarded with a nice horse cutlet.

One evening a careless attendant forgot to lock the cage. Leo wandered through the door that leads to the orchestra pit and scared the living daylights out of the musicians who broke all records getting out of the pit.

There were very few spectators for this particular performance but one unfortunate man was sitting in the front row with his knees touching the curtained rail that separates the front seats from the orchestra pit. He was paralyzed when a lion's head rose from behind the curtain a few inches from his face and stared at him mournfully. The petrified spectator was unable to move a muscle, which was all to the good, as the lion, fed up with the scant response to his offered friendship, jumped down calmly and returned to his cage.

Meanwhile the ushers carried out the spectator, stiff with fright after his horrendous experience, and later, in an interview with the press, he swore by the soul of his mother that he would never enter a theatre again as long as he lived. When asked by the reporters just what he had felt at the moment, he said the only thing that entered his mind was that the lion had foul breath.

The poor old lion was docked his horse cutlet that night which was rather unjust.

During his first few weeks in Buenos Aires Raymond had arranged with a large furniture manufacturing company, John Wright & Sons, Ltd., to build a number of new illusions. Among them was the Beetle illusion that we had brought half finished from Brazil. One day I met one of the sons, Arturo Wright, in a cafe and he told me that Raymond had left this material behind and offered it to me at cost, including the crate they made for it. I thought this was just the thing I needed to start a small show as it was a time killer, and with the rest of the small stuff I had, I could fill in the necessary two hours.

An acquaintance of mine, Mr. Walter Gaulke, a Kansan with a Churchillian jaw and stare, ran the New York Film Exchange in the Calle Tucuman. He was a shrewd business man and had made a small fortune in wheat. He was running the Film Exchange as a sideline. I needed about a 1,000 pesos (roughly $500) to complete the illusion and buy some scenery and a few props. I interested Gaulke in backing me. Spreer and I finished the illusion and he was to play my old part handling the magnet. I doped out a simple code in Spanish that used only about ten words. This code was based on the words, "This, that, these, those, here and there" of which there are many variations in Spanish, "Ese, Eso, Este, esta, aquel, aquello, aqui, aca, ahi, alli and alla." Any grammatical errors I might make would be attributed to my being a foreigner. Using Zancig's technique the code was a little marvel and was widely copied in later years by Latin American mind readers.

I made an Egyptian act of it and called it Isis, the Scarab, with a preamble about the beetle being discovered in a sealed tomb of an Egyptian Pharaoh, which caused many a head to nod wisely.

The illusion worked perfectly and we opened at the Coliseo Theatre doing our first full evening's show. However, the show wasn't strong enough to fill an evening's entertainment, even though I stretched the illusion out by answering written questions thrown into a bowl of fire. These were actually transmitted to Spreer by telephone from the wings by Hilda. But after a half an hour of the Beetle, the audience got sick of it and the show dragged on to a weary finish. We lasted a week with poor audiences. The last night Raymond was sitting in the front row with a wolf grin and gave me the horse laugh. Two weeks later he played the Coliseo to terrible business and *I* sat in the first row with a wolf grin and gave *him* the horse laugh. I played a few picture houses with Isis as the main attraction, but the act didn't click and Gaulke lost his money on this deal.

Hilda had not given up her job and one evening she came home late. I made a sarcastic remark and when I was through, she looked at me with that quiet way of hers and said, "I am late because I visited a doctor after work and you will soon be a father." At these words I was speechless for one of the few times in my life. I remember thinking how different my father's marriage had been. He had already made a name for himself and was a well-to-do man when I was born. I regretted having invested Gaulke's loan in one illusion and wondered when I would learn to do things right.

CHAPTER 25

One bright morning, some weeks later, I was shaken to the core by seeing the whole town papered with attractive lithographs that read, "Thurston Presents Dante. Opening at the Casino on Friday." They were the same lithos Thurston had used with the little red devils, and I knew them all by heart.

I rushed over to the threatre and as I walked in, I was greeted by the familiar smell of the big time magic show. Dante was sitting in the first row and the stage was full of people setting up the props. Everything was running very smoothly, just like the old Thurston show. Dante's sons were most efficient assistants, his daughter did the main illusions, and Mrs. Dante was in charge of the orchestra.

I introduced myself to Dante and we chatted for a while. Then I noticed that there seemed to be some delay as no one on the show spoke Spanish and they were having trouble with the stagehands. I offered to interpret and Dante jumped at my suggestion, and as I knew the stagehands of the Casino quite well, we got along fine and all difficulties were straightened out.

Dante looked the part of a magician with his mane of hair which was just beginning to turn white and his satanic mustache and goatee a la Herrmann. He also had that audacious drive that I admired so much and nothing seemed to faze him. He gave me tickets for the opening night, and Hilda, Spreer and I were there good and early.

All in all it was a thrilling experience. A fast, flashy and exciting magic show in the grand manner and the style of Thurston, but on a smaller scale. Instead of the levitation, he did a good Asrah and presented many of his own creations, including the Vanishing Horse, the Barber Shop, Backstage, an excellent Sawing a Woman, Crushing a Woman, Black and

White, the Prisoner's Escape and his own version of the Spirit Cabinet. Among the small tricks, he did ball manipulation, Tarbell's Rope and the Linking Rings.

He spoke English on the stage without an interpreter and the audience loved it. As the show was self-explanatory and had speed and rhythm, he played to capacity houses for over a month. He gave magic a tremendous boost in Buenos Aires, which was good for everybody.

I was in a quandary. It seemed that the more full night's shows I saw, the less I knew about the secret of their success. I had blamed Raymond's poor business in South America to his lack of Spanish, but here was Dante speaking English and packing them in. Raymond's personality was every bit as imposing as Dante's, so it couldn't be that. The first time Raymond had played these countries he had a great success with a much smaller show. Li-Ho-Chang had packed them in among the smaller towns but in the big capitals such as Buenos Aires and Rio he did only fair business. I figured that his special style was geared to the small town audience. I wondered what would happen to Dante in the small towns. I also wondered what was the right path for me to take. One thing I did know; the Okito pantomimic stlye for a complete evening show would never do.

Every night after the show Dante and I would go to Kessler's German Restaurant, and over a meal that lasted two hours, we would talk. He was an entertaining talker and made me laugh with his tales of magicians—especially when he would start in on Danish Acquavit and beer. We usually would wind up in the market place at dawn to buy fresh shrimps which we ate sitting in the gutter. I often left him at his hotel well after the sun was up. He was a great character.

Sometimes when he was a few over the eight he would get somewhat aggressive and at times got into some nasty fights with people whose faces he didn't like. He was particularly bitter about Houdini but never told me why. Once when I mentioned something about Houdini's death, he snarled, "That was about the best thing that happened to him, the son of a bitch."

Our friendship nearly ended one night at Kessler's when I pointed out a flaw in the presentation of his Modern Cabinet, which was a brother to the one I had hid in on the night of my escape. A careless assistant had left the curtain partly open on at least two occasions that I saw and exposed the girl coming through the hinged partition.

With his eyes stopped down to f.22, he gazed at me a bit

unsteadily. "This proves to me that you know nothing of magic as my cabinet works on a different principle." I told him that I had been doing the illusion for years with Raymond and at the mention of Raymond's name he blew up and started to get violent. I got up to go but he calmed down and apologized and talk drifted to less dangerous subjects. But the next day I made a point of having a good squint at the illusion and it was exactly the same as Raymond's.

Dante was very closemouthed about his illusions, for which I couldn't blame him. Our discussions were mostly about the merits or otherwise of other illusionists. He liked to call Goldin, "that packing case magician," and claimed that Goldin had stolen every illusion he had done in his life, whereas, he, Dante, had invented all his illusions. I thought it best to keep my mouth shut and not get him into an aggressive mood.

One of the most barefaced acts I have ever seen in my life happened during Dante's season at the Casino. An Argentine magician named Faluggi, whom I had heard of but never seen, was working the provinces with a small show, mainly card manipulations, and he had saved up quite a bit of money. His one ambition in life became to own a big show, although he had no technical knowledge of big stage illusions and no way of finding out how they were done. He got the mistaken idea that if he were to see the illusions over and over again he could solve the inner workings. Then all he needed were the approximate outside measurements.

Thereupon he engaged an "avante-scene" box at the Casino for two weeks and stayed there every night with a carpenter and drew sketches of all Dante's illusions.

After a few nights of this, Dante began to get suspicious and asked the house manager who this guy was. The manager had been bribed to say that Faluggi was a great caricaturist on a leading paper and was doing a big layout for a double spread in one of the Sunday editions.

Dante swallowed this story whole, and it was funny to see Dante from the stage, bowing and smiling to Faluggi, who in turn stood up and made a tremendous bow of respect to "el maestro Dante"—and went right on making his plans. When Dante finally found out the truth, it was too late. Faluggi had what he wanted—or thought he did. But to see magic performed and to build illusions on the strength of it are two different matters. Faluggi and his carpenter started building illusions from the outside in and got into a hell of a mess, and in not one instance did they have the correct modus operandi.

Later I saw Faluggi's debut in the Astral Theatre and not one illusion worked properly. He was laughed off the stage. The only thing that saved him was his card work which was of the old school but done well. He did a very clever disappearance of a borrowed watch in a newspaper rolled into a cone. Faluggi died many years ago, but his son Polo does a small but very clean show with his wife in the Argentine provinces.

After the brilliant Casino season Dante went over to the Coliseo at popular prices, but business was poor and he left the Argentine for Russia. From there he played all over Europe and England with outstanding success.

A week or so after he left I had a phone call from the manager of the Coliseo to come over. In the cellar of the theatre Dante had left half a dozen illusions thrown into a corner. Among these things was a Multiple Production table that was three times as heavy as Okito's and didn't work. There was also a cannon such as Goldin used for his Arab illusion; but everything was bulky and heavy and it wasn't worth carting away. They burned it as junk. Again I was convinced that Okito was right and that his "cardboard" show had something greatly in its favor.

Dante's show had a profound effect on me and the plan for my future show was beginning to take place in my mind. At times I was terribly discouraged as I knew how hard it was to get a show of Dante's calibre going. I knew that Dante had been handed the show on a silver platter from Thurston, but that didn't alter the fact that he had made it a top-notch production. I am afraid I forgot about the simple Li-Ho-Chang show and the big money it made.

I was still doing the act and working club dates and I organized a variety company with a ventriloquist, acrobats and a line of girls and we made a tour of the province of Buenos Aires which abruptly ended one February night in 1928. In a small town called Bragado I received a telegram from Buenos Aires informing me that Hilda had given birth to a son.

I didn't wait for the express but left on a milk train and arrived early the following morning. I rushed up to the room over the tailor's shop on the corner of Maipu and Viamonte Streets to get my first glimpse of a quiet, red-faced young man with a rather philosophic expression. I was a bit sore at the Bamberg tribe at the moment and decided to break with the constant Davids and Tobiases. We named the boy Robert Douglas with a fervent hope that he wouldn't go into show business, but when he became a man, he would find a more peaceful and secure way of life.

He was a wonderful baby and rarely ever cried, which for Hilda and me was a godsend as we lived mostly in hotels. When the little fellow was about six months old we moved to a round room in a tower on the thirteenth floor of an apartment building on the corner of Cordoba and Esmeralda Streets. We could see the whole city of Buenos Aires from any of the four round windows. Hilda did the cooking, and with my club dates and her job, we were not rich but we were happy, and we had the kid, which was a lot of fun.

Hilda Seagle Bamberg (circa 1930).

CHAPTER 26

And then it was that Moira really took a hand in things.

One evening I was walking with Spreer on the Avenida de Mayo and he suggested we take a streetcar home to the Cordoba which was about eight blocks away. It was rather early and the theatres hadn't finished yet so I said it might be a good idea to walk home through the theatre district to see if we could pick up some work.

We cut through to the Calle Corrientes and alongside the old Empire Theatre we saw Walter Gaulke holding up the wall. Since the debacle of the "Isis" show we hadn't exactly been bosom pals and I greeted him with some diffidence. He was waiting for some friend who was late and I suppose it was sheer boredom that made him enter into conversation with me.

"Hi, are you still around?" was his opening line. This remark did not lead to brilliant repartee, but the guy was loaded and I gave him the idiot grin. He had seen the Dante show and as a businessman was impressed by the money it made.

"Why don't you do a show like that," he said, "instead of fooling around with that bug?"

"I could do it," I said. "I know how all those tricks are done and how to build them. But do you realize the kind of money that takes?"

"I can imagine," said he, "but you'll never get anywhere with that piss-ant show you've got. Besides, it doesn't have to be so big. With half that crap Dante carts around you could still have an impressive show. How much would you need?"

"I can't say offhand but I can make up an estimate in a few days."

"Do that," he said, "and come to see me at my office. It might be throwing good money after bad, but I just might take a

161

chance if I like it.''

We talked for a few minutes longer and then his tardy friend (God bless him) showed up, and with a two fingered salute, he was gone.

When I banged on the door of our tower flat, Hilda was sore at my dragging Spreer up there at that time of night, but she calmed down when I gave her the news. Spreer and I were wildly excited and woke up the baby. Hilda let us blow off steam for a while and then said, ''I have to get up early to go to work while you loafers can sleep till noon. Out!'' After showing Spreer through the door she promptly went to sleep and I talked it over with Bobby.

The next few days were hectic. I made out interminable lists with every trick and illusion I had ever seen in my life and argued the pros and cons with Spreer day and night. I made a careful study of all the big shows I had ever seen and what made them click or fail. I finally came up with a combination of the best of Okito, Thurston, Selbit, Dante and Raymond. It was to be a Chinese show with patter a la Li-Ho-Chang.

We estimated that about ten big stage illusions and twenty stage tricks, a set of scenery, a traveller and some Chinese costumes would come to about 10,000 pesos (roughly $5,000), providing we built all the apparatus ourselves. When the outline of the show was completed on paper I was ready to rush over and show it to Gaulke, but Hilda took a firm hand in the business at this point.

''Look at it from a businessman's point of view,'' she said. ''That list you have there is a living beautiful thing to you, but to Gaulke it's just a bunch of expensive props that he can't visualize. He is a busy man and has no time for long, drawn-out explanations, and besides, in his office he will be interrupted constantly with phone calls and people waiting to see him, so he won't get a clear picture of what you're trying to sell. And it's almost certain he'll freeze when he sees that 10,000 peso total.''

''I could see him at his home,'' I suggested.

''That's no good. Look, why don't you invite him here to lunch on Saturday?'' she said. ''I'll prepare a fried chicken and you won't say one word about the business during the meal. Later, when he is mellowed by a bottle of Trapiche, you can go into your spiel.''

That sounded like good sense to me and Gaulke accepted the invitation. Hilda put on a swell meal and what with the

Trapiche, the baby cooing and the loving couple at their best, the stage setting was complete, and Gaulke's heart should have melted. When the meal was over he sat back and sighed and patted his belly and we thought it was in the bag.

"Thank you for a splendid lunch which I really enjoyed. A man doesn't get much home cooking down here when he is a bachelor like me, which I suppose you found out," he said looking at Hilda. "Y'know this whole setup seems to be arranged with the idea of softening me up."

Hilda and I exchanged dismayed glances.

"The idea was mine," said Hilda. "I work in a business office at the Burroughs Company and I know how hard it is to get ten minutes of Mr. Jackson's time."

"I know Jackson well," said Gaulke.

"I have great faith in David's ideas," she continued, "and this plan of his will take some time to explain. I thought it would be better to talk it over here rather than in your office. This is not a thing to be looked at from a motion picture distributor's standpoint. This is a purely creative theatrical venture."

Glauke looked at her pensively. "You're a smart little woman," he said and turned to me. "You're a lucky guy to have a girl like that. Show me the papers."

I talked for a solid hour, painting an exotic picture which must have dazed him, and when I was through, he sat back in his chair and sipped his cognac, thinking it over.

"Ten thousand pesos is a lot of jack," he said finally. "How do I know you can do all this? Maybe it's just a wild dream that looks good on paper. The bug deal was not so hot. I'm already a thousand in the hole."

I tried to explain that the Beetle was just one small act and would be a strong feature as part of a complete show. I gave him an outline of my experience in the theatre and my background. I even went so far as to mention my times with Thurston and Houdini.

"Never heard of 'em," he said getting up to go. "The only big show of that kind I ever saw was Dante. Well, let me mull it over for a coupla days. Come to my office on Tuesday morning. Thanks again for the lunch." And he was gone.

"What do you think?" I asked Hilda.

"I don't know," she said. "He's a very shrewd man and nobody's fool. Just keep your fingers crossed."

The next two days were as full of suspense as a Hitchcock drama. On Tuesday morning I went to his office and was kept waiting outside for over half an hour, which gave me plenty of time to die over and over again.

When I was ushered in through the door marked "Private" I found him sitting glumly at his desk.

"H'ya," he said without a smile and then apropos of nothing, "Nothin' but headaches, the bastards." He fiddled around with some papers for a while and then, "Maybe I'm a sucker for falling for this deal but I'll play along with it."

Gratefully, I started to thank him but was cut short.

"Under certain conditions," he went on. "In the first place I'm not giving you the money in a lump sum. I'm going to dole it out as you need it, and I reserve the right to inspect the work as it goes along. If I'm not satisfied, I'll stop right there."

I didn't speak. I just nodded.

"If and when the show opens, you'll pay me the invested capital as soon as you can, and I reserve the right to put my personal representative in the box office. During the time the capital is being deducted, I will receive ten percent of your share of the take after salaries and expenses are deducted. You will not receive a salary as you are on a percentage basis. After the debt is paid in full, I will continue to get ten percent of the profits for one year whether or not it be a percentage deal or a straight salary. Is that acceptable?"

I hastened to reply that it was wonderful.

"Don't be in too much of a goddamned hurry," he said. "Talk it over with your wife, who is a far better businessman than you are. In fact, she's so darn good that I want her to handle all the accounts. I talked to Jackson and he said she is tops. You may be a great artiste, but like most actors, a lousy businessman. Show people seem to me like a bunch of whores— come easy, go easy and to hell with tomorrow."

I was so happy that all I could do was give him the idiot grin.

"Take these figures with you," he said handing me a paper, "and show them to the little woman and come back tomorrow. If you agree, we'll draw up a contract."

I couldn't wait for Hilda to get home that evening so I went to her office. Hilda studied the paper carefully and then said thoughtfully, "I think it's a fair and generous offer. It's better than I expected. You know he's taking a big chance and stands to lose his money. So grab it and put everything you've got into this venture to justify this man's faith in you."

The next morning I signed the contract and the first thing I did was to buy a drawing board, paper, pencils, and thumbtacks. Following my father's method of construction, the first step was a complete set of plans and drawings of the illusions and tricks I intended to do.

Lists were made of all the illusions I had ever seen, including the impracticable useless junk that sometimes passes for a stage illusion. By elimination I boiled it down to a selection of proven hit illusions of widely different effects to obtain versatility and balance for the show.

I had to be right the first time because I had no money for experimentation or trying to be too original. Yet I was wise enough to know that the show should not be a carbon copy of other shows and must have a touch of originality. As I was in no position to invent new illusions, I would have to change the presentation of good, proven material in order to achieve a successful production.

It's funny what the power of money can do. I changed from an irresponsible youth to a man in those days. The responsibility was all mine.

Surprisingly, many of the magicians I had been in contact with knew nothing, or very little, of the technique of magic and it was a sad fact that even some of the "greats" had presented some terrible stinkers in their time. We all made mistakes, but one has to have the courage, when he sees that an illusion is hopeless, to take it out and chop it up for firewood. Whether they had a tin ear or just didn't give a damn, many magicians would present the most ill-conceived devices, and some magicians would have the nerve to break them in without a rehearsal, hoping for the best. The tin-ear league would allow an excellent trick to fail for lack of rehearsal and then throw it out as no good.

At first I toyed around with the idea of the Maskelyne levitation which would have been a sensation in these countries, but I realized that it was not an illusion to be set up in most of the theatres of Latin America. Besides, it needed four men to handle it, not to mention that it would use up most of my capital to build, so that was out although I was a bit downcast about it. Aga and Asrah had been presented by every magician who had played these parts so I decided to do no levitation at all.

It took me well over a month to get the final plans in order after long arguments and discussions with Spreer over innumerable coffees into the small hours of the morning. Hilda laughed about it and said I was arguing with myself really as I had the last word anyway. But finally it was done and we were ready to start construction.

Chang.

CHAPTER 27

In the meantime, Spreer chased around town and got the address and price list of every hardware store, tinsmith, nickel-plater, and metal spinner within a radius of five miles.

I rented a large cellar which was entered from the street through a low door that was built for a midget. Our workshop-cellar was near the tower where I lived. It was a corner house at the Calle Paraguay and Esmeralda, just a few blocks from Harrod's department store where we bought a lot of our material. I engaged a carpenter from the province of Entre Rios and a painter named Leonidas Mivie who was also a wood carver. Spreer was in charge of all the metal work. I did the supervising and final assembling of the illusions and tricks.

Okito's remarkable comeback had placed him as the highest paid magician in Europe and he was in good humor. I had written him of my good fortune and he sent me an encouraging letter telling that he was changing his act and if I could use his Sofa and Lantern illusions he would be glad to ship them to me. This unexpected gift made a change in my overall plan but after this gesture I felt like a heel in copying his exclusive tricks. I had no alternative, however, as his were the cream of stage magic and I could find no substitutes.

I wrote him a long letter and told him the truth, asking his permission to do these things, knowing deep down in my heart that if he refused I would do them anyway. I explained to him that I intended working only in the Spanish-speaking countries and would never conflict with him.

To my joy and relief he wrote back and gave me full permission to use anything I wanted and offered to send plans for sizes. This letter tore me to pieces. I just couldn't figure out this man of extremes. When I was with him, he wouldn't give me as much as a pocket trick and seemed dead set against my becoming a magician. Now he not only sent two expensive and beautiful illusions, but practically gave me his whole act. I was touched and grateful and wrote him a thankful letter and was rewarded with a series of long letters giving me helpful advice on construction which was of inestimable value to me and saved me many pesos.

I now had a head start with two stage-tested illusions. I decided to build the rest of the big stage illusions and began with the opening presentation illusion first.

I had the conviction that a magician should appear in some mysterious way and not just walk out cold. Thurston's novel opening from the giant book had always impressed me, but it wasn't an illusion and no attempt had been made to present it as such. By combining Thurston's book with the gateway Li-Ho-Chang used for his flash appearance, and eliminating the black art, I came upon a mystifying and flashy opening that I have used continually without any change.

My second illusion was a spectacular cremation. For this I used the basic principle of the Noah's Ark Illusion but in reverse. Instead of an appearance, it was used for the disappearance of a girl who was apparently burned alive. My improvement on this illusion was the grilled, openwork front door through which the shrouded girl was visible until she suddenly burst into flames and reduced to a smoking skeleton. It was a lightweight and easily set up illusion yet looked massive and heavy from the front. You see, I was learning.

The substitution trunk a la Raymond came next but with a decidedly improved trap that allowed us to do it even faster than he had. Also this trunk was built slightly out of square to prevent the trap from binding on the sides and leaving marks on the lining.

Two illusions were required for the next number which was a pantomimic sketch a la Okito entitled The Death God of Tibet, a combined magical and quick change sketch reminiscent of Thurston's raincoat and whisker dramas. One of the illusions used in this act was the Girl From the Light invented by Cyril Yettmah of London and used by Raymond. However, notwithstanding the ingenious principle involved, the illusion had a grave defect which was the wide platform on which the box made of paper-covered frames rested. It was obvious that a girl could be hidden behind the box and be resting on the platform. I designed a platform that was flush with the box, employing a sliding shelf which made the illusion a puzzler even for the magicians. It also cut down on a lot of extra weight.

The second illusion of this sketch was a simple cabinet for the exchange of a person but with the advantage that the front and back doors could be opened, allowing a clear view right through. The thin platform that this illusion rested on, doubled for the production of the Chinese Water Bowl.

In Tarbell's course there is a clever little illusion called Three Kings and a Queen which employs three giant cards. This we changed to three screens with large vase-shaped cutouts in them. The "vase" itself was brightly designed calico which rolled up on thin roller shades and gave the effect of the girl instantaneously appearing in a triangular screen.

I also built Selbit's Human Pin Cushion illusion, in which a girl is placed in a tall shallow cabinet, "perforated" with thirty walking sticks and finally pulled through them by hoisting her into the air with a block and tackle. However, I changed the walking sticks to long steel spikes, which was far more effective.

The large wheeled platform that served for the Death God cabinet and Water Bowl production was again used as the base for an easy to set up "one-man" spirit cabinet, using a radically new principle to hide the girl who operated the "spiritualistic phenomena."

The last of the big illusions was the Vampire, an elaborate escape, somewhat like the Stroubeika illusion, but employing a purely mechanical release. Spreer did a fine job on this illusion.

In fact, Spreer was invaluable to me in those days and really did a wonderful job. Raymond never knew what he lost when Spreer left. He had never had a chance to do anything right on the Raymond show, but I gave him carte blanche, and as long as he stuck to the general idea, I let him have a free rein. I never saw a man so happy in his work.

Altogether I had eleven big stage illusions: light, compact, easy to set up and relatively cheap to build. As each illusion was finished, a crate was made for it. This sometimes required a lot of planning, but it was worth the trouble because illusions get damaged in transportation—very rarely when in use on the stage. We also had the lids of the crates removable, and the inside of a lid was painted with a gaudy painting that was used for lobby display.

Gaulke would pay us a surprise visit now and then. What he saw seemed to satisfy him and there were times he wouldn't show up for weeks. We worked six days a week from eight in the morning to seven at night. I would have worked Sundays also, if I could have gotten away with it but my employees drew the line. We had one distressing experience when both the carpenter and the painter didn't show up for two days. Always the comedian, I had thought it a great gag to switch chewing gum for Ex-Lax. As they didn't know what the cause was, they both thought they were desperately ill and stayed home. That cured me of fooling around. I should have remembered Pop's practical joke with Wong. I decided to leave the gags to Joe Miller.

I had written a letter to Herman telling him of my windfall and a few weeks later I received a phone call to stop by at the British Consulate to pick up a letter. In those days I had my mail addressed to the Consulate where I had a good friend, Mr. Caldwell. When I got there he was holding a letter in his hand and looking at me as if I were insane.

"What's all this nonsense about?" he said, handing me the letter. It was addressed to Dr. Fu Manchu, care of David T. Bamberg. I knew at once what it was and opened the letter. After reading it I showed Caldwell a part where Herman prescribed recipes for deadly nightshade and hemlock cocktails. Then Caldwell knew I was nuts. I got a good laugh out of it but the name Fu Manchu stuck in my mind. From then on I was called Fu Manchu at the Consulate and a lot of corny kidding went on.

Once the big illusions were packed we started on the small stuff. I explored the toy shops of Buenos Aires and was fortunate to find a celluloid ball slightly smaller than my father's. I used his same technique for covering it but tried to be too original and instead of gold paper, I used an imitation pearl paper which was very delicate and pretty but something was wrong. It didn't have the look of Okito's golden sphere. Later on I changed it to gold and left it at that. I suppose the pearl effect made it look too much like a bubble.

We made four folding plywood tables suitably tricked. The Water Bowl, Multiple Production, the Bowl of Gobi, the Pigeon Catching, the Aerial Fishing, the Duck Vanish and Reappearance, the Mat Trick, the Three Nested Boxes and Dove, Soup Plate and Silks, Linking Rings, Egg Bag, a new Cut and Restored Rope, the Thurston version of the Rising Cards, and the Torn and Restored paper trick were all to be used in the show.

Looking back over the years, I am very proud of this efficient selection of some of the greatest magical effects known. The show had wonderful balance and could hold its own anywhere. I bought a very flashy collection of genuine Chinese stage costumes from Wong's "El Celeste Imperio" (The Celestial Empire), the biggest oriental importers in town. These costumes cost me almost a third of my capital, but they were worth it. Most of the assistants in an illusion show, including Thurston's and Dante's, were very poorly dressed and it had always been a matter that no one ever paid much attention to. But the beautiful Chinese robes solved the problem perfectly and I had a well dressed show.

My scenery was bright orange, with dragons and Chinese warriors painted on it. The traveller was of the same sateen material but with different motifs.

The patter for the show was typed out and learned by heart. Hilda took over the musical arrangements.

After six months of hard work, the show was complete down to the last detail; but instead of telling Gaulke I stalled around like a finicky old maid. The truth was that now everything was ready, I had cold feet. The idea of opening with a giant show terrified me. Hilda was the first to get wise to my finagling and quietly had a talk with Gaulke behind my back. The next thing I knew Gaulke showed up in the cellar one morning.

"Well, how's it goin'?" he asked innocently.

"Oh, fine, fine...fine. Just a few details here and there and it'll be set."

"How long d'ya need for rehearsals?" he asked.

"At least fifteen days, maybe more. It's all new and I have to break in the people and so on. If possible on an empty stage."

"U'huh. D'ya think you could open about the first of March?"

I made a quick calculation. This was the end of January and March seemed far away. "Yeah, I guess so," I said.

"Great," said Gaulke rubbing his hands. "I've arranged your opening for the San Martin Theatre for March first. That'll give you plenty of time for those last details and more than enough time for rehearsals. My pictures are running there now and the manager said you can have the stage all day long until you open. How's that?"

A cold iron hand shook my intestines. "Wonderful," I said with a ghastly grin. "Just wonderful."

"Fine. That's settled," he said. "On Monday we'll have the stuff carted over to the theatre. I'll have a big truck here at eight o'clock. Ciao! Be seein' ya." And he was gone.

I cursed myself. How had I ever gotten into this nerve-racking business? The old man had been right. Why hadn't I stuck to the peaceful shadow act? Why did I have to go around looking for grief? Look at all those happy people selling ribbon over the counter at Harrods. No worry, no responsibility. . .nothing. Just happiness. Damn it!

Early Monday morning the truck showed up with two hefty baggage men. The first crate they picked up was the cremation, the biggest of all, and carried it up the steps. When they got it to that lousy midget door, the crate couldn't pass. This was the one calculation we hadn't taken into account. All we could do was to unpack the illusion, knock the crate apart, repack and hammer it together on the sidewalk, with dark looks from a strolling cop who was silenced with ten pesos. Three crates had to be taken apart, but all the rest went through easily. Finally, when we got to the theatre about three hours late, the street was packed with parked cars. A city ordinance prohibited unloading after ten o'clock so the big truck had to spend the night in a garage and I was charged for two full days, which made a great start. Feverishly I started looking around for good omens.

Before nine o'clock the following morning all the stuff was on the stage. As the dressing rooms were unoccupied, we set up all the tricks and then the big illusions which took us nearly the whole day until just before the picture started.

For the first time I saw all my props together. I had a thrill of pride. A pleasant glow of optimism set in and I was rarin' to go. This strange sensation the theatre has on me has lasted all my life. No matter how bad things are I get a tremendous lift and can think better on a stage. It makes me feel safe and is home, a refuge where nothing bad can ever happen to me. Radio, motion pictures, television leave me cold. They are mechanical things run by strangers. The theatre is my first and only love. There is nothing in all show business to touch it. It gets under your skin. In a purely monetary sense it may be the poorest of the family, but it's warm and it lives and you feel the excitement of it.

So I started rehearsals with a high heart, and after a couple of weeks the show began to take form. One morning the house manager, Senor Gea, asked for the copy for the programme and the ads for the newspapers. I told him I'd have them ready the next morning.

That night I shoved a nice white sheet of paper into the typewriter and suddenly realized that I didn't have a name. That was one little detail I had completely overlooked.

Syko was out. It had to be Chinese. But what? Names ran through my head. Chung-Ling-Fu? No, too confusing. Okito Jr.? Worse. I got out a map of China and pored over it. Chang-Hai? Too contrived. No, it had to be something alliterative; something easy to remember. Something pronounced the same in all languages. I suppose it had been in the back of my mind all the time, but I suddenly remembered Herman and his insidious devil doctor, Fu Manchu. Now there was a name indeed. It was unknown in South America and so without further thought I typed, FU MANCHU.

In later years I found that it had been a mistake to adopt this name, but then it was too late to do anything about it. I had made the same error that Houdini made when he copped Houdin's name and added an i.

I made up an exotic programme and gave it to the manager and forgot about it. Gaulke took over and had half a dozen colored lithographs made and took charge of the advertising from the Film Exchange. Hilda worked on the music score and cue sheets.

Li-Ho-Chang wore a mandarin hat during his show, without a pigtail. I copied Okito and wore a half-bald wig with a long queue. I looked like a perfect half-wit in it. My father had small eyes, but I had two saucers that were impossible to shape into almonds. I used this silly makeup for the opening, but after a week or so I threw out the wig and fastened the queue directly to the mandarin hat, which was much better.

The show began to take shape in spite of my propensity to interrupt the rehearsal of a scene to putter around with some unimportant detail. It was a habit I found hard to get rid of and a very bad thing for rehearsals.

A week or so before the opening I left the tower room one morning and when I stepped into the street, I was greeted with a display of lithos and posters in bright red and black announcing the debut of the great Chinese magician, Fu Manchu, at the San Martin. I just stood and stared at them. It seemed like it was another person—not me.

For the moment I was elated but this was immediately followed by the grandfather of all cold feet attacks in the history of show business. I felt like that time with the spider in the Matto Grosso. I died a hundred deaths and had thoughts of locking myself in some convenient toilet and cutting my throat.

I got to the theatre looking like a six-weeks-old corpse. Everybody in the show rushed up to me with bright faces and asked me if I'd seen it. Yeah! I thought gloomily, I'd seen it, goddammit!

Those last few days of rehearsal were terrible. I didn't know it then from lack of experience, but the show was over-rehearsed. I got on my own and everyone else's nerves. It was really bad. I yapped at everybody and nothing was right, although they did their best and took my ill-humor without a squawk. I had thought Okito to be a pest in rehearsals but I had him beat. I have a suspicion it was Hilda who, understanding my nervous tension, had told everyone to overlook my bad temper. Hilda would brush off my trenchant remarks with a shrug and absorb my ill humor without a word.

On my part, this was just sheer funk. Stage fright and nervousness are usually caused by lack of rehearsal. A magician is forced to think of two things at the same time, the mechanics of the trick and patter that goes with it. Therefore, the trick must be rehearsed until it becomes second nature and requires no conscious thought.

The average patter of the average magician is really a guide or a reminder to his actions. There is an old Hebrew saying, "The magician mutters and knows not what he mutters." If a magician says, "I will place this silk in this empty glass" he is doing little more than rehearsing the trick in front of an audience. The ideal patter, of course, is not something memorized and then delivered mechanically, but rather a studied spontaneity which gives the effect of clever ad-libbing. This was one of Will Rogers' strong points, his apparently unstudied monologue.

When the magician completely masters the trick, and the patter has been tailored to it, only then can he give an easy, convincing, spontaneous presentation. Insecurity is the chief culprit of stage fright and jitters on the stage.

Even today, after so many years in the theatre, I get butterflies in the stomach before a debut; but they usually disappear when the curtain rises. If rehearsal is adequate, the nervous tension of the whole cast will be at a minimum. Infallibly, a nervous performer makes an audience nervous, and in turn they often release their tension by laughter and ridicule, or even catcalls from the gallery. (An old actor's dodge and a good remedy for stage fright consists of moistening the lips with the tip of the tongue as it is claimed that fear causes the mouth to become dry.)

The misdireciton necessary for the "critical moment" of a trick depends on rehearsal, and one gets to the point where one can kid the audience while passing the danger spots; but it must not be overdone as this leads to overconfidence, which in turn leads to a mechanical delivery. Occasionally after performing the same trick hundreds of times, I began thinking about what I would do after the show, while mechanically pattering away. Then I would suddenly wake up to what I was doing and be at a loss to remember at what point of the trick I was working. I would then repeat my monologue, much to the surprise of the maestro. This may be the main reason I built so many new illusions and tricks and wrote so many different shows in later years. I suppose I did this more for my sake than for the audiences, as I felt I was getting stale and into a rut.

When the opening night finally came, I was a wreck. Lots of people kindly came to my dressing room to wish me luck. I mentally and boorishly wished them to hell. The call boy came in fifteen minutes before curtain time and asked permission to give "la primera" (the first bell of three before the overture).

Well, that was it. Just before the opening music started, Hilda came over and pressed my hand. She didn't say a word and she didn't have to. I wasn't that stupid.

CHAPTER 28

For a moment after I stepped out of the book and took my opening bow, I had the strange detached feeling that I was in another world or that this was a dream. Everybody looked strange. Even the props looked strange and unfamiliar. In a mechanical way I went into the series of productions and small tricks that made up the first ten minutes of the show and it was here that the rehearsals paid off. It went like clockwork and gave me time to get myself in hand. By the time I got to my first talking trick I was completely at ease and a surprising calmness and zest came over me and transmitted itself to the company. Even during the Floating Ball, my hands were rock steady and I got a big hand at the end of it.

The show ran without a hitch and, wonder of wonders, it even ran on time. The equilibrium of the show was good and there was no need, as so often happens after a debut, to cut out or change certain tricks. A couple of my ideas were not up to expectations, but on the whole the show played unchanged all the time we were in the San Martin.

The house was quite filled, due in part, to all the free passes we had handed out, and it was an appreciative audience who laughed and applauded at the right places. Gaulke was in the right avant-scene box, almost on the stage, with his cronies. He was beaming. All of my friends in Buenos Aires were out front and helped to boost the general enthusiasm. Caldwell, of the Consulate, sat there looking like this was a personal triumph of his and the British Empire's.

For the first time I enjoyed that exhilarating feeling an actor gets when he knows he has his audience. Only the theatre can give you that. The show built up to a strong finish and at the finale we had eight curtain calls.

After the final curtain Hilda grabbed me around the neck and couldn't talk for her tears. I nearly passed out and someone brought me a chair and a brandy. I vaguely remember a lot of people on the stage but I had that detached feeling again. Nothing seemed real—the flowers, the noise, the congratulations, Gaulke strutting around like a proud father and holding forth to his pals who had their doubts about this crazy venture, not even the boys covering the illusions for the night. Finally I was alone in my dressing room, removing my grease paint.

A while later Hilda and the manager came in with the bordereaux and the money. In spite of the advertising the paid attendance had been poor. They had sold less than 300 orchestra seats and few boxes (the upper floor were very poor indeed); but the manager was happy and said the show was in for a long run. For my share that night I got 440 pesos—a fortune.

Gaulke was bursting with pride and invited us all to supper. We really needed it. I, at least, hadn't eaten decently for two weeks. The wine flowed and we acted like a bunch of kids. I suppose by today's standards such corny antics would be frowned on, but it was wonderful and a fitting end to an unforgettable evening.

When we got home in the early hours of the morning I had a fit of the blackest depression and started to worry about the future.

The press treated me kindly, and although there were no raves, there were no brickbats. It was more or less like Dante's press and I was accepted as an illusionist.

Just as the house manager had predicted, the word got around and we did a good business for seventeen days but had to cut the season short as another company was booked for the theatre. After a week or so we could do the show with our eyes closed and backwards, and it began to get that indefinable professional touch so characteristic of the big-time magic show. I was really in now and on a footing with the big boys of the business, and don't think I didn't love it.

At the end of the run I brought Gaulke his share of the receipts and what money I could spare to pay off the debt. He checked the accounts and the money and turned his grim Churchillian stare on me which I had never expected to see again. He looked me up and down.

"You certainly don't look like a successful magician," he said. "You're not working the shop anymore, so why do you go around in those clothes?"

I admitted that my suit was a bit threadbare but it was all I had.

"Why didn't you buy a suit with the money I advanced you?"

"I thought that the money was not for personal use," I said.

"How much you got now?"

"Enough to coast along until I get further bookings."

"You open in the Medrano the week after next," he said, and picking up the money from his desk, he handed me about half. "Here. Go out and get yourself some decent clothes and buy that little woman anything her heart desires."

Together with Spreer, who had earned it for his hard work, we raided the Casa Tow on Florida Street, and stocked ourselves from head to foot. Hilda cut a wide swath through the exclusive women's shops and I had never seen her looking so lovely. Little Bobby got a wondrous collection of bibs.

For the next few months we played the larger picture houses in Buenos Aires and the suburbs. In those days it was possible to make a deal in a movie house and suspend the picture as talkies had not yet come in and there were no bulky loudspeakers.

Okito, who was in Paris again, was delighted with my success and had Latscha make him a beautiful seven stone lithograph of a large head in semi-profile. As a present to me he had an extra hundred printed with my name instead of his and he sent them to me. I always hung up one of these lovely lithos in the theatre lobby and it was in the Florida Theatre that one of them was the cause of a very funny incident.

We were doing two shows a day there and one day after the first show there was a knock on my door. I opened to find a Chinese gentleman standing there.

"Do you speak English?" he inquired politely.

I said I did.

"I just caught your show," he went on to say, "and I thought it was very good, but there are one or two things, no matter how disagreeable, that I must say. I have a very dear friend whose name is Okito, a very famous Chinese magician, whom you have no doubt heard of. It seems to me that many of your tricks are a direct copy of Okito's. I also noticed that the affiche over the box office in the lobby has your name but Okito's face. I don't know if you are aware that this sort of thing is considered unethical in the magical profession."

"I agree with you," I said, "but that affiche was a gift to me from Okito, and as far as the tricks are concerned, my father

178

gave me permission to use them.''

"Your father?'' he exclaimed.

"Yes. My name is David Bamberg and Okito is my father.''

He clapped his hand to his head. "How stupid of me. I should have known. How can you ever forgive me?'' He held out his hand. "My name is Long Tack Sam.''

I told him that I knew of him by reputation and made a mental note of writing to Okito and letting him know what a good friend he had in Mr. Long.

We had a long chat about magic and magicians. He told me he was opening in the Casino the following week. Just before he left he spotted my linking rings, picked them up and did the most amazing routine that I had ever seen, finishing up with his wonderful swimming fish and flying dragon figures. After seeing that, I realized I had a lot to learn. The old boys could still show me a thing or two.

We became good friends. I had the pleasure of meeting his wife, who was Austrian, and his two daughters. I caught his outstanding act twice at the Casino. That was the only time I ever saw this great artiste and modest gentleman.

Shortly after, I had an offer from the Brazilian impresario, Serador, for a percentage deal for a tour of his theatres in Rio, Sao Paulo and Porto Alegre. I talked it over with Gaulke and he was enthusiastic about the deal and advised me to go. He also had me open an account in the Bank of Boston instead of using my wardrobe trunk as a safety vault.

My knowledge of Portuguese, such as it was, served me well in Rio where we opened in the Gloria Theatre. The cariocas are a fun loving, exuberant people and my outlandish Chinese-Portuguese took their fancy. The show was an instant hit. In fact, after the Rio date which consisted of three theatres, I was able to send Gaulke a check for 4,000 pesos.

Business was equally good in Sao Paulo and held up well in Porto Alegre. On the way home I stopped over in Montevideo and, for the first time, took over as my own impresario at the Solis Theatre, one of the best houses in Montevideo. The Uruguayan peso was the highest monetary unit in South America, being on a par with the U.S. dollar. I could have taken the theatre for an indefinite time but I was a little scared at my temerity and took it for only fifteen days. Business was marvelous and I could have kicked myself after the run was over, but it was too late as the theatre was booked.

When I returned to Buenos Aires, Gaulke told me the story of the 4,000 peso check I sent from Rio. When he received it he thought I had made a mistake and spoke to the manager of the Boston Bank who was a friend of his.

"Look, Larry," he said, "this crazy kid has never had any money in his life and he's a little mixed up, I think he wanted to send me 400 pesos and the durn-fool makes out a check for 4,000. There is no attempt of fraud here. It's just foolish kid stuff. What do I do?"

So before presenting the check the manager checked my account and informed Gaulke that the check was good as I had sent over 7,000 pesos. Gaulke nearly dropped dead. He used this story to goad a few people he had backed in other ventures which had not panned out well and this did nothing to make me popular in certain quarters.

Most of the larger theatres had big lobbies and I thought it would be a good idea to have some sort of sensational illusion that could be exhibited free to attract the passing crowds. I built a headless woman illusion but with a new twist. A headless girl lay on a thin operating table and from her neck ran two rubber tubes with glass tubing insertions at intervals that ran to an icebox in which the girl's head rested on an electrical coil. When a blood pump was started the legs and arms of the girl gestured to accompany the talking head in the icebox.

The thing worked beautifully and just before the final touches I got an offer to play Chile, so I packed it carefully with the intention of using it after my return and stored it in a garage. But I made the mistake of showing it first to an Egyptian mentalist by the name of Prof. Bernardo. When I returned from Chile I found that Bernardo had built a duplicate and was presenting it in a side show in the Parque Japones, a local Luna Park. He was doing a thriving business and all Buenos Aires was talking about this illusion.

I was so disgusted that I foolishly destroyed my model, but I was so angry at the time that I didn't stop to think clearly.

It was in July, mid-winter on that continent, when we opened in Santiago, Chile after a four day trip over the Andes range, white with snow and ice. My impresario, Herr Mewe, a German-Chileno, introduced me to the owners of the leading newspaper *El Mercurio,* who generously gave me full spreads in their afternoon papers in Santiago and Valparaiso. In the latter town I became friendly with the boys on the *La Estrella,* the evening paper, and they gave me a buildup of full pages for ten days running, just before and after the debut, without charging us a cent. To top off this friendly gesture, they made me foreign theatrical correspondent for *El Mercurio*. With this sensational publicity we did a wonderful business, and in connection with the Ratanpura Tea Company, we arranged a "challenge." For the first time, I ventured to do a nailed packing box escape and was able to appreciate the powerful attraction that any illusion with a hint of danger has upon the public. However, I never got very far with the escapes as I lacked Houdini's stamina and physique. My scrawny frame looked like hell in a bathing suit. The night I did the escape in Valparaiso we had the biggest gate of the whole Chilean tour, over a thousand dollars.

By this time Gaulke had been paid back his capital in full and was now on a ten percent share. In his affectionate letters to us, he always called us the "square shootin' kids" and "my children" and often said that it wasn't the money that made him so happy but the fact we had vindicated his faith in us. In the long run Gaulke tripled his capital. This business may seem like small peanuts compared to today's standards, but in those days when the average workingman's salary was about a dollar a day, it was big business.

My personal representative at that time was a young man named Gaby who promptly established himself as one of the family. Hilda would arise fairly early in the morning and take Bobby for his breakfast, letting me sleep until noon. Gaby developed the irritating habit of waking me by shaking the bed and hollering, "Get up you lazy so and so."

In the little town of Quillota I was rudely awakened with a loud crash and the shaking bed and furiously shouted "Dejate de joder, hombre," when I suddenly realized it was still night and the room was heaving like a ship. Hilda was sitting up in bed terrified. The room was occasionally illuminated with what seemed to be flashes of lightning. It didn't take long for it to dawn on me that this was an earthquake. I remembered that the safest place was to stand inside a door frame and not rush into the street as the walls usually fell out. My first thought was for Bobby but I couldn't make it to the door of his adjoining room as the rocking of the floor made walking impossible. The quake lasted for only thirty seconds but it seemed much longer. We could hear the crash of falling things and the panicky screaming going on outside when abruptly the shaking stopped and a heavy downpour of rain started.

The connecting door to Bobby's room was jammed. I

hammered on it but no sound came from inside. The light had been cut off but with the aid of matches I started out of our room into the patio when the blasted quake began again. It was much shorter and less violent than the first shock, so I was able to get out to Bobby's room only to find it empty. I rushed out and found him almost at once, sitting in the patio in a river of wine.

The bodega of the hotel had two walls stacked with full wine bottles and the opposite walls were stacked with the empty ones. By some whim of the quake, not one of the empty bottles fell down. Only the full bottles had been smashed, causing a flood of wine to seep under the bodega door and into the patio where young Robert D. Bamberg was having himself a hell of a time splashing around in his original version of wine and water trick. He was soaked to the skin. In spite of the fact that the quake might start again and the hotel fall on our ears, Hilda carried Bobby to our room and changed him after a good rubdown. The kid stank like a two-bit Bowery stew-bum but he loved this new game and wanted to play it again.

After a few more slight tremors things quieted down. We made our way to the dining room which was lighted with an old kerosene lamp. We found Spreer and Gaby along with the rest of the hotel guests. It was just after three in the morning and there was no use going out as the town was pitch black and the rain was still pouring down.

Just after dawn the rain stopped and we made our way to the theatre, passing a number of collapsed houses on the way. The main doors of the theatre were still locked so we went around to the back and found a hole in the wall big enough to drive a truck through.

I knew just what to expect. All my illusions were on wheels on an inclined stage. Considering that and all the delicate props and glassware we used, I could see my profits from this tour dwindling like magic. But what we did find staggers the imagination. Not a single prop had moved! In spite of the severe shaking, not even a table had tipped over. In my dressing room the glasses and pitchers and bowls that I used were intact. Everything was all right, except for one thing. The linking rings had fallen from a table to the floor after the trick anyway. They were built for this kind of treatment. When I picked them up, I found one ring of the chain of three connected rings was split open and twisted as if a giant had done it. Figure that one out! The floor of the dressing room, by the way, was hardwood, the same as the stage. It has been a lifelong mystery to me how a quarter-inch thick steel ring with a welded joint could be torn apart like that. I never could find a reasonable explanation for this phenomenon.

Needless to say, we packed as fast as we could and got out of town. The evening papers from Santiago mentioned that a slight shock had caused little damage in the Quillota region. What the hell was a real earthquake like in that area?

Back in Santiago we were due for some more free publicity when the Chinese minister lodged a complaint affirming that one of my sketches, the Opium Dream, and my use of a pigtail were derogatory to the Chinese people. The queue had been a mark of slavery and had been abolished since the 1912 revolution. The minister was perfectly right, of course, but I stubbornly refused to change the sketch or cut off the pigtail. The resultant publicity was good for another season in Santiago. Years later in Tampico, Mexico, I had the whole Chinese colony on my neck and was finally forced to change my ways. Another contretemps I had in later years was over the swastika, an ancient oriental symbol, which I frequently used as a design on my props and scenery and even embroidered on some of my costumes. Because of this I was accused of being a Nazi sympathizer. I had to paint out the swastikas while I cursed Herr Schickelgruber and his motley crew.

After a tour through the beautiful southern Chilean lake country, where the scenery is even more beautiful than in Switzerland, we left for Mendoza on the Argentine side of the Andes and played Cordoba and Rosario on the way back to Buenos Aires. It was in Rosario that I had the good fortune to meet Leslie Briant, his wife Violet and their two sons, Frank and Ronald, for the first time. This was the beginning of a lifelong friendship with this enthusiastic amateur magician.

CHAPTER 29

When I returned to Buenos Aires I had saved up quite a bit of money and we rented a nice apartment directly opposite the Politeama Theatre on the Calle Corrientes, which is Buenos Aires' Broadway. It was fun to be able to buy furniture and things without having to worry about the prices.

Hilda and Gaulke teamed up to keep a watchful eye on me to prevent me from going into unsound business ventures which were offered from all sides.

From local actors I heard that very few magicians had ever played the Republic of Paraguay and my exotic show should do well there. I decided to play on spec, as I did in Montevideo, and took the river boat from Buenos Aires for a six day trip up the Parana River to Asuncion, the old colonial-style, semi-tropical capital of about 150,000 population.

At the dock, large baskets of oranges were being loaded onto freighters by short, stocky Guarani women who balanced these enormous loads on their heads. The men sat around in the shade, checking and sometimes dozing off in the heat. The ship's purser explained this situation.

"You must understand, senor," he said, "that many years ago Paraguay was one of the biggest and most powerful countries in South America; but they made the mistake of taking on Argentina, Brazil, and Bolivia single-handedly in a war that lasted seven years and left it a very small country of thick jungles and the great Chaco desert. The male population was decimated to the point of seven women for every man. This makes it a very pleasant place for the foreigner to visit and also explains the reason why the women do all the work."

Those actors in Buenos Aires had been right and the show was a complete novelty. We needed armed police to hold back the crowds who stormed the box office. The house manager would bring in a night's take in a basket and Hilda would spend half the night sorting out those filthy sticky bills.

In spite of the heat we kept away from swimming in the river for fear of the piranha, the fresh-water cannibal fish that is all head and teeth and is considered to be far more dangerous than the shark or the barracudas. Any human or animal unlucky enough to fall into a pack of these marine monsters is devoured in a few minutes.

We played Asuncion for six weeks, and on the way back to Buenos Aires, played all the river towns. At one place called Tres Esquinas, near Formosa, they had never seen a magician before. I had great expectations, but to my surprise, the show was a complete flop. They just didn't understand what I was doing and it made no sense to them. The only thing that caused any comment was a white rabbit I had, which somebody promptly stole.

Back in Buenos Aires, I found that an Italian magician named Maieroni was playing the Politeama Theatre, just across the street from my flat, with a full night's show. Spreer and I went to see the show that night. The show was really worth seeing as he was a throwback to the old days of the last century having an old-fashioned magic show that I had read about but never seen. Il Commendattore Maieroni, as he billed himself, was a stocky man with a great shock of black hair and a fierce mustache that overhung his tremendous tomb-like teeth—which he displayed in what he thought was a smile and scared the children half to death.

In spite of his looking like a scare mask, he was a pleasant and charming performer. I was delighted to see him do the original version of the Bridal Chamber illusion and the original of an illusion that Raymond had called Boy Scout, in which a small trunk was placed in a cabinet and the curtains drawn. When the cabinet was wheeled around and the curtains opened, the tiny toy trunk had expanded into a normal-sized one which was opened and a girl dressed as a Boy Scout stepped forth. Maieroni's prop was even more ancient than Raymond's version, and it was funny to hear the orchestra blow its brains out in an effort to kill the noise the expanding trunk made.

The Italian colony of Buenos Aires is huge and they turned out in force to honor their compatriot and he did good business. It was a pity that I couldn't understand most of his patter as he spoke in Italian. Although there is a similarity to Spanish, he talked so fast I could make out less than half of what he said. One of his tricks had a shattering effect on the audience and was the talk of Buenos Aires. It was the old, original version of the Inexhaustible Hat, from which he produced the usual silks, boxes, clocks, cups and cannon balls. He finished by producing a paper coil which he spun and wound around his wand until he had a great loose bundle of paper which he threw onto the stage just in front of the run down. He produced one more cannon ball, showed the hat empty, and took his bow. Then, almost as an afterthought, he picked up the paper ribbon bundle and from it he extracted a naked, kicking baby. There was a great shout from the audience as the Italians love kids and it was truly a most simpatico effect which brought the house down.

I paid a visit to this great old timer and he was very friendly. Unfortunately, as he only spoke Italian, our conversations didn't get very far.

Magicians rained on Buenos Aires and the next one to show up was the fabulous Max Malini with his son, Ozzie. This man was a living legend even at that time.

There are certain regions on earth that seem to breed first-class magicians. The Austro-Hungarian Empire was such a place. Houdini, Goldin, Carl Rosini and Max Malini all came from there or near there, and it would be difficult to find a greater magical quartet.

I was playing the Paramount Theatre at the time, and one night after the show, there was a knock and I opened my dressing room door to find a short, fat, bald-headed man with a huge cigar stuck in his face. This was Max Malini, who introduced himself, sat down and watched me as I removed my makeup.

"So you're Okito's boy, huh? Vell, vell. He iss a goot friendt of mine. I am glat to see you getting along so goot." He removed his cigar and tapped the ash thoughtfully. "You vant my candid opinion of your show?"

I said I would, preening myself for the coming compliments.

"It ain't a *bad* show," he said, "but I don't like it. Now vait a minute and lemme explain. You're too much like your old man. You're too mechanical. Eferything is boxes. You don't do no manipulations. Efen the paper trick is mechanical. De oder piece is stuck on der back. Vy don't you palm it? Look, I show you."

He took out a pack of cigarettes, seemed to change his mind, and took one of mine from the pack on the makeup table. He slit it open lengthwise, threw out the tobacco, and proceeded to do the sweetest paper tear and restoration that I had ever seen. I knew he swiped one of my cigarettes beforehand and was bluffing, but that didn't alter the fact that he did it beautifully.

"Vell," he asked, "vot you tink of dat?"

I told him that it was marvelous but insisted that the principle could not be applied to my larger, stage-sized paper. He insisted it could but he didn't offer to show me how.

After the Paramount Theatre I had a layoff for a couple of weeks that coincided with Malini's stay in Buenos Aires. We were together every day and I saw him in action many times. Malini was not a man given to fraternizing with fellow magicians and he particularly detested amateurs. For some inexplicable reason he cottoned to me and took me along everywhere he went, even going so far as taking me up to his hotel room to show me a collection of clever fakes he had picked up. I still cherish a small hollow wooden ball he gave me for color changing a silk.

I had a good chance to study this remarkable man. I have mentioned before the audacious type. Unquestionably, Malini was the king. Beside him Houdini was a shrinking violet. I have never seen a man in show business with such colossal crust.

Malini was at his best in a bar or at a table. Much has been written about his misdirection, but for me he had something that surpassed that. He was never in a hurry and would wait patiently his chance to spring unawares. The effect on the spectators when he casually, without fanfare lifted a hat to show a brick on the table, was devastating. It was this sort of thing that people talked about for months after he was gone.

At the risk of making continued controversy I maintain that he was not a great manipulator, nor a crack card man. Some of the card moves I saw him do were the crudest things imaginable, but no one noticed as his acting ability covered up for him.

His egg bag was excellent and he made the most of it. The first time I saw him work, he took me completely unaware and fooled me greatly; but after two or three shows I was prepared for him and understood his subtle technique. He could be compared to Zancig in the sense that no one could do his tricks the way he did them. His tricks were directly based on his extraordinary personality and mannerisms. He was something very special and his tricks fit his personality.

His last show in Buenos Aires was a full evening's entertainment in a small theatre of the British community. He invited me to come and told me to pay attention to the "real" Chinese Water Bowl production that he had learned in China, which he claimed was the proper way to do the trick and not as I was doing it.

The first two parts of his show were up to the Malini standard and his spectacular Card Stabbing routine was a lesson to any magician.

The third part of his show was announced as oriental magic and I anxiously awaited the Water Bowl production. When I saw it I seriously suspected Malini of having a tin ear. Very rarely have I ever seen anything quite as bad as that.

He waddled on stage wearing a long mandarin robe that dragged on the floor. He also wore a little round Chinese hat. He looked so funny that the audience burst out in laughter but he paid no attention. He showed a cloth empty by twisting it into a rope and banging it on a table. Then he stepped forward a step or so and addressed the audience and, obviously for my benefit, he said, "Dis trick vot I am going to do now I vos teached in China. I don't need no big stage and a lot of assistants and fancy scenery to do it. I admit I ain't Chesus Christ but I'm better dan a lot of oders vot call themselves machicians." Those were his very words.

Then he proceeded to spread the cloth over his shoulders and squatting on the stage fumbled around for what seemed an eternity, pulling and jerking at something under the cloth, and grunting with a red face. It was so funny that the audience started laughing again but he gave them the Malini stare and they shut up. Finally something went "bop" and he stood up and jerked the cloth away to display a low flat bowl like a washing basin. Picking up a dipper, he scooped water out of it and took a bow.

It may be, of course, that in this particular show the thing had gone wrong and later when he asked what I thought of it, I diplomatically replied that it seemed a trifle slow.

"Vell, maybe," he said, "but dat's the right vay to do itd."

So what the hell.

The rest of the "Chinese" magic he did was almost as bad as the bowl. It seemed a pity to ruin such a fine performance with such a poor ending.

But, all in all, Malini was a great performer and it was a privilege to have known him and to have been his friend even for such a short time.

A characteristic of this man's strange personality was revealed in his departure from Buenos Aires. Things hadn't gone well for him but as he was a man who liked good living, he had taken rooms at the best hotel in town and run up a bill which he couldn't pay.

"Look," he said to the manager of the hotel, "I'm the great Malini, de greatest machician in the vurld. I tell you vot I do. I got contracts for Chile. I gif you my void ven I get there, I send you de money first thing."

How he bamboozled the manager into agreeing to this, I'll never know, but the man agreed and no doubt mentally kissed his money good-bye. Two weeks later Malini sent the full amount from Santiago, including generous tips for the hotel employees. That was Malini.

I often envied his way of living off a few simple tricks that took him all over the world and even permitted him to appear before royalty. Often I remember his favorite saying to me, "Vot the hell you vant to cart all dat junk around for? Do it de easy vay." I didn't have the colossal nerve. All of us have our own way of doing things and that perhaps is why the history of magic is so fascinating.

After Malini came a French magician named Rhyss, "Satan's Bartender," who played the Casino with his original act of producing any drink called for from a glass pitcher filled with water. It was a sensational act and new for Buenos Aires. It created a lot of comment. His closing number—visibly changing a vase of water to ink while it was held in the hands of a spectator—was pure magic. At that time I didn't know the secret of the delayed-action process he used and it drove me crazy.

Rhyss saw my show and, surprisingly, he had never seen the cut and restored rope and was just as crazy about that as I was about his ink trick. The upshot was that we swapped tricks. I believe I got the better of the bargain, by obtaining one of the most mystifying tricks in the whole realm of magic.

A few weeks after Rhyss came Linga Singh, a genuine Hindu magician, also at the Casino. He had a rich stage setting and appeared in a howdah on the back of an elephant. His feature illusion was the production of two girls from a metal vase filled with water. He did the Indian Sand trick in the original version, the Dizzy Limit illusion and a levitation. He was a very friendly man and we spent many pleasant days together. Some years later my friend Cyro wrote me from England that when Linga Singh died he ordered in his will that all his props and illusions be burnt on the Heath in Birmingham so that the layman could not get hold of his secrets.

After such a wave of magic I got my first symptoms of expansion fever and decided to build some new illusions for the show. I didn't really need them as I had only played five countries. The rest of the world was still open for me, but I had that "world's greatest" itch which is an incurable disease with first symptoms being a slight swelling of the head.

The Dizzy Limit illusion, which was the disappearance of a girl in a large net, had always appealed to me, but its one drawback was the heavy wooden scaffolding used to support the net. We constructed a light and thin affair that could be hoisted into the air with an off stage block and tackle. Instead of the girl, I vanished a "gorilla," after reading that this was the way gorillas are captured in Africa. I had the "gorilla" appear from an African hut, which was a box-like arrangement using the same platform used for the Girl from the Light illusion. The whole setup required very little extra baggage.

Linga Singh had raved about a new illusion presented by Amac in England, called Find the Lady, and described the effect to me in detail. I could see that this illusion was a natural for any country in the world. It was Three Card Monte on a large scale, using giant cards which passed in front of a girl. The audience had to guess which card they thought the girl was behind and they were always wrong. Finally the girl vanished.

Linga Singh told me that he had inside information that the three stools used for the girl to stand on were, in reality, small "sphinx" tables with mirrors at a 45 degree angle, which allowed the girl to shoot up and down through three stage traps. Common sense told me that this explanation was highly improbable as no theatre in the world would allow anyone to cut three traps in a line for a magic effect. Other explanations from friends of mine bordered on the absurd, and all contradicted each other. One of the solutions sent to me in good faith was the ridiculous version which was later published in *Greater Magic*—the girl being up behind a black border, with a complicated crane affair in the grid.

Then I received a letter from Okito who wrote that there were rumors from "first hand" sources that Amac was disgusted with show business and was storing his act and going into another business. I immediately wrote a letter to Amac and told him I was interested in this illusion for South America, wanted exclusive rights, and asked for his terms. I never had a reply.

I still didn't know how the illusion was worked, so I figured out a way of my own, and by a process of elimination I came on what I thought could be the only possile solution. In 1931 we built the illusion and it was a sensational hit from the first night. It was a light, easy to set up illusion and a great time killer, besides being something off the beaten track. I consider it one of the world's best illusions, but it requires a lot of rehearsal and is rather a delicate and tricky thing at best.

The first talking pictures in Buenos Aires created a furor and the theatres began to feel the pinch immediately. All the movie theatres were vying to be first in their neighborhood and they cluttered up their stages with heavy beam scaffoldings in which outsize loudspeakers hung. Most of these primitive contraptions were immovable and put an end to a lucrative field. Within a short time over eighty percent of the stages in Buenos Aires were unusable, and the old system of renting a theatre for a week or playing together with a picture in a one hour variety act was out. In a few of the big houses they had the sense to hang the loudspeakers on rails so they could be pulled to one side, leaving the stage free.

Variety was also badly hit. The Casino was turned into a revue house and very few acts were imported from Europe. That was the end of variety in South America. On a lesser scale, the same thing was happening in Europe and Okito was feeling the pinch and was looking around for new worlds to conquer.

Like all show people, I had the silly habit of exaggerating my profits. For instance, I had written to Okito from Chile and told him that I made a $1,000 in one night with the packing box escape. This was a gross misrepresentation. In the first place, I was on a percentage basis, and after expenses and taxes, my cut came to about $400; and we only had such big gates once in a while. All show people do this kind of bluffing and theatre managers are worse. There's an old story about this.

A third-rate theatrical company put on "Hamlet" and the take was $8. The manager was standing glumly outside the theatre when a rival manager came up to him and said, "How did it go?"

"Terrible," said the first manager, "terrible. $16."

When Okito received my letters telling him about these thousand dollar-a-night deals, he realized he was wasting his time in Europe—when the streets of Latin America were paved with 24 karat gold. He wrote me a most enthusiastic letter telling me the time had come to team up and do a two-man show to be billed as "Okito Presents Fu Manchu." I was to be publicly named (at every show) to be his successor, a la Kellar-Thurston.

When would I learn to keep my tremendous mouth shut? If he had only given me some previous warning, I could have written to tell him to hold off for a while, but he was already on the high seas when his letter arrived. To make matters worse, he had booked his and Marie's passage to Montevideo as the Argentine Consulate had refused him visas for lack of a signed contract.

He brought his whole show with him and had many new and clever effects. He completely fooled me with a new and ingenious trick that Goldin had given him, which had been invented by a Scottish magician, Fred (Caird) Smith of Dundee. The effect was a wooden frame with two holes drilled on either side. A solid wooden cube with a hole drilled through it was placed in the frame so that all the holes were aligned and a silk ribbon was threaded through. The cube was then pulled from the frame leaving the ribbon intact. He made me a present of this splendid trick and I wrote a comedy, a pseudo-scientific story, around it and presented it as the Mystery of the Fourth Dimension. It became one of the comedy hits of the show. In later years I used the same principle for the Thief of Bagdad trick which was so widely copied.

He also brought me his latest eight glasses of water on a tray production. This ingenious trick is described in detail in his book, *Okito On Magic*. Its only drawback was the constant breakage of the glasses. Transparent plastic glasses hadn't been invented. An amateur magician named Henry Solanas told me that in his father's emporium on the Avenida Santa Fe they were selling imported unbreakable glasses which could be thrown to the floor without fear as they bounced. Okito and I rushed over to the store to see this marvel and Solanas, with the air of a professor, tossed two of these glasses to the stone floor where they collided and with a thunderous clap dissolved into dust.

Okito went just as crazy over Bobby as my grandfather had been over me. After his long and expensive trip and his high hopes, I didn't have the heart to tell him things were going from bad to worse in show business, hoping that things would take a turn for the better. We planned a two-hour show with him doing his complete act and me the big illusions and the talking for both of us.

Without a doubt it was the most luxurious magical production that had ever been seen on any stage. The old maestro was still in his prime. I decided to start with the province of Buenos

Aires, which is the most heavily populated region of the republic, with dozens of fair-sized towns within easy reach of one another, including the provincial capital of La Plata. Talkies hadn't reached these towns yet and I was new in that part of the country and things looked hopeful. Leaving Bobby with an Argentine family named Resta in the Barrio Flores, we left for La Plata and opened there to heartwarming business.

One of the small towns we played was Pigue. A boy in short pants haunted the theatre there and made himself generally useful running errands and not missing a show. This little boy was the son of the mayor, though we didn't know that. This experience started a tremendous interest in magic which lasted all the boy's life. His name was Carlos Colombi and he became Argentina's amateur magician, winner of various prizes and awards including *The Sphinx* medal for his Phantom Flame trick. Rarely have I met a magician as dedicated as Carlos.

Okito was favorably impressed with the size of my show but decided that some of the props could stand improvement and he got to work. He made me a new ball, a duplicate of his, and also figured out a very fine comedy routine for the Vampire Escape illusion using for the finish a duck from the spectator's back a la Thurston. Once in a while he would take a sarcastic sideswipe at me when he inquired about the improved Duck Vanish and the "tableless" sawing I had talked so much about but never done anything about.

But when he saw the Find the Lady illusion he was flabbergasted.

"How did you figure dat out? Who told you?" he asked.

"Nobody," I said, "I just figured it was the only possible way it could be done. I still don't know how Amac does it, but I wouldn't change my system for his now."

From that day on our relationship underwent a subtle change. He seemed to have a new respect for my ideas and a new and totally unexpected (but very agreeable) camaraderie sprung up between us. For me it was very pleasing and most flattering and I felt that at last I was accepted as one of the boys and not just a snotty assistant. He was also very favorably impressed with most of my illusions and the cremation especially caught his fancy. He declared it the best he had ever seen. This was all milk and honey for me and I lapped it up, as I knew that he was a tough critic. The fact that I was his son meant nothing when it came to magic.

Moira woke up and belched.

We were in Chivilcoy and Okito woke me up one morning to tell me it was snowing. It never snows in this part of the country, much less in mid-summer. I looked out the window to find the plaza covered with snow. It was falling heavily, but the strange part was our room temperature was stifling. I dressed and went outside to have a look at this phenomenon.

We soon discovered that the "snow" was powdered pumice and covered the town; but where was it coming from? We soon found out on the radio. A volcano hundreds of miles away in the Andes had literally blown its top. The greater part of Argentina, Chile, Bolivia, Paraguay, and parts of Peru, Uruguay and southern Brazil were covered with a thick carpet of volcanic ash that extended over five hundred miles into the Atlantic Ocean.

It turned out to be a major disaster for the Argentine as the crops were ruined and the lush pampas grass destroyed, causing the death of cattle by the hundreds of thousands. The rivers and streams were choked, practically wrecking the economy of the country. The only people who benefitted from this disaster were the firms that sold cleaning powder like Old Dutch Cleanser. They stocked up huge warehouses of the pumice and over the years made a fortune from it.

Our ill-fated tour ended then and there and we returned to Buenos Aires. Gaulke was worried about the future and told me that Argentina was in for a bad time and advised me to get out as soon as possible.

There was only one way to go, north. So we decided to play Brazil on spec.

I sold all the furniture and sublet the flat. We arranged passage on a boat leaving for Rio Grande do Sul and from the upper deck took a long sad look at this generous, democratic country to which both Okito and I owed so much. Bobby's little pals from the Barrio Flores were at the dock to see us off. Bobby was a very quiet child who spoke very little so Hilda and I were surprised and broke into laughter when he climbed up the rail and in a high treble burst into a popular tango that goes, "Adios, muchachos, companeros de mi vida" (Good-bye companions of my life) for his little pals below. It really was adios as the little gaucho never saw Argentina again.

The Brazilian tour started badly. We opened in the Municiple Theatre of Rio Grande do Sul and from the start of the show I felt an undercurrent of hostility and sullenness in the audience. I didn't know that a bad political situation was brewing and the theatre was full of rowdies looking for trouble.

The blowup came when I inadvertently used the Spanish word "paquete," instead of the Brazilian term "pacote" which means packet. Paquete in Brazil is a four letter word that one never mentions to a lady. Therefore, when I asked a woman to examine the paquete of needles, for the needle trick, a loud murmur of indignation went up. As a border town they understood Spanish quite well, and as a foreigner, my mistake was pardonable; but they were on the lookout for trouble and they made a big production of it. I made the mistake of trying to apologize for my mistake but they wouldn't let me finish. I suddenly lost my temper and told 'em all to go to hell. That did it. We had a blasted riot on hand and we had to get out of town under police escort.

From there we went to a town with the unbelievable name of Pelotas (Balls). The local manager of the theatre advertised us as, "At Last and for the First Time—Okito and Fu Manchu in Pelotas," which had the double meaning of Okito and Fu Manchu naked. There was a lot of sniggering going on and I foolishly made a wisecrack about it to the mayor of the town, which did us no good. We left town quickly.

We then went to the state capital of Porto Alegre where we did fairly good business, but the same sulky brooding atmosphere was noticeable everywhere. After a couple of weeks we were happy to get out of it. Skipping all the small towns of Santa Catarina, we jumped to Sao Paulo where we opened at the beautiful Sant'Anna Theatre to excellent business. This was the first big stage we had worked and we went all out and gave them everything we had.

It didn't last long. A fortnight or so after our opening the civil war started. What we first thought to be a typical two-day South American revolution turned into a long, knock-down-and-drag-out war that lasted over three months.

The rich coffee state of Sao Paulo had made a secret pact with the southern states of Santa Catarina and Rio Grande do Sul to revolt against the federal government in Rio de Janeiro. Sao Paulo started hostilities, but the southern states betrayed Sao Paulo and joined the government forces, thereby hemming in the state of Sao Paulo from all sides.

We kept on at the Sant'Anna but only playing the weekends. This just about paid our expenses. After a month of this we closed down and then played every theatre and movie house in town until there were none left to work. Okito came down with a double hernia and had to have an operation. The money

I had brought with me was dwindling rapidly and there was no way of getting any money through from Buenos Aires until after the war.

Food was beginning to get short. Very little bread, no butter, eggs or meat. We were back (to Okito's disgust) on the old black bean and rice routine. To top it off, a feud started between Hilda and my father; and although I knew that Hilda was in the right, I tried to be neutral and was looked on as a traitor by both sides.

Okito was fed up and made me a present of South America and bought two tickets on the first boat leaving for France once the war was over.

Sao Paulo put up a valiant fight but it couldn't lick the whole country and after the battle of Campinas, the end was in sight. The day Sao Paulo surrendered the infuriated mob sacked the town, smashing shop windows and setting fire to public buildings. I was with Hilda in the tearoom on the fifth floor of Mappin and Webbs in the Praca de Sa and from the window saw the mindless mob sack the windows of the beautiful shops. The police tried to drive them off and the town was under constant gunfire. Some fool tried to hit a plane with a hand thrown grenade from the roof of the building and it fell into the plaza killing many people. Hilda and I made it back to the hotel without having our heads blown off and we didn't leave the building for three days.

But at last things calmed down and it was over. Okito took the first train down to Santos where he and Marie caught the boat for Europe.

I was left with my original company. We went to Rio where we opened in the El Dorado Theatre and, as Rio was in an optimistic mood over its victory, we did a booming business.

After Rio I had to make up my mind what to do. It would be suicide to go north as summer and the rainy season was starting. The Guianas were risky for show business and the first stop would be the Port of Spain in Trinidad. From there it was just a step to Venezuela and Colombia. However, there was no passenger boat service and we would have to go to New Orleans and make connections from there. To return to Argentina was obviously out, so what to do?

Spain. That was my logical step, and from there to Portugal and Africa. I booked passages on the S.S. Alcantara that touched the Port of Vigo on its way home.

On board was an English girl, Lily Nettleton, who had a bit of bad luck with a folding theatrical venture in Rio. She was on her way home to London. She was at loose ends, and as I needed another assistant to take Marie's place, I offered her a job. She accepted, little dreaming she would be part of the show for the next fifteen years.

The Great Raymond (inscribed to Arthur Felsman, Chicago magic dealer).

CHAPTER 30

From Rio's tropical heat we plunged into the bitter cold of the Spanish province of Galicia, where we arrived in Vigo in December 1932. I was completely unknown in Spain and my South American press books didn't mean much as the provinces looked to Madrid for their shows. We had a difficult time persuading the manager of a chain of theatres in Galicia to give us a trial date. Finally, after a lot of haggling and misgivings on the part of the management, they gave us three week days starting on Tuesday the 13th, which corresponds to our Friday the 13th. It is a bad day for the theatre in a country as superstitious as Spain. To top it off, my posters had a yellow background, which is also considered fatal in theatrical circles there.

We opened to half a house of gimlet-eyed Gallegos but I gave them everything I had. It was the best and fastest show I had ever given, and before the first half of the show was over, I knew I had them in the bag. The press reports the next day were excellent and the people began to come. Like old Finnegan of those long ago New York days, the management did a right-about change and offered to suspend the picture for the weekend and started chattering about a tour of the province and the adjoining province of Asturias. Show business!

Of course, we stayed on and did a S.R.O. business and later played the tour ending up in La Coruna. We could have gone on playing northern Spain but I knew that if I could get to Madrid or Barcelona and the show clicked I would get better percentages in these towns later. I sent my representative, Marchese, a Uruguayan, to Madrid and he returned a few days later with the bad news that Madrid was out of the question as the theatres were booked solid until the spring. The only thing

I could do was a forty minute act in the Circo Price (previously named the Circo Parrish where Okito's first wife had been killed) but I decided against that.

Marchese said that there was a slight chance of getting a theatre in Barcelona, and even if that failed we could play the small towns of Cataluna until one was free. I knew this was theatrical suicide but I agreed. We crossed picturesque Spain to that wonderful Mediterranean port.

Barcelona was a wide open city at that time and no one ever seemed to sleep. The principal avenues, the Ramblas and the Paseo de Gracia, were crowded with strollers until dawn.

The theatrical center was the famous Paralelo with its many theatres, cinemas, cabarets, music halls and dance restaurants, with people sitting in the crowded street cafes, each with its own orchestra, and many customers dancing in the streets. This was a far gayer city than Paris. I had a suspicion that theatres were at a premium and that we were destined for the small towns.

The last theatre at the very end of the Paralelo near the Conde de Asalto was the Apolo, where an asinine revue was playing to the poorest houses of any theatre on the line. Senor Lluch, the impresario of the Apolo, was negotiating with a top-notch Madrilenos revue, but as they were still doing a S.R.O business in Madrid, no date for their debut in Barcelona could be set.

Lluch examined my press books, photographs and the reports from Galicia and Asturais with an unenthusiastic eye, and finally told us noncommittally that he would let us know his decision in a few days. Actually he was stalling for time as he had his eye on another show drawing good houses in Valencia.

For ten days we hung around the theatre, waiting for news until the early hours of each morning. One freezing February night (rare in Barcelona), he called us into his office. The deal he offered us was deplorable. We could only have the theatre for a limited time. As he had neither dealings with nor, to be honest, faith in a magic show, he refused to be our impresario. We could rent the theatre for a nominal sum and he was to get twelve percent of the gross. We were to pay all expenses, advertising, orchestra, spotlight men, transportation and salaries. All he provided was the theatre, light, stagehands, electricians, ushers and the box office crew. Take it or leave it and no haggling.

I asked for an hour to decide. Marchese and I sat at a table in a small cafe alongside the theatre and brooded. With my usual lack of audacity and faith in myself, I was for chucking the whole lousy deal and heading for the small towns.

"Look, amigo," I said to Marchese, "we just don't have the money to swing the deal. How can I guarantee him the rent he wants? Where do we get the dough for the pre-debut advertising? And suppose the show flops? Then what? The poorhouse?"

"Have you forgotten the Solis deal in Montevideo with half the show you have now?"

"That was different," I replied. "I was loaded then."

"Well," he said. "Esta bien. You're the boss; but if I were you, I'd take a chance."

"*You'd* take a chance? It's easy for you to talk. What have you got to lose? This isn't easy-going America. This is hard, penny-pinching Europe and I don't want any truck with the sheriff."

"Wait a minute," he said brightly. "If I can get the newspapers to hold off payment until after the debut, will you take a chance?"

I thought it over. "All right," I said. "Have it your way, but stop by the cemetery and pick me out a nice plot."

After this cheerful conversation we went back to the theatre and signed what I thought was my death warrant. I don't know how he did it but Marchese got credit everywhere. Newspapers, printers, posters and goodness knows what else. I was startled one morning to see the town papered with posters that read "L'Mago Xines Fu Manxu." I started to run a temperature until someone told me it meant the "Chinese magician—Fu Manchu" in Catalan.

With a terrible case of cold feet up to my neck, we opened on a Thursday night to a full house and received a smattering of applause as I stepped from the book and took my opening bow. Yet within ten minutes I had the electric feeling that the audience was with me. I liked them and they liked me. They laughed themselves sick with my pseudo-Chinese patter, and all my gags were new for Barcelona. The show was an outstanding success with twelve curtain calls at the finish. I had to give a short speech of thanks. We were in.

Marchese gloated over the press reports the next day when they outdid themselves in praising the show. The most important newspaper in Barcelona, *La Vanguardia,* said it was the greatest and most novel illusion show ever seen in Spain and "Fu Manchu is an exceptional actor and comedian of the first rank."

The word spread and the Apolo became the main theatrical attraction of Barcelona. In view of the thousands of people who were turned away from the box office, we had the temerity to raise our prices, and they still came in droves.

The Opera, the Spanish Zarzuela Company, Mme. Nijinska and her ballet, Margarita Xirgu, Spain's first lady of the theatre, the revues and the famous Feijoo Circue all took second place to us in box office. Money poured in and we were doing two shows a day, three on Saturdays and Sundays, ending at two-thirty in the morning. Marchese went around with an "I-told-you-so" smirk and archly inquired when I was ready to open in Reus, (a small Catalan town), but I cheerfully took his ribbing as he had taught me to be such a blasted pessimist.

When our contract expired, Lluch refused to extend unless we made a new deal on a straight percentage basis. The shoe was on the other foot now and a hard-hearted Marchese worked the chastened Lluch down to thirty-two percent and the season continued. If Okito had seen this, he would have gone off his rocker. It was a pity such a thing hadn't happened in Buenos Aires when Gaulke was getting his cut. I wrote to Gaulke and told him all about it but, strangely, he never answered my letters.

The Barcelona Magic Club, known as the A.C.A.I. (Agrupacio Catalana d'Aficionats al Ilusionismo) showed up in force and I was elected honorary member of their society and made some very good friends. (One of the members of the club was Senor Areny-Plandolit, ex-President of the Republic of Andorra, a tiny country between Spain and France.)

In spite of our good business we had to close, as Lluch had signed with the Madrid revue and wanted the theatre. It was a better deal for Lluch as I was getting the lion's share of my contract with him.

So with regret we planned a big festival for our despidida, the closing night which in Spain is called "El Broche de Oro" (The Golden Brooch) and signifies a happy ending to a good season. It was a giant show with the personal appearances of the leading stars of Spanish show business and lasted until past three in the morning. It was a brilliant night which was completely spoiled by an ugly incident that happened at the very end.

In order to understand the cause of this incident I must explain that I spoke no Catalan, the difficult language of Cataluna, and that the proud Catalanos do not consider themselves to be Spanish. I had been taught a few words and I used them as a gag in the show. A duck would stroll onto the stage and interrupt me with its quacking. I would say to an assistant in Catalan, "Agaf' il anac" ("Grab that duck") which got a roar from the audience. During my farewell speech that night, while I was thanking them for the wonderful season, someone in the gallery shouted "Speak in Catalan." I told the audience, regretably, I only spoke two or three words, but would make it a point to learn as fast as I could for future seasons. To my surprise, the audience took up the cry and insisted that I talk Catalan. What I didn't know was that a local paper called *The Black Bee* had published an article stating I was born in Reus and my family name was Garcia y Garcia. The audience took my denials the wrong way and was convinced that I was a Catalan ashamed of my birth. Many of them stood up and walked out and the night was spoiled.

The next morning I visited the leading newspapers with my passport to prove I was a foreigner. I received columns of publicity but the populace still refused to believe me. Even today in Latin America many people think I am a Catalan, which is very flattering but also embarrassing.

From Barcelona we went to the Balearic Islands, then to Valencia and other towns in southeastern Spain until summer started. I decided to take a holiday for three months and return to Barcelona, open a shop to store the material and build some new illusions. That was my idea of a holiday but I had a severe case of "expanding fever" again.

Hilda had sense and took this opportunity to take a trip to New York with Bobby to visit her family.

The first illusion we built was a finish for the Mat Trick, in which a girl with huge butterfly wings was produced from the cloths that were pulled from the mat. This was to be my closing illusion and was based on the principle of the Dress Trunk illusion but used a cage for the ducks instead of the trunk. A very pretty switch.

Then we designed a special Doll House type of illusion for the presentation of the "gorilla" that vanished in the net. One nice detail was a concealed air pump to inflate the rubber chest of the gorilla so that he appeared to be twice the size of the tiny hut from which he appeared.

My constant changing of costumes during the show was a very strong feature. I wondered what would happen if I changed the stage settings for all the major illusions and sketches. This was the most radical idea I had ever had. I got in touch with the renowned scenic painters, Asensi-Morales and had them design eight sets of exotic scenery. The first colored sketch they showed me was a breathtaking Chinese palace interior in red, black and gold. I fell so much in love with it that I had a duplicate setting made for Okito and sent it to him. Some time later Marie told me that when he hung it for the first time, he sat for an hour in the empty theatre as tears ran down his cheeks.

Asensi-Morales painted me a wonderful Egyptian setting for Isis, the Scarab; a wild African scene for the gorilla illusion and specially tricked scenery for the Find the Lady illusion, which allowed me to use full light for the first time. The closing set was a huge Chinese dragon in a jewel cave. The monster's eyes moved and it breathed fire and smoke.

I threw out all my stock music and had a special score written for the show by the well-known composer, Maestro Padilla, who had written the popular song "Valencia."

I took on some new assistants, including a member of the Barcelona Magic Club, Miguel Carbonell, who was a skilled wood carver and carpenter. Along with Spreer I now had the makings of the team which in later years was to be of inestimable value to me when we really went on to big productions in Mexico.

All the new illusions and scenery were finished by the time Hilda returned from New York; but before rehearsals I decided to take a short trip to Ryswyk, a suburb of The Hague, where my father had bought a house at 35 Huis te Hoornkade. Spreer, Bobby and I left for Paris and from there to Holland.

The family reunion was a happy one. Dorothy had come over from Vienna for a few days between shows. She had made quite a name for herself in Viennese revues and musical comedies under the name of Dixie Poole and was the star attraction of the Femina Revue from 1930 to 1935. She was the first in Austria to sing popular American song hits in English, which she belted out like Ethel Merman.

This was the last time the family was ever to be together. The shadow of the Axis was already creeping forward, but we did not understand and would listen to clown Hitler rant on the radio and laugh.

One little incident that happened always gives me a nostalgic laugh. Pop had a running gag with Bobby, and every time he would give the child a sweet or a toy, he would say "Kiss me for dat," and like all these crazy little things it got to be a household word.

Okito's home was beautiful and richly furnished. He autocratically demanded that everything be clean and neat, and there would be a song and dance over a broken cup.

One afternoon my mother extended the dining room table to put in an extra leaf and my brother Donny, who was about fourteen at the time, sat on one end of the table and it suddenly gave way with a loud crack. Donny landed on the floor with half the table on top of him. There was an ominous silence as the old man began to get white patches on the sides of his nose. He was just on the point of going into hysterics when Bobby said in a loud voice, "Kiss me for that."

We were speechless for a moment, then everyone, including the old man, burst out laughing. Okito picked up Bobby and did a crazy dance with him, laughing his head off. This silly little story always gives me a kick and knot in the throat when I think of it, because a few years later little Donald would be a prisoner in a German concentration camp condemned to be shot, Dorothy a refugee in Switzerland, Okito's sister Eva and his brothers Neddy and Simon frozen to death in a filthy freight car on their way to deportation to Poland, and Okito himself a ruined man, who was to lose his home, his life savings and his show.

My mother cried when we had to go and begged me to leave Bobby with her, but I knew Hilda wouldn't want that. I promised to come back again soon and left for Paris where I was joined by Spreer, who had visited his father in Danzig. The next day we were in Barcelona and rarin' to go. Marchese had gone back to Uruguay and my new manager, Paco Diaz, an Andalucian from Malaga, had signed a contract for me to open in Madrid at the Zarzuela Theatre, one of the best houses in Madrid.

Yet cautious "Cold-Foot Dave" insisted on breaking in the new show in a small Catalan town called Figueras. This paid off as the opening night was very disjointed. After three days I straightened everything out and we were ready to open in Madrid.

CHAPTER 31

Madrid! A cabalistic word in the world of the theatre. Madrid was renowned for the most exacting audiences in all of Europe and Latin America. It stood in a class by itself: the Madrilenos took their theatre seriously and stood for no nonsense. There were no half measures; it was either first class or nothing. An artiste who made the grade in the Madrid of those days was consecrated for all of Spain and the Americas. There is one story of a company who produced a new play at the Teatro Pavon. After the first act the public left the theatre en masse, and when the curtain went up on the second act, the astonished cast found not a soul in the house.

The Zarzuela was considered one of the leading theatres of Madrid and it was very difficult to obtain. My manager, Paco, had discovered through the theatrical grapevine that the impresario, Paco Torres, had lost a lot of money the previous season and was on the point of bankruptcy, unable to finance the big production he had in mind for the coming season. In spite of his bad situation he was completely cold to the idea of having a magician in the theatre for the first time. Our Barcelona success did not impress him at all. He called it a fluke. The proper place for a magician was in the Circo Price.

Paco finally wore him down and with great misgivings he signed a contract, but with a clause that specifically stated that if the show was not up to certain standards, he had the right to cancel us without notice. He was to be the sole judge. With this sword hanging over my head I opened in Madrid, knowing that if I made good the doors of all Spain, Western Europe and North Africa were open to me.

This time I had confidence in the show and knew that things *had* to go right but, just the same, I was as nervous as a rat before curtain time and behaved as if I had never been on a stage in my life. Paco did nothing to help when he came rushing backstage with sparkling eyes to inform me that the house was sold out and included the tough press, artistes, and some of Spain's greatest authors and playwrights. This made me all the more nervous and I rudely sent him to hell. I often wonder what magnetic power the stage has to make one go through these awful moments? It's a masochistic business at best.

As usual, the moment I stepped out of the book my nerves miraculously vanished and again I had that éclat that I felt in Barcelona; that surge of inward rejoicing when you know that your audience is with you. It's hard to describe, but a bond of sympathy arises between the audience and the actor. The first act went over smoothly and the curtain descended on a wave of applause.

There was only a ten minute interval between acts, and I needed every minute of it to prepare the second part and solve all the little problems that crop up on an opening night. I was therefore rather annoyed when my dressing room was overrun with reporters and their interminable questions. I wished that they had waited until after the show when I could spare them all the time they wanted. I prayed to heaven that they'd get out, as a very long interval cools off an audience considerably. I didn't know that in Madrid it was considered a mark of honor for the press to interview an artiste between acts. A first night audience understood this and went out for coffee while the interval sometimes stretched to twenty or more minutes. Nobody had told me this, perhaps because they never dreamed it would happen to me, and the reporters must have thought me a bit of an oaf with my nervous off-hand replies. Finally they left, with the exception of one elderly man who raved on and on and patted my cheek with great enthusiasm until, to my great relief, this kindly old gentleman also left. Not until after the show did I discover that this man was Spain's greatest dramaturgist, Don Jacinto Benavente.

The second act went over just as well as the first, and they even applauded the stage settings—a custom in Madrid. At the final curtain I received an ovation and vainglorious as it is to say it, I must confess that it was a memorable night and it's still talked about in Spain and in theatrical circles all over Latin America.

The delighted impresario, Paco Torres, gave me a rib-cracking Spanish abrazo and insisted on taking me to the Cafe Castilla in the Plaza del Rey, where the critics and intellectuals gathered until the early hours of the morning. As I walked into the cafe I was greeted with smiles and bows from all the tables. The word had spread, and I drank it in with joy in my heart.

I was invited to the table of the owner and director of the morning paper, *A.B.C.* whose caricaturist, Sirio, a slender black-haired Cuban with an ulcer, drew the caricature of me with the rabbit and the duck which later became my trademark. Sirio and I became good friends. He initiated me into the mysteries of Madrileno life.

All the Madrid newspapers reviewed the show with raves, and in his article Don Jacinoto wrote, in part, "Fu Manchu's humour is so subtle that many a local playwright could use his jokes as a curtain for a second act."

I was invited to parties of intellectuals and pseudo-intellectuals who discovered hidden meanings and art in things that I had always thought to be simple. They saw symbolism in the floating ball and in my handshadows. One tall thin girl saw me as a man who dominated space and wanted me to caress her body as I caressed the golden sphere. At these meetings I desperately tried to think of something clever to say but rarely thought of anything, and my unusual silence was taken for profundity.

I would like to say that all this adulation had no effect on me, but the truth is, like all inbred hams, I ate it up and began to act like a longhair. Later, when I came down to earth, I realized that all I had was a first-class magical production. It was unrealistic to compare it to the really great stage plays and other, higher art forms, but as I was the Lion of Madrid for the moment, I was flattered and cocky. I really enjoyed it because, during this brief moment of glory, the world was mine and its women seemed to be thrown in as part of the gift.

During the show one night I was doing my silk routine and happened to glance at the lower front box and nearly dropped my *fake* when I saw the head and shoulders of a beautiful woman apparently floating in the air. This was an illusion worthy of my show. This pale, raven-haired beauty with her classical Spanish features, wore a low-cut black velvet evening gown which faded into the dark of the box, giving the illusion of a disembodied head. She wore pearls in her ears and one huge single pearl hung on her bosom. She was alone in the box and I couldn't take my eyes off her. When the audience noticed it, I had to dissimulate and steal a glance only now and then. After the final curtain, when the house lights came up, I looked at the box and she was gone.

The next evening she was there again and once more I stole those sidelong glances. This went on for a few nights until she became an obsession. I would spy through the peep hole in the house curtain before the show. I never saw her come in or leave the box, but when I stepped out of the book, there she was.

One night, after the show, I was removing my grease paint and brooding on "la dama misteriosa" when the doorman brought me a note. It read, "Te espero" ("I await thee"). It was not signed but I knew whom it was from. I dressed rapidly and from the stage door that led to the narrow side street, I saw a parked car. I walked over and saw a uniformed chauffeur who looked straight ahead without a glance at me. The rear door of the car opened and I got in. The car started without an order.

I started to speak to this dream woman but she placed her fingertips to my lips and I understood I was to keep silent. We drove for quite some time and finally stopped outside one of those old Moorish portals on the outskirts of Madrid. Through a small door in the portal we crossed a patio and went up a lot of winding dark stairs to a tastefully furnished boudoir with only a single reddish light burning.

Again I started to speak and once more she pressed my lips for silence. Not a single word was spoken. It was uncanny. When I tore myself away, I found the chauffeur waiting to drive me to the Cafe Castilla where I was the object of many knowing looks and raised eyebrows. I still didn't speak and this caused great speculation. The next evening, when I stepped from the book, I had a bright smile ready, but my dream woman wasn't there and I never saw her again.

I asked Paco Torres, in confidence, who she was and he replied, "It is better for all concerned that you do not mention this matter to anyone. Just think of it as a cherished memory and do not try to find out who she is. De acuerdo?" How discreet they were in Madrid!

After the Madrid season all Spain was open to me. We could pick and choose our dates. Paco was flooded with offers from every corner of the peninsula and as far away as Mexico, even from Buenos Aires.

From Madrid we went to Sevilla where we opened at the Teatro Cervantes. Business there was just as good as in Madrid. One morning, at about two o'clock, I was awakened by a hammering on my door. When I opened it, in marched my manager,

Paco Diaz, accompanied by five men. Introductions were mumbled but I didn't catch a single name. Two of these men, poker-faced individuals, sat down without saying a word. Another young Andalucian produced a guitar and started to play, while the fourth young man, a handsome lad, sang flamenco.

Flamenco is something that takes quite a lot of understanding, especially to a foreigner who has never heard it before. It is an acquired taste that grows on one. During this recital the fifth man, a short, sharp-featured person, would break into loud "olés" and clap his hands, accompanied by the two poker-faced men and Paco.

After half an hour of this the sharp-featured man entertained with songs from the old Zarzuelas in a beautiful tenor, after which they insisted I get dressed and took me to a tasca in old Sevilla. There we feasted on boquerones and Mansanilla (sherry) until five o'clock in the morning. We broke up with vows of eternal friendship. I didn't know who they were but they were great guys. I was beginning to love this country.

Months later in Madrid some of the press boys asked me if it was true what happened in Sevilla.

"We had a great season," I replied.

"Yes, we know that. But is it true that the Nino Marchena and Marcos Redondo sang for you privately in your hotel room?"

"Some people sang," I said, "but I don't know who they were."

This was a sacrilege and they stared at me speechless.

That bloody fool of a Paco hadn't explained to me that El Nino Marchena was the most famous flamenco singer in Spain. He and the renowned Marcos Redondo were the idols of the Spanish public and, to top it off, the two poker-faced guys were two of the most famous matadores in the world.

This was a good story, indeed, and widely circulated. I was instantly christened "El Bruto Ingles." Both Nino Marchena and Marcos Redondo took it as a great joke.

From Sevilla we went to Malaga, Granada and other ports in Andalucia. When we arrived in Gibraltar from La Linea, my company merrily stepped over the border but I was refused admittance! I raised hell and loftily told the officer in charge that I was a British subject.

"Exactly," said the official, "that's why you can't come in. Gibraltar is a British Crown Colony. In an emergency all these other people can be compelled to leave. But once *you* cross the line, there is no possible way to get you out. Therefore, you don't come in.''

I explained that I was to open the next day in the Theatre Royal and when my week was up I would cheerfully leave. I offered to sign an affidavit to this effect.

''An affidavit would mean nothing if you decided to stay. But there is a way. It's a question of good faith. If you give me your word of honor that you will leave the day after your engagement, you can enter Gib.''

''You have it,'' I said, ''but supposing I broke my word. Then what?''

''It's been tried before and it doesn't work. We couldn't turn you out, but you'd be sent to Coventry. Not a soul would speak to you and no shop would serve you. Rather disheartening, what?''

So we opened and had a fine week on the Rock which is a charming place. We had to cut out the flashes and fire effects from the show as the British fire laws were very strict. For the first time in years I couldn't smoke in the theatre. The Rock is a free port so I took advantage of thc chcap prices to buy some excellent English lighting equipment and bulbs, some fine Chinese costumes and a portable typewriter. The boys on the show had a great time buying Scotch and tobacco at a third of the price charged in Spain. From the Rock we took the short trip to the African coast.

CHAPTER 32

Our first stop was in Ceuta, Spanish Morocco. As we had two days free before the opening I toured the bazaars and market places with my 16mm movie camera, looking for street magicians. I took shots of a few snake swallowers and one street magician who did a skillful cup and ball routine, Indian style, sitting on the ground and using the small wooden cups with knobs to grasp between the middle fingers. Although this man was very adept, he was, as usual, considered a beggar. For the first time I saw race hatred at close range. All the Jewish houses had a green Star of David on the door and the Arabs' doors were marked with a red crescent. I saw many a cold-eyed Arab spit violently on a door having a star. One could feel the murderous hatred they had for the Jews in the bazaars, where they watched them like hawks, just waiting for an excuse to start something. In those days there was nowhere for Jews to go and it was sad to see how they took all this humiliation.

I had been given a letter of introduction to the Commander of the 3rd Spanish Infantry in Ceuta, Commander Gonzalo Ramajos Ortigosa. He received me very cordially and invited me on a trip into the wild Riffien country where the revolutionist Abd-El-Krim had led the Spanish army on a wild chase a short time before. The Riffiens were a sullen lot and cold hard stares followed us wherever we went. It was here that I had, for the first time, a bowl of Cous-Cous and I hope to god I never have it again. It's a mixture of lamb and rice which I had a hard time swallowing. It was so unbelievably gooey it stuck in my throat. We called it Arabian haggis.

From Ceuta we went to Tetuan where I met an amateur magician, Senor Luis Llanso, owner of the largest cork plantations in those parts. We spent quite some time together. He taught me to drive a car and we nearly came to grief when I smacked into a donkey on a mountain road on the way to Tangiers.

One morning Lieutenant Colonel Lopez-Bravo of the Spanish-Moroccan Army called at my hotel and told me that a lower box had been reserved that evening for the Sultan's nephew, the Caliph Abd-Essalam Mohammed El-Hach. He begged me under no circumstances to approach the royal box, nor address myself to His Highness. That understood, he bowed, and left.

All went well until the sketch of the Death God of Tibet in which Lily, my English assistant, had to bow down on her bent knees to the shadow appearing in the cabinet. In order not to obstruct the audience's view, she always made this reverence a little to one side. As bad luck would have it, His Highness was presented with a view of a plump British backside.

I heard a murmur from the audience and, glancing at Lily, understood the situation in a flash. I whispered to her to stand up and bow from the waist, but because of the music, she couldn't make out what I was saying. She made things worse by going into a sort of undulation that caused her fanny to wave from side to side.

His Highness didn't bat an eyelash and the rest of the sheiks sat like mummies; but from the opposite box the military glowered at us with murderous glances. At the end of the show the Caliph and his party abruptly left the box with a polite bow to the Spanish officials.

Lopez-Bravo burst into my dressing room with a face like a thundercloud. "Sanatisima Madre de Dios," he wailed in anguish. "How in the devil could you let a thing like that happen? The political situation there is so delicate that this can cause trouble. They may even think it done on purpose to insult him publicly."

"I'm frightfully sorry," I said. "But you know it wasn't intentional. Can't you talk with him and explain?"

"Explain what? You don't know these people. It takes weeks to get an audience with a man like that." The distracted officer left, saying he would do what he could. The next morning he was back at my hotel.

"I had a talk with a close friend of the Caliph," he said gloomily, "and His Highness wishes to see you at three this afternoon. I'll call for you."

We arrived in an army car at the Mezquita Grande, the Caliph's palace at three o'clock on the dot. We were ushered into

a large room, which like all Arab dwellings, was symmetrical—
one half of the room like a mirror reflection of the other half.

On a large carpet in the exact center of the room was a low
table with low stools and cushions around it. On the table were
cakes, a kipi pipe or two, and the usual thick Arabian coffee,
the sight of which cheered Lopez-Bravo up a bit.

The Caliph was sitting on a low divan with two strapping
Moroccans standing behind him while another man squatted
at his side.

Lopez-Bravo introduced me as the squatting man interpreted.
The Caliph bowed and offered us the cakes and coffee. Lopez-
Bravo heaved a sigh of relief as breaking the bread is an Arabic
sign of friendship.

I explained that no suggestion of disrespect to His Highness
had been intended. True, it was an unpardonable faux pas and
my only excuse was that Lily had unthinkingly played her role
as she always did. If anyone was to blame it was me and I begged
his indulgence.

The explanation satisfied him and he graciously bowed and,
through the interpreter, he asked me a lot of questions about
magic and the stage in general. We had a very pleasant half
hour and he laughed heartily when I told the story of Robert-
Houdin with the Light and Heavy Chest in Algiers.

When he arose we knew the visit was over, but just as we
were about to go, he said he would like to see me alone for a
moment, then suddenly lifted his burnoose to display golf pants
and gaudy Scotch socks. He watched for my surprise and burst
into laughter.

"My dear chap," he said in perfect Oxford English, "you
must forgive all the protocol, but I am a martyr to convention
and just between you and me, it gets frightfully tiresome at times.
I was educated in England and spent many happy years there.
I thought your show was wonderful and I would greatly
appreciate it if you would teach me a small trick or two."

With the air of a magician he produced a deck of cards from
his pocket and I showed him a few good non-manipulative card
tricks. At one point I heard giggling somewhere but, looking
around, saw no one. He smiled and pointed up to some open
lattice work, "They're spying?" he said.

"Who's spying?" I asked with visions of Eric Ambler
characters in the offing.

"The women," he replied. "What you would call my harem."

Lucky stiff, I thought.

We were together almost an hour while Lopez-Bravo suffered in the other room and no doubt wondered what in hell was going on. He seemed relieved when he saw me return safe and sound. As we left His Highness made me a present of a kipi pipe and a beautiful hand-hammered brass tray which I have used in my show ever since.

On my last day in Tetuan the Sultan visited the city and in the parade he sat in an open carriage with a tremendous umbrella over him. Alongside the carriage, on a beautiful white horse, rode the Caliph looking straight ahead. He must have spotted me on the balcony outside my hotel room, for as he passed by, he gave me a solemn poker-faced wink.

Our North African tour ended in Tangiers. On my return to the Spanish mainland at Cadiz I bought a Willys Knight and toured the Extremadura on my way to Portugal. Paco had booked the Coliseo de Recreos in Lisbon, the same theatre where I had started out with Raymond six years before.

At the border town of Jerez de la Frontera are the famous Domecq distilleries. The attendance in the local theatre for the first two days was rather weak, but the house manager, with a mysterious smile, said not to worry as the house would be sold out for Friday night. Why Friday, of all days?

I soon found out. On Friday afternoon one of the Domecq sons called for us and took the entire company for a tour of the distilleries. He plied us with samples of all their products, ending up in a cellar which held ancient vats of cognac from Napoleonic times. Here we all had a dram of cognac and, loaded with bottles of Fundador, we returned to the theatre in a mellow mood for the show.

The house was packed that night as this was what they were waiting for. It was a standard gag in the town and it happened to every company that played there. It didn't take much to make me drunk and I was plenty high. It was the craziest show we ever gave—climaxed by the Sacred Beetle Isis flying around the glass backwards! Then, at the finish, a gay and carefree Spreer stood up from behind the illusion and waved the magnet in his hand, saying, "What! No applause for me?" Curtain!

Lisbon brought back memories. A cycle had been completed. I hadn't heard anything about Raymond or Li-Ho-Chang for years and I wondered where they were.

On the vast stage of the Coliseo my whole setup looked like a doll house outfit. The proscenium alone was bigger than most stages and the first row was a long way from the house curtain.

The Coliseo had the largest seating capacity of any theatre in Europe, yet the acoustics were good. In those days we had no mikes and used pure lung power.

Oversized theatres are not good for magic shows which are essentially intimate performances; and, too, half a house, which would be the equivalent of a full house in any other theatre, seemed empty in this giant place. It was psychologically bad for business and with some misgivings I opened.

The night of our debut the usual noise of a restless audience was absent and I tried to see into the hall through the spy hole in the house curtain, but it had none. Well, I thought, the flop had to come some day, but it's a pity it had to happen in a big capital like Lisbon.

The third bell rang and the overture started. When I stepped out of the book I got the shock of my life. The house was packed to the gallery, with people standing up in the back. What fooled me was the iron curtain which had cut off all sight and sound of the hall from the stage and which was lifted during the overture.

With the exception of the night of the packing box escape in Chile, I had never worked to such a crowd before. I expected trouble from the last rows and gallery, which surely couldn't hear or clearly see what was going on; but I need not have worried as everything went fine. In fact the huge apron off the stage helped me to improve the show.

During the floating ball I was so far away from the first row that, at one point of the trick, I walked down as near to the footlights as the thread would allow. The effect was stunning as I left the stage proper and was surrounded in front and both sides by spectators. This was impulsive enough, but to top it, Hilda, a tiny woman, who brought on the box for the finale of the ball sinking into it, walked diagonally forward with the thread just brushing over the top of her head, thereby eliminating any suspicion of a thread. The trick received a roar of applause and was the topic of the town, with everybody swearing it was done by magnetism or compressed air or other crazy ideas. I didn't enlighten them and said yes to everybody. That stopped them from thinking any further.

From that day on I kept the move of bringing the ball down to the footlights. In some theatres I even floated it over the run down and over the heads of the people close to the aisle in the first rows.

We had a record-breaking month in Lisbon. Both Goldin and

Chefalo, who were booked in rival theatres, postponed their engagements for a later date. This was a wise move. If they had got there first, I would have done the same. Nevertheless, it was a pleasant feeling to know that I had stopped two of the big boys in their tracks. Who could have imagined six years before that I would be playing opposition to Goldin and Chefalo?

I was contracted for a return engagement to Madrid but Goldin beat me and opened in the Zarzuela, which was poor timing for him. As a crafty old-timer he should have known that at least a year has to go by before another magician can make a killing. In later years I was to have this same experience with Chefalo, Chang, Dante and Kalanag.

A distressing experience happened one night on the stage of the Coliseo. As usual, during the substitution trunk illusion, I invited a committee on stage. One of them acted very strangely and I saw at once that something was wrong with him mentally. I told Spreer in a whisper to keep an eye on him. I asked one of the committee for the loan of his jacket, but before the person could remove it, the nervous character yanked his own jacket off and handed it to me. I had no alternative but to use it.

All went well until the moment came for the change. I told the committee to look at their watches and count two seconds. At the count of "one" the nervous spectator jumped to his feet and came toward me. As I had to go on with the trick, I shouted "two" and rapidly closed the curtains of the tent in his face— and Spreer stepped out.

I dived through the trap and locked myself in. Even from the inside of the trunk I could hear shouts and blows from the outside. I banged on the side of the trunk with the handcuffs as a signal to open but nobody paid any attention. I could hear confused sounds and was beginning to get worried as I didn't have too much air in the trunk. Finally I heard the locks being opened and the lid was flipped up. The tapes on the sack were cut and when I was released, the first thing I saw was a pale and frightened Hilda and Spreer with a cut on his face. When I turned my back to the audience to display my handcuffed wrists, I saw the tent torn to ribbons and the framework bent out of shape. The committee was gone, including the nervous owner of the jacket. As I had no time to ask questions, I got on with the show and later got the full story.

The nervous man had only been released from a mental institution the previous day and his mother thought it would be nice for him to see a show. When I asked for a committee he had rushed up onto the stage before she could stop him. It seems that the shock of seeing me vanish before his eyes and Spreer appear in my place, was too much for him. His violent reaction consisted of tearing the tent apart looking for me. It took four stagehands to overpower him and he was taken out through the stage door. He managed to break free and attacked two policemen who had come running up. In a fearful fight, he had been shot dead. The newspapers made a lot of it, and one paper tastelessly said that my trunk trick was so sensational that it drove people mad, but this was all grist for the box office.

After Lisbon, we played Oporto and Coimbra and returned to the Coliseo for another two week "farewell" season, then returned to Spain through Asturias, the Basque provinces and Castilla la Vieja. From there we went to the Teatro Chueco in Madrid.

My first night in Madrid I went to see the Goldin show at the Zarzuela. There is no doubt that he was a sensational illusionist and his show included a lot of new illusions and tricks, including the Canary in the Lightbulb, the Indian Rope trick, and the appearance of a girl in a motorcycle sidecar, which was then driven at top speed up a long ramp and vanished into thin air. He also did Living Shadows, which were handshadows that turned into living animals; the circular buzz saw for Sawing a Woman in Two; the Vanishing Arab who was tied to the mouth of a cannon and blasted into nothing; Walking Through a Plate Glass Mirror; the Vanishing Piano and Player and Walking Away From Your Shadow.

All in all it was a very good show and, with the exception of the Indian Rope Trick and the Arab and Cannon, which were stinkers, it was original and well paced. I knew I had been lucky to have played Madrid first.

The one real advantage I had over my competitors was that I could speak the language of the country. In a full evening's show this makes an enormous difference. Goldin carried far more sensational illusions than I did, and the overall effect was overpowering, but after an hour or so it reached the saturation point and became boring. In fact, many people got up and left the theatre before the show was over. Due to the lack of patter the show had no balance, and although it was a magical education for a magician, it was too much for the average spectator. Goldin had been at his best with his one hour vaudeville act.

Goldin's original idea for a Circular Saw Illusion was brilliant but was marred by the crudely made and over-thick table the girl rested on. In his advertising material Goldin had the table carefully blocked out and the result was miraculous, but when one saw the actual apparatus on the stage it was a letdown.

This constant and universal use of the levitation table as a means to hide portions of a person had been the cause of the differences between Okito and me. Goldin had spent much time and money on this effect and it had given him lots of headaches. He presented it for the first time in the Palais d'ete in Brussels in October of 1930. In this primitive model the giant circular saw was attached directly to the electric motor, not on a long axle like the model he presented in Madrid. On his opening night the saw broke away from the motor and spun down onto the stage where it hit the footlights and bounced over the heads of the musicians and hit a spectator on the shoulder injuring him badly. There was an unholy row in the theatre and Goldin was taken to jail where he spent three days. He was finally released after paying damages and costs.

After the show I visited him in his dressing room and found a tired and depressed man sitting dejectedly in an armchair. We had a desultory conversation and he congratulated me on my success in this same theatre and found it hard to believe that the "Bamberg Kid" had done it. "Who would haf beliefed it," he said. I told him that I thought his show was extraordinary and that his big illusions were far more sensational than mine—but the main reason for his poor season in Madrid was the infallible law of the big illusion show: he who gets there first is the kingpin. Another maxim of the theatre is that two magicians working at the same time cancel each other out. At any given place, any magician is the "world's greatest" at that moment, yet it takes an audience a year or so to forget and accept another, no matter how good he may be.

Most impresarios know that and refuse to engage a magic show soon after the termination of a previously successful magic show. In an interview published in *Heraldo de Madrid* on June 12, 1934, Paco Torres, the impresario of the Zarzuela, stated that his losses the previous season had been fabulous. The only show that had made money was the Fu Manchu show. He went on to say, "With Fu Manchu I made up a lot of my losses as his was the only show to make any profit last year. Later I booked Goldin, and lost heavily as I feared I would."

"Why did you book him then?"

"I thought I could do another Fu Manchu season, but the public was satiated with magic."

But the word had spread that Spain was a big field for magic and other full evening shows came in for a share. Apart from Goldin, the biggest of these shows was a Greek magician, Anastasius Kasfikis (actually a Russian with a Greek passport), whose main attraction was the circular saw illusion copied from Goldin. Knowing it was useless to play Madrid for the moment, he tried to cut off Goldin in as many towns in the Extremadura as he could.

My season at the Chueca Theatre in Madrid was short and the money was nothing to be compared with the first season, so we decided to go to Cordoba. Because of all the new opposition it was very hush-hush, like a bloody cloak-and-dagger mystery. In fact, it was so top secret that the manager of the rival theatre in Cordoba knew nothing of our coming and booked Goldin for the same week! Somehow Kasfikis got wind of the deal and, skipping Cordoba, he booked Salamanca where I was booked for the week after.

In his hurry to get to Salamanca he loaded his truck badly and on the Valladolid Highway, near Tordesillas, the crates began to topple. The driver of the truck extended his arms to protect his head, thereby losing control of the truck which left the road and hit a mound of sand. Kasfikis, who was sitting alongside him, received the full weight of the buzzsaw crate on his head, killing him instantly. He was the only one hurt in this accident and his wife, who escaped without a scratch, took over the show and worked it under the name of "Cleopatra, The Goddess of the Nile."

Goldin and I split the theatre-going public of Cordoba and both did poorly. A good show town was wasted for no good reason.

From there Goldin went south and I went north and we never played opposition again.

The political situation in Spain was becoming restless, and during our week in Oviedo, shots were fired which did our business no good. These, I believe, were the first shots of the Civil War which was to start much later.

Theatre is a delicate business and anything out of the ordinary upsets it, whether it be a political situation or too many magicians. I don't know why, but business slacked off, and although I was not actually losing, I was close to it. So from San Sebastian I decided to jump to Barcelona, breaking the journey in Zaragoza where an ugly incident made me decide to leave Europe and accept an offer from a Mexican impresario.

We arrived in Zaragoza the day before we were to open at El Teatro Circo and that night I went to see the French Ballet for its last performance. After the first act there was an over long interval and the few spectators were beginning to fuss. I went backstage to see what had happened.

There was a fearful argument going on between the dancers and the impresario, the gist of which was the ballet hadn't been paid and they refused to allow the curtain to go up until they had their money. The tough goons of the Guardia Civil with their black lacquered hats were called in and they ordered the ballet to start at once. They refused and all at once the Guardia Civil men went into action and beat the male dancers into submission with their rubber truncheons, leaving several on the floor badly bloodied up. The ballet gave in and finished the show somehow. Then they were taken to jail where they spent the next few days.

It seemed like the theatre was jinxed. We opened the next day to the worst business we had in all of Spain. I was heartily glad to get out of town and back to Barcelona where we opened in the old Apolo again. With the new illusions and scenery we did a short but good season, followed by a popular-priced season in the Novedades Theatre which was later destroyed in the Civil War.

One evening I had a visit from a good friend whom I had met in Madrid, Jesus Marroquin, captain of the S.S. Habana and formerly commander of the royal yacht of Alfonso XIII. Captain Marroquin was a rabid monarchist and in touch with the ex-King, who was in exile. Don Jesus told me in confidence that something tremendous was brewing and advised me to get out of Spain as soon as I could. I told him of my Mexican offer and he said to grab it; he would be happy to take me on his next trip to Veracruz, his last port of call. The S.S. Habana was in drydock in Bilbao but was scheduled to sail in two weeks time. Paco cabled Mexico and closed the deal.

Moira gave a slight smile.

I had all my money in pesetas in a bank in Barcelona and one Saturday morning I was on my way to the bank, which closed at noon, to change this money into American dollars. In the Plaza Cataluna a Chilean friend of mine, Jose Casajuana Ochoa, owner of the Chile cinema in Valparaiso, was sitting at a sidewalk table of the Cafe Leon de Oro and invited me for coffee. I told him I was in a hurry but he insisted, so I sat down. While we were talking I felt a tap on my shoulder and looked up to see another South American friend, Senor Clemente Lococo. He had been my impresario at the Astral Theatre in Buenos Aires when I had played there with Josephine Baker.

Senor Lococo sat down with us and told me he was building the biggest cinema in Latin America, a huge opera on the Calle Corrientes. Time was getting short and I had to get to the bank. I was on the point of getting up and making my excuses when Lococo said, "You remember Walter Gaulke, no?"

"How could I ever forget him?" I replied with a smile.

"Have you heard from him lately?"

"No," I said, "he didn't answer any of my letters and I haven't written for some time."

"I've got some bad news for you," he said slowly. "Gaulke's dead."

I was too stunned to say anything.

"That's only part of the story," he went on. "He never answered your letters because he was in jail and when he got out he died broke."

"Valgame Dios!" I cried. "I knew nothing of this. What happened?"

"Gaulke trusted people too much and he made the mistake of signing a blank check which was filled in for an amount he didn't have and, being a stubborn man, he refused to ask his friends for aid and was jailed. Pleurisy set in from his damp cell and shortly after his release he died. A collection was taken up in the American colony to bury him but his grave doesn't even have a tombstone. The whole business was sordid and unjust as he was a very wonderful person."

I sat at the table for a considerable time, bitterly reproaching myself for not having kept in closer touch with my benefactor. I had been in a position to be of considerable help to him if I had known of his trouble, but now it was too late. When I finally looked at my watch, the bank had been closed for a long time, but to hell with it. I'd go on Monday.

I was still in a rotten mood when I arrived at the bank on Monday morning, but my blues turned to black when I learned to my dismay that there was no quotation for dollars. President Roosevelt had declared a moratorium and the U.S. banks were closed. This was inconceivable. Was this mighty nation bankrupt? Impossible! We had read of the depression but it was so far away we never imagined that things could be so bad. I thought for the moment of buying English pounds or Swiss francs but I had a few days before the boat sailed and I decided to wait before I did anything.

It was lucky for me that I waited because in a few days came the news that the dollar had been devaluated as America went off the gold standard. I got nearly forty percent more for my pesetas and saved the loss of thousands of dollars—all because I had been delayed in the Cafe Leon de Oro on Saturday morning.

On this note we said good-bye to that wonderful country Spain and from the port of Bilbao we sailed for Mexico.

Teatro Esperanza Iris, whose manager, Señor Molina, mysteriously disappeared. The Iris (now Teatro de la Ciudad) was one of the first theatres that David Bamberg played in Mexico City (1934), and it was at the Iris in 1953 that he gave his last Mexico City performance.

CHAPTER 33

Captain Marroquin went out of his way to make things pleasant for us. He insisted on my paying for third-class passages and charged me nothing for the baggage. The moment we sailed he moved the entire company into first class and reserved for Hilda and me a deluxe suite with a private deck.

Don Jesus was a tall, thin, wiry man with sharp features and short cropped iron gray hair and ice blue eyes. He looked far more like an English sea captain than a Spaniard. Every evening, before dinner, he would invite me to his cabin and pull aside a small curtain to expose an autographed photo of King Alfonso XIII and from a small barrel would pour two glasses of excellent cognac and proceed to drink a toast to his Majesty's health.

On board was also La Banda del Empastre, a Spanish orchestra on its way to Mexico to liven up the bull ring. We had fiestas that sometimes started at the crack of dawn! It was the happiest sea voyage I had ever had in my life and we were sorry when it ended.

Marroquin used his influence in Veracruz with the Mexican customs who were plenty tough and with the port authorities, so we were given every consideration. When I said good-bye to Don Jesus I gave him a silver Mexican charro sombrero and a sarape de Saltilla. He, in turn, made me a present of my first electric razor.

I had no news of him during the Spanish Civil War, but when I returned to Spain in 1955 I was told that he had been in the thick of things and been blown to pieces by a hand grenade. Many friends of mine died violently in those unhappy years.

I had been warned beforehand by Marroquin that I would have to declare how much money I was bringing into the country; but I figured it was nobody's business how much money I had, especially as I didn't expect to spend it there. I bought a box of chocolates in the barber shop and concealed the high denomination bills in sterling and dollars under the usual cardboard double bottom that most chocolate boxes have. Young Bobby marched off the boat with this prize packet under his arm and Hilda kept a sharp eye on him. It was my intention to rent a safe deposit box in a bank in Mexico City and only use this money for an emergency.

Our impresario, Senor Rafael Torres-Belena, proved to be Spanish and told me that he regularly received the Madrid newspapers. He had been so impressed by the reviews and the length of time we had played the Zarzuela that it had convinced him to bring us to Mexico. He was also representative for the Spanish Society of Authors, and as I was getting a ten percent cut of the gross for my author's right, he would be glad to handle it for me.

We took the night train to Mexico City and it was obvious that we were back in the plentiful lands of America. Pineapples in Spain were only for the wealthy. I once saw a pineapple draped in a red velvet cloth like a crown jewel in a Madrid store window. When the train stopped for a few minutes in Cordoba, Miguel my Catalan assistant, saw an Indian woman selling baskets of pineapples. He asked the price and she said, ''Un toston''—fifty cents Mexican. Miguel was delighted, gave her the coin and started to select the fattest pineapple in the basket, whereupon she said that all the pineapples including the basket cost a toston. Miguel was flabbergasted. Grabbing the basket he locked himself in his bunk and gorged on pineapple until he was sick. He had to be helped off the train the next morning when we got to Mexico City, and then it took him another two days to get used to the rarified air at nearly 3,000 feet above sea level.

I fell in love at first sight with Mexico City, that quaint and charming city with its picturesque people. Over the years I grew to appreciate all the friendly and openhearted Mexicans.

Unfortunately, things started badly in Mexico. On my way from the railway station to the hotel I didn't see a single poster or bill announcing our debut in three days' time. Belena had the weak excuse that he was waiting for my lithographs to start the publicity. The newspapers carried small, unimaginative ads for a bearded midget blowing a trumpet, which was a leftover cut he had from some extinct show. I was so disgusted with this meager and stupid publicity that I refused to open, and had my first of many fights with Belena who said that if I wanted more publicity I could pay for it out of my pocket. There was no clause in our contract as to the minimum of publicity he was obliged to make as this problem had never arisen before. This was a fine way to start off in a new country. I had no alternative but to use up the greater part of the expensive lithographs I had brought from Spain and Portugal. He refused to pay one cent for this expensive advertising.

To make matters worse, the old Lirico Theatre was on a side street and I knew I would have to do something out of the ordinary to get people to come. With our constant bickering this miserly man defeated every idea I had to stir up interest in the debut. Everything went wrong and finally I opened to a half-full house on a rainy night. The audience wasn't any too enthusiastic and, for the first time, I thought I had a healthy flop on my hands and I wasn't too happy about it.

Torres-Belena sat in the last row with a glum face and walked out in disgust before it was over. He offered to sell his share of the business to his partner for 7,000 peso, but his partner had even less faith and told Belena he was getting out while the getting was good. That same night Belena chased around Mexico City trying to get some sucker to take over, but no one wanted to take a chance. As a last resort he offered the deal to me for 5,000 pesos, but as I was born a blasted idiot in financial matters, I didn't take him up on it. For that I deserve to be nibbled to death by ducks.

Then one of those freak events, which the theatre breeds on, happened. The press was marvelous and we got columns of free publicity. The exotic Chinese costumes and scenery appealed to color-loving Mexicans of Aztecan descent. Slowly they started to come and in a week's time it was an avalanche. The theatre was sold out twice daily for a week in advance and that went on for four months. Belena made so much money that he was able to buy the theatre which he later remodeled and placed a bronze plaque in the lobby dedicated to me. He suddenly went nuts, and to make up for his previous churlishness, he had the programmes printed on silk. Gold and silver amulets of Sirio's caricature of me were given to favored friends, and he launched a publicity campaign that is still remembered in Mexico.

My safe deposit was loaded with Mexican centenario gold pieces, for after that dollar scare in Barcelona, I was leery of all paper money. I wanted everything in hard cash.

Once you have the momentum and the excitement going for you, you must keep it going or it fades very quickly. As I was on my way to becoming a fairly wealthy man I began to get a little out of hand. The truth was I couldn't get used to making money so fast and I didn't know what to do with it.

After two hard shows a day and three on Saturday and Sunday, without a single day's rest, my greatest joy was to go to a restaurant after the show and whoop it up till all hours of the morning. Hilda didn't like it and usually I was on my own and would greet the rising sun, a la Dante, on my way home to the flat we had in the Colonia Roma.

One night I was dining with Adriana LaMar and Ramon Pereda, a pair of Mexican movie stars, when a handsome Mexican woman paused for a moment at our table, placed a wrapped package in front of me and left without a word. Adriana and Ramon grinned as I opened the package to find a hand-tooled set of Mexican leather work consisting of a wallet, a billfold and a purse. A small white card read, "Mme. Ruth."

A Mexican motorcycle cop, El Huero, who doubled as a prompter in the theatre, nearly choked over his beer as he explained to me that Mme. Ruth was the Polly Adler of Mexico and ran the most luxurious bordello in town. I made a big mistake when I wrapped up the gift and gave it to the proprietor of the restaurant to return to her if she came back. I knew very little of the hot Mexican temperament, but I was to learn.

A few nights later I got a nudge in the ribs from the Huero and looked up to see Mme. Ruth staring furiously at me. Suddenly she dived into her handbag and came out holding a gun.

"Cabron. Son of the great whoremother," she spat, "no one scorns Ruth."

It was the first time in my life that anyone had pointed a gun at me. I was scared stiff but the Huero jumped up and grabbed the gun and in a rapid fire Mexican dialogue reasoned with her. She calmed down and finally extended her hand and we shook on it. I invited her to sit down and she insisted on ordering champagne to seal our friendship. I thought everything was all right, but I didn't know my restless Ruth.

The next night the whole first row of the theatre, much to Belena's horror, was filled with Ruth and her girls. Never have I had such an audience. They screamed with delight and had the whole theatre in an uproar. We all had a hell of a time. What a night that was.

While in Madrid, I had made friends with Maria Tereza

Montoya, one of Mexico's leading actresses, and her husband Ricardo Mondragon and his brother Jorge. They had returned to Mexico and Jorge was at my table every night. One evening, after the show, Jorge showed up at the theatre with a gargoyle smile.

"Will you accept *my* invitation tonight?" he asked.

"With pleasure and with many thanks," I replied in my best Spanish.

"Magnifico!" he said and hailed a taxi. We drove out to the Calle Insurgentes and stopped in front of a large mansion. We were ushered into a large salon by a colored maid. We sat down while I wondered what kind of a restaurant this was when in walked Ruth dressed to kill and wearing all her jewels. I shot a glance at the double-crossing Jorge but he was busy studying an Aztec idol.

There was nothing for me to do but give my idiot grin and, after a drink, Ruth led us to the dining room where we had a marvelous meal. After our giant repast I sat back with a contented sigh. It was good to be alive.

"My house is closed for business tonight," said Ruth, patting my hand. "Everything is for you."

"Very nice of you," I said lamely, thinking, everything what?

"My girls enjoyed your show so much that they wish to repay your finas stenciones. There is no doubt," she continued getting up, "that you are un artista excepcional, but I also, in my small way, put on some very artistic shows. Come!"

She led us into a large room with mirrored walls and on a podium in the center was a tableau of gorgeous nude women.

"The espectaculo will now commence," said Ruth, clapping her hands.

What a night *that* was.

There is a phenomenon in show business that sometimes lifts a hit show out of all proportion to its real value and often this mass hysteria gets out of hand and in retrospect seems rather silly. Be that as it may, no one knows how it begins or how long it will last. Something like this was happening to me in Mexico.

Reams of newspaper and magazine articles appeared. Candy bars using my name were sold. My photo advertised soft drinks, toothpaste and beauty cream, of which I was given a large stock that I didn't use but tried out on our dog—with no noticeable improvement. General Juan Jose Mendez, chief of the Mexican police, made me an honorary officer. I was called on to give my profound views of world affairs of which I knew damned little and cared less. My greatest asset, of course, was my one-track mind and my burning fervor to improve the show.

After the Lirico season we played the Politeama Theatre and the Palacio de las Bellas Artes, Mexico's beautiful opera house with the famous illuminated crystal house curtain made by Tiffanys of New York. In this palace the house was sold out for a week in advance. It still wasn't enough and from there we played the Iris Theatre for another six weeks.

The house manager of the Iris, a very courteous person, Senor Molina, vanished on Sunday night after the show and with him vanished the week's take. The police sent out a nationwide search for him and had all the borders watched, but he had disappeared without a trace.

I got a lot of good-natured ribbing from the press about the Great Molina escape act—with the loot—and although it was good publicity, it wasn't worth a week's take.

The drinking water in Mexico has a strange taste for a newcomer but one gets used to it; the water in the Iris, however, went from bad to worse, and finally we had to have bottled water sent in. The theatre management sent for the sanitation authorities to make an investigation and to their horror they found the body of poor Molina stuffed into the main water tank on the roof of the theatre. Mexico has an excellent police force and they found the criminals and even retrieved the money.

After the Iris we left for our tour of the Mexican states, starting in Guadalajara, the capital of Jalisco.

The theatre I played in Queretero is famous for being the site where the Emperor Maximilian was tried and condemned to death. My dressing room was the one he had used during his trial and a short distance from the theatre is the hill where he was shot. It was an eerie sensation to sit at the dressing table while making up for the show and imagine what had happened in that room in that fateful year 1867.

A few miles from Zacatecas, high in the mountains of northern Mexico, we arrived one evening at a small town whose name I have forgotten and have no wish to remember. To get there one has to make a hair-raising trip by bus over some cliffhanging roads that make a man old before his time.

We came in rather late at night and the boys, to save time, left most of the baggage in the vestibule of the theatre and carried the props piecemeal to the stage. We were terribly late and didn't have time to set up some of the big heavy stuff. We did a small show, filling the time with small magic.

When I arrived at the theatre the next day I found Spreer and Miguel standing outside looking like a couple of ghosts. They motioned me to follow them backstage, stepping like men walking on eggs. Spreer glided over to the back door of the stage, and opening it, invited me to look out. I did so and nearly collapsed. Below me was a sheer drop of two or three hundred feet. The stage of the theatre was propped to the side of this cliff with a few diagonal supporting beams. Had we brought the full weight of the show and hung all the sets, the stage would surely have given way. When I thought how calmly I had given the show the night before, while hanging in space, I nearly threw up! I told the boys to clear the stage and carefully pack, and in spite of the manager's threat to sue me, I left town.

It was during this tour that I played for the first time to a large Indian population. As the illiteracy rate was very high in those days, I devised special cartoon-like advertising which was most effective. In later years the boom of Mexican talking pictures in Latin America was largely due to the fact that the majority of the Indian population could not follow foreign pictures with Spanish subtitles.

Theatre conditions were often quite primitive. In Merida, the capital of Yucatan, the stage cellar was a pool of water and a rough catwalk arrangement had been set up to get around it. A specialty dance number on my show used a trap and one night the ballerina became hysterical and swore she had seen a sea monster under the stage. What she had seen was a huge black snake coiled in one corner. The manager calmly explained that it was there to exterminate the rats.

I hadn't had news of Li-Ho-Chang for years and had been told that he quit show business and was in the States. Imagine my surprise to see him sitting in the first row on my opening night in Monterrey. After the show he came backstage and called it a "dream show" and warned me never to change it: leave it just as it was as I had a sure fire money maker. He was in a poor financial situation and explained that he had lost the bulk of his capital in a talking picture deal in South America. He had invested heavily in the old Vitaphone system that used records for synchronization but found that most of the cinemas were unequipped for sound, and as the pictures he had brought down were very poor, he had gone broke. He still had his props stored in El Paso, on the Texas border, but was too discouraged to start all over again. However, after seeing my show, he got the old fever again and thought maybe he could do something.

It's fascinating how the wheel turns. Here was the same situation as in the old days of the Comedia Theatre in Buenos Aires, but reversed.

A few days later I received a letter from Neuvo Laredo in Texas in which Chang wrote in part, "You are the talk of Mexico and so famous that even the American managers talk about you and this makes it harder for me as I am a has-been and am in an awful position as I am already in Mexico but no one will take up my bond and I don't know which way to turn. I would like to be your manager and this would give me great pleasure as I think I have three or more years of activity."

I wrote to him to come along as I had faith in him as a businessman, but he never answered my letter. He played the little towns and villages in northern Mexico and put up his own bond. He made a most remarkable comeback and in a short time had a bigger and better show than he had ever had. He shortened his name to Chang and had more success and made more money than he ever had in the past. In later years he told me that my show had inspired him just as his show had inspired me so many years before, and he took my style as a model for his future productions.

When I returned to Mexico City we played the Iris again and I knew that the time had come to leave Mexico; but I was crazy about that country so I decided to stay and build a new show for the coming season. I rented a large house in the Calle Magnolia as a workshop and stored all my material there. Chang had warned me not to touch the show but I went against everybody's advice, and with a terrible attack of "expansion fever" I tampered with the gold mine and thereby opened the door to a lot of grief and unhappiness.

Lower left to right: **Zancig, Theo and David Bamberg.**

Two theatrical photographs taken of David Bamberg during his first tour of Spain in 1933. He is still wearing the pigtail. (See page 198 and following.)

Four portraits of David Bamberg taken in Mexico City, 1934.

Fu Manchu in lights.

Fu Manchu billing at the Teatro Nacional in Buenos Aires, Argentina, 1947.

Okito producing a handkerchief for the Silks and Soup Plate Trick, photographed in performance at a magicians' convention in Chicago, 1947.

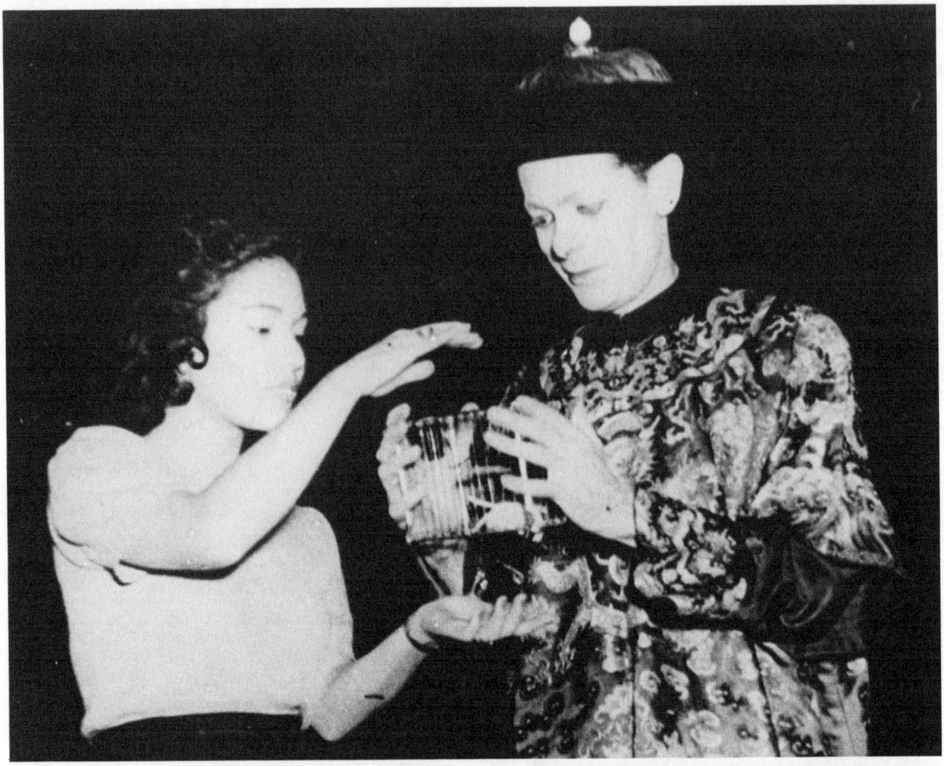

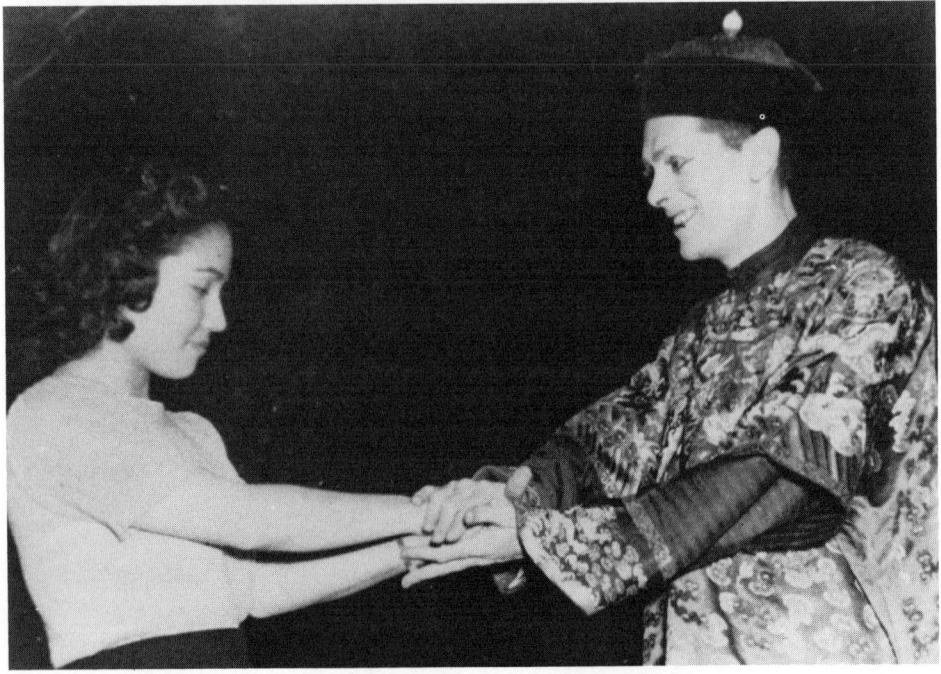

David Bamberg causing the bird cage to vanish from the hands of an assisting spectator.

Khelmis, principal female assistant on the Fu Manchu show from 1951 to 1956.

David performing the rope trick originated by Harlan Tarbell of Chicago. David, Okito, and Dante were among the many magicians who made a success of this cut and restored rope illusion.

A stage filled with apparatus used in the Fu Manchu show.

The Bamberg Mat trick.

The production of a human butterfly, introduced in Spain as a climax to the Mat Trick. (See page 202.)

David Bamberg, just before stealing the glass in the Thief of Baghdad trick. Photographed during a performance at the Teatro Nacional in Buenos Aires.

David releasing the glass from the ribbon at the moment of the "disturbance" in the theatre box. The trick was performed in the aisle with members of the audience holding the ends of the ribbon. (See page 307.)

Cesareo Pelaez performing his version of the Thief of Baghdad in the Beverly, Massachusetts, production of "Le Grand David and His Own Spectacular Magic Company."

Top to bottom: **Seth Bartlett, David Bull, and Cesareo Pelaez of Le Grand David Company, which carries on the Bamberg tradition.**

CHAPTER 34

Perhaps I should explain my mental and emotional state in 1935. The show was practically the same one I had started out with in 1929 but with a far more elaborate presentation, a few new illusions, and by this time I had plenty of theatrical savvy. After thousands of shows I was getting increasingly mechanical as the same routine and patter were repeated night after night. Despite the advice of people who understood show business, and advised me to leave the show alone on the theory that as long as it made money it should be handled with kid gloves, I paid no attention. I knew it was true; many magicians hadn't changed a trick or a line for over thirty years as they feared to fool around with a breadwinner.

I felt I had to change. Even the studied spontaneity that was my forte was getting stale. The show could have gone on for years if I had taken a world tour. Actually, I had only played a few South American countries, Spain, Portugal and Mexico, which had taken me six years; so the show was good for another ten years, at least, as I had the rest of the world open. England alone, with her hundreds of theatres and variety halls and with the greatest magic-loving public on earth, was a potential gold mine. All the biggest illusionists who had played England on spec had succeeded and many of them made fortunes. England was a magician's dream, but I didn't go. In retrospect, I could kick myself, but I had other ideas.

The truth is I was sick of the show and sick of myself. The show completely dominated me and was first above all other things. I know nothing of psychiatry or such matters, but I suspect that I was developing a split personality. In private life I was rather shy and timid, not too much of a mixer. I began to hate crowds, noise and inane cocktail conversation. The one exception was the nightly gabfest in the restaurant after the show. But even this began to pall in time.

As the magician Fu Manchu I was exactly the opposite. I was completely at ease on the stage and delighted in addressing large audiences. In private life, any trifling accident would upset me, but on the stage even an inadvertent failure of a trick didn't phase me, and by fast thinking I always managed to cover up any difficulty. I could make split-second decisions on the stage, whereas off stage I had to think things over carefully to make up my mind.

Off stage, I was so nervous that people stared at my trembling hands in lighting a cigarette or lifting a cup of coffee, and any contretemps made the trembling worse. I would jump out of my skin when the telephone rang or somebody knocked on the door. Yet in front of an audience of a thousand people I could do the floating ball with a rock steady hand, without a tremor. The roof could fall in as far as I cared. My assistants marvelled at the completely relaxed Fu Manchu and the high-strung, terrible tempered Dave. Maybe Fu was a safety valve. When the boys wanted a favor or a raise, they never asked Dave but always the good natured Fu in the theatre.

I had developed a fine theatrical sense. There were times when I wrote a new sequence for the show which read fine as I studied it, but the moment I was in front of an audience I automatically sensed, even as I was talking, that it was wrong. I would ad-lib and change it and I was usually right. Most of my best gags and lines were ad-libbed during the show. This would drive my comic crazy and I would have to whisper his reply through the side of my mouth, like a ventriloquist.

Finally the Fu character completely dominated my other self and I lost my nervousness to a large degree. So more for my own peace of mind rather than from necessity I began to plan the new show. I wanted it to be radically new and to bring something to magic that it had rarely known before. A brand new outlook.

My first idea was a three part magical sketch, A Flight to the Moon, based on science-fiction. This was a story of the future, in which a man reduced to atoms is projected through space to materialize on the moon. He finds it inhabited by huge robots built by the moon men, who, when their atmosphere, water and vegetation begin to die out, transplant their brains to these metallic monsters which can continue living in a dying world.

The last of the moon men, a being with a huge head and withered body, was to tell the story of the injustice of man to man, the curse of war and so on, which was supposed to be a satirical resume of what was happening on earth. This, I fondly believed, was serious theatre combined with great magical effects.

My Sawing a Woman had to be different. Why not do a dramatic version of Edgar Allan Poe's *The Pit and the Pendulum* and have a razor-sharp blade slowly swing down and cut the victim in two? So I dreamed up a plot in which Nayland Smith, Fu Manchu's mortal enemy, was tied to a post while I talked of Chinese tortures. Tableaux of these dreadful deeds were to be seen in the background on a revolving stage: beautiful girls being boiled alive in glass tanks of steaming, bubbling water and other horrible tortures so vividly described in Flores' *Jardin de los Suplicious.*

Ah! One must not neglect politics, so a sketch was written around the Checker Cabinet trick, taking a slap at the fascists and bewailing the predicament of Haile Selassie. A new spirit cabinet on a gigantic scale was also conceived, with a plot based on Conan Doyle's *Land of Mist.* And so forth and so on.

I showed my final scripts to some of the best Mexican playwrights and theatrical critics and, perhaps because they did not wish to offend me, as the Mexicans are among the world's politest people, they all agreed that it was a great step forward in the theatre. My ideas would place magic on a level with serious plays. The more people I showed them to, the more enthusiasm I encountered. I was sure that I had discovered a new theatre form that could not fail.

Now you know what "bloody fool" means.

Leaving the boys to start on the rough carpentry work, I took a short trip to Hollywood while Hilda took Bobby to New York for a vacation.

The train arrived in Los Angeles in the evening, and as I had not advised anyone of my trip, I was completely on my own for the first night. I decided to go to Grauman's Chinese Theatre which I had heard so much about.

I didn't know how to get there from my hotel so I approached the first man I saw and said, "I beg your pardon, but could you..." but he turned away with a sour stare and kept on going. What a sullen sod, I thought, as I went up to another man and began, "I beg your pardon, but..." and I was cut off with a snarled, "Beat it." What the hell was going on? Finally it dawned on me that my approach had been that of a panhandler and they had just recovered from the depression. The next time I said to a passing man, "Hey, you! Where's Grauman's Theatre?" and the guy cheerfully showed me the way.

The following morning the first thing I did was to go and see Floyd Thayer. I bought several things from him, including a well-made collapsing chair. He invited me to his home and I dined with him. Then he took me along to the Pacific Coast Convention of Magicians where I met Caryl Fleming, Laurie Ireland (who sold me a clever folding cage), Charles E. Miller, Dariel Fitzkee, Bill Larsen and many other magicians. Harry Mendoza took me under his wing and helped me to obtain a marvelous collection of Chinese stage costumes through a friend of his at Paramount Studios. There I had the pleasure of meeting Carl Brisson again. The gorgeous collection of oriental robes were sold to me for a very fair price. I spent about $5,000 for all the costumes I bought in Los Angeles and, with what I already had, I was on the way to having one of the largest collections of Chinese robes in the world. I had over three hundred genuine costumes, some dating back nearly two centuries, including Chinese warrior costumes. My collection was topped by a robe embroidered for Li-Hung-Chang, eldest son of the Empress of China.

I once saw the movie, "55 Days in Peking" which depicted the royal court of China in the days of the Boxer Rebellion in 1900. In the picture the costumes are magnificent and undoubtedly genuine; every single one of them I have in my collection, even those worn by the Empress.

Thanks to Harry Mendoza I had a wonderful time in Hollywood and hated to leave after ten days there.

Upon my return to Mexico City I got down to hard work and we started on the moon sketch. This was divided into three parts. First, there was an elaborate set of a futuristic scientific laboratory complete with television. The illusion in the center was a machine for reducing a man to atoms and projecting him into space. This illusion was based on controlled dimmer lighting on perforated aluminum screens.

The second scene showed the universe with a trick effect of atoms in ray form leaping from the earth to the moon.

The third part was a fantastic moonscape with a ten-foot-high mechanical robot that was controlled in part by a short wave radio in its head.

Salvador Tarrazona, the renowned Spanish painter, designed

and painted the sets in which we had to combine art and trickery. Television had not yet been perfected, so to get the effect of TV moon close-ups, we filmed a large model of the moon with a Kodak 16mm Special. This film was projected by mirrors on a translucent oval in the set which was supposed to be an electronic telescope. Understand that this was in 1935 and most of these things were still in the future!

The basic plot of the sketch was simple by today's standards. In my gigantic, light-flashing laboratory there was some pseudo-scientific dialogue between a white-frocked assistant and myself. To prove my theory of outer space I stepped into the atom time machine armed with an electronic death-ray gun. When the assistant threw the switch a series of long sparks and flashing lights were set in motion and slowly I dissolved before the spectators eyes.

The second part was a purely scenic bridge-over effect of the atomic "rays" rushing from the earth to the moon. It was contrived with a box-like gadget that ran behind the drop and gave the spark-like effect through a series of punched out holes in the scenery.

The moon set was breathtakingly impressive, using semi-solid flats in bas-relief to represent silver gorges and caves and, with blue, violet and green lighting, gave a stunning out-of-this-world effect.

The giant robot was made of aluminum and copper. By opening the doors in its chest, back and legs, one could see completely through its maze of operating gears, wheels and springs.

This illusion alone took over nine months to perfect. We wasted more time on it than it was worth. Owing to its great bulk, it shuffled along rather than walked. It was really nothing more than a tour-de-force that I had to get out of my system.

Today transistor transmitters and receivers no larger than a cigarette box are common, but in those days ultra-short wave radio was in a purely experimental stage. We had to experiment and construct our own model and I believe I was the first to use short-wave radio for mind reading.

The receiver was built into the head of the robot and, through earphones, I directed Spreer, who was concealed inside the monster. The transmitter was hung from a harness concealed under my Chinese robe. Through a microphone on my wrist, hidden by my long mandarin sleeves, anything the audience whispered to me was picked up by Spreer. It worked perfectly up to a distance of nearly a hundred feet.

In Cuernavaca, a small town near Mexico City, we had twenty Indian women embroider the front drop, using Mei Lan-fang's painting of the Bodhisattva P'uhsien, the seated Buddha on a jewel-studded elephant. This drop took six months to complete and used over ten pounds of artificial jewels, brass and metallic ornaments.

When the time came to make the plans for the sawing illusion, I was up against the eternal problem of the thick table to conceal the girl. As I sweated through all kinds of impossible solutions, I could feel the shadow of Okito grinning over my shoulder and my mind went back to the old days in London when I had lambasted Goldin. So now what, little man?

Some unknown American solved the problem for me. The 16th of September is Mexico's "Fourth of July." As the big parade went by on Avenida Jaurez I saw a typical American tourist with a cardboard periscopic contraption through which he was watching the parade. I edged over to him and asked permission to have a look through, and in a flash the solution to my sawing illusion was revealed.

I went to the shop, but as it was a holiday no one was there. I had all afternoon to make up a miniature model out of old scrap plywood and bits of mirror. When it was finished I hid it in a corner of the shop and covered it with an old cloth.

The next morning I bought an articulated doll and when I got to the shop all the boys were already at work. Without saying anything I put my model table on a large crate and placed the doll on the little table, sinking its body into the trap and leaving only the legs and head resting on table level. Then I stretched a piece of cloth from the doll's neck to its knees to give the semblance of a body. Only then did I invite the boys in to have a look. They stared at it for a while, and when I asked them what they thought of it, they seemed puzzled.

"I don't understand what I'm supposed to say," said Miguel. "It's just a doll resting on a table. So what?"

Sweet music! I snatched the cloth dress away and still no response. They thought it was a doll's head at one end and the legs at the other. I lifted the doll from the table and have never seen such a flabbergasted bunch of guys in my life. Miguel, in particular, couldn't believe it and picked up the crude little table and studied it and crooned over it for a while.

"This is, without a doubt, the darndest thing I've ever seen in my life. Why didn't somebody think of this before?" he said. He was so enthusiastic about it that he begged me to relieve him from the work he was doing and allow him to design and supervise the construction of the illusion. Cheerfully I gave him the go-ahead and he made a first mock-up of old plywood and scrap material. It looked like a breeze until we hit a nasty snag. The sides of the table, even when painted dead black, seemed to disappear when viewed from a certain side angle. That meant it would have to be worked so far backstage that it wasn't a trick anymore. I had visions of Okito doing a triumphant war dance and my million-dollar idea going down the drain.

We worked on it until the problem was solved by the painstaking cutting of an intricate design in the two side walls of the table, and it turned out to be perfect. Spreer did a fine job on the mechanism for swinging and gradually lowering the steel blade, and I took charge of the faked half-body that the girl wore.

Without a doubt this was the best illusion we had invented and Ted Annemann, when he returned from seeing my show in Havana some time later, highlighted it above all the rest of the show in an article he wrote in his magazine *Jinx*. I purposely said nothing to Okito as I wanted to surprise him some day.

To complete the sketch of The Pit and the Pendulum we constructed a tricked post that allowed the ropes which bound Nayland Smith to fall to the floor at a wave of hand. This post also contained the mechanism for the appearance of a knife alongside Smith's head, which seemed to be the same knife that I "threw" from a distance.

The revolving stage on a large platform for the torture scenes completed the sketch, and with the fancifully inspired set by Tarrazona, it was a magician's dream.

The next illusion we built was one of those pipe dreams of my youth from the old London days—a giant Chinese fan that opened to produce a girl.

Apart from the robot, the most elaborate and expensive illusion we built was the Chinese Bazaar, based on the old Bridal Chamber illusion but with a modified principle. This huge illusion required three crates for packing—and I could see Okito squirming! The effect was a cabinet on wheels which was revolved with the doors open to show it empty. It "transformed" into a Chinese shop filled with costumes, lanterns, tables, lamps and vases and the final production of four girls in beautifully sequined oriental robes. This was the most beautiful prop I ever built.

The Haunted Window was an innovation in spirit cabinets and utilized an entirely new principle for the concealment of the assistants. The effect was similar to the Maskelyne version with a large window set into an aperature of a gloomy, ruined castle. This was also designed by Tarrazona and employed colored light-changing effects to bring out the demons and skeletons, concealed in the stones and rocks. The combination of the Kleigl special-effect projectors for floating ghosts and skeletons, a spectacular inferno of fire and witches and demons flying about, made the overall effect remarkable.

The sketch started with an assistant going to sleep in an old four-poster bed, the curtains of which closed mysteriously by themselves. Afterwards two demons rushed out carrying the sleeping assistant to the haunted castle.

The haunted window frame detached itself from the scenery and folded forward and the triple folding windows opened to show it empty. When the windows were closed again a dim light appeared inside and the shadow of a miser carrying a bag of gold appeared. The figure of a robber seemed to emerge from the floor and, stabbing the old man in the back, stole the gold. In getting away, the robber knocked over a lamp which exploded, causing a fire to start, in which one could see the vague forms of people in the flames. However, when the windows were opened, the cabinet was empty.

At that point we went into a regular spirit routine but with a new twist. The stooge's handkerchief visibly grew bigger and turned into a ghost. This was followed by a luminous vampire which flew down from the border drop and battled with an enormous luminous spider that suddenly turned and jumped out over the heads of the audience. At the same moment a large luminous hand clutched at the people in the front rows and boxes and was joined by flying ghosts and skeletons that did a wild luminous dance over the audience.

The Triple Escape followed. It was the substitution trunk enhanced by enclosing it in two canvas covers which were laced together with rope. This was placed on a low platform and a heavy Chinese tea chest was fitted over it and padlocked at eight points. The change was made at the same speed as the simple trunk, but the effect was far greater and the impact on the audience was enormous.

My Pagoda illusion, which was a switch on the Dress Trunk, was an imposing prop I built because I loved pagodas. Unfortunately, it was not a good nor effective illusion and after a month or so I threw it out.

After my success with the sawing illusion I wanted to solve the weak spot in the Duck Vanish to justify my criticism in London in 1920. Fifteen years had gone by and I still hadn't figured it out; but one night, just before going to sleep and for no good reason at all, I had an idea which I thought might work. When I made the final drawings it looked so good on paper that I skipped the mock model, took a chance and built the apparatus from scratch. It worked perfectly and was far superior to the old duck vanish as the obviously loaded board was done away with. I did not write a word about it to my father, knowing that I would see him one of these days. I meant to keep it a secret until then. It may seem mean on my part not to have explained these things to my father, but it was the ham in me that wanted to fool him. I had a healthy respect for his knowledge of magic and there was nothing in the world I wanted more than to baffle him just once.

My duck vanish was small and only good for the vanish of two ducks so I combined it with the Thurston (LeRoy) trick of exchanging the heads of a duck and a rooster but using a white duck and a black duck for the effect. Miguel carved two lifelike duck heads from wood and I used a Jack Gwynne type of production box for the reappearance of the two ducks and it made a fine combination.

Another trick included was a growing rose bush effect based on the Indian Mango Tree trick, which I later described in *The Sphinx*.

I had always loved the Indian Sand trick as something off the beaten path, but the dull colored sands (due to the preparation) never appealed to me. I experimented and finally substituted white powdered marble for yellowish sea sand. I obtained bright, vivid colors and by combining a chemical water-to-ink-to-water effect in a large glass bowl, I had a startling finish for this classic, which had always been slightly anticlimactic. This presentation was very favorably received and commented upon by the magicians who saw my show in the Cervantes Theatre in New York in 1937.

With a double arc-lamp I was able to present my hand shadows in colors, using the same system that Max Holden had used many years before in vaudeville, before he gave up his act to open his magic store in New York.

Louis Nicola's appearing doll in the Glad Eye trick followed, along with a number of other small effects.

Miguel carved a beautiful set of break-apart Chinese furniture that consisted of two armchairs and a large center table. In later years Okito converted one of these chairs for the de Kolta vanishing lady illusion.

A portable switchboard for the control of the projection machines, general lighting, special effects, flashes, and U.V. light and a remote control for other spots and special lighting effects were constructed. An amplification system with loud speakers for sound and incidental music effects were also added. This was something rather radical in those days and it was the first time it was used in Latin America for stage shows.

A whole new score was written for the show and one of my numbers, called "Mujer de mil Ilusion," became very popular and was played over the radio and used by Mexican dance orchestras.

David Bamberg in his dressing room in Havana, Cuba, in 1936, with the Prince of Asturias, eldest son of King Alfonso XIII of Spain. The Prince, an ardent magic fan, died the following year in an automobile accident in Florida. Standing in the background, two impressarios of the Teatro Nacional.

CHAPTER 35

I was living it up and wading through my capital like a maniac. Soon all the money I had made in Mexico was gone and I had already dipped heavily into the safe deposit box for the dollars and pounds I had brought from Spain. But I had dived into this deal with my eyes open and I had no other alternative than to finish.

I had cut off completely from Belena, who was impresario of his own theatre now, but I had never liked him and hoped that I would not have to do any business with him in the future.

Another Mexican impresario named Juan Toledo rented the Lirico from Belena and brought Chang to Mexico City for a season at popular prices. Toledo had the original idea of calling the show "A Voyage to Hell" and the novelty of a trip by train to the netherworld captured the public's imagination and they did a good business. Chang used the multiple scenery and the change of costumes gimmick which considerably improved his show. He added a few new illusions and tricks that he had brought from the States. Shortly after, he left for South America and ended up in Buenos Aires where he did a great season in the Avenida.

Time flew by and I was developing the same complex that I had in Buenos Aires when I opened with the first show in 1929. I was stalling around and worrying over small details and spending money too freely.

A petulant perverseness had overtaken me and estranged me from my real friends who wished me well and inclined me towards the backslappers and hangers-on who always gravitate to a "success."

To make matters worse I became involved with Mexico's top ballerina, Eva Beltri, the star of Augustin Lara's Revue at the

Fabregas Theatre. Hilda soon found out and on the night of our thirteenth wedding anniversary we fought it out, the result being that she left for New York, taking Bobby with her.

Alfonso Bedoya, a Mexican film actor, who was later to play the part of a bandit in John Huston's "Treasure of the Sierra Madre" and who loved Bobby, tried to reconcile us and made dire predictions for the future. He was one of the few who was skeptical about the script of the new show and said, "Frankly, I think it's too arty and it's not for you. I realize that magic is your vocation, even more than your profession, but you mustn't let it dominate your whole life—even if you are a magician by birth. There are more important things in the world than magic."

I fought with him, too. The deeper I got into this thing, the more stubborn and unreasonable I became.

Finally, in April, 1936, we hauled six huge truckloads of baggage to the Iris Theatre where I was to open in three weeks. When I saw this enormous display set up on the stage and running over into the passageways of the theatre, I had the supreme thrill of knowing that I had the biggest magic and illusion show on earth. What I didn't know was the headaches and troubles I would have with it.

The theatre was running pictures and I only had the mornings and early afternoons for stage rehearsals, although some of the evenings we rehearsed in the large patio beside the dressing rooms.

The show was so complicated that I wasn't satisfied with rehearsals and had to postpone my debut twice, much to the annoyance of the management who had to get pictures at the last moment to fill in the time. The big motion picture companies didn't like to be played around with and gave the theatre the poorest B pictures they had.

I couldn't put my finger on it but I felt that something was sour somewhere, yet it was impossible for me to get an objective slant on the show.

Always on the lookout for omens, I got a fat one. One evening after the picture I called a dress rehearsal. I was in my dressing room binding my ankles with ribbon in the Chinese manner, with one foot on a chair. All at once I had a dizzy spell and the room seemed to turn around. I realized I had been overdoing it as I grasped the chair back to steady myself. Then I noticed that a scimitar hanging on the wall was swaying from side to side. I knew it was one of those oscillating tremors so common in Mexico, but not nearly as dangerous as the house-toppling trepidation shocks. Still it was enough to send me flying out into the street half-dressed. Maybe this shook some sense into me for I decided to stop stalling and, repeating my superstition-defying debut in Vigo, I set the opening for Friday the 13th of May.

The house was jam-packed and the show opened to a good start when the house curtain rose to display my embroidered front drop which drew a round of applause from the expectant audience.

For the first half hour the show ran at a steady pace and with very favorable audience reaction. I began to get the feeling that I had a hit on my hands; but when we got to the Moon sketch things began to bog down, and I started to lose my audience.

To make matters worse, the short wave radio didn't work and Spreer heard nothing but a constant roar in his earphones. There was a lot of stalling around with the audience getting colder by the moment. I switched to the old Isis talking code in a loud voice so that Spreer could hear me. The robot was able to do a few tests but nothing compared to the ones that had been rehearsed using the mike. I couldn't understand as the thing had worked perfectly during all the rehearsals and now it went haywire. (After the show we tried it out and it worked again. The second night it failed during the show and we discovered that the neon lights in the lobby and the big neon sign outside was the cause. These had never been turned on during rehearsals.)

I now had a completely apathetic audience on my hands. The Pit and Pendulum sketch lifted them slightly from their lethargy, but not as much as I hoped. The actual illusion itself, the cutting of the girl in two, got a good hand. The Haunted Window opened to a slow start but the ghostly ending got the reaction I had wanted.

From there on it was a slow letdown but the finale was saved by the sensational Triple Escape which got a big hand.

For the first fifteen minutes of a show the audience is a group that can be molded easily, and if you give them the slightest indication that they are going to be entertained, you can play with them at your will. But after that time they either go along with you or split into small groups that never join together again.

The final curtain came down on polite, scattered applause and at this moment I learned, the hard way, that failure is the norm of the theatre—not success. Of course, my backslapping pals went into ecstasies and acclaimed it the greatest extravaganza ever seen in Mexico, but in my heart I knew it had been a flop. I knew that the magic spell was broken and that I'd lost them. My worst fears were realized when the press reviews came out the next morning.

All the leading Mexican newspapers were fair and impartial. They spoke highly of the settings, costumes, lighting and the high quality of the magic in general; but they really criticized me for the script.

Universal, the leading morning paper, said in part, "The fact that Fu Manchu uses a complicated and imposing robot for a telepathic act modifies nothing and is basically the same thing we have seen before. We find the whole show too mechanicl and drawn out."

Excelsior, on a par with *Universal,* advised me to go back to the old show and said, "The production itself is extraordinary in presentation and luxury but the main thing is missing—the old simpatico Fu Manchu is not there." In that statement they had a point, as I had given up the old Chinese accent and spoke correct Spanish, which had been another mistake.

I had made the same mistake that Chaplin made in his later pictures when he injected a lot of homespun philosophy that no one cared about. It was the baggy pants and pratfalls they wanted to see and not a lot of bad histrionics. My cherished dialogue with the "moon man" about the curse of war and man's injustice to man fell flat.

The man who put his finger on the weak spot of the show was Juan Toledo, Chang's former impresario. "When people pay to see a magic show they want just that and nothing more," he said. "They come to see tricks and be fooled and resent anything else."

In my dreams of being a magical Eugene O'Neill, I had written the dreariest drivel without one original thought of my own. Just a hackneyed hodgepodge gleaned from things that had been said before and much better.

This was not a case for simple rewriting. This required a major surgical operation to bring the dead to life. I did the fastest job of cutting and changing in the history of show business in order to save the show. I had to cut to the bone to get some sort of rhythm and speed into it.

With the exception of the King Blackbeard political satire, almost the entire dialogue was thrown out. My beloved patter for the opening of the Haunted Widow was beheaded with one blow of the ax!

On Broadway the thing would have been thrown out after the first night but as I was the producer I hung on by the skin of my teeth.

Fortunately, the magic and the illusions were good and owing to my big name in Mexico and the large following I had, I managed to keep going.

I worked like a slave on it and managed to keep going for six weeks. With daily changes that drove my actors and assistants crazy I weeded out the worst and put back a few sure-fire hits from the old show until I had a well paced production. I took it on the road for a few months to the larger cities but it was too bulky and top heavy to make much profit so I returned to Mexico City to open in the Arbeu Theatre at popular prices. Only then did I start to make money again, nothing like my Lirico business, but enough to get me back on my feet. I was once again learning the hard way, after not following my own advice in my article on Stage Presentation in *Greater Magic*.

All in all it was better this happened when I was a young man of thirty and could take the blow, rather than in later years when the energy, fire and ambition start to cool.

One curious fact that I learned in those months was how happy it made people when I hit the skids. Most of those backslapping friends vanished.

With this experience I should have learned something, but the fact remains that I was never a first-night hit writer. Every show I ever wrote was terrible on the opening night. It always took me at least a week or ten days to get it into shape. The one exception was the straight comedy magic show I produced in that same Arbeu Theatre in 1945, which was a smash hit from the first night and practically never changed.

Another ogre was rearing its head, in the shape of labor unions in the theatre. They were beginning to make life miserable for the impresario and, after a ten day wildcat strike of the stagehands in the Arbeu, I decided the time had come to leave this splendid, hospitable country that I had grown to love. I arranged for my debut in Cuba.

CHAPTER 36

The old wide open Havana of the pre-Castro days was one of the most captivating and gayest cities in the world, with a personality all its own.

From the first day I felt at home in Cuba and got along fine with those fun-loving, amicable people. The spectacular press of the sensation-loving Habaneros outdid itself in its build-up for our debut at the Teatro Nacional, in the heart of Havana. *La Marina,* Havana's leading newspaper, gave me a full page spread in the Sunday rotogravure section, calling me the "Emperor of Magicians."

So it was not surprising that the show was sold out for days in advance. After my bitter lesson in Mexico I took no chances and combined the best of the old and new show for the opening night.

The debut was triumphal and they greeted the show with wild enthusiasm, which started the old box office clicking. (You'll say, "He's blowing his horn again," and your darn tootin' I am!) A friend of mine, an American employed by the Havana Telephone Company, told me that in the morning hours from ten to twelve there was a sudden, heavy traffic on the lines; and in order to find out why, they listened and discovered that it was the teenage girls calling each other to discuss the show. When teenagers fall for a show, you know you're in!

I had only signed a month's contract with the Nacional but they extended my contract. They kept postponing the Astaire-Rogers film booked to follow me, until M.G.M. tried to force them to close me down. However, we made a deal with them. The last two weeks I split the bill with the picture, giving a one hour show. Yet the scalpers were getting double price for downstairs seats and as M.G.M. frowned on this practice, we had to close. Scalpers in those countries have been the ruin of many theatrical seasons.

I met some interesting people in Havana, including Octavus Roy Cohen, whose comic Negro stories of the deep South were so popular in *The Saturday Evening Post* in the 1920s and 30s. He was not interested in writing detective stories and wanted to write a novel. He thought the life story of a magician would be a good plot and we talked it over for days while he made notes; but he never got around to writing it as he died shortly after. (Years later William Lindsay Gresham wrote his magnificent *Nightmare Alley,* the first book of its kind to truly convey the character of a side show magician and mind reader. Hollywood made a film of the book, starring Tyrone Power, but as usual they made a monkey of it just as they did with that silly Houdini picture.)

Visiting Havana at that time was the Prince of Asturias, eldest son of Alfonso XIII, presumptive heir to the Spanish throne, and a good friend of Captain Marroquin. He spent many evenings in my dressing room talking magic with me over a bottle of Scotch, and we usually ended up in the "Miami" restaurant in the early morning. His Highness was afflicted with hemophilia and it took him ten minutes to climb the stairs to my first floor dressing room.

One evening a newsboy was racing down the back street of the theatre shouting the news. The Prince stood up, and looking out of the window, said to me, "Life is so unjust. I am heir to the throne of Spain but I would give anything in the world to be that ragged boy."

I could think of nothing to say so I fiddled around with my makeup and pretended I hadn't heard. Soon after he left for the States and was tragically killed by an automobile accident in which he bled to death.

After Havana we played the whole island as far as Santiago and visited some of the large sugar and tobacco plantations. We returned to Havana to the Teatro Payrets where we did another season at cheaper prices.

The manager of the Cervantes Theatre, a Spanish-speaking house in New York, offered me a two week engagement in his theatre with a tour of the U.S. to follow and I happily signed the contract.

It had been fourteen years since Hilda and I had left New York for our great adventure and I hadn't seen the city since. We sailed into New York harbor on the S.S. Oriente and my heart pounded when I saw the familiar skyscraper skyline. I had visions of "Local boy makes good" running through my head.

Dear little Hilda and good old Herman were at the dock to meet me and at last I was out of the doghouse. I went to live at Hilda's apartment on Riverside Drive. Nothing seemed to have changed very much. The kids were still skating on the sidewalks and playing ball in the street. It was good to be back. Bobby was at a military academy in Peekskill and we planned to go up and visit him the first chance I had.

My first headache in New York was the customs who went through every single piece of baggage and even took measurements of sticks, put lead seals on the costumes and scenery and held me up for over a week.

Headache number two occurred when I had all the trunks and crates loaded on six trucks and ready for the trip to the theatre. A man came up to me and said, "Is that all theatrical baggage?"

"Yes," I said. "It is. Why?"

"You'll have to unload it. Them trucks don't belong to the union and can't haul theatre props."

"Why didn't someone tell me this before, instead of waiting until it was loaded?"

"That ain't my lookout," said the guy, shrugging his shoulders.

So I was forced to unload, but I had to pay the trucks a dollar for each piece. After the union trucks were loaded I found that their price was two dollars for each piece, so it cost me more to haul the baggage from 57th Street to 110th Street than it cost me from Havana to New York. All this made me very happy.

The third pain in the neck was the night before I opened. A greasy drip came to my dressing room and told me that my embroidered front curtain was a "woik of art" and must be worth a fortune.

"Very nice of you to say so," I said, rather pleased.

"Is it insured?" he asked.

"Only for fire. Why?"

He tch-tched. "Wooden it be a crime if some joik was to throw acid on it or cut it up or sumpin'."

"Who would do that?" I inquired.

"Ya never know. They's all kindsa screwballs aroun'. But I can guarantee pertection an' fer fifty bucks nobody's gonna fool aroun' wit yer props."

I delicately told him to get the hell out.

A few minutes later my manager came flying into my dressing room looking like something out of my Haunted Window. He asked me if I had taken leave of my senses.

"You know who that guy is?" he screeched.

"No. And I don't care."

"That's Jake the Jerk (or something similar) and if ya don't pay him, *he's* the guy wots going to do the doity woik."

So I had to shell out fifty pieces of lettuce. Three jeers for the Bronx!

Headache number four: A man with a blowtorch showed up and asked me if my scenery was fireproofed and I lied and said it was. So he went to work with his blowtorch on the back of my beautiful front drop and after burning a nice black hole in it he said, "Whoever did this job doesn't know his business. It'll have to be done over."

I told him in a hoarse voice that I had over forty sets hanging there. He said not to worry as he had a machine to spray the liquid on and it could all be done in one day.

The first painted drop they sprayed started the paint running and almost ruined a lovely backdrop. I knew the guy was only doing his duty, and to a certain extent it was a great thing, but I blew up and wanted to quit right there. I told the boys to start packing, but the house manager called the blowtorch artist to one side and convinced him to spray all my drops from the back very lightly, leaving them flame-proof. Then he stamped each drop with the official approval seal.

Headache number five happened a few nights after my debut. I had just left the theatre after the show when Miguel caught up with me on the street and asked me if I had seen my friend who was waiting for me.

"What friend? There was no one waiting for me when I left." We returned to the darkened stage and Miguel put on the light. There, up against the wall, just behind the sawing table, was the Great Nicola. He informed me that he was waiting for me to come out of my dressing room as he wanted to invite me to supper, but he had "lost" his way on the stage and hadn't seen me go out. I wondered if he seriously thought I would swallow such a lie but I gave him a wolf smile and the matter was passed off. Fortunately, as a precautionary measure, we always removed the gimmick from the sawing table after the show and kept it in my dressing room, so Nicola must have been a sadly puzzled man. This was one of the very few times I met

Nicola, who had the misfortune, some years later, to lose all of his equipment when his ship sank after hitting a mine off the coast of Singapore.

I was a bit scared on my opening night as the theatre was full of magicians, including most of the top-notch men in the business. The one man above all that I wanted to be there was my boyhood idol, Howard Thurston, but he had passed on. I always regretted that he never saw my show.

The opening night must have seemed rather weird to the lay audience when the magicians would appear to applaud at the wrong time. They were applauding the technique and not the trick itself. Still it was a grand night and one that I will never forget.

After the show Hilda, Herman, Uncle Emile, who was my musical director, John Mulholland, Dorothy Wolf, Al Baker, Ted Annemann and Sam Horowitz joined me in Rigg's Restaurant where we waited for the morning editions to appear.

Since I had been away Mulholland had taken over *The Sphinx* and had made it the leading magical magazine in the world. For him it was a labor of love and a rather thankless job that cost him much of his time, money and health. We became very close friends and he disclosed to me many of his subtle secrets. I found him to be a kindred soul, like Okito, and it was a delight to study this man's technique. Rarely did I find such a perfectionist as John. He took me along to a private engagement he gave in Long Island. What I did with six truckloads of props he did with two suitcases, and entertained them for two solid hours. It was an education in magic with a charming style that I used many, many years later when I did lecture-magic shows of my own in the Argentine.

Theo Annemann also became a very close friend and showed me much of his extraordinary technique in mentalism. His was a subtle technique comparable to Mulholland's but using different methods.

John was kind enough to write about the show in *The Sphinx* and in part he said, ''To me, the whole show was the realization of the dream of what a magic show should be...a liberal education in magic.'' Sweet music coming from a man of his standing in the profession, and it made all that hard work over the years justified. Perhaps I appreciate it more today than I did then.

Always the ham at heart, I wanted to impress the American magicians and put on a three hour show for the debut.

Annemann said in the *Jinx*, "Those who have seen it opine that it is the most beautifully dressed show to hit these shores. The opening ran almost three hours and the illusions, for the most part worked into sketches, are of a type, and carry an atmosphere totally different from what American audiences have seen...the boys are running around in circles and seeing the show three times in a row. By the way, I wonder who the first louse will be to steal his idea on the buzz saw illusion...three days after the show opened U.F. Grant had a total of forty-one calls for the colored sand trick."

Jean Hugard told me he had cried when he saw the show. Dean Frederick Eugene Powell embraced me and told me it was the climax of all magical productions.

You can imagine this sort of thing went to my head. It wasn't that these fine magicians couldn't do a show like mine; it was the fact that I had been my own boss in foreign countries where working conditions were different. I could experiment and do practically what I liked, while they were geared to American show business which was run on an entirely different basis. Theatre conditions in the U.S. were so difficult it was next to impossible to produce a show like mine. I found that out quickly when the unions clamped down on me.

However, this appreciation from the crack men of magic was the greatest artistic satisfaction I had ever had, and I still prize a file of the wonderful letters sent to me.

Variety gave me a two column review and said, in part, "He has a sparkling personality and there hasn't been anyone around in years who has the possibility of carrying on with the big magic show tradition."

Uncle Edward saw the first show a few days after the opening and between shows, in my dressing room, he announced that it wasn't true and that he would have to see it again. As a gag I changed the second show that night and added all the other illusions I had. I suppose he must have been annoyed and thought me a smart aleck because he never came around again. I never saw or heard from him after that.

Dear old Herman was my inseparable companion. The night I was elected to membership in the Society of American Magicians, he was elected along with me and remained a good member until his untimely death in 1940. I never had a friend the same as my boyhood pal. When he went away, part of me went with him.

To be back in New York in the thick of magic was like the old

St. George's Hall days in London. I heard talk about a very hush-hush magic society but no one seemed to know much about it. I was as much in the dark as anyone until I received a letter from Dai Vernon, who was secretary of this unpublicized, exclusive club called The Academy of the Art of Magic, informing me that I had been elected to membership. There were only twelve members in the club and its object was according recognition by election to its fellowship to those who by character and ability have added outstanding distinction to the art of magic. The twelve members at that time were: Al Baker; David Bamberg; Richard Cardini; Arthur Finlay; Paul Fox; S. Leo Horowitz; J. Warren Keene; Nate Leipsig; Max Malini; Charles E. Miller; Garrick M. Spencer; D. W. Vernon.

I attended some memorable sessions and was privileged to see high quality manipulative magic far superior to anything I had ever seen before. I hadn't been around for years and most of it was new for me and they took a keen delight in driving me crazy. Dai Vernon made me suffer for a time with the new "Do As I Do" card trick which had me baffled because of the many variations they used; but finally Dai took pity on me and explained it. Sam Horowitz had developed a new style over the years, entirely different from Vernon's but just as effective, and he gave me many a sleepless hour, and any evening with Al Baker and Nate Leipsig was something never to be forgotten. It was the beginning of the modern school of manipulation, in which apparently no moves are made and things seem to happen of their own accord. The first time I saw the Brain Wave trick by Dai I nearly did a French Drop. There was no doubt the American school of card manipulation was the finest in the world.

The show clicked and I was approached by Lee Shubert, Max Gordon and Norman Bel Geddes for a broadway production but I was high-pressured into signing a contract with the William Morris Agency with a guarantee of $2,000 a week minimum, even for layoffs. It was a terrible mistake as they began to break down the show to a fifty minute vaudeville act to play in combination with pictures. They drove me to distraction with their constant demands to change the routine around. One day one of the big shots in the Morris Agency told me to cut out what he called "that mechanical scene," which was my opening Multiple Production, one of the strongest tricks in the show. I complied and after the show another big shot came backstage and asked me if I was nuts cutting out the flashiest trick! They tore the show to pieces, but of course they had a point as they wanted to gear it to American standards.

I played Hartford, Connecticut, and the Earl Theatre in Philadelphia and made at least a dozen changes to please them. Then they wanted me to open in Chicago with only the Triple Escape in an eight minute act. By this time I was fed up and refused to go. The resulting rumpus cost them $4,000 for layoffs and they weren't happy.

To be perfectly honest, they weren't entirely to blame. The truth was the show in English lost something. Fu Manchu was gone and The Great Manchu, a hybrid personage, had taken over. I just couldn't feel the part in English. The definite pseudo-Chinese-Spanish type was lost, and with it went the essence and most of the comedy. I was unknown in the U.S. and had to start pioneering all over again to create a personality suitable for American audiences. I knew I couldn't do it with a ten minute act.

Another thing that influenced me greatly was the fact that in Latin America I was a big shot in show business and could write my own ticket, but in the U.S. I was just another act.

Leonidoff, artistic director of Radio City Music Hall, wanted me to do the floating ball in one of his stage attractions and we mulled it over. However, the massive stage with its huge settings and light, sky-blue background was not suitable for the ball trick and we got nowhere. I did have the pleasure of meeting my father's old assistant, Erich Rach, again. He was in charge of the complicated light and electronic system of the Radio City stage. He took me on a tour of that marvelous theatre and told me there was nothing in stagecraft that they couldn't do.

Harry Latz wanted to back me for a Broadway season and had previously sent Sam Margules to Torreon, Mexico, to see the show and make arrangements, but as I had lost faith in the Manchu character I refused the offer.

Through a New York agent I was offered the Fuller Circuit in Australia. At the turn of the century, my maternal grandfather, C.W. Poole, had a young bill poster named Ben Fuller. One day this ambitious chap got fed up with the brush and paste-pail and decided to try his luck in faraway Australia. Twenty years later he had the biggest chain of theatres in the country and was knighted by King Geroge V as Sir Benjamin Fuller.

Somehow he had found out that I was C.W.'s grandson and offered me a tour of his circuit on excellent terms, and with the condition that I could do the full evening's show just as I had in Latin America, I was happy to accept his offer.

Moira, in the guise of Chang, showed up in New York just two weeks before I was to sail. He convinced me that the world was ripe for war and advised me to stick to America and not get in Australia or the Far East should hostilities break out. He said my show was new for all South America and he had so much faith in me, he offered to be my impresario for a year.

He was right. Japan was waging war in China. The European situation was uncertain, and Spain was in a terrible civil war. What Chang said made sense. I cancelled the Australian tour and accepted his offer. He arranged my debut in San Juan, Puerto Rico for the following month.

I went up to Peekskill to visit Bobby who looked wonderful. He told me he was very happy in the Academy. Hilda didn't want to go on the tour but she did agree to take charge of the company and rented a house on Staten Island where they lived for a month. I broke my contract with William Morris Agency, much to their relief, and went ahead to Puerto Rico by way of Havana.

Poster for David Bamberg's second Mexican movie, "The Headless Woman" (1944). (See page 292.)

CHAPTER 37

One has the illusion of floating through the center of the city when the boat docks in Havana. I was glad to be back and the tourists on board were startled when I burst into a whoop of laughter at a name on a warehouse that read, Sabanon Y Papada, which in English would be Messrs. Chilblain and Dewlap, even better than Potash and Perlmutter.

Chefalo, the Italian magician, was playing the Comedia Theatre, but as it was stifling summer season, he was doing very poor business. The show was good. His assistants were midgets and one giant, over seven feet tall, who carried two of the midgets in his arms in the streets as a novel advertisement.

His two main illusions were the Chariot illusion (appearance of two girls from an empty chariot) and the Girl From the Drum illusion which he invented and used for years. One of Chefalo's specialties was his ingenious steps for the getaway of his assistant. He was constantly improving his accessory and the last steps he used, in Buenos Aires in 1963, were the best ever for this type of apparatus.

We were together quite a lot. He told me he was on his way down to Buenos Aires and would be ahead of me all the way down the Pacific coast to Chile. We agreed that there was no sense in one of those jumping-jack tours just to cut the other guy's throat so we stuck to our original plans, and the result being that I was more than six months behind him; it didn't affect my business at all and he did well. If his show had been a bit faster and more modern, he would have done even better.

I spent two weeks in Havana as the guest of Senor Correa, owner of the Eden Cabaret, and he explained his plans for opening a new type of outdoor nightclub for the tourist trade. The site for this place was a beautiful spot just a few miles out of

Havana, to be known as the Tropicana. It would have the finest imported acts, a chorus line of the most beautiful girls in Cuba, and the added attraction of gambling. He wanted me to go into this deal with him and direct the artistic angle, but I didn't have the money required for such a partnership and had to refuse. The Tropicana became the most famous nightclub in the world and made a fortune for Correa. That's show business.

When I arrived in Puerto Rico I found that Chang had already sent his representatives ahead. His personal manager was Senor Salvador Fernandez, a Guatemalan who had been with Chang for years and, to my surprise, his other representative was the blond Olivia, who had been out of show business for years. She had changed so greatly that at first I didn't recognize her.

A few days later my company and baggage arrived by boat direct from New York, and Eva Beltri, the Mexican dancer, arrived by plane from Mexico City. We opened at the Municipal Theatre and the season opened on a sour note. Fernandez and Paco Diaz, my representative, couldn't agree on the advertising. Puerto Rico was the most Americanized of all Latin American countries, with the exception of Panama, and neither Diaz nor Fernandez handled the business properly. There was so much bickering both Olivia and Paco Diaz quit and left the country. This left me with Fernandez as my personal manager and, taking over the publicity myself, business picked up and the last two weeks were good.

Our next stop was Caracas, Venezuela, the rich oil country. We played all the towns as far as Marcaibo and from there to the Dutch West Indies. There I was prepared to use the few words of Dutch that I knew, but found that the language used was Papimiento, a mixture of various languages. In Curacao many people still remembered my grandfather from Holland.

The next logical stops were Jamaica, Santo Domingo and Haiti, but Fernandez informed me that they were "no good for show business" at that time. I was rather surprised as I had always thought they were great show countries. We skipped directly to Panama and the American Zone where we opened in the Nacional Theatre. After an uninspiring season in Panama Fernandez again told me "on good authority" that Colombia was "very bad" and said that it would be wiser "to save it" for some future time when things picked up. I knew that Chang had made a fortune in this country and I was very disappointed. We then sailed directly from Panama to Ecuador.

The heat was stifling in the port town of Guayaquil, almost on the equator and, stripped to the waist, we hung all the scenery and took out all the costumes for an airing after the long sea trip. We got to the hotel at three in the morning to catch a few hours sleep before the debut the next day.

I was awakened by blood-chilling screams from Eva and found the hotel room swarming with locusts. I phoned down to the desk and asked what the hell was going on. They told me it was one of those terrible locust plagues that Ecuador is subject to and to pack all my silk shirts as locusts loved silk. Silk? I was out of that hotel like a shot, and rousing the boys in the pension where they were staying, we rushed to the theatre. We found it locked and no night watchman on hand. On my responsibility the boys broke open the stage door and found the insects dropping from the flies onto the stage. There was an open space, for the ventilation, between the zinc roof and the walls of the stage, and the locust swarm was inside the grid and eating its way down. Spreer and I threw the costumes into trunks and locked them while the rest of the boys struck the scenery. The boys' hands were raw from the rough ropes and especially the heavy embroidered front drop that required four to five stagehands to lift. We managed to fold the big drop, constantly sweeping the locusts off with brooms, and packed it in its trunk. After that we lowered and folded all the sets and put them in a dressing room without a window. We sealed all the cracks of the door and the keyhole with sticking plaster. Then we got busy killing locusts. The stage was a shambles, with locust juice all over the place. About ten o'clock in the morning the manager of the theatre showed up and was most indignant that we had broken his door to get in. He didn't worry about the show, of course; all he could think about was a two-bit lock.

Yet the worst was still to come. After the locusts came a tremendous thing called the fever bug, a type of giant flying beetle whose bite is slightly poisonous and causes a high fever. These loathsome things were all over town. There was nothing to do but wait until the wind changed when they would fly off. The town literally stunk with squashed insects, and in one area around the lighthouse, the dead bugs were two feet deep.

We didn't leave the hotel room for three days and even ate our meals in bed, under a thick mosquito netting. Even then they got in, and every time Eva saw a locust, she would go into hysterics, until I had a yen to throttle her.

At last it ended and we opened. Everything was forgotten

when we did a record-smashing business, which I sorely needed as I was scraping the bottom of the money barrel again.

From Guayaquil we took the train to Quito, up that hair-raising pass known as the Devil's Nose, where trains shuttle up the sheer sides of a cliff. Some wag had painted on one of the slopes, "Abandon hope all ye who enter here" which did us a lot of good.

The Sucre Theatre in Quito was a lovely colonial theatre and I was able to present the show as I had in Havana. Chefalo, for some reason, had skipped Ecuador and they hadn't seen a big magic show for years. It was like the good old times all over again and everything was rosey. It was always easy to forget the past when the money started rolling in.

My political skit, King Blackbeard, was the outstanding comedy trick in the show and it became so popular that the President of the Republic, General Alberto Enriquez, his cabinet and diplomatic corps, and the majority of foreign ambassadors attended a special gala show in the President's honor. The political situation in Europe was getting worse and the Ecuatorianos loved my critical slaps at Hitler and Mussolini. After the show the President came backstage to congratulate me and give me an autographed photo.

I left little Ecuador with regret, but I was to return there many times, always with good business. I had another "sure" country on my list.

We returned to Guayaquil and sailed for Callao, the port of Lima, Peru. Fernandez had booked the best theatre in town, the Municipal, the opera house of Lima. We papered the town and paraded the streets in Chinese costume for the benefit of the large Chinese colony there and the debut was a sellout.

Maybe I'm superstitious at heart but I think there are good luck towns and bad luck towns. Almost every time I played Lima something happened there that wasn't good.

The house was packed to the rafters on that opening night but I could feel an undercurrent in the audience just like the time in Rio Grande do Sul, Brazil, when I needed a police escort to leave town. They applauded my tricks but they seemed to be waiting for something and it didn't take me long to find out what it was.

When I started the King Blackbeard trick there was a sudden cold silence and about half way through the skit groups of furious, fist shaking, red-faced men got to their feet and shouted "communista" and "sin verguenza" with a shrill "imperialista" here and there. I had a nice little riot on my hands. The police swarmed in and it seemed odd that so many cops were at hand so quickly, and although the offenders were thrown out, the damage was done and the show fell flat. I was forced to take out the trick for the season.

I visited the leading newspapers the next day and explained that anyone who was an anti-Nazi or anti-fascist was not necessarily a communist. The U.S. and England were anti-Nazis but that didn't make them lovers of Russia. They explained to me that the fascist element in Quito had tipped off the breathren in Lima about my skit. The scandal they had created in the theatre did not represent the majority of Limenos. The police had been tipped off and the only one who hadn't known about it was the magician and mind reader, Fu Manchu.

People were afraid of more riots and business was only fair. Even when the President came to see the show it didn't help and we left Lima without fanfare.

I went directly to Santiago de Chile. Being in my old neighborhood again, we did a terrific business and King Blackbeard was hailed with delight. This skit still earned me a lot of political enemies that were to do me harm in the future. It's better to keep magic and politics apart as far as possible in these countries, especially as a foreigner, but who could reason with me in those days?

Chang's impresario, Ramiro de la Presa, a Cuban, was waiting for me in Santiago. He had brought along an American orchestra leader named Jack Obermann with his wife and also a sister act, two cute Argentine twins, Tita and Lola, who were so identical that right away I had visions of several hot illusions.

Ramiro told me that he had arranged the National Theatre in Buenos Aires for my debut, but instead of making the long jump from Santiago we would have to play Mendoza and Cordoba on the way.

We did an excellent business in Chile and the newspapers were just as generous as they had been the first time. Everyone seemed to go out of their way to make us comfortable and happy. I loved Chile and was always happy to play there.

Back again over the Andes to Mendoza; but this time it was almost the end of summer. There was no ice and snow and it was a pleasant trip. In Mendoza we inaugurated a new theatre alongside the Casino. The management offered a grand fiesta in the lobby after the show with huge bowls of "punche" which was fruit, drowned in good wine from the rich vineyards of Mendoza and San Juan. Fernandez, not a drinking man, dipped into the bowl too often and, in a tearful mood, had a row with Ramiro, thus the inside story of my South American tour came out.

It was all perfectly legitimate from a Latin American business standpoint, but I had been played for a sucker all along the line. Chang had booked the opposition circuit in Australia (the Rickard circuit and the J.C. Williamson Theatres Ltd.) and wanted to get there first. That's why he had sold me on the South American deal. Fernandez had skipped Jamaica, Santo Domingo and Colombia as he was "saving" it for some future time and didn't want the territory "burned out."

When I arrived in Buenos Aires I found the situation even worse. Chang had just finished a long season at the Avenida Theatre and was about to leave for Australia and the Far East. To make things tougher, my impresario in the National Theatre, Senor Enrique Muscio, had also arranged for Chefalo to open in the Broadway Theatre, only two weeks before my opening— with the Million Dollar Mystery as the chief attraction!

If ever a place was "burned-out" for magic, it was Buenos Aires at that time. This whole crummy deal was considered fair play in theatrical circles and there was nothing I could do about it. It did teach me, however, that one shouldn't mix friendship with business. I took it and kept my mouth shut, but if they wanted to play games, I figured one day I could show them a second deal of my own.

Buenos Aires had changed. The Calle Corrientes was now a wide avenue. Two great "diagonales" had been cut right through the heart of town. The old Teatro Buenos Aires where I had worked with Raymond, the Comedia where I had first seen Li-Ho-Chang, and the Teatro Sarmiento were torn down to make way for the Avenida 9 de Julio with the huge obelisk right in the center of town. The population was now five million and it was still growing.

What saved me in Buenos Aires was the National Theatre being next to the obelisk on the main street. It can be compared to Broadway and 42nd Street in importance. Seven theatres had been demolished in this big face-lifting job and houses were at a premium.

The Broadway Theatre, on Corriente, was a picture house and Chefalo had it for only two weeks. I went to see his show and was terribly disappointed with the Million Dollar Mystery, a much talked about illusion invented by Selbit. Chefalo, for some technical reason, had built a spider-web affair made of copper tubing behind the production box, which was close to the backdrop due to the wide stage. From the center of the house it was no illusion at all. Chefalo was disgusted but he had to do it as it had been heavily advertised. I saw it later in another theatre under better conditions, but perhaps I was prejudiced. I still thought it a rather silly illusion, although the basic principle is useful for other effects.

We did a three months' season at the National with average audiences on weekdays but packed houses on Saturdays and Sundays. From the National we went over to the new Teatro Comedia (an old house renamed) and it was there, a few days after our opening, that a careless employee left a stage trap door open between the hanging drapes. On coming into the theatre early one afternoon I stepped right into the trap and fell fifteen feet into the cellar. I just missed being killed by a piece of sawed-off iron girder that projected from the trap about eight inches. Luckily, I fell straight down and landed on my feet but badly twisted both my ankles. After about half an hour someone found me and I was rushed to a hospital where my legs were injected and bound. I was out of the show for three days, which did not do business any good as a break in the beginning of a season is nearly always fatal. The papers made much of "the magician who vanished through his own trap," but I was not amused. When I could work again, we did one of those dragged-out seasons that finally bogged down to nothing. We changed to another theatre on the Calle Corrientes, the Comico, which was across from the Broadway. Here things were much better. From there we went to the Boedo Theatre.

I took over the Solis Theatre again in Montevideo and did well, then played the River Plate towns before returning to Buenos Aires where I opened in the Mayo Theatre. From there, of all places, I played the Avenida Theatre, which was Chang's stronghold. It was there that the force of Madrid was felt. The Spanish colony had either seen me or read about me in the Spanish papers and we did a wonderful season, thanks to the old Teatro Zarzuela.

In spite of everything, I had played over a year in the city of Buenos Aires and it was time to get out. But where? I didn't need the seer Chang to tell that Europe was almost at the boiling point. Spain was still at war and Africa was too risky. Brazil was still a dead end. I had no alternative but to go north again. There was only one sensible solution. Start in La Paz, Bolivia, where a magic show hadn't played for years; then play through

Peru to Ecuador and Colombia, where I had great success and, thanks to Chang, was now open for me. I would go from there up through Central America, all new countries for me, to Mexico.

Ramiro de la Presa, Chang's impresario, had a fight with Chang and had stayed behind in Buenos Aires. He offered to be my impresario for this return trip as he wanted to get back to his native Cuba.

This would seem senseless after all the trouble I had with these people, but I accepted chiefly because Ramiro was an excellent publicity man and dreamed up all kinds of stunts. He had been my publicity man in the Solis in Montevideo and had thought up a fantastic extravaganza for the combined celebration of Uruguay's independence day with the signing of the peace treaty that ended the Chaco war between Bolivia and Paraguay. We had four special backdrops painted for this show and they depicted scenes from history and included the statues of Generals Artigas and Urquiza. A lineup of extras, dressed in the old grenadier guards regalia, stood in front of a drop painted with a huge army in perspective behind them, while I produced from an empty drum, flags of the twenty-one South American Republics.

On the 18th of July, following the finish of this patriotic display, the ambassadors of Bolivia and Paraguay were invited onto the stage to shake hands while I produced a white dove as a symbol of peace. As luck would have it, the dove flew into the air and settled on the shoulder of the Bolivian ambassador, just as he was embracing the Paraguayan diplomat! The audience thought it was a trick and that the dove was trained. There was a great roar of appreciation and the audience, including the President of Uruguay, stood up en masse and cheered. Tears were in the eyes of many a tough old gaucho and the show was stopped cold as anything after that would be anticlimactic.

When the Bolivian ambassador returned to La Paz he told the story to the press and the newspapers were full of the incident, so I had very little trouble getting the government owned Municipal Theatre for my debut.

We left Buenos Aires by train for Bolivia, passing through and playing the northern Argentine towns of Santiago del Estero, Tucuman, Salta and Jujuy on the way to the frontier.

From the moment I stepped off the train in La Paz I was in the spotlight and my debut was unforgettable. The President of the Republic, a tall, handsome young man with the Germanic name of Busch, was in the presidential box, with his staff and when he clasped his hands in a sign of friendship to me, it brought the house down. It was one of those debuts where everything goes right. After the show the President came backstage and complimented me on the Montevideo affair and asked me why I hadn't done the pigeon trick. Sad to relate, a few months later he was assassinated, as was General Enriquez, the President of Ecuador, who was practically cut in two by machine gun bullets.

It took me quite some time to become acclimatized in La Paz, which is the highest capital in the world with the exception of Lhasa in Tibet. After the Triple Escape I would get dizzy spells and one night while doing the water bowl production I felt dizzy and made a false step in getting up on the platform with the heavy load and was ruptured. This was the first of a series of hernias that have plagued me all my life.

I had never been up in the altiplano before and it was interesting to see the colorful cholos with their llamas and their white varnished hats. It was customary for the Indian women to buy a new skirt of a contrasting color every year, and wear one on top of the other until some of them wore over thirty skirts.

A laughable incident happened the day before I opened in the Municipal. The streets of La Paz are very steep and with the high altitude, a newcomer has to go slow. I was on my way from the hotel to the theatre and stopped on a corner to watch four sturdy cholos carrying a piano through the street, supporting it with leather thongs stretched over their foreheads. I had never seen such a thing and stood there watching them until they reached the foot of a steep street where they rested for a moment, easing the piano down in the middle of the road, blocking traffic. Suddenly a man rushed out of a corner cantina and belabored the cholos with a short whip and there was a terrible argument in Guarani which I didn't understand. After a while the brute with the whip returned to the cantina.

I had never seen a man thrashed with a whip before and it angered me. I should have known better than to get mixed up in these things, but I walked over the cholos and asked if they spoke Spanish. One of them explained that the jerk with the whip was an overseer and they had been promised a few pesos to carry the heavy piano across town. In one of my quixotic moods I indignantly told them that if they would leave the blasted piano where it was in the middle of the street I would pay them double. They stared at me as if I were insane but accepted the offer by acclamation and trotted off down a side street and out of my life forever.

I continued my long climb to the theatre highly pleased with my Boy Scout deed and imagining the overseer's rage when he found the abandoned piano. When I finally got to the theatre I found the administrador calmly chewing coca-leaf and when I inquired if everything was in order he said, "Everything's fine except that I'm afraid your orchestra rehearsal will be late because the piano we rented hasn't shown up yet."

Moral: No te metas en que no te improta! (Don't interfere where it is not important.)

We had a great season in La Paz and I was beginning to go on the gold standard again. We played a couple of other Bolivian towns and then left for Peru, taking the small steamer that makes the trip to Puno, Peru on the world's highest lake, Titicaca, dotted with its strange Islands of the Sun. My mania for omens was satisfied when two things happened. We were playing poker on board when a card fell off the table and landed face up on the deck. It was the ace of spades, the death card. (In fortune telling, the ace of spades signifies sickness or death and is considered the unluckiest card in the pack. In 1615 James I of England placed a tax on cards and the government enforced this tax by prohibiting anyone but themselves to manufacture the ace of spades. Card makers could only complete their packs by purchasing the ace of spades from the government. Forging the ace of spades was punishable by death and the superstition of the black ace lives on. In Argentina the ace of hearts was taxed by the government and carried the official stamp.)

The second incident happened in my hotel room when we arrived in Puno, a tiny town where the lights are cut off at midnight. There were some candles in the room and I lighted three of them and was petrified by a goosefleshing shriek from Eva who doused one of the candles and told me that in Mexico it was a sign of death to have three lighted candles in a room.

Hogwash! I thought as I went to sleep, only to be awakened early the next morning by a banging on the door. I opened it to find a little Indian boy who said, "El tren se suicido, senor."

"What the hell is he talking about?" I said to Eva, "The train committed suicide? Does he mean there was a train wreck?"

I tried to question the frightened boy but that was all I could get out of him until Eva took over and finally comprehended that someone in our company had been injured.

I dressed hurriedly and finished just as Fernandez appeared, pale as a ghost, saying that Ramiro de la Presa had been killed by the narrow-gauge train that ran from the dock to the main station in town. The locomotive had been pushing a line of freight cars backwards and as Ramiro was deaf, he didn't hear the warning whistle as he crossed the track. The end car knocked him down and five freight cars ran over him before the train could be stopped. By a strange twist of fate it was Peru's national holiday, July 22, and the locomotive was draped with the flags of America that Ramiro had loved so much.

For some reason, perhaps because I was the head of the company, the police insisted I attend the autopsy, which was performed in an open patio, but as they started to cut across the hairline to tear away the scalp I became violently sick and walked out. The whole town turned up for the funeral and he was buried in a niche in a high wall overlooking the lake.

I wanted to suspend the one show we had planned for Puno but a committee headed by the mayor pleaded with us to give the performance and I agreed, but I cut out all the comedy. It was a very stuffy show but they liked it.

We took the mountain train to Arequipa. Ramiro had been arranging the business in Lima, but had left no notes or papers concerning the people he had been dealing with. I sent Fernandez ahead but opened in Arequipa without anyone to control the door and lost a great deal. Fernandez returned ten days later with a contract for the same Municipal Theatre where I had the riot on the way down. He also informed me that the little Puno newspaper had mixed up and sent a report to the Associated Press that *I* had been killed—so I was mourned in most of the Latin American countries. Later I read my obituary in a Buenos Aires' paper and it was a scary thing to read.

We opened in Lima—without King Blackbeard—and business began to boom. I still thought Peru was unlucky for me after what happened to poor Ramiro, but I thought that whatever misfortune was to happen to us had already happened and from now on it would be plain sailing. And then, a few days after the debut, England declared war on Germany! For the first few days Lima was panicky as we all expected a tremendous onslaught, but when nothing happened the city settled down to the old routine. Still, it didn't do my business any good as the theatre is always the first to suffer. I changed over to the Segura Theatre, with lowered prices, and was saved.

It was in the Segura that I had a Peruvian sculptor do a life size head of me in clay. He did a fine job and from that head we made papier-mache masks of my face and using an assistant who was roughly my size and build, I had a perfect double. I broke in a new illusion, which I called the Third Man, which was an instant success. The day after war was declared I reported to the British Consulate and offered my services. I was told that they had no instructions as yet, but if I wanted to go to England at my own expense and take a physical I "might" be accepted. They thought that England had no need of manpower for the moment but there was one thing I could do: keep my eyes and ears open and report anything that might be of use. I agreed, and when I told them I understood German, they were delighted and told me to mix with the German speaking people as much as possible. I did and got a bloody bad name for it—all for the cause.

Then there was the problem of Spreer. He had been a faithful employee for thirteen years. Was I suppose to throw him out on his neck? He had absolutely no interest in politics and less in Hitler; in fact, he had often said that he thought Germany was going the wrong way and his one worry was what would happen to his father who was of Jewish extraction. There was nowhere for Spreer to go. If he lost his job with me he would be deported to Germany as he only had a three months' visa for Peru. I decided to do nothing and wait to see what happened.

After Lima we trekked through the Inca country, through sandy wastelands and deserts that stretch from Chiquicamata to southern Ecuador, playing the coastal towns of Trujillo, Chicalayo, Talara (the oil center), and Piura on the frontier, then crossed the bay to Guayaquil, Ecuador. Considering that we had been there such a short time before, we did exceptional business. This time I picked up a few shrunken Indian heads, including a very rare one of a white man with a blonde beard.

It was good to be back in Ecuador again after those days on a desert so parched that for miles on end not a living thing could be seen. The nights, however, were spectacular. Never have I seen so many stars in the sky. It was like looking through a telescope with untold thousands of stars that could be seen with the naked eye, and on that lonely desert it was all the more eerie.

Again we took that awesome trip up the Devil's Nose to Quito and played the same theatre for the same people and it was getting to be a family affair. I left Quito with love in my heart that turned to ice as we went over the mountain trails on the way to the Colombian frontier.

Our first stop was the border town of Pasto. The theatre there was very small and we set up a half show. The performance went over all right but after the show, when we went to a cafe and ordered tintos (black coffee), we got black looks from the men sitting around the tables. One drunken Indio tried to start a fight. We shoved him away and the situation became tense. The patron of the cafe sent for a policeman, but when he came in the first thing he told us was to remove our ties. It just happened that we were wearing blue neckties and in Colombia there are two rival political parties, the Blues and the Reds, and the necktie is their identity. From that time on in Colombia we were careful of our choice of neckwear. Even our girls packed their blue and red dresses.

If I thought that the trip from Quito to Pasto had been bad, I was in for a surprise. It was U.S. Highway No. 1 compared to the so-called road built by the Colombian army in thirty days that led to Popayan. It was a dirt road just wide enough for one car to pass at a time and used a telephone and chain system to hold back any truck coming the opposite way. Sometimes one waited for hours. Some of the precipices were so deep and the road in such a bad shape that I often got out of the car and made my way on foot. That trip brought out a phobia of heights that has never left me to this day.

It was on this trip that we passed through the valley of the ''White Indians'' with their blonde hair and blue eyes which some claim started with a Norwegian settler.

At one stop I was scared out of a year's growth by a giant centipede, fully fifteen inches long, that travelled with the speed of a race horse. The creature ran up and fastened itself on the arm of a young Indian who shouted something and then held perfectly still. It seemed like an eternity until a woman came running up with a hot flat iron and held it about two inches above the centipede. When the monster felt the heat it lifted its legs and started to move. At this instant the boy gave it a quick side flick with the edge of his hand, knocking it to the ground where it was instantly crushed with a stone. The Indians claim this is the only way to deal with these creatures, as once they get their claws into a human being there is no way to remove them without a poisonous and sometimes deadly sting.

Another Indian remedy, which greatly impressed me, I saw used near Buenaventura some time later. A naked Indian tot, about three years old, had the misfortune to sit on a brazier of smouldering charcoal, burning his little bottom terribly. The native woman immediately emptied bags of salt into a pile and sat the screaming child in the middle of it. After a few minutes the child quieted down and they told me there would not even be a scar to show for his mishap. Since that time, when I have slight burns, I have applied salt and it certainly does relieve the pain.

CHAPTER 38

Moira works in strange ways and through a gift to a Colombian bishop my parents were saved from the Nazis.

In Popayan I made the acquaintance of Don Guillermo Valencia, poet and man of letters greatly revered in Colombia, and his son, who at the time of writing this is president of Colombia. Don Guillermo was kind enough to write a very fine comment on the show which was invaluable to me for publicity as his name carried great weight in Latin America.

It was through him that I was introduced to the Bishop of Popayan, a charming and most influential man in a country that is even more Catholic than Spain.

One of Eva's most prized possessions was a small half-inch square of cloth cut from the coat of the Mexican martyr saint, Padre Pro. He was brutally shot to death by the revolutionists, and this bit of blood-stained cloth came from the coat he was wearing. Eva generously presented this relic to the Bishop who was greatly pleased. We also arranged to give a free matinee show for the poor Catholic children.

A few days later an order came through from Bogota, signed by the Minister of the Interior, exempting me from the crippling thirty-three percent theatre tax if I would agree to give these matinees all over the country. I agreed and wrote him a letter of thanks to which he replied and said that he would be delighted to see me when I visited Bogota. From Popayan we went to Cali and up the valley of the Cauca to Medellin, touching some of the river port towns of the Magdalena River. I had been under the impression that I was hard-bitten by this time, but no one had ever told me about the interior of Colombia or those trips on the Mississippi-type paddle wheelers and being stuck on sand bars for days at a time.

One small town called Honda is considered to be one of the hottest spots in South America. Even sitting quietly there, with no exertion of any kind, is like sitting in a Turkish bath. I spent the night wrapped in a bed sheet which I would soak under the shower and then lie down and doze, but soon I was ready for the cooling shower again. For a guy as thin as I was this was really debilitating.

During the night, attracted by the light, the screens of the doors and windows were covered with insects the size of those blown-up models you see in museums. Giant praying mantis, huge grasshopper-like things, my old pals the outsize spiders and one thing that looked like a broken twig with green leaves for wings—nature's finest job of camouflage. I was told it was poisonous.

I had seen the native huts with open windows and no doors and would somebody please explain to me how anyone can sleep on the floor with that unholy crew creeping and crawling about? When I mentioned it to the patron of the hotel, he laughed and told me I was a great wit. I never did understand the joke. I wonder why Noah didn't step on those things.

Now comes a priceless bit. Russia had declared war on Finland and we gave benefit shows in aid of the Finnish Red Cross. A couple of years later Russia was our ally again and somebody found out about those shows, so I was called anti-Allied. You can't mix magic with anything.

There were very few shows in Colombia at that time and my chief opposition was Pat O'Brien, the movie actor, who used to rush over to watch the vanishing bird cage, which was driving him crazy.

Finally we got to Bogota and opened at the Faenza Theatre, where I had the pleasure of meeting Carl Jones, the publisher of magic books, from Minneapolis. Carl and Mrs. Jones had come down especially to see the show and we spent many happy days, with Carl doing tricks for my assistants behind the front drop while I was working on the stage!

I paid that visit to the Minister of the Interior and he was most courteous. We talked about the war and I said that it looked like a phony one and I didn't think much would happen. He told me to stop kidding myself; when things really started, it would be world-shaking. When I told him that my parents lived in Holland, not far from the German frontier, he advised me to get them out as quickly as possible. He said that if he could be of any help he would be delighted. I took him up on it and requested three visas for Colombia for my mother, father and brother. He said he would attend to it at once.

Holland was laboring under the delusion, as was much of the rest of the world, that nothing was going to happen. The phony war had lulled them into a false sense of security. In his letters Okito reminded me that Germany had respected Holland's neutrality in the First World War and he believed they had nothing to worry about.

I sent him a long and alarming cable which apparently scared him, for he sold the house for a ridiculously low price, stored his show in the cellar of a friend and, carrying just a wardrobe trunk, he cabled me he was leaving. When the cable arrived I had a bad moment or two as I remembered the time in Buenos Aires when I had influenced his coming over on what turned out to be a disastrous business venture. I prayed I hadn't made another mistake, because this time he had sold almost everything he owned.

But time has proved that this was the most prudent thing I ever did in my life. My father told me later that the Colombian Embassy in The Hague had given him the red carpet treatment as the Minister of the Exterior had given express orders to treat my family as V.I.P.'s. The Embassy even arranged passage for them on the Conte Biancamano, sailing from Genoa on its last trip to the Americas, where it was interned in Panama for the duration.

My brother was refused permission to leave Holland as Dutch law stated that all children of Hollanders were Dutch subjects. In spite of being born in New York, he was drafted as a sergeant of the grenadiers. My sister was married and went to Switzerland.

They left just in time. The Conte Biancamano arrived at Curacao, Dutch West Indies, on May 10, 1940, the very day Hitler invaded Holland. From that day on we had no more news of Donald, but at least my parent were safe in America.

Meanwhile, I changed theatres in Bogota and played the Municipal Theatre for a season with good business and from there took a trip through the eastern part of Colombia, as far as Cucuta on the Venezuelan frontier. This little town is famous for the nearby emerald mines; both crude and cut stones were sold in the streets. I visited one of these mines, was given an uncut stone as a present, and saw the miner dig it out of the "well" where the precious stones are found. It was quite large, but after I had it cut and polished, it was reduced to less than a tenth of its original size, yet it was worth about five hundred dollars.

While in Cucuta I received news that my parents had landed in Baranquila, Colombia's largest Caribbean port, and were taking the river steamer to Puerto Wilches, the port of Bucaramanga, where we would meet.

They arrived there first and a few days later our meeting in the old Rosendal Hotel was one of wild joy and backslapping. We certainly got together in the darndest places.

Okito had not seen my new show and my mother had never seen me work as a Chinese magician at all. It was a pity they had to see the show on such a small stage as I had to cut it considerably. I couldn't wait for the debut and had the boys set up the sawing illusion and the duck vanish and told Okito to sit in the front row.

The ham in me demanded balm for those sarcastic remarks of his over the years. I did the duck vanish first. He sat there with no expression on his long, intelligent face. Then he said, "Do it again, I don't get it." Sweet music! I did it again. "I still don't get it," he said, coming up onto the stage. I showed him the gimmick. "Gott! Vy did I neffer come on this idea?" was all he said—but it was enough.

But greater joy was in store for me. I returned him to the front row and did the sawing—not the whole sketch, just the actual cutting of the girl. He slowly walked up onto the stage and put his hand on my shoulder and said, "I vish my father vos here to see this. Vot would I hafe giffen to haf had such an illusion in my time. It iss extraordinary."

He inspected the gimmick and right away his inventive mind started to get busy and he suggested improvements and undertook to carry them out.

That night he saw the full show sitting in a box with my mother and after the show he said to me, "What I have seen tonight is the climax of all the Bambergs."

Another effect that intrigued him was the walking forward to the footlights with the floating ball.

Years later Robert Lund asked a group of prominent magicians to name the eight acts they would like to see on an all-time magic bill. There were no restrictions except that the list be limited to eight performers.

"Let me point out that I have had the great advantage and opportunity of seeing many old-time performers as a youth," Okito prefaced his reply to the questionnaire, "acts that never appeared in the United States. I have selected eight performers I have witnessed. I consider these the great masters, the fine experts, both for the general theatre-goer and the connoisseur alike.''

Okito's list: Compars (Carl) Herrmann, Buatier de Kolta, L'Homme Masque (Jose Antenor Gago y Zavala), David Devant, Servais LeRoy, Max Malini, Cardini and Fu Manchu.

''There are others deserving of the name master magician,'' Okito concluded, ''but you asked for only eight, and there they are.''

It was a great compliment coming from him and a far cry from the old St. George's Hall days in London when I had been scragged for opening my mouth.

As a further aside, let me retell two delightful stories Okito told me of how he outwitted the Russian customs and government.

The first time, just after the post World-War I inflation, he had unwittingly taken a number of unset diamonds with him, but was informed by other artistes that if they were found on him at the frontier, they would be confiscated as they hadn't been declared. He considered that for a while and then took a block of wood about four inches square, sawed off a quarter of it, and from the larger piece hollowed out a space big enough to hold the diamonds packed in cotton wool. He glued the quarter piece back on and let it dry overnight in a clamp. The next day he worked the block into a perfect cube, drilled a half-inch hole right through the middle of it, gave it a splendid paint and decorative job. Next he sawed up his old die for the Block and Frame trick and burned the pieces. He mussed the new die up so it looked like a used prop, and at the Polish frontier, when his baggage was being inspected, he had the colossal nerve to do the trick for the guards—even passing everything for examination. Of course this was absolutely unnecessary, but it pleased his perverse sense of humor.

The other time was far more serious. All foreign acts playing in the Russian State Theatres were engaged by the government and paid in either dollars or pounds as no artiste wanted rubles. Okito played in Leningrad, Moscow and Odessa and was paid every week in white five pound notes which looked like tissue paper. (In spite of their simple appearance, I have been told that British high denomination notes are among the most difficult in the world to counterfeit.) Shortly before leaving Russia, Okito was informed that no foreign currency was allowed to be taken out of the country. One had the choice of leaving the money in banks or buying Russian made articles. There was nothing Okito wanted to buy as most of the goods were of a very inferior quality, and to leave the money behind in a bank was out of the question as he had no intention of returning. So what to do? This time it wasn't like the diamond deal because the government knew he had the money and exactly how much. Okito was furious.

"Who the hell would have gone to that godforsaken hole if he knew beforehand that he couldn't take the money out?" he said to me.

He decided to take a long-shot chance. He had arranged a tour of Egypt and Morocco to follow his Russian engagement and craftily signed a contract with an acrobat playing on the same bill with him, who was leaving Russia a few days before him. Okito insisted that the acrobat wait for him in Warsaw, where they would leave together for Trieste. Without telling the acrobat, Okito spread his pounds between the protective canvas cover and the bottom of one of the man's suitcases.

Okito knew that the acrobat would have no trouble getting through the customs as these acts were notoriously underpaid and rarely managed to save anything. The only real danger lay in the acrobat finding the money and running off with it, but Okito figured this was better than leaving it in Russia.

Everything went as planned and the acrobat left for Warsaw and wired Okito when he arrived.

Now was the time for Okito to go into his great cloak and dagger act. One evening, just before leaving for the theatre, he broke the lock of the cheap wooden wardrobe in his room, making it appear as if it had been forced and wiped away all fingerprints with a towel. After the show, when he returned to his room and "discovered" that he had been "robbed," he put on a heart-rending act and, of course, the police were called in. However, Okito had under-estimated the Soviet police and a dour inspector examined the wardrobe lock carefully and then requested Okito to open his American wardrobe trunk and just as carefully examined the Yale lock.

"I cannot understand why you hid your money in a wardrobe with a cheap lock that can be opened with a hairpin when you have such a solid trunk with an excellent lock."

"Exactly," answered Okito, who had not read Poe's *Purloined Letter* in vain. "I thought that a thief might try to force the trunk lock but would never dream that anything of value would be in the wardrobe."

"Oh! So you expected to be robbed?"

"No! But one has to take precautions. Maybe I was trying to be too clever. I think now that I made a bad mistake. The thief came to steal clothes and found the money by accident."

The police-inspector studied Okito for a long moment and after a few formalities he took his departure with a cold "good-night." Okito knew they hadn't swallowed his story and was further convinced when he arrived at the Russo-Polish frontier. Everyone of the company was stripped and searched. All the trunks and crates were unpacked and in some cases the linings were ripped out and a few of the props X-rayed. They held him up for three days and his heart was in his mouth when he thought of the possibility of the acrobat getting tired of waiting and wandering off somewhere. Finally the customs were defeated and he was allowed to cross the frontier.

The acrobat was waiting for him in Warsaw and when Okito dramatically removed the canvas cover of the suitcase and displayed the loot, the poor acrobat nearly had an attack. "You had no right to do that. Suppose they had found it?" he wailed, "I would have been accused of theft."

Okito told him that if the money had been discovered, Okito would have owned up and taken his chances as they couldn't do much to a man for stealing his own money. I think Okito was wrong on this point, and if the trick had been discovered, they would both have been in deep trouble. Happily, it turned out well and some time later Okito sent a sarcastic letter to the Russian government which ruined any chance of his ever returning.

My mother was happy to be in South America but she under-mined her health worrying about Donald. She suffered greatly in the following six years.

In Barranquila I got the news that my boyhood friend Her-man had died. I had been in constant touch with him as he was night operator on the South American lines of All America Cables and at night, when the lines were slack, we chatted for a few moments now and then. His death affected me greatly and both my father and mother remembered him with love.

We played the Caribbean ports of Santa Marta and Cienaga and returned to Puerto Cabello where we took a Dutch boat sailing for Costa Rica. For the first time we felt the war when the portholes were covered and no lights were allowed on deck at night for fear of submarines. Two trips later that ship was torpedoed and sunk.

San Jose de Costa Rica was a beautiful little city nestled in the hills of the most democratic country of Latin America. I was fortunate to obtain the Nacional Theatre, Costa Rica's beautiful opera house. We did splendid sell-out business and ended a long season with a gala performance attended by President Guardia and his lady. The proceeds of the evening went to the home for crippled children.

From the Nacional we went over to the Reventos Teatre for a season of popular prices. It was here that I presented a special show for children's matinees called "Pinocho en China." I had always had the conviction that the big show was not suitable for small children, being geared for adults, both in intricate magical effects and dialogue. "Pinocho" was a magical fairy tale. We used the same illusions as the big show but with a simple, easy-to-follow plot which included Pinocho (a puppet), Aladin, a witch, a comedy king and queen, a pretty princess, Patote (an oversized baby) and a monkey. The continuity of the play was helped by the use of sets projected on a white sheet and the actors in silhouette, interspersed with the regular full stage settings. This novel form of children's show was so popular that the Walt Disney picture, "Pinnochio," which opened at the same time there, made less than half the money we did.

There were no roads in the Central American jungles and mountains in those days. Leaving Costa Rica by way of the Pacific port of Punta Arenas, we took a small coastal steamer to Managua, Nicaragua. We lived in a large hotel with a big swimming pool. Okito was delighted with the carefree life we led in these countries. Especially fine, from his point of view, were the large stages of the Municipal Theatres, where one was free to do as he liked. We tried all sorts of experiments and new illusions during the day, always adding a new bit here and there to make the show better and more novel.

Again we took a tiny coast steamer to the little port of Amapola, Honduras, and then up the mountain to Tegucigalpa, where Okito ran up against black magic for the first time in his life. Belief in voodooism, macumba and other forms of black magic were common in Latin America, and in some places they threw a dead toad or a vampire bat from the upper gallery boxes to cross my path and take away my "magical powers." In Tegucigalpa they threw down black flowers that cast a spell to drive out the demons which they thought I possessed and which were responsible for my magic. Had I sold talismans and

275

horoscopes I could have made a fortune in those places.

The Indian population liked straight magic without comedy. They took things seriously, which was proven by what happened one "Dia de los Inocentes" (Day of the Innocents) which falls on the 28th of December and is equivalent to April Fool's Day. The comic strip of "Tarzan of the Apes" was followed avidly by the whole population of one town in northern Colombia. As a gag, the newspaper which was running the strip had a cartoonist fake an adventure for "Inocentes" day in which Tarzan was attacked by a tribe of African savages. In the last picture of the strip Tarzan looked like a porcupine with fifty spears sticking out of his back like so many quills, and last caption bewailed the death of the great jungle warrior. The gag backfired when infuriated Tarzan fans attacked the offending paper with stones and almost burned the place down!

It was in the ghostly old Teatro Nacional of Tegucigalpa that I was inspired to write the short story, "The Weird Adventure of Doctor Q" which was published in *The Sphinx* magazine. Later I received a letter from Floyd Thayer in Los Angeles who was quite upset because I had "killed" his mythical wonder worker (created by the mentalist Alexander) by having Dr. Q perform the spirit cabinet routine on the evening of the Day of the Dead (November 2) and be carried off by an audience of zombies who had attended the show en masse, coming from their nearby graveyard. Nice, cheerful stuff and, although it was a tongue-in-the-cheek story, it was surprising how seriously it was taken in certain quarters.

Taxes were high in Honduras. When making out our tax report to get our exit permit for El Salvador, my manager Fernandez padded the expense account as much as he dared. His estimate for duck fodder was a wonder to behold. His statement was returned by the Internal Revenue people with a sarcastic note asking him if the ducks had a suite in the Ritz-Carlton hotel and, if so, under what names were they registered!

And so to El Salvador, the smallest of the Latin American republics, which we entered through the Port of La Union, where the nearby cluster of seven volcanos kept the tiny country constantly trembling. We opened in the capital city of San Salvador to a surprisingly sophisticated audience.

One evening before leaving El Salvador I attended a small circus. One of the acts was an oriental magician who did a cute little act in the ring. His closing number was a cremation illusion, exactly like the one I had used in the original Fu Manchu show. It was the first time I had seen anyone use the visible vanish of the shrouded figure just before the explosion. After the show I went back to ask him how he had come on the idea and was surprised to find out that it was my original apparatus he was using! I had sold it many years before to someone in Sao Paulo, during the revolution days, and here it had popped up—after changing hands half a dozen times—in a small circus in Central America.

We left El Salvador by road to Guatemala, the only country left before my goal, Mexico. But Guatemala was to be our stumbling block. Jorge Ubico, the iron-fisted dictator with the Napoleonic complex had banned all foreign theatrical companies for over fourteen years. Fernandez, a Guatemalan himself, knew this and had craftily prepared a scrapbook filled with Fu Manchu programmes from Argentina to El Salvador, all bearing advertisements stating that Guatemala's coffee was the finest in the world. (This is true. It is the champagne of coffees, but owing to the small crop it is only used for blending.)

With this impressive, thick album Fernandez hoped to soften the dictator's heart. A day or two after we arrived in Guatemala City we were received by Ubico in the presidential palace and were courteously invited to pure Guatemalan coffee while Ubico studied the scrapbook carefully, asking a question now and then. Finally he slapped the book shut and thanked us for our ''desinteresado'' support of Guatemala and smilingly told us the answer was no. He expressed regret that he could not break his ruling, and we were eased out with a handshake and a bow to return to the hotel with the saddest faces in town.

That afternoon an army officer appeared at our hotel bearing a sack of excellent coffee, a gift from the President, and a note informing us that he had given the order for free transportation for our company and baggage from the Salvadorean to the Mexican frontier. We were grateful for this attention and took advantage of it. (As long as Ubico was in power no foreign artist played Guatemala. Only a year after his death did foreign companies start to come in.)

A couple of days later, when leaving the hotel to take the train to the Mexican border, I asked a small boy who was always hanging around the hotel to get me a ''coche,'' a term used for an automobile in all Latin America.

''A big one or a small one?'' asked the boy.

''Any kind, and pronto,'' I answered.

The kid flew off but took so long that, afraid of missing the train, I hailed a passsing "coche" and was driven to the station with my bags. Just a few minutes before the train started the kid came running down the platform with a suckling pig in his arms.

"I got him cheap, senor," he panted, "two Quetzales."

There was quite an argument until Fernandez laughingly explained to me that a "coche" in Guatemala is a pig and I had to give the kid a "Quetzal," and told him to return the pig to the market.

One has to be careful of the double-meaning words in Latin America as I already knew from my Rio Grande do Sul fiasco.

In Guatemala, "paloma" (dove) is a vulgar word. In Chile, a "gondola" is a streetcar. In Mexico City, a "huila" is a blonde. In northern Mexico a harlot. In Cuba, "papaya" is a fruit, but in Havana it is a vulgarity. In Mexico, "cajeta" is a carmel candy, but in Argentina it is unmentionable. In Chile, "la polla," is the national lottery. In Spain it is part of the male anatomy. In all the Americas and Spain the verb, "coger" means to grasp, to take and is one the of the most common words in Spanish. But in Argentina it means sexual intercourse.

All these niceties have to be learned so that one does not have a riot on hand on the opening night.

After a four day trip through lovely southern Mexico we arrived back in Mexico City after a four year absence.

CHAPTER 39

The Mexicans have a saying, "Como Mexico no hay dos!" (There is no second Mexico) and they're right. I spent the happiest years of my life there and I was overjoyed to be back. My first few days were given to visiting old friends. The tequilla flowed freely.

Juan Toledo, Chang's ex-impresario, had taken over the Arbeu Theatre and was my combined impresario and publicity agent. Toledito, as he was affectionately known in Mexico, was a very short man, less than five feet tall, but with boundless energy. He was one of the very few impresarios in Latin America that had a special feel for magic. He loved magic shows and was impresario of nearly every magic show that played Mexico. It was he who had dreamed up the "Voyage to Hell" show that Chang did for so many years.

I had practically nothing new to offer Mexico and Toledito advised me to play the show without all the heavy dialogue. Defying the old taboo about two magicians on one show, Okito did his complete act, using my props and costumes. The novelty of father and son "challenging" each other was very well received by the family-loving Mexicans and we did a wonderful business which I really needed as I didn't have too much cash.

We stayed for three months in the Arbeu Theatre and then made a tour of the country. By coincidence I was playing the little town of Uruapan, close to where the volcano Paracutin was born, and when I went out to see it, the "baby" was only a few meters high but already blowing off steam and melted rock.

In Aguascalientes business was so good that we had to stay over for another day, postponing our debut in Tolima which was destroyed by a terrible earthquake the very day we were to open! The terrific shock was felt all over the country except for one

279

spot—Aguascalientes.

We played a lot of towns on the Mexican-U.S. border—Nogales and Tombstone, Arizona and Juarez, El Paso and Loredo in Texas—and never once did we see a bandit or a cowboy. I was offered another season for Mexico City at the Follies Theatre to be followed by the Alameda with Carmen Amaya. So from Chihuahua we went back to Mexico City where we opened a shop to build two new illusions for the new season.

Okito built me a fine illusion that was a cross between Thurston's Vampire and Karston's Battle of the Toy Soldiers, but instead of using the mirror principle or Thurston's risky loading of the girl creeping behind the cloth, we decided to use a trap. Until this time I had never used a trap in my show as many stages were unsuitable for them, but after a careful study we decided that the theatres where a trap could be used far outnumbered the others. It was a practical prop that Okito built for me and could be used on any stage with a minimum of bother and could be adapted to any previous trap cut in the stage. This device opened up a whole new field of illusionary effects and very rarely did we hit a stage where we could not use it.

With the new illusion and the addition of a new version of the Fasola Sack illusion, we played the two dates successfully. We were preparing for a tour of California, booked by Frank Fauce, when Pearl Harbor was attacked. Later, with the double-cross of Russia by the Nazis, everything went haywire and show business, as usual, was the first to take a beating. I was forced to store the show.

One day, out of the blue, appeared an unhappy Chang. He told me that his Australian tour had been badly timed. He had signed up with the Williamson Theatres, agreeing to pay his own fares and baggage. Williamson's had only one theatre in Sydney, which was booked ahead for seven months, so Chang had jumped around the country which cost him a fortune and, to top it, Nicola jumped in from New Zealand and cut him off. Disgusted, Chang left for the Philippines, but the country was seething with rumors of war, which was considered inevitable, and show business was in a bad state. He returned to America, and Mexico was first on his list for a tour of Latin America, but he found to his dismay that I had just finished three seasons in Mexico City. Things were exactly like the Buenos Aires' deal but in reverse this time.

Chang had brought some beautiful costumes with him from

the Orient and opened for a short season at the Bellas Artes, followed by a short season at the Arbeu at ridiculously low prices; but it was no use and he had to close down.

One afternoon Chang and I were walking along Avenida Juarez, glumly talking about the future, when an old Mexican lady stopped dead in front of us and stared at Chang.

"I beg your pardon, senor," she said politely, "but aren't you Chang, the magician?

"I saw your show the other night and I want to tell you how much I enjoyed it. I have never seen such a beautiful show in my life."

Chang, highly pleased, bowed to the lady and shot a side glance at me to see how I was taking it.

"A thousand thanks, senora," said he. "Which trick did you like the best?"

"I liked them all but, above everything, I adore that trick with the little cage and the canary bird that goes up your sleeve," she said innocently.

I choked and Chang did a color change and, mumbling an adios, walked on, looking like something dragged out of a Nebraska fossil bed.

Soon after this Chang left Mexico, taking Fernandez with him as his manager, and worked his way slowly down to the Argentine. I didn't envy him as travelling in normal times was bad enough but now, with shipping tied up, it would be an inferno. A letter to me from Fernandez, posted from the interior of Colombia, bore me out. He wrote that it had been the worst experience of his life.

Although I didn't have such hardships, my situation wasn't very good either. I had played Mexico to death and, except for the United States, the rest of the world was cut off. I had to think of something to do as I had the responsibility of my parents and six assistants. Miguel, the Catalan boy, had stayed in Buenos Aires but I still had all the rest. Lily, after so many years with me left for Colombia to marry an Englishman who had a candy factory, but no one else seemed in a hurry to do anything. As we only had a six months visa for Mexico I had to do some quick thinking.

To make matters worse, my health was in a bad state. With the hernia and the strenuous tour from Buenos Aires, I was practically a walking skeleton. One morning I was sitting in bed with my door open when the Beltri family doctor, Guillermo Bosque, head of the Mexican Faculty of Medicine, popped his head into my room.

"Which do you prefer," he asked, "mahogany or cedar?"

"What?"

"Your coffin," he said, cheerfully. "I may be mistaken but I give you, at most, six months."

He scared the hell out of me and arranged a visit to his clinic the next morning. After a lot of blood tests and X-rays, I heard the verdict. Complete rest and medical care for at least a year. No smoking, no late hours, no running around, no booze and no women. Just take it easy and, above all, don't worry.

The problem was extremely simple. All I had to do was to throw my parents out on their necks, fire all the faithful assistants who had been with me for years, store the props, and sit down and bask in the sun. Just like that! So what did I do? I kept right on working.

Hitler proved his military genius once again when one of his submarines sunk an unarmed Mexican freighter and for his pains he got Mexico and almost all the rest of Latin America on his neck. Hitler laughed at the Latin American military but he couldn't sneer at the potential for the combined republics with their vast natural resources of grain, minerals and livestock, all at the disposal of the United States.

Mexico's declaration of war made things tough for Spreer. Although he was not sent to the prison camp at Perote, he was confined to the limits of Mexico City and made a good living repairing machinery and doing special jobs. He lived with his wife, a Cuban girl, in the back rooms of the house I had rented for the combined workshop and storage place for the show. The rest of the boys got work in the theatres as stagehands or as prop-men in the motion picture studios. My only real expense was the Hotel Toledo where my parents lived.

An intimate friend of mine, Don Vincente Miranda, owner of the largest nightclub in Mexico City, El Patio, offered me a three months' engagement to do a show of about twenty minutes at a salary that would more than cover all my expenses. After two and three full evening shows a day, this was easy for me. I worked with Don Vincente for over a year as combined performer and master of ceremonies.

It was here that I first met Orson Welles, who came in one night with Dolores del Rio. After the show he invited me to his table. To my surprise he gave me a resume of the Bamberg history and it didn't take us long to get down to card tricks, which we ended at 5 a.m. with Dolores fast asleep in her chair. In later years I was privileged to become quite good friends with this amazing personality.

Senor Manuel Davalos, publicity manager for Mexico's best selling cigarettes, Delicados, wanted to put on a radio show based on magic amd mystery and asked me if I had any ideas. I kicked it around for a few weeks but was unable to come up with anything original; but I liked the idea of a radio show and looked around for some other angle.

Those were the days of the big American broadcasts with comedians like Jack Benny, Bob Hope, Fred Allen, Edgar Bergen and other top-flight men doing excellent comedy programmes. Surprisingly, very little in this line had been attempted on Mexican radio. I suggested an American type gag show to Senor Davalos, based on a fictitious nightclub to be known as El Club Delicados and using a couple of big name guest stars every week. Each programme was to have two six-minute comedy sketches about a travelling magician and his lethargic and brainless girl assistant.

Davalos liked the idea but could find few scriptwriters for this type of gag show and the few sketches that were tendered were so bad that we almost gave up the idea. I knew it wasn't easy and that the big name American comedians, with very few exceptions, paid their gag writers extremely high salaries. One afternoon I was pointing out to a writer just where he was going wrong on a script when Davalos suggested that I write the programmes myself. I had never done this kind of thing before and started off by trying to translate the gags on the U.S. broadcast, but as many of the gags were a play on words or had a double meaning, I found that I could use less than ten percent.

Finally I woke up to the fact that I didn't need all this expensive brand new material. I procured an American gag file and some joke books (including Copeland's *Ten Thousand Jokes*) and, choosing a theme, I would look up the jokes to fit it. In this way I wrote twenty comedy skits that were instantly accepted by Davalos. My great good luck was that the majority of these gags were new for Mexico. With a bit of judicious switching around of the old and the new, and an occasional original gag of my own (very rarely!), it was a tight and funny show. The girl who played the lazy assistant was Cuca Escobar, known as ''Cuca, la telefonista.''

Among the name stars who appeared were Jorge Negrete, Augustin Lara, Chucho Martinez Gil, Tito Guizar, Elvira Rios, Militza Korjus, Cochita Martinez, Arturo de Cerdoba, Gonzalo

Curiel, Pedro Vargas, Tona la Negra and three of the biggest name bands in Mexico. We gave two prime time one-hour shows on Tuesdays and Fridays.

From the first broadcast the show clicked and soon became the number one hit show on the Mexican radio network XEW for over three years. My health improved and I began to put on weight, but Dr. Bosque advised me to have a hernia operation. The show was cut in wax for a few weeks, the operation was a success and for the first time in ages I hadn't a care in the world. I was beginning to learn how the other half lived and bought myself a Chrysler. I would drive up for weekends to Cuernavaca and Taxco and it was then that I realized what I had missed in my life. Although I had made a tremendous amount of money in the theatre, I never got any fun out of it and only now was I learning to live.

It was during one of these broadcasts on XEW that I introduced Maria Felix to Augustin Lara. Her car was under repair and I loaned her mine which she promptly smacked into a milk truck. She came over to the studio to apologize and return me the keys. In the tunnel that leads from the studio stage to the foyer of the building, we ran into Lara, and Maria told him that his music fascinated her. Lara bowed and thanked her in his princely manner.

The next morning I had a phone call from her. She excitedly told me to come over at once to her apartment in the Calle Londres. When I arrived she took me into her living room. There was a huge stack of Lara's records, a lovely phonograph, and a pure white baby grand piano wrapped in cellophane with a big pink silk bow. A card read, "May I have the pleasure of playing and dedicating some of my musical poems to the most beautiful woman in Mexico?" and was signed, "Augustin." What woman could resist that? Six months later she was married to Lara and shortly after he composed one of his greatest song hits, "Maria Bonita," which he played for the first time on my programme.

During my last year with XEW I wrote and directed a half-hour series called, "The Crime Museum" which were the adventures of a magician-detective. In one of the first of these stories I used Orson Welles' "War of the Worlds" technique with a realistic broadcast of a sound engineer murdered during the programme. It was realistic enough to have doctors and nurses phone the studio. The police and an ambulance showed up and nearly wrecked the show, but the resulting publicity was very gratifying.

The American motion picture industry was running on a war basis and the few pictures that were coming down to Mexico were mostly war stories. The majority of picture houses were playing reruns of vintage movies. The Mexican movie industry was just starting and the largest company at that time was Films Mundiales, whose president was Senor Augustin Fink. At a board of directors meeting my name was brought up as a possible cinema actor for a series of full-length mystery stories. After a long conference with Senor Fink I signed a contract to do three magician-detective thrillers; then followed months of stalling and time wasting looking for likely stories. It was the gag writer story all over again. There were no scriptwriters who specialized in detective plots at that time and most of the stories offered were impossible nonsense and even the passable plots didn't ring true.

Ramon Navarro, formerly M.G.M.'s top star and now with Films Mundiales, advised me to write my own stories, or at least write a synopsis that a professional writer could adapt to the cinema form. This was good advice, but first I had to learn something of motion picture technique, of which I knew nothing. At that time there were only two major studios in Mexico and I spent all my days there watching and learning.

A great new field for Spanish-speaking pictures had sprung up in the Latin American countries and the U.S. government generously supplied this fledgling industry with millions of feet of raw film, even to the extent of depriving the major Hollywood studios. As much as forty million feet a year was supplied, besides sending down the latest equipment and crack technicians— including Walt Disney and Lee DeForrest (inventor of the radio tube). Walt Disney taught me to run a special stop-projector for rushes and I spent quite some time with Mr. DeForrest, who initiated me into the mysteries of the soundtrack. I was not a sound engineer by any means but I gained a good understanding of what could be done. The whole thing fascinated me so much that I wanted to have a general, all-around knowledge of motion picture technique. It was just like magic inasmuch as one should have a good background before starting anything.

Emilio "Indio" Fernandez, Mexico's top director, was with our outfit and was writing the script for Dolores del Rio's first Mexican production. He allowed me to be in on his story conferences with the top Mexican writers and I began to learn how to do an adaptation of a novel for a shooting script.

I had the good fortune to meet Norman Foster who was making his first Mexican picture with Ricardo Montalban. I became a close friend of Norman and his wife, Sally Blaine (Loretta Young's sister). He had just finished the Hollywood production of Eric Ambler's "Journey Into Fear," starring Orson Welles, Joseph Cotten and Dolores del Rio. As this type of picture was right up my alley, I practically lived at Norman's home and it was he who taught me more of film technique than anyone else. Norman was a combined actor-writer-director and it was a great stroke of fortune to be a friend of this generous man whose advice was literally worth gold in those days.

Okito was very keen on this motion picture deal and his Sherlock Holmes' complex was a great help in many ways. We started addressing each other as Holmes and Watson and this kept up as long as he lived. All my letters to him in the future started with, "My Dear Holmes."

After three or four months of getting familiar with motion picture technique, which was so very different from the theatre, I felt that I knew a little about the business and at least could hold my own in a studio. I knew that if I waited for Films Mundiales to get me three scripts I would have time to grow a long white beard. I sketched out three rough outlines, in synopsis form, for the magician-detective character they wanted and submitted them to Fink. They were immediately accepted. Although none of these stories would ever set the world on fire, they were superior to anything that had been offered. In order to save money, the company decided to shoot all three stories together to save on production costs. The scripts called for a luxurious Chinese home and a theatre in all three pictures. My producer, Senor Subervielle, advised me to join the Screen Guild and then, with the director, Senor Rene Cardona, go right into the three shooting scripts, complete with breakdowns. I don't think that anyone in the history of the movies started off with the responsibility that I had with no practical experience in this line of work.

The first story, "El Espectro de la Novia" (The Spectre Bride), was based on an old legend of a beautiful young girl accidently locked in a wooden chest on her wedding night. She suffocated to death and returned as a ghost to haunt her deranged bridegroom. There was a lot of fake spiritualism in the plot and some good sound magic in it, including the Chung Ling Soo bullet catching tragedy and Houdini's Chinese Water Torture Cell, using the alleged Raymond-Houdini story of the buckshot in the handcuffs which almost cost the magician (me) his life. All very sensational stuff and with enough truth in it to make it appear plausible.

The second story was "La Mujer Sin Cabeza" (The Headless Woman) with a black-magic background and combining the Substitution Trunk with the Headless Woman illusion. This story was set in a waxwork museum, and the mystery was based on a number of wax heads and the four cork gimmick that I had suggested to Octavus Roy Cohen, in Havana, which he never used.

The third story was "El As Negro" (The Black Ace), a cloak-and-dagger drama with international spies and seers. This picture had a variety-hall background with magic, handshadows, mentalism and a ventriloquist whose gags had a double meaning and were picked up by spies in the audience. A lot of time was saved by writing these stories directly for the screen and after three months of hard work, Rene and I had them ready for shooting.

I met a lot of American movie stars, including Bette Davis and Errol Flynn. John Wayne took time out to teach me how to stage a fake fight and showed me some of the tricks he had used with Randolph Scott in their realistic fight scenes. Another man who taught me many movie tricks and camera angles for hair-raising adventures was Charlie Stevens, a Hollywood heavy who specialized in westerns and was contracted for The Black Ace. Ramon Navarro and Antonio Moreno, my childhood idol in Brooklyn, gave me invaluable advice on screen acting, which is very different from stage acting.

Gaby Figueroa, Mexico's top camera man (winner of a first prize in Cannes), was in charge of the cameras and Howard Randall was in charge of sound.

Unbelievable as it may sound, I had done all this work without ever making a screen test. The first thing Gaby wanted before actual shooting was a test for my "camera angles" and one evening after fininshing Ramon Navarro's picture, he was ready for me and I made my test. All my years of the theatre and radio went for nothing as I trembled like a novice in front of that cold lens. In the close-ups especially of my hands, it looked as though I had the St. Vitus dance, and with my stuttery lines, fluffs and general all-over stiffness, it was appalling. I was in such a blue funk that I couldn't control myself. Fink, Gaby, Subervielle and Rene looked like the end of the world was at hand. There was too much time and money sunk in this deal to stop now and they went into a huddle that lasted half the night.

I knew that the test had been bad but I didn't know how bad and they refused to let me see the rushes (daily takes) and it was Rene Cardona who solved the disagreeable situation by putting on the best act of his career. The next morning he showed up at the office as if nothing had happened.

"How were the tests?" was the first thing I asked. "Pretty bad, huh?"

"So-so," he lied. "You were a little nervous, but that happens to everybody."

"I never expected anything like that to happen to me."

Rene waved a dismissing hand, "We're used to that sort of thing and discount it. We look for other things and I can tell you in confidence that the producers are very pleased."

I stared at him open-mouthed. I knew it had been terrible, but then again perhaps it wasn't as bad as I thought. I swallowed his story because I wanted to believe it.

"Of course," he continued, "you'll have to ease up a little and let some of that tension out; but I, for one, think you'll make a great screen actor."

"You've taken a great load off my mind," I said thankfully. "When do we start production?"

That stopped him. "Well, he said after a long pause, "before we go into the actual shooting there are a couple of long scenes, like that one in the passageway outside your dressing room with the kid, that's not quite clear in my mind. I mean, I'm not sure of my camera action here and can't decide whether to shoot it in a one long dolly-shot or break it up into two or three short shots."

This was pure hogwash but I didn't know enough about direction to see it.

"Therefore," he went on, "I'd like to run over these scenes with you a few times before we start filming. How about it?"

I said I would be delighted.

The next morning on stage number 1, the whole crew was on hand and I was made up and wearing an old dressing gown. I arrived on the set to hear Rene saying in a loud voice (for my benefit I found out later) that this was just a camera and light rehearsal, but he wanted everything exactly as if it were being shot. Gaby came over with his light meter and started adjusting spots and floods and finally he seemed satisfied.

"Don't bother to wear a Chinese robe for this rehearsal," Rene said to me. "That dressing gown is good enough."

That fooled me, as I was supposed to wear a mandarin robe for this scene, but Rene had made a change or two in the script without my knowledge. We went through the whole scene with the kid and when it was over Rene did a lot of comedy chin-pulling and thinking and asked Gaby what he thought about it. Gaby shrugged his shoulders and after a word with the sound engineer he said it was all right. Rene ordered us to do it just once more, but told me to come out of my dressing room after mentally counting three from the word "action."

I returned to my dressing room and closed the door and waited for the signal. I didn't know that Rene had the cameras rolling on this shot and when I heard "action" I waited for three seconds and opening the door I stepped out into the corridor and went into my part.

"Cut," said Rene. "Very good. Very good indeed. Now let's do it it just once more before we start rolling. Make it better this time."

Again we went through the scene and Rene seemed highly pleased with himself. "Now," he said, "we'll try it with camera."

That awful trembling of the previous day beset me again and although I managed to get through the scene, I knew it was a bad performance; but surprisingly, Rene seemed very satisfied and said, "That's all for today, Fu. Be on the set tomorrow at 8." He spent the rest of the day taking shots in which I did not appear.

At eight the next morning I was made up and waiting for Rene. He came charging in about nine o'clock, waving his heavily red-penciled script. He informed me that he was shooting some close shots of other actors and all he needed from me was my voice on the sound track. I was secretly relieved as I still had camera fright in my soul and any delay of the fateful moment was welcome. The cameras started rolling and it was a boring repetitious morning with nobody seeming to be satisfied—the director, cameramen, sound and electricians all griping at the same time. About eleven thirty Rene called for a break.

"Come with me," he said. "I want you to see something." We went over to the rush room, a small fifty seat theatre where they showed the daily takes for selection. When I entered the room I found Augustin Fink and Felipe Subervielle already there, sitting with Ramon Navarro and Pedro Armendariz, a popular Mexican film star. Gaby and Howard Randall came in just after we did and sat down alongside Rene. I wondered what they were going to show. Rene phoned the projectionist to get started and the lights dimmed, and suddenly, for the first time in my life, I saw myself on the screen.

They say that everyone is disappointed when they see themselves for the first time on the screen but this is the understatement of all time. Never had I seen such a repellent character. I don't know what I had thought myself to be. I had always imagined a good-looking young man with a resonant voice like Herbert Lom, but what I saw was devastating—full of smirks and facial gestures, with a high pitched voice and a marked accent. I suffered through ten minutes of this as they ran it twice (so I thought), with it seeming to get worse instead of better. Then they ran it a third time and it was really awful as I paraded around like a wooden board and overacted everything. Then I realized that the dogs had fooled me. I was seeing the two "rehearsals" and the first take.

The rest of the day's work I didn't even see as I brooded there in the dark; but finally it was over and everyone started to talk at once. Rene was sore about the camera movement, Gaby sore about the lighting, Randall in a rage about the sound and nobody said a word to me. Finally I could stand it no longer. I told Randall that his sound was rotten, that wasn't my voice at all.

"How was the kid's voice?" he asked me. "And Medel's?" (Medel was the comedian in my pictures.)

"Their voices are perfect," I said. "It's just my voice that's bad."

"Use your head," said Randall. "If Medel's voice is perfect then your voice is perfectly recorded too."

I was dazed and made a mental note to lower my voice a full octave.

The producers were smiling and waved happily at me. Ramon Navarro came over and shook my hand saying, "Muy, muy bien."

Rene threw his arm over my shoulder and said, "I knew you could do it. Are you happy now?"

"No," I said. "I think it stinks."

He took me to a corner of the theatre and sat me down beside him. "Look, Fu," he said seriously, "I'm going to tell you the god's honest truth. The tests we made of you were so bad that the company was at the point of chucking the whole deal. But I've seen you many times on the stage and I have faith in you. I convinced them to let me pull that comedy act yesterday and you can see for yourself how superior the first two takes are compared to the last in which you are camera-conscious and stiff. But the first two takes prove you can do it."

"I thought they were terrible too."

"That's only natural. Every actor feels the same when he sees his first picture. Believe me when I say that I'm very satisfied and so are the producers. So come on and let's get to work."

On the way back to the set I realized that he had told the truth. I was making a monkey out of myself in front of everybody and decided to get over that panic I had for the camera.

On my first scene that day I let them have a beautiful baritone from a half smiling dead-pan face that I thought would rival George Raft.

"Cut!" cried Randall. "What the hell are you mumbling for? Lift that voice! Recia! Keep it up."

Rene came over. "Now what? Are you paralyzed? Where's all that facial expression you had yesterday? Forget that goddamned camera and be yourself." He opened his arms and spoke to the studio in general. "It's the last time I ever let a ham see the rushes. Not even Paul Muni."

Let's draw a curtain over the rest of it. I improved, but I never really got over my camera-consciousness and was never completely at ease in a movie studio. Perhaps the difficulty of having to memorize my lines in perfect Spanish for the day's takes had something to do with it, but I found it difficult to combine words and action. I always had that uneasy squeamish feeling in my stomach.

I worked very hard and did my best. We had been given half a million pesos and a three months' time limit to make the three pictures. With careful planning and Orson's advice for "cutting paper before, to save cutting celluloid after," we finished the pictures two weeks before the time limit—and a "first" in the Mexican movie industry—using only 420,000 pesos, thereby saving the company 80,000 pesos.

Although I thought we had done a great thing in saving the company all this time and money, I soon found out how wrong I was. In my ignorance I had made some enemies because I had prevented "the mordida" (the bite), the customary "looking-the-other-way," thus allowing certain people to get away with a lot of petty graft, which is considered part of the game and not looked upon as dishonesty. One director told me that I would never make another picture again in Mexico and that I was out.

But just like my other business, if your product sells, you're not out. My first picture opened at the Paslacio Chino, one of the leading picture houses in Mexico City and had excellent press reviews and did good business. The three films paid for themselves many times over and helped to pay for some of the losses the company had on the "art" films that had cost millions. Even today I sometimes see these old pictures on television and they hold their own with pictures of that period.

"The Specter Bride" was the first picture to be released and the Reverend Padre Heredia, a Jesuit priest and author of several books exposing fraudulent mediums, took the picture as an example of what he had so profusely written about. His letters praising the film were published in the leading newspapers and helped to promote it greatly.

"The Headless Woman" was the second to be released and its theme of the absurdity of black magic and superstition again appealed to Padre Heredia and once more I had the church and the press on my side.

But it was "The Black Ace," to my mind the poorest of the three pictures, which was to have the greatest publicity, due to a series of bizarre events that made headlines in the papers.

From the very start "The Black Ace" was tagged as a hard luck picture. During the filming, Rene's mother died in Cuba and he went to Havana, leaving another director in his place, who was on the job for only three days, when he was poisoned by eating spoiled seafood. Nobody wanted to take his place. The word spread that we had a jinx picture on our hands and Gaby took over until Rene returned.

Then a fakir, Harry, who had played a small part in the picture, tried a publicity stunt (not connected with the picture) by being nailed to a cross. He died of blood poisoning from the nails and this tragedy was immediately tied to the picture.

Altogether twelve people either died or were seriously ill during the shooting of the film, but the sensational payoff came with the thirteenth victim.

The promising young actor, Mario Tenorio, who played the young lover in the picture, was shot to death on the opening night of "The Black Ace" in the Savoy Theatre. A jealous husband found Mario sitting in the first balcony with his wife. That did it! There was a panic in the theatre that ended with a police chase and ambulances. The resultant newspaper headlines packed the theatre as all wanted to see the thirteenth victim. It was a grisly affair but it made the producers happy.

In spite of all this publicity Films Mundiales didn't care to extend my contract as they claimed that three detective pictures were enough for the moment. I was free.

I hadn't made much money on this deal and, except for my salary as an actor, I had only the author's rights, which I sold back to the company for a straight sum. I had been seven months with the company but only three months on pay. With all my expenses and the bluff that goes with being a movie star, I wasn't too well off. Fortunately, I still had my radio programme.

I produced a second radio programme with Edmundo Santos, who was Walt Disney's dubber for the Spanish speaking version of his full-length feature films. This series was a satire on the movie studios and it became quite popular for a time.

Then one day I received a letter from Fernandez, who was in southern Colombia with Chang, bemoaning the fact that Mexican films were killing show business in South America, although the exhibitors were making a fortune.

At the time Mexican films had little distribution. Outside of Mexico City they were rented for a flat rate to exhibitors in the country and sold outright for a fixed sum, usually before the film was made, to the other Latin American countries. Most of the companies used this system to help finance the film. For the exclusive rights to a film Colombia would pay $5,000, Venezuela $7,000 and so on, according to the market. It all added up to a respectable sum of money. I wrote to some theatrical impresarios in various countries and they all answered with the same story: sellouts everywhere and fortunes being made.

I had a talk with Senor Menendez, business manager for Films Mundiales, and he told me that every time they worked on a percentage deal in any of the interior towns of Mexico, they lost heavily. I remembered a certain town in Mexico where I had played with my show in 1941. I had arrived there the day before my debut and that evening attended the theatre where they were showing a Films Mundiales' picture. I couldn't get in as the house was jammed with people standing in the aisles. I checked the exact date and asked Menendez to have a look at the receipt for that day. He looked it up in the files and said that they had run the picture on a percentage basis but business had been poor and the company received only 42 pesos. According to my estimate they must have taken in well over 3,000 pesos for the three exhibitions of the film that day. No wonder the producers paid such poor salaries!

I did a spot of detective work of my own and dug up a few more facts, and armed with this data, I had a talk with one of the big money men in the Mexican film industry. He studied my examples of box office "double-lifting" which was not news to him. At first he was inclined to regard my information as being exaggerated. He explained to me that for any single Mexican film company to have its own distribution was out of the question. In the first place they would have to release at least fifty full-length A and B pictures a year, along with newsreels and shorts, to obtain "block-booking" like the big American companies. I realized after talking to this man that I knew less than nothing about finance but, in any case, he thanked me and told me he would study the situation.

The grapevine was soon agog with the news that certain big shots had been sent to Central and South America. I had a pretty good suspicion of what was going on and shortly after there was a small sized revolution in the film industry, with mergers of the biggest producers and a steep thirty-three percent of the gross deal with Colombia Pictures of Hollywood to distribute through their well organized company. The resultant profits increased enormously for Mexican producers.

Although I had nothing whatever to do with this deal, the word went around that I had been in the know from the beginning and had made some good connections. A rash of new companies sprang up, anxious to climb on the bandwagon. One of these outfits, called Astro (Star) Films and backed by a popular cosmetic firm, contracted me for two pictures at a much better salary and percentage deal than the previous films. Rene Cardona and a few others who knew how to make pictures went over to this company. I had a much freer hand to write and adapt my story ideas. I decided to stick to mystery stories and stay clear of dramatic vehicles for many reasons, the most obvious being the bathos that was an essential ingredient of a successful dramatic film in those days, but I had no feeling for these tear-jerkers. I preferred to stick to what I knew.

Every once in awhile I would pay a visit to my first love, the show. The boys, under Okito's direction, were building new crates and repairing and painting the props for some future day. It always cheered me up to visit the shop and be surrounded by my old faithful trappings. I knew that one day when all this high-falutin' nonsense was over, I would be back "sawing" beautiful women again.

I wore myself out trying to think of some angle or sensational gimmick for my next picture. After the super publicity of "The Black Ace," what could anyone do? The producer at Astro Films would pop his head into my office every once in awhile to see me sitting in a trance, sprawled in a chair, and gazing at a blank wall. This made him very happy.

Then, for some obscure reason that I could never explain, I got two ideas at the same time and they both looked good to me. The first idea was murder in a movie studio and the gimmick was to put Astro Film on the map. The picture was to start with silent shots of the old days, when pictures were made in the back lot. In one of the scenes of this Mexican charro (cowboy) plot a real glass bottle was switched for a wax one and in a fight an actor was seriously injured, leaving him feeble-minded. The story then jumped twenty years to the present and the modern industry was depicted in a series of montage shots. It was here that the gimmick came in. We built a false front with a big sign reading Astro Films giving the impression that our studios were the size of Warner Brothers, whereas we had no studio and rented stages for our productions. The injured actor of the silent days was now a porter in this mythical studio and the plot developed from there.

The second story was to be titled "The Crime Museum." It was my good fortune to be a close friend of Senor Teodoro Gonzalez, a detective-inspector of the Mexican police, and the discoverer of the paraffin-wax-test used in many parts of the world today for determining, by the minute powder marks that are imbedded in the hands, if a person had fired a gun. Senor Gonzalez' test became famous when he proved that a girl had committed suicide, thus proving the innocence of her fiance who had been accused of murder. Senor Gonzalez allowed me to go over the files and examine some of the gruesome objects in the Black Museum at headquarters. Here the plot for "The Crime Museum," which later co-starred Katy Jurado in one of her first parts, was born and accepted by the company.

For some technical reason they decided to make "The Crime Museum" first. It was then that I wrote the radio series under the same title which was a great plug. So instead of loafing the day away, I was now writing a movie script and two weekly radio mysteries at the same time.

Just about this time I had my wallet stolen in a bus and had to keep my mouth shut as the resultant publicity of the great detective-magician having his wallet lifted would be the last kind of advertising we wanted. An example of this bad type of publicity was a well-known mentalist by the name of Fassman who had the habit of rushing over to the casino after a show to play his day's take on the roulette table. Naturally, when this seer, "who sees-all-and-knows-all," played a number, everyone, Fassman included, usually lost their shirt. In spite of this, there were a few who swore that he could read the future like an open book.

We could have saved a lot of money on production for "The Crime Museum," as Norman Foster offered me the use of some of his sets from a picture he was making, if I cared to shoot at night, using different camera angles. Even by paying extra time for night work, this was an enormous savings as stages were hard to get. Unfortunately, the union stopped us and we had to wait until there was free time between two super productions to squeeze in our picture.

Both films made money for the company, but two films of that kind for such a small outfit was enough, and as I still refused to make potboilers, I was out.

By this time I was Mexico's Hitchcock and it didn't take long before I had an offer for another whodunit from a very big organization. Okito gave me a good idea for a plot based on a short story that he read in a *True Detective* magazine and, together with Norman Foster, we wrote a comedy-mystery which Norman was to direct. The company accepted the script, but just as we were to go into production Norman was offered a very powerful dramatic bullfight script, "La Hora de la Verdad." He wisely accepted what turned out to be one of the best "torero" films, starring Ricardo Montalban, ever made in Mexico. I worked for a time with Norman on this picture, matching the bullfight sequences from the newsreels to his actual shots of Ricardo in the bullring. This was where the stop projector that Walt Disney had brought down came in handy.

The picture that we had written together, "Gooseflesh," was turned over to one of those "cut-in-camera" fiends who think they need no shooting script and carry everything in their head. The result was that no one could cut it, and it was so changed around that they held it in the can for years before it was released. Fortunately, by this time, I was very far from Mexico and was in no danger of being lynched for this stinker. I saw it on television and I never got over it.

With the exception of Emilio "Indio" Fernandez and a few others, all Mexican pictures were made with an eye on the old sure-fire-box-office formula. Any departure was vetoed by the producers as too risky. A few years later the Italian "neo-realism" films proved that highly dramatic and artistic films could be made on a shoestring; but we weren't ready for that kind of thing just yet. I mention this because three ideas of mine with a gimmick in each of these ideas were used with success by American and European directors.

In one of my scripts the camera was to act as the detective's eyes in an attempt to make the audience feel they were the detective and the camera was their eyes. The detective is never seen and only his voice is heard. The producers told me I had a screw loose and I got a collective razzing! A few years later Robert Montgomery used this very same technique for his "Lady in the Lake," Raymond Chandler's powerful detective story. It was acclaimed by the critics as an artistic triumph.

My second gimmick was a picture with a double ending. It was to be a murder story in which the audience was tricked into believing they knew who the murderer was right from the beginning. An innocent person was electrocuted and the real murderer got away. The picture ended on this note, a very unsatisfied audience got up to go, when a voice bellowed from the screen saying, "Wait. It's not over. We feel just like you do...but what really happened is this..." and the picture started again, showing that the executed person was really the murderer and had gotten what was coming to him while the suspected person was just trying to cover up to prevent an innocent person from sordid publicity.

The producers choked on that one. Too radical! Too far-fetched! Now I had two screws loose. Again the horse laugh. Years later a Hollywood director heard about it and produced it with the result that the press spoke highly of the novelty gimmick involved.

The third time they thought that all my screws had fallen out. I wrote a synopsis for a film divided into three acts like a stage play. This film was to be titled "Viewpoint." The first act shows the trials of a young wife and what a rotter her husband is (her viewpoint). The second act is an exact repetition of the first, but here we see that the husband is a long suffering good guy and the wife a shrew (his viewpoint). The third act, again a repetition of the first two, is the point of view of a third person and proves that both husband and wife are right and wrong and both to blame. Do I have to say what the comments were when they read that one over? They didn't even laugh—

they just looked. Time marches on and years later this theme was filmed in France. The critics raved about the novel approach.

Admittedly, each of these ideas was a tour de force. That was my specialty in the theatre and in movies. I always used some gimmick either as an added attraction or a novel ending. I believed that in motion pictures, just as in magic, everything fell into two simple categories: a different method of doing a known effect or a new effect employing a known method.

Near the end of the filming of the "Gooseflesh" epic, I did a scene on a narrow ledge of a bell tower of an old church. I lost my footing and fell in a sandpile with a nice double hernia to show for it. After the picture I set a date for another operation.

Orson Welles was in and out of Mexico frequently at that time and we were together quite a lot. A good friend of mine, a young Anglo-Mexican girl, told me she had been "operated on" for a swollen appendix by a doctor who had died over a hundred years before and cured people through the aid of a spirit medium. This girl had a faint white scar where the "invisible" knife had cut. She swore this story was true and her mother corroborated every detail.

The day before I was to be operated, I mentioned this story to Orson. His eyes flashed as he cajoled me into postponing my operation in order to try the spirit doctor. I wasn't at all keen on the idea, but Orson had his way and I postponed my operation for a few days.

That evening I drove my girlfriend, her mother and Orson to the medium's house in a rather poor neighborhood in the suburbs of the city. On the way we decided not to use our real names. Orson was to be "Mr. Smith" and I was Mr. F. Amber." (Forever bAMBERg!)

When we drove up, a lot of kids gathered around the car, and although it was quite dark, I feared that they would recognize us, but apparently they didn't. We were ushered in by the medium herself, a short, stout woman wearing a long sleeved sweater with wide pockets. She told us her control was an Indian doctor who had died nearly a century before. She sat on a sofa and after a long pause she jumped up and, plucking a bunch of dead, dried stems from a vase, she waved them in the air, bending and twisting her body all the while and then, suddenly, she broke the packet of stems in half close to Orson's face as the perfume of fresh flowers permeated the air. Then she went into a trance and in a passable imitation of an old man's voice she told of his past triumphs while she passed her hands over my body, finally stopping at the groin where I had my inguinal hernias. I felt like a blasted idiot during all this but Orson sat there with a deadpan face and hawk eyes.

The medium started weaving and waving around again, picking up the dead stems and throwing them into the air all around her. During one of these gyrations she came quite close to Orson, who, just at that moment, leaned over to pick up one of the stems and accidently brushed against her. She returned to the sofa and continued with the mediumistic ritual for awhile. Then she put her hands in the pockets of her sweater and instantly she came out of her trance. Her eyes darted to the floor, then to Orson, who was sitting without any expression, and then asking to be excused for a moment, she hurriedly left the room. After a long pause she returned and mentioned something about a powerful magical influence that emanated from one of us. She glared at Orson, and continued saying that this had destroyed her contact with her Indian doctor and we were politely asked to leave.

When we got to the car the kids were still there and shouting my name. We figured she had found out who we were but had mistaken Orson for me.

I left the girl and her mother at their home and drove Orson to his hotel. He invited me up to his room and the first thing he did was to take a small glass phial from his pocket and hold it under my nose. It was the same smell of fresh flowers from the medium's seance. Orson was as happy as a school boy as he showed me how he had picked her pocket when he had "accidently" brushed against her. I must say his timing was perfect as I didn't see him swipe the phial, and I have an eye for that sort of thing. He went through the flower routine in his room, using the artifical flowers the Hotel Majestic provided. All that remained for me to do was call the hospital and make new arrangements. I've often wondered what would have happened if Orson hadn't copped the phial.

Occasionally Orson, his wife Rita Hayworth, and I would have a late supper at some night spot. On one of these occasions Orson predicted that when the war ended, and Hollywood was on its feet again, the Mexican film industry would take a terrible beating in spite of its having captured seventy-five percent of the Latin American market. He advised me to write a new show just in case. What he said made sense as I knew that there were so many independent producers working on a shoestring that any strong opposition would burst the bubble. I began to make notes and rough outlines for a new magical production.

My double hernia operation was a success and after I left the hospital I had a month to rest. I went to Cuernavaca where I wrote a new play in which I combined movie technique with stage illusions. The plot was about a famous magician who is kidnapped. A street fakir who resembles the magician greatly, is forced to take his place and, by magic, breaks up a gangster organization. When I got back to Mexico City and re-read it, I burned it and was back where I had started.

A few days later I was having lunch with Norman Foster and a producer friend of his at Bellinghausen's Restaurant. We had a table next to the large window that faces the street. Suddenly the room began to rock, and looking out the window, we saw the trees waving like a storm at sea. This severe quake lasted almost a minute and we were lucky that the plate glass window did not shatter. We finished our lunch in record time. I was driving back to town when the quake started again. I almost lost control of the skidding car. I was just beside the huge Latin American building at that moment; it swayed like a palm tree and I expected it to fall on me, but the quake stopped suddenly. I was able to make my way slowly downtown to my producer's offices, in a building on the Calle Artes. I took the elevator up to the fifth floor and just as I stepped from the elevator, it started again. This time I lost my footing and fell, with the result that the stitches of my hernia on the right side broke. By this time my belly was beginning to look like a road map of Guatemala and I was so disgusted I decided to wear a truss and to hell with it. About that time Norman was shooting his final corrida shots in the bullring in the Calle Durango and had his cameras and technicians inside the stockade in order to shoot the bulls close up, at eye level. Silverio Perez, one of Mexico's ace matadors, had been terribly gored just a short time before. I visited him in the hospital and he told me that the bull's horn had entered his groin up to nearly half its length. I quickly realized that my hernia was nothing compared to this so I decided to have another operation at the first opportunity.

CHAPTER 40

It was on my fortieth birthday that a little incident happened that had no significance at the time but which was to be the clue for my new show in the future. A young American magician, whose name I can not recall, was suffering from tuberculosis and had come to Mexico City to benefit from its high, dry climate. In order to pay his expenses he had brought along a little magic act, using the stock tricks of the time, including Al Baker's Rice Bowls, the Harlequin Cigarette, Al Baker's Diminishing Cards, the Razor Blade trick, the color changing silk, the match to flower and other small effects which were most effective for a small club act. This chap spoke no Spanish and couldn't get a date in Mexico. On this day he came to me with his little suitcase of magic and told me he wanted to go to Arizona. He needed fare and offered to sell me his little outfit. I had no use for it, but in order to help the guy, I bought it. I never heard of him again. I took the stuff over to the shop and showed it to Okito, who sniffed and put the suitcase on a shelf and forgot it. I thought I might one day sell it to some amateur.

I hadn't seen anything new in magic for years and then Maury Kains and Harry Mendoza visited Mexico City and started the old fires burning with demonstrations of the latest in American magic. They gave me many good ideas and gags. Maury and I remembered the old "Krazy-Kat" days in Brooklyn and we had some nostalgic laughs over our old Spanish of those days. Harry told me about the new type of "hellzapoppin" shows that were so successful in the U.S. and this seemed to me to be the kind of show that I needed. Something fast, silly and gay to counteract the dreary war years.

Dante opened at the Iris Theatre and I was invited to attend the debut by Dona Esperanza Iris, a former musical comedy star and owner of the theatre. We sat in her private box.

Dante's new show was called "Sim Sala Bim." He had many new illusions and effects, all presented with the familiar Dante touch. I also noticed that he had changed nearly all his assistants since the time I had seen him in Buenos Aires. It was a first class magic show but something had happened to it, just like the Thurston show. Dante wasn't the same man and the fire and pep were lacking. He was still a first class performer but he worked with a sort of "be-damned-to-you" listlessness which gave the impression of not caring about anything. He did the full evening's show in English and a few of us in the audience enjoyed his gags, but the laughter as well as the applause was sporadic. It is true that he had also performed in English in Buenos Aires with great success, but Buenos Aires was far more cosmopolitan than Mexico City. (At least it was in the 1920s.)

Between the first and second acts a most embarrassing thing happened. Dona Esperanza, always one to bask in the limelight, stood up in her box and took a bow, getting a big hand. Then, in her theatrical way, she dragged me forward to take a bow. The audience gave me an ovation and some half-wit in the gallery shouted, "Fu Manchu, si! Dante, no!" Several people picked up the cry. This was really an awful thing to happen on a colleague's debut. I sat down fast and, believe me, I was very angry about the whole silly thing.

The magic and illusions of the second part were just as good, if not better, than the first part, but Dante's apathy had its effect and at the final curtain there was scattered applause and a couple of forced curtain calls.

I went backstage to his dressing room and found him sitting at his makeup table with a huge stein of beer before him. He received me quite cordially. I made no mention of the incident in the theatre and neither did he, which was good. We talked about old times and things that had happened since we had last met when suddenly he drawled, "I heard that you had a pretty good little act in the last years. Still doing it?"

I didn't know if he was kidding or not, because as an old timer he knew the difference between an act and a full night's show. I went along with him and told him I had stored the show as I was doing movie work. I mentioned three or four of my films and gave him a brief description of the magical sequences in them.

"You're a goddam liar," he commented. "Why did you give

up magic? Couldn't you make the grade?"

I saw no sense in prolonging the conversation so with some excuse I wished him luck and departed. A few days later I met him on the street and he asked why I hadn't come around any more. He invited me to a dinner held in his honor and went out of his way to be charming and agreeable. Dante was certainly a complex character.

I saw his show a few times and really enjoyed it. Dante with his snow white mane and beard was an imposing personality and looked every inch the magician. I got the old theatre fever again just looking at him. I wanted Okito to come and see the show but he was angry for some reason and refused.

Every six months we would have to go through that time wasting routine of having our immigration permits extended and finally, through a friend of mine, Don Maximino Avila-Camacho brother of the President of Mexico, I was introduced to the foreign minister, Senor Miguel Aleman—who became the next president. He kindly obtained "residencia," which permitted us to stay in Mexico permanently, with the right to apply for Mexican citizenship if we cared to. This was a big load off our minds.

For the next few months I did very little work, except for the benefit shows we gave for the war effort and my radio programmes.

Before starting on the new show I thought it was just as well to have one last joust with the hernia. During my convalescence I could figure out just what props we had to build. I implored my doctor to graft in part of the hull of an armor-plated battleship to prevent a recurrence of another hernia and he promised to do what he could.

It was during this operation that I learned not to pull gags on doctors. My doctor and I were pals by this time and we called each other by our Christian names. Just before entering the hospital someone gave me one of those thin flat rubber bags which are inflated and placed under a pillow, ready for some victim to sit on with a resultant disastrous noise. I took this joke noisemaker with me to the hospital and the day after my operation, just before the doctor's daily visit, I inflated it and held it under my armpit. When the doctor came in and asked me how I felt I let him have it. For a moment he was startled out of his wits, but after calming down and shaking his head, he said, "That's very bad," and went out of the room.

I was laughing myself silly (and, believe me, it hurts to laugh after an operation) when the nurse came in with a tray on which rested a rubber tube that looked like a boa constrictor.

"What's that for?" I asked with a big grin.

"Gas!" said the nurse. Take my word for it: if you have any ideas for a comedy act, don't try it out in a hospital.

Okito thought it was very funny but he always did have a perverted sense of humor.

The remaining ten days in the hospital I behaved myself and worked on my script. The basic idea for this new show was a series of magical comedy blackouts. I wanted to avoid any great expense due to building a lot of new illusions. Most of the ones I had would serve admirably for the sketches I had in mind. However, it was vital to have at least two or three new effects that could be heavily advertised as a bait to get the people in.

The illusionary effect that gave the show its title, "The Fire Dragon," was not really an illusion at all, but an exotic dance number. It was purely a U.V. (black-light) fantasy employing a luminous dragon similar to the ones used by the Chinese to celebrate their New Year. It consisted of a large fire-breathing dragon's head with ten girls wrapped in capes to form the snake-like body painted in bright, fluorescent colors. The dancer who played the part of the magician for this scene was dressed in a duplicate of one of my mandarin robes, dyed with U.V. colors. He brandished a luminous scimitar with which he fought the wildly twisting dragon, finally cutting it into nine pieces. These turned into flames, went into a fire dance and then flickered out. This number turned out to be so successful that I kept it in the show for almost twenty years, and even used it as one of the dance numbers in "Satan's Daughter" in 1953.

Ultra-violet effects are a great asset to any magic show but must not be overdone. Except for the Fire Dragon and the Spirit Cabinet routine, I had only one more luminous effect. This was also a dance number of ten girls wearing differently colored skeleton costumes, which began with a slow macabre dance of the skeletons emerging from a coffin and ended with a wild rhumba to a blood stirring African drum beat.

While sitting in bed in the hospital poring over my lists of tricks and illusions and endeavoring to work them into blackouts, I suddenly remembered the suitcase of small tricks I had bought. Could these be used for some kind of a routine? I had always liked Oswald Williams' little comedy routine of the egg and the silk, and I had often thought this idea could be expanded into a short sketch. I mulled over this idea off and on for days, but discarded one plot after another until I remembered an experience in Buenos Aires just as I was starting out on my own. At that time there was only one magic shop in town, owned by the Literas brothers. The Bazar Yankee, as it was called, imported novelties from all over the world. In their magic department they had listed quite a number of stock tricks and accessories. Sometimes I would pop over for some small article and inquire of Senor Literas if he had it in stock. Usually we would go into the "Yes! We have no bananas" routine. If I asked him for a thumb tip he would say, "Yes! You mean a sort of metal thimble painted flesh color to represent a thumb?"

"Exactly." I said hopefully.

"Sorry. We never stock them."

Almost every time I went to the Bazar Yankee to buy something we went through this same routine and they never had anything I wanted. It got to be a running gag and I never forgot it.

This train of thought led to the idea of a sketch in which I played the part of the magic dealer and the comic played a poor ham-handed slob with a burning ambition to be a great magician. The gimmick was that he would ask me if I sold a certain trick and by way of illustration actually perform it. I would then repeat the trick, or a variation of it, as a confirmation that I understood what he wanted. After all this rigamarole I would say, "I never heard of it," or "I don't have it."

This basic idea adapted itself to some beautiful routining and pay-offs and included all the tricks in the suitcase and many other small effects totaling about fifteen minutes duration.

I showed the sketch to Okito but at first he didn't care for the idea as he thought there was too much clowning in it and it would be harmful to the dignity of a big stage illusionist. (Dai Vernon expressed it well when he said, "Comedy born of bewilderment is the only comedy that should be in magic.") Okito had a point, or was it that you can't teach an old magician new tricks? I thought that times were changing and that comedy magic had come to stay although there was a danger of over-doing it.

I argued with Okito that it was just an experiment which would cost very little to produce. If it didn't click, little harm would be done and it could be thrown out. Once my father knew my mind was made up he went along with it and even gave me a wonderful suggestion. "You haf that beautiful trap I made for you," he said. "Vy not use the de Kolta vanishing voman illusion for a finale and instead of the girl you vanish the bone-headed client?'' This was a brilliant idea and I jumped at it with the result that Okito converted one of my carved Chinese chairs into a de Kolta chair and, as usual, did a masterly job. It worked like a dream and gave the sketch a punch finish that couldn't be bettered.

The comedian I had in mind for the show was a young Mexican, Freddy Romero, who did a comedy acrobatic act with his wife Sonia, which included some well-performed small magic. He performed the vanishing cane, using a ''profonde'' in his evening dress coattails for the getaway of the cane and employing misdirection that many a big-time professional would envy. Freddy fell in love with ''The Magic Bazar,'' as I called it (bazar is Spanish for bazaar) and suggested some funny running gags such as the foot-on-the-stool business and the growing flower. Freddy's characterization of the dim-witted client was superbly conceived and as a trained acrobat he did some spectacular prat-falls that brought the house down.

The whole sketch looked marvellous on paper but you can never tell in the theatre. I bitterly remembered some of my past flops so I had a cheap paper backdrop painted. Paper scenery is allowed and widely used in Spain and Latin America. The sketch needed a tricked counter with various wells and traps so we made a provisional one from old 2 x 2's and covered the resulting frames with painted paper. With the exception of the chair illusion (which could always be used) we spent only a few pesos on the whole thing.

After that we built a combined Rehearsal and Backstage sketch with a very funny comedy situation and a very fine illusion.

Maury Kains suggested the 20th Century Brassiere trick, which was new at the time, and also the Lesson in Magic trick, using a record for teaching a magician a new trick and leaving him in the lurch at the crucial moment. Harry Mendoza had taught me his single card stabbing with a dagger that I used most successfully in combination with the record trick. We combined the expanding egg with the vanishing birdcage to bring back the canary, and using a new type of black-net fan, made the trick much surer to perform.

The banknote in the orange was worked into a sketch about a tempermental movie director, and the vanishing wand was changed to the vanishing orchestra leader's baton using the original Okito getaway which had never been used by anyone else. In went the old circus trick of the dancing spoon in the bottle combined with some sight gags that made it a high spot in the show. Card manipulation was combined with a sling-shot bit for the blackout of the smashed spotlight.

The old die-and-ribbon trick was changed for the glass plate version and was titled The Thief of Bagdad. The Hellozapoppin effect of throwing a woman from an upper box (a dummy) after a terrible fight was combined with the trick and it turned out to be the most sensational presentation in the show, with many people coming back to see this number—and trying to catch me when I stole the glass plate.

El Circo Magico (The Magic Circus) was next on the list and was a series of illusions, tricks and gags using clowns and acrobats. A special "vertical" levitation was built for suspending a girl in the air at the finish of a comedy strong-man act. A prop horse with two men inside was used for a quick change illusion and a clown was vanished in midair using the Fasola Sack illusion. This sketch was done in a specially painted circus tent set, complete with trapeze and circus ring and was excellent for children's matinees.

The Magician's Nightmare was a black art routine supposedly being the dream of a magician being haunted by all the halves of the women he had sawn in two. He was chased by dismembered legs, arms and half bodies!

The Third Man illusion was changed to a quick-change number called The Eternal Triangle, using a "backless" cabinet for the first time. At no time did any of the actors leave the stage or the sight of the audience. This was a new principle in stage magic.

After so many years my scenery began to show white lines where the paint had worn off in the creases due to constant folding for transportation. It was in bad shape. I was in a quandary as to whether I should have the sets re-touched or new sets made when the matter was solved in a dramatic fashion.

Senor Magin Banda was a Mexican artist with a marvellous sense of exotic scenery. Without telling me, he painted a fantasy combination of Oriental and Aztecan art which he hung in a local theatre. He invited me to inspect it, telling me he had painted it on the off chance that I would like it, but I was under no obligation. The set was a dream fantasy and I fell in love with it, but feared the price would be too high. When he told me his price was 300 pesos I could hardly believe it. I made a deal with him to paint me twenty new sets, which were all spectacular, and some of them were even cheaper as he washed the old backdrops to remove the paint and used this still strong canvas. In the years to come Magin Banda became Mexico's finest scenic artist. His work was used by all the ballet and opera companies in the Palacio de las Bellas Artes.

We rented the Arbeu Theatre for rehearsals, with Norman Foster directing many of the new sketches. During rehearsals an incident happened in an old mansion about a block away from the theatre. In this house lived two old eccentric spinster sisters who had the local fame of being witches as they were rarely ever seen. All their groceries were left in a basket outside the door of the patio wall and bills were paid by mail.

One morning the police, suspicious because the food basket had not been collected, broke in and found the two women brutally murdered in a room full of stuffed owls and other weird props. During their search for clues the police discovered thousands of dollars, pounds, liras, francs and pesetas hidden in mattresses, books, under the floor boards and in other odd places. Some of the money was so old it was out of circulation and valueless. Some of it had been eaten by rats and vermin.

I immediately wrote a short, grisly sketch for my U.V. ghost routine for the morbid-minded in the audience and added it to the show.

I repeat what I have mentioned previously. I am not a first-night hit writer and usually have to do a lot of rewriting after the debut, but this show was the one great exception to the rule. Perhaps because it had no plot and was just a series of sketches tacked together, or it may have been that the public was hungry for a comedy show after so many war years. All the publicity I had been getting with my radio shows and films obviously helped. All these circumstances together made the show a smash hit from the first night—and that night it ran twenty minutes overtime due to laughs and applause. Those were something I didn't know how to cut. The only solution was to speed up and make the show tighter. There were moments when the show was stopped cold and couldn't go on. It was, without a doubt, the best opening I ever had.

The show ran for five months without a break, except for the two days I suspended when President Roosevelt died. I never imagined that I could have surpassed my Lirico record in Mexico City, but this show did just that and made far more money. This wasn't like the movie deals—this was a daily box office deal with cash on the line every night. It was always in the theatre that I was in the big money. The show lasted eight years and was a hit in every country I played. It did five years in the city of Buenos Aires alone, which is a world's record for any magic show. But I am getting ahead of my story.

My mother had her own box and didn't miss a show. It certainly helped take her mind off Donald, whose unknown fate was getting her down. Sometimes, from the stage, I would go into an imitation of the marked mannerisms of Okito and she would laugh with the tears running down her face. The audience would look at her and wonder what she was laughing about as it didn't strike them as being very funny. Looking back over the years, I honestly believe that show kept my mother alive. Without fail, between shows, she would pop into my dressing room with a little paper bag from the delicatessen with some little snack I liked and coax me to eat it. Then, as she was leaving, she would often say, "Dave, do the Pop bit tonight."

Orson saw the show many times and declared it ready for Broadway. In a letter to me Harry Mendoza said, "Orson Welles returned from Mexico and told everyone you had the greatest show he had ever seen. With your charming personality and the new magic comedy angle, you sold them one hundred percent. This is a swell compliment coming from him."

One night, during the Magic Bazar sketch, I was surprised when Orson and Rita walked onto the stage and did some magic. The audience loved it as they were very popular in Mexico.

One evening Rita Hayworth showed up a few minutes before curtain time and wanted a front row seat. As the house was sold out, I prevailed upon the management to put an extra chair in the aisle, well down front. This was against the fire laws, but for Rita—what the hell—there were no rules. She wore a wonderful piled up hairdo that evening and took her seat to the great joy of the guy sitting alongside her. But we forgot all about the flying skeleton routine and during the blackout, when the boys came rushing down the aisles twirling the luminous skeletons hanging from the perch, one of the skeleton's feet got tangled in her coiffure with disastrous results. When they finally got untangled, and the light went up, she was a mess. Never in my life did I get such a black look. After the show in my dressing room, I had my hairdresser fix her up. He did such an artistic job that Rita was very pleased. Later the hairdresser went to Hollywood on Rita's recommendation.

Summing up the show, the Magic Bazar took pride of place. It was a twenty minute act of constant laughs. Through the years a lot of revising, cutting and adding new tricks and effects was only natural, but basically it was the same sketch that we opened with. It acquired a rhythm and polish that only comes with constant repetition, and the timing, that illusive ingredient and the soul of a fast skit like this, was perfect. Another advantage of the Magic Bazar was that it lent itself to constant changes and additions without harming the whole. Its possibilities were unlimited and any new effect could be added at a moment's notice. It was the most valuable sketch I ever had in any show.

After the first week in the Arbeu I had a special set painted, representing the interior of a magic store with outsized and fantastic apparatus on display. A new counter was constructed of plywood with all sorts of gadgets and traps to make the working easier. To think that all this came about by a chance accident of buying a little suitcase of stock tricks!

Another interesting point of the Magic Bazar was that it allowed two magicians to work without conflicting. That had been one of Okito's main objections to the sketch. He pointed out what a failure the ''Triple Alliance'' had been when LeRoy performed on the stage, another famous magician performed in the audience and still another in the balcony, all doing the same tricks. In the Magic Bazar there was no element of challenge. Although the comic played the part of an inept imbecile, the audience could appreciate his adroitness and skill as a manipulator and the whole sketch was psychologically sound. After the debut Okito changed his opinion and called it ''a show in itself.'' It became his favorite and he made many suggestions for gags and ideas which were all accepted with thanks.

The other two outstanding successes of the show were the Fire Dragon and the Thief of Bagdad, but all the rest of the new stuff held up beautifully, making it a fast, funny and entertaining show. So now I was in the position of having a hit show on my hands and nowhere to go with it. We closed soon after V-E Day, and as we thought the war with Japan would last for years, I regretfully stored the show and went back to motion pictures.

I was in the money again so I didn't break my neck trying to get a story finished. I took my time and wrote two detective yarns. Both of them were refused by the producers, and although some people advised me to produce them myself, I was afraid to take the chance, knowing how long it took to get one's money back. The first story was the straight detective story with the trick ending which I mentioned before. They said it was too radical. The other was a comedy-detective story ridiculing the famous screen monsters—a comedy show like the Munsters and the Addams family which became popular on television. My story was about a magician who discovers four famous horror-merchants living in a cheap boardinghouse. Frankenstein was the porter who answered the door and attended to salesmen who froze when they saw a butler with the screws in his neck. Dracula was getting old and had lost his teeth and was using a badly fitting dental plate with long fangs which were constantly falling out. He was now depending on blood banks instead of beautiful damsels. The invisible man never ventured out of the house as he either froze or was sunburned and was fed up with people shoving, pushing or stepping on his invisible feet. The wolf man was also afraid to leave the house because a great dane was in love with him. The magician takes these four misfits as his assistants in a detective agency with the story ending like a Marx Brothers' comedy. Senor Carlos Villareas, who played Dracula in the first Spanish talkies made in Hollywood, was to play the part in my picture and I was in touch with Bela Lugosi for the Frankenstein part, but they rejected the story and it ended in the trash can. I still think it would make a funny film.

I was forced to stick to the old box office formula. Mediocrity was the norm and the majority of picture-goers delighted in it. On that quicksand foundation I wrote a couple of stinkers that were accepted.

Before we went into production, the war with Japan ended—with a greater surprise than when it had started. We knew it wouldn't take long for American industry to get back into full swing and the motion picture industry would be one of the first. The Mexican film industry stood still for a while and took stock of itself; they decided to make fewer but better pictures. Some of the farsighted lads thought the Americans might make some of their films in Mexico, as the costs were much lower, and a giant studio was built in Churubusco. This proved to be true. In later years many good pictures were made in Mexico by major American film companies working with the Mexicans.

Both my pictures were cancelled for the time being, along with many others, and there was a general air of uncertainty for a while.

The word of my new show had spread and I was not surprised when one day my ex-manager Fernandez arrived in Mexico, with a young and pretty bride. Fernandez told me that when he heard I was in the theatre again he had quit the Chang show in Buenos Aires and, with his seventeen-year-old Argentine wife, had made the long voyage around Cape Horn, up the west coast of South America, through the Panama Canal, to Tampico in the Gulf of Mexico. He was very disappointed when I told him I had no intention of leaving Mexico.

One great day in October, thanks to the International Red Cross, my mother received news that Donald was safe—but her joy was quickly dispelled by the terrible story he told in his first letter. He wrote that after the Dutch Army had surrendered he had joined the resistance movement. As he spoke perfect English and German he was contacted by the British for under-cover work. In August, 1941, he was betrayed by a Dutchman and on October 15 sentenced to death. For the next thirteen months he was kept in a death cell, but because of his youth the sentence was commuted to life imprisonment. He spent the next four years in two jails and eleven concentration camps, including the infamous Buchenwald, Dachau, Neuengamme and Gross-Rosen. Of the two hundred odd Dutchmen that were arrested with him, only three survived and one of them died shortly after the liberation. He had developed tuberculosis during this time and was unable to work after being freed. We sent him all the food packages and financial assistance possible. Later we learned that my father's sister Eve and his two brothers Ned-dy and Simon had frozen to death in a freight car on their way to a concentration camp in Poland.

My mother developed a guilt complex, stemming from the fact that she had spent the war years in comfort and her boy had suffered so terribly. We tried to convince her that it would have done no good for her to have remained in Holland during that fearful time, but she blamed herself for his misfortune and her health began to fail.

To make matters worse, Fernandez' young wife, Matilde, died of gastectasis, leaving Fernandez in an awful state and with a burning desire to get away from Mexico to forget. Without my knowledge and abetted by Okito, who was also anxious to leave Mexico, Fernandez contacted the Nacional Theatre in Havana and they made an offer.

In the meantime Ricardo Montalban and other Mexican film stars had been approached by Metro-Goldwyn-Mayer with a tempting seven year contract for Hollywood. Norman Foster was dead against it but Ricardo signed anyway and shortly after married Georgiana Young, Sally's younger sister.

I was contacted by a representative for a similar seven year contract with a $2,000 a week minimum and was just on the point of accepting when I was discouraged by some of the actors who had previous experience in this deal. When I argued that it was a sure two grand a week deal, work or not, one actor said to me "Listen, babe in the woods, they'll tear your heart out. They'll miscast you in a picture or two, and if you don't make the grade, they'll have you hanging around, month after month, doing nothing and unable to work with anyone else as they have you under contract."

"Maybe so, but they'd still have to pay me over $700,000."

"Less taxes," he said. "Sure they'll pay, but it's the kiss of death. Those birds have it all figured out. How long do you think a real artiste could stand laying off for years at a time, even with a guaranteed paycheck? The time comes when a guy is ready to do anything to have his contract broken."

I could see what he meant when Ricardo was promptly miscast in his first film, a bathing suit epic with Esther Williams. It made no use of his undeniable dramatic talent, which in the long run was to save him. He made some good films.

I was at a crossroads. These dire warnings had soured me on the Hollywood deal but to travel again with the big show didn't appeal to me either. I was happy in Mexico and for the first time in my life I felt secure. I hated the thought of giving it all up.

Fernandez painted a brilliant picture of what would happen in Cuba after five years of theatrical stagnation and was sure the the first big show to play there would make a killing.

I compromised and accepted the Havana deal, but with the understanding that I would return to Mexico immediately after. To this day I don't know if I did right or not. I have often wondered what would have happened if I had refused the Havana business.

There were no passenger boats to Havana yet but Fernandez arranged with a cockleshell freighter to take the baggage and two of my assistants but with no guarantee for time of arrival. They were touching Mexican gulf ports to pick up freight and figured that the trip would take more or less a month. With some misgiving I gave the green light, the crates were loaded on board and away she sailed, for better or worse.

Okito insisted on going along, but my mother preferred to stay in Mexico for the short time we would be away. She went to live with some good friends of ours, the Honey family.

Finally the day came to take the plane to Havana and I said goodbye to my mother, little knowing that I would never see her again.

CHAPTER 41

The Havana deal started off badly. There was no sign of the boat and Fernandez would spend hours at the docks waiting for some news of the blasted ship. Havana was bursting with war dollars and the days slipped by with us loafing around town. I visited my friend Senor Correa at his new Tropicana nightclub which had proved to be a gold mine.

My first headache was with the Centro Gallego, owners of a whole block in the center of Havana, right alongside the Capitol building, which included the Nacional Theatre and the imposing Galician Club. Fernandez hadn't a proper contract and they backed down when they found out the expense involved in bringing the show from Mexico and the high cost of advertising. Senor Duran, the Centro Gallego's representative and manager of the Nacional, regretfully said that if we wanted to open, we would have to take over the theatre as our own impresario. They offered very fair terms and I had no alternative but to agree. I had no fear of losing, but it was a jolt to have to spend over ten thousand dollars for advertising and bringing the show to Havana, not to mention our expenses while waiting for the snail-boat to arrive. I cursed the day I left dear old Mexico and my easy life there.

When the boat finally arrived we rushed the material over to the theatre, went into rehearsals, and set a date for debut. The theater-starved Cubanos raided the box office and the theatre was sold out for two weeks in advance; but scalpers bought up the choicest seats and were selling them for double the price and there was nothing we could do about it. The police stepped in and we were hauled off to jail to explain why no tickets could be had at the announced price. We explained that we had nothing to do with it, that this sort of thing was against our interest. We were freed of all blame, but the scalpers kept at it and made a tremendous killing.

The show was a hit and it seemed like all Havana showed up, including the outlying towns which had special bus services to the theatre. The show was one constant roar of laughter from start to finish and we were doing two and three shows a day. On weekdays we did from three to four thousand dollars; on Saturdays and Sundays over five thousand. The Centro Gallego was sick about it, but there was nothing they could do but sit back and mope.

Okito went crazy about this wide open city with its marvellous tropical climate and I had never seen him so happy. He had made friends with a fervid amateur magician, Senor Tortosa, president of the Corona Cigar Company, who provided Okito with boxes of the same Corona-Coronas that were made for Winston Churchill. As Okito had always been a heavy cigar smoker, this was nirvana. After the first month at the Nacional, Okito opened with his act. All a real artiste needs is an appreciative audience to make him feel twenty years younger.

One day Ramiro de la Presa's brother, who lived in Havana, told me that Chang had passed through on a trip, had seen our show and had left immediately after. "Oh! Oh!" I thought. "The old merry-go-round is starting again," but I didn't really care very much because I was set on returning to Mexico. That's what I thought!

From a financial standpoint, Havana became the most successful venture of my whole career. We grossed well over $100,000. My pictures were playing in Cuba and the island was ripe for a wonderful tour. Then I did one of those hare brained things that I always did when I was flush.

Fernandez showed up one morning at my hotel with that old cloak-and-dagger look that I knew so well and went into a melodrama. He had it "at first hand" that Chang was going to open in Caracas, Venezuela, with a copy of my show and cut me off from South America.

"So what?" I said. "He's welcome to it. In the first place I don't think he can do that type of show and, even if he can, it doesn't matter to me as I am going back to Mexico right after we play the island. Y pronto!"

"What?" squawked a horrified Fernandez. "Do you realize what you are saying? Have you ever made so much money in your life as now? Do you know that Caracas is better than Havana? They haven't seen a decent show for years and they stink with money. You can't let a chance like this slip through your fingers.''

"Where's Chang now?''

"I don't know. I suppose in Buenos Aires.''

"Then how the hell can he get to Caracas so fast and with an entirely new show? Or is he a real magician now?''

Fernandez left my hotel looking like a condemned man but he wasn't finished yet. Together with his conspirator, Okito, they almost wept at the thought of Chang sweeping up all those million dollar bills lying on the streets of Caracas just waiting for some Chinese magician to pick them up. Eventually they wore me down and I agreed to play Venezuela but after that, back home to Mexico.

Instead of playing the island of Cuba I made one of those world-shaking bonehead decisions and arranged with another nutshell boat to take the baggage to La Guaira. Once again, the captain made no promises as to arrival as he had to touch the Caribbean ports of Haiti, Santo Domingo and Puerto Rico, and perhaps a stop at Trinidad before touching La Guaira. How long? Maybe a month—maybe more. In spite of this we loaded the baggage and with three new Cuban assistants, they set forth for the South American mainland.

I contracted a chorus line of six Cuban girls for Caracas and with Freddy Romero, Sonia, Okito, Eva and some of my assistants (Spreer had remained in Mexico), I chartered a plane for Caracas. I felt the loss of Spreer and Miguel keenly as none of the assistants I had on the show now knew anything about magic. The old team was split up. Although I could do all the necessary repairs on the show, it wasn't like the old days when someone would have a fresh idea and the three of us would tackle it from every angle and worry it into a workable illusion. Okito was actually in charge of all new construction, but as each day passed our separate outlooks on magic, or rather the presentation of magic, became more divergent. He claimed that I was over doing the comedy angle and relegating magic to second place. He may have been right from a purist's standpoint, but I had discovered a box office formula that was successful, as the crowded theatres proved. Okito claimed that in these show starved days, just after the war, any magic show, comedy or not, could do the same amount of business; but that I couldn't prove. All I knew was that I had a solid show and was afraid to tamper with it. I knew from former experience how hard it was to write such a money-maker.

I didn't know what all the rush was to get to Caracas. I should have waited in Havana for a few weeks where I would have had far less expenses. I had ten Cubans on my hands and in Havana they would have cost me very little for salaries. In Caracas I had to pay full salaries in a country three times as expensive as Cuba. Venezuela always was one of the most expensive countries in the world, and as the boat took over a month to get to La Guaira, the deal cost me a small fortune. At this time I held the world's championship as the worst business man on earth. Finally the boat showed up, with the boys looking like toasted skeletons and with horrendous tales of hurricanes and the ship springing a leak off the coast of Santo Domingo.

We opened in the Nacional Theatre where I was forced to be impresario again, but I must say that Fernandez had been right about one thing; the town was full of money. We repeated the Havana success with even greater profits as we charged higher prices and there was no scalping.

In Caracas I had the pleasure of meeting and becoming friendly with Spain's greatest matador, Manolete. I invited him to see the show and he had the wits half scared out of him when the girl was apparently thrown out of the upper box in the Thief of Bagdad trick. He stood up and gripped the rail of his box when the dummy sailed through he air. That night, after the show, he told me he was always nervous, and every time he stepped into the bullring he was scared stiff. He laughed when I told him I was paying him back in part for the scares he had given me in his corridas. He was considered by many to be the greatest bullfighter who ever lived. Several months later, he was gored to death in a small Spanish town.

Rumors sprang up that the American dollar was wobbling again and although this was sheer nonsense, "Old Chief Cold-Foot" sat in the front row and believed it. We made a study of all South American currencies and came to the conclusion that the most solid of all the countries financially was Argentina. I sent nearly $75,000 to a bank in Buenos Aires where I hoped it would be safe and collect interest. A new energetic president had just been elected, Juan Domingo Peron, and a bright future was predicted.

Okito did his act for the last time in the Nacional Theatre in Caracas in June, 1946. He had lost his American citizenship by staying away too many years and was trying to get permission to enter the U.S. again. Eventually it was arranged and in Caracas he told me he was leaving and would try to get his act together again. I gave him his plane fare to New York and $3,000 to get his material from Holland, and when the season closed in Caracas, we said good bye. I can still remember him clearly as he wished me luck, standing in the door of my hotel room. Just before he closed the door he looked at me and said, ''Gott bless you, Dafe,'' and then he was gone. That was the last time I was to see him. Slowly, one by one, the people who loved me were drifting out of my life, but I never realized it until it was too late.

Letters from Mexico, especially from Norman, warned me that things were rather rugged in the film industry and if I could hold off for a while, it would get better. There were no ships to Mexico as yet and we decided to play the interior of Venezuela, as far as Maracaibo, and then down to San Cristobal on the Colombian frontier, cross over to Cucuta and so to Bogota.

In Maracaibo I had my first bad business since I opened with the new show. On the opening night they sold so many tickets that the people were standing in the aisles like sardines in that tropical heat. The seated spectators protested as the standing people cut off their view of the stage and, finally, most of the audience had to stand up to see the show. It was impossible to do the skeleton act, and with all the protests and noise, they couldn't hear what we were saying. The show was a disaster and the audience very dissatisfied. The foolish manager was proud that he had broken all records on that night but never stopped to realize that by doing so he had killed the season in a town noted for being a great show town.

Business in Colombia was wonderful and we went from town to town making money everywhere. Only once in a lifetime does one have such a continual winning streak and I had to play along with it. It would have been insanity to stop. I was on my way to being a millionaire (in South American currency) and you don't throw away a thing like that casually. We went south to Ecuador where it was the same story over again, and from Guayaquil we left for Lima, Peru.

Lima! My jinx town. I wondered what would happen this time. We opened at the Municipal and things started beautifully. We had crowded houses. On the morning of October 26, I received a cable from Mexico that my mother had passed away. Her last letters to me had been quite cheerful as she was in constant touch with Donald. Suddenly her health failed and in a few days she was gone. I sat for most of that day in the cathedral of Lima. It was there I said farewell to the kindest soul I have ever known.

The season dragged on and after the Municipal we took over the Teatro Segura for a season of popular prices. Across the street from the Segura was a restaurant owned by a friend of mine, Senor Leon de Mozart, where we had supper every night after the show to relax after the tension of the theatre. One night Macao, one of my Cuban assistants, rushed up to my table with the startling news that the theatre was afire. "It had to be Lima," was the thought that ran through my head as we ran over to the theatre and saw smoke coming up through the roof of the stage.

We managed to get into the theatre and to the stage where the smoke was not too thick and, looking up, we saw the red flicker of flames in the grid. Luckily the scenery hadn't caught fire as yet and we still had a little time to salvage something. I ran to my dressing room and opened the trunk which contained the books of travellers cheques and other valuables. I gave the order to get the Chinese costumes out first. The boys dragged the heavy trunks out into the street and then they started wheeling out the heavy illusions.

One of my boys climbed up into the grid to cut the ropes of the scenery, hoping at least to save the big embroidered front drop. He shouted frantically for me to come up. I shouted back for him to cut out the nonsense and come down at once, but all he did was laugh and wave his arms, crying, "Falsa alarma! No hay peligre."

I climbed up the iron rungs sunk in the wall and up to the bridge where I was rewarded with the most perfect optical illusion I have ever sen. The roofs of most theatres in South America were corrugated zinc with an open space of about a yard between the walls of the theatre and the roof to allow air to circulate. The fire was actually a full block away from the theatre, but the wind was blowing the smoke toward us and it drifted through the open space where air currents forced it down to the stage. The flames of the burning building were reflected on the under side of the bare metal roof and from below it gave the perfect illusion of a burning grid. A few sparks added to the reality and this was the only danger we had. Two of our boys stayed up in the bridge to keep watch.

We dragged all the material back into the theatre again and after explanations to the police, who had shown up to see what all the fuss was, we returned to the restaurant and celebrated our good luck with a few piscos.

For the rest of the season our business was good and from

Peru we jumped to Santiago de Chile where we opened in the Santa Lucia Theatre. I had the opportunity of meeting old friends who I hadn't seen in years. It was here that I had to break in a new comedian as Freddy Romero and Sonia had returned to Mexico from Lima. The new comic, Rodolfo Areu, was also Mexican, and although his style was different from Romero's, as he was formerly a circus clown, he was quite a success.

When Fernandez returned to Santiago from Buenos Aires, where he had arranged the Teatro National for the official season of 1947, he informed me that after a long tour of Brazil, Chang had returned to Buenos Aires. He had played a summer season at the Avenida Theatre and was still there. We were back playing the cat and mouse game again, but this time I wasn't afraid as my show was so entirely different from all other magic shows; I didn't care who played before me.

We flew straight to Buenos Aires from Santiago and I found that Chang was splitting the bill with Cleopatra (the widow of Kasfikis who had been killed in Spain) and was doing a variety show with a lot of imported acts. Miguel was with him as chief assistant but was leaving the show and asked me if I had something for him in my show. I told him I would think it over.

I found a disagreeable financial situation in the Argentine as Peron had frozen all foreign currency bank accounts. The strange thing was that one could send all the money he wished *out* of the country, but it was forbidden to bring fresh money *in*, as the banks were full! I didn't understand exactly what was going on, but it was clear that my $75,000 was frozen and I couldn't touch it. It didn't worry me at the moment because I didn't need it, and as the Argentine peso was 4.20 to the dollar, I made no effort to get it out.

Just as I had surmised, Chang's season in the Avenida had no effect on our business and we had a splendid season. However, I was forced to make a change in the show, as the new comic, Areu, was deaf. This made it hard at times as I had to stick exactly to the dialogue without changing a single line for fear of getting a non sequitur answer. I knew that I would have to make a change and started looking around for another comedian, but for my particular type of show they are not easy to find. I thought of Miguel for the part and although he was not an acrobat, he did have a kind of dry humor. I thought with training I could make a good comic out of him and I called him over to talk. At first he demurred as he had never done a comic part in his life; but I talked him into letting me direct him and have a try at it. We rehearsed for weeks and the result was Micalet—which was the name I gave him—became the best comedian I ever had. He developed a dead pan fathead type with a Catalan accent that was really funny.

News from Mexico was bad. Just as Orson had predicted, the industry was going through a tough time and the Americans were rapidly taking over their lost markets again. Europe was getting on its feet and the Italians were starting to make the "neo-realismo" films that were to be such a sensation. There was also a lot of talk about something new called television but no one knew exactly what effect it would have on the theatre and the movies, although it should have been obvious to any clear thinking person. I decided to hold off on Mexico for a while and completely forgot that to retain my Mexican residence I had to return within two years to get an extension; but time slipped by and when I woke up, it was too late.

While we were still in the National, Chang decided to go to Spain instead of continuing in South America, which was pretty well played out for the moment. His choice was a wise one as he did very well there and made enough money to realize one of the dreams of his life—a magical circus. He bought a beautiful tent with aluminum walls, complete with trucks and trailers. From Spain he went to Caracas with his new venture, but unfortunately was swindled by a person he trusted and lost the whole property.

After the National I went over to Chang's old stronghold, the Avenida Theatre just as summer was starting again. New theatre regulations came into being, including a one-day-a-week rest, normally a Monday, which usually is a slack day anyway. Although the impresarios raised hell, we found out eventually that it was a good thing for everybody and even helped to increase business. Another municipal edict was the abolition of the "vermouth" show, that six o'clock show that was always poorly attended and did nothing but tire out the artistes. The new law called for one show on weekdays and two on Saturdays, Sundays and holidays. One show a day was not enough to meet expenses so when we opened in the Apolo, I got around the law by dividing the show into "secciones," that is to say we gave two separate acts of an hour and a half duration with a fifteen minute interval. Both shows were different so a customer could see the first or the second act or both if they wished. This new system had amazing results, and it wasn't long until half the theatres in Buenos Aires followed suit—a practice still used in all the revue houses.

A Brazilian impresario offered me a tour right up to the Amazon country, and although Chang had been there less than a year before, I knew from the Buenos Aires business that I need have no fears so I accepted. Eva wasn't keen on Brazil for some reason, and after having been with me for nearly twelve years, she decided to go home to Mexico.

We sailed from Buenos Aires and arrived in Rio de Janeiro in March, 1948, opening at the old Carlos Gomez Theatre. Rio hadn't changed at all over the years and it was still the old fun-loving, gay place it always had been. My comedy show was perfect for it. We had a grand time and from Rio we went north to play all the towns I had worked with Raymond over twenty years before.

In Forteleza, right on the end of the hump of South America, my son Bob, who had just gotten out of the army, flew down to pay me a visit. He was studying physics at Cornell at that time with expectations of becoming a teacher. I was very happy to see him and we had much to talk about. He loved the show but said he had no interest in show business, and although he liked magic as a hobby, he wouldn't care to be a professional. With him the long line of Bambergs as magicians ended after a saga of 250 years.

Bob brought six Weller beer bottles with him and using the Brunel White Hat I immediately incorporated them into the Magic Bazar as a running gag. It was a hit from the start and every time I would say, "I haven't got it!" (when the comic requested a trick) he would produce a bottle of beer from his hat and say, "Good! Then let's have a drink!" As silly as this sounds, it became a catchword everywhere we went.

Another effect I tried when Bob was with me was the Show Boxing bit, in which the comic tries to do handshadows as I have done them and ends up by having a fight with his own shadow which refuses to obey him.

Bob had a good sense of humor and planned a funny gag for the boys on the show. The day he arrived all the boys were at the airport to meet him, and when he stepped off the plane they expected us to go into one of those back-slapping "abrazos" that are the custom in these countries. They were surprised when we shook hands in the usual Anglo-American way, without displaying our emotions to outsiders. I overheard snatches of "cold blooded Americans" and so forth. When it was time for

Bob to go from the city of Belem de Para at the mouth of the Amazon River, back to New York, we planned a comedy act for the benefit of the boys. We said our good byes in the hotel and did all the back-slapping and embracing in private, but when we got to the airport with all the boys there to see him off, Bob shook hands with all of them, gave each of them an "abrazo," but to me he gave a casual two fingered salute saying, "Be seeing you!"—and hopped on the plane. The boys never got over it and talked about it for months.

From the Amazon we worked our way back south and played in Bahia, the first South American city I had ever visited. On the walls of the stage were still the old programmes of Li-Ho-Chang and Raymond pasted alongside each other, and for auld lang syne I pasted one of mine along with them.

While having lunch in the hotel in Bahia, who should walk into the dining room but Dai Vernon. He was on his way to Buenos Aires on a Moore-McCormack cruise and had stopped over in Bahia for the day. He had seen my posters in the streets and found me at the hotel. We spent the day together but he couldn't stay to see the show as the boat left that evening for Rio. Dai told me that a number of good magicians had been contracted by the Moore-McCormack lines to give shows on board and all were going to Buenos Aires. I saw to it that Dai was given a nice reception by the local Argentine magicians and amateurs.

It was also here in Bahia that I engaged a strikingly beautiful brunette, Vanette, to do all the main illusions of the show. She was a descendent of the Baron of Bahia at the time of Dom Pedro II.

On the way to Victoria the company went by boat with the baggage, but Vanette and I took a plane. About half an hour out of Bahia flying over the jungle, the plane caught fire, and after fifteen horrendous minutes, the pilot made a forced landing with one engine. That experience soured me on planes and I didn't have the nerve to fly again for eight years—and then only because it was absolutely necessary.

We played Rio again in another theatre, then to Sao Paulo and south through dozens of small towns right through to Uruguayana. I went to Paraguay again, and after a very good season returned down the river to Buenos Aires after a year's absence.

CHAPTER 42

We opened at the Casino Theatre for a four month's run and went back to the National for another three months. For the next three years we played nearly every theatre in Buenos Aires.

These were great magic years for the Argentine amateurs. Thanks to the Moore-McCormack Lines they had the opportunity of seeing many of the greatest American magicians. In addition to Dai Vernon we had a chance to study the techique of Sam Horowitz (who made the trip over sixty times in a period of ten years working under the name of Mohammed Bey), Francis Carlyle, who took the Buenos Aires' nightclubs by storm, Dr. Stanley Jaks with his subtle and amazing mental effects, Milbourne Christopher with his original rope routines, and many others. Manipulative magic and basic principles had changed since I had been in New York and I was completely baffled by some of the tricks these men did. Carlos Colombi, the little boy of Pigue so many years before, was now living in Buenos Aires and was my constant companion at this time and perhaps he, more than anyone else, appreciated the high class magic we saw performed week after week.

All these men were most generous with their secrets. Dai and Sam gave lectures explaining in detail the latest and best in modern magic and advanced the art in this country by fifty years. Les Briant said to me after seeing Dai do impromptu magic at a dinner table, "Dai Vernon doesn't do tricks—he does miracles." He went on to explain, "I have seen hundreds of card tricks which are obviously just card tricks with accent on the word trick. But when I see a man slowly take a card and with no discernible movement, change it for another—that, for me, is magic." I had the utmost respect for Briant's opinion on magic; perhaps because he was, like Okito, hard of hearing, his powers of observation were very keen. Nothing distracted his attention, which made him a dangerous spectator for any magician.

Briant refused to do any magic in front of these masters but one night, after prodding, he finally consented to do a small effect. He had a deck shuffled and a few cards selected and placed face down on the table. He then removed a small scarab from a pillbox and proceeded to divine and match the facedown cards. This stopped everyone cold. Only later did we discover that, with his scarab misdirection, he had rung in a marked deck on us and we fell for it line and sinker!

Leslie Briant had a great sense of humor and his Waldorf-Astoria hoax is a gem that must be told. During those years Les was in the legal department of the bank of London and South America. Every magician who came to Buenos Aires would look him up. Just around the corner from the bank, in the Calle Cangallo, was a crummy little joint with the imposing name of the Waldorf-Astoria. They served coffee on little round tables. The only reason Briant went there was because it was near the bank. When a magician visited him, Briant would invite the fellow to have a coffee at this dump. However, in his articles in *The Sphinx* over the years, he would mention that the "great so-and-so and I had a magical session at the round table of the Waldorf-Astoria." The American magicians reading this had visions of some fabulous South American palace! When a new magician would visit Buenos Aires for the first time and look up Briant at the bank, he would say, "Have you time to pop over to the Waldorf for a snort?" They would gleefully accept and it was wonderful to see their faces when they entered the Waldorf-Astoria and saw the battered tables. No one ever gave the gag away and it kept up for years.

Many magicians, including Sam Horowitz and Milbourne Christopher, honored me by appearing in my Magic Bazar sketch in various theatres.

When Stanley Jaks came down to Buenos Aires he found a kindred spirit in Juan Kappelmacher, an Austrian chemist and former member of the Vienna Magic Circle, who resided in the city. Juan had been a good friend of mine for many years and was the inventor of some wonderful plastic apparatus for magic.

Dai, Sam, Vanette and I were together in Rio de Janeiro during the Mardi Gras week, and in an article in *The Sphinx* entitled, "I Learn a Card Trick," I told how Dai was almost knifed by a fanatic dressed as a skeleton when Dai triend to defend a sarong clad Vanette from a crowd of youths. Dai held them off while Vanette, Sam and I escaped through an empty building. Dai aged ten years in ten minutes and from then on never left the beat.

During my tour of Brazil and Paraguay, the Argentine peso started dropping, and when I returned to Buenos Aires the peso had dropped to 15 to the dollar. When I finally managed to get my frozen money from the bank, I had lost thousands of dollars. The real seriousness of that loss didn't hit me until years later when I needed that money. Gaulke had been right with that crack about artistes being like a bunch of whores—come easy, go easy.

In 1950 I got the old expanding fever again. I decided to make a change, or at least add a few new effects to relieve the monotony. I laid off for a few weeks, opened a shop, and had the good fortune to be helped by Frank Cleaver, an English amateur magician and first class mechanic, who was associated with the British Railways in Argentina. Another friend of mine, Senor Hector Belucci, an Argentine magician known as Yadu and inventor and constructor of some remarkable illusions, also kindly lent me a hand. With Miguel we had a wonderful team and overhauled the show and made a lot of necessary repairs. Colombi took charge of advertising and lobby display material.

A radical change was made in the Pendulum illusion and a tree-cutting saw was substituted for the swinging blade and the table itself considerably reduced in size. A new and improved ''body'' was constructed for the girl, which made her appear half nude and greatly enhanced the effect. The sketch itself was changed to a parody of Don Juan Tenorio, which was a poetic travesty of the old Spanish theatre of the nineteenth century.

Most of all I needed a new, sensational illusion that I could advertise and use as a strong finale for the show. Thurston's Iasia illusion for the vanish of a girl over the heads of the audience seemed likely but without the shortcomings the Thurston illusion had. I wanted to do the effect with a much lighter and easier setup. After considering and discarding various basic principles, I came up with what is known as my Atomic Woman illusion. In this effect a girl is seated on a trapeze in a large Chinese lantern, which is swung up and over the heads of the audience. A second lantern, folded flat on a thin stand, is at center stage and also hoisted into the air. A shot is fired and the lanterns collapse with a loud explosion and a flash of fire and smoke. The girl is seen to vanish from the latern over the audience and appears sitting on a trapeze in the second lantern on the stage. This illusion, using only one girl, turned out to be a most sensational closing number.

A few new comedy effects were added to the show. One of them was a water pail that was kicked offstage, flew all around the theatre, and fell from the flies, just missing the comic's head. Many complicated theories were given by people to explain this silly gag and many thought I used complicated stereophonic sound equipment. In fact, it was only a tin can dragged around with a cord by a stooge.

A really funny gag that went into the Magic Bazar was a collapsing piano stool, in which the large center screw perforated the seat—to the obvious discomfort of the comic.

We incorporated a floating table routine into the Haunted Window sketch, using the "chopped-off" hand gag when the comic tried to duplicate the effect.

A new Chinese dance number was added which consisted of four "rickshaws," a girl sitting in each, pulled by coolie girls. The rickshaws visually transformed into parasols, followed by a luminous dance routine.

It was while we were building this new addition to the show that television came to Buenos Aires. Channel seven opened with great fanfare, but the programmes were so poor and the sets so expensive, it was a flop and did no harm to the theatre. By this initial failure we were lulled into believing that television would never be serious competition, and it was not until ten years later when three new channels opened that we began to feel their effect.

We opened at the Smart Theatre with the new show, and for the Magic Circus I engaged some foreign variety acts, including the Guttenberg Trio (eccentric musical comedians) and a very good acrobatic act. The season lasted four months and the next year we did another four months at the same theatre. The Atomic Woman clicked from the first night and never needed any changes.

We played in and around Buenos Aires for the next two years, establishing a record for a magic show that has never been equalled. I have no record of the exact number of performances we gave but it ran into the thousands, until Buenos Aires finally got tired of us and I had to look for new worlds to conquer. The grind was getting me down anyway. I was on my feet for eight or ten hours a day, at full speed, and as I was not the type to rest between shows, I was a nervous wreck every weekend. To make things even merrier, I had a coughing spell one day, brought on by too much cigarette smoking, and my hernia returned.

The only other full evening's magic show to appear in Buenos Aires in those two years was a German-Brazilian magician named Cantarelli, who opened in the Casino; but it was a slow show, his props were ungainly and old-fashioned and he closed after two weeks of very poor business.

The political situation was getting bad and a lot of new impositions were slapped on the theatre, including a full day's take for one of Eva Peron's social security projects. The value of the peso was dropping constantly.

A good offer came from Bolivia and I accepted. We started to form a company when a lot of things happened at once. Miguel, whose cousins had a small factory for the manufacture of metal bottle cappers, was offered a steady job as foreman and he quit the show. Vanette pined for Brazil and she, too, left. Two of my best girl assistants got married and, without warning, Chang arrived and opened in the Avenida Theatre.

I had to work fast so I engaged the Guttenberg Trio to do their act and double on the show. Pinky took over the part of the comic and as he was a trained circus comedian and acrobat, he was quite good. His wife, Hilde, did the illusions and his brother Joe who was about my size and build, played my double in the illusions. It was quite a good setup, but I still didn't have a chief girl assistant for the big illusions.

There are certain girls (very hard to find) who are cut out for stage illusion work and every magician, at one time or another, has had one of these rare jewels. The assistant problem for a travelling show is a very difficult one as there is no future in this kind of work and it is only natural that after a certain length of time they find something better. This is fine for the assistant but hard on the magician when he loses a trained artiste who has been with him for years. A good assistant knows all the details of the show and even a lot of things the magician himself is ignorant of as he is out front while the assistants are setting and preparing backstage. They develop a routine that builds up over the years.

For example, on closing nights the boys would stack the open crates on the floor against the walls, quickly pack the illusions as they left the stage, and never miss a cue for their own appearance onstage again. With this system the big show was packed and ready to leave the theatre an hour after the final curtain.

On opening days it was the same thing. When I got to the theatre after lunch the show was set up, the scenery hung, the traps cut and everything was ready for a quick show and orchestra rehearsal. When a magician loses one of these train-ed people, the entire show suffers. The girl who did the main illusions developed an agility that was little short of marvellous. There were times, during the Atomic Woman illusion, that I thought the girl couldn't possibly have made it to her spot in time, but it never once failed. The assistants took a great pride in breaking their own records, and when I saw a girl dive through a trap, without the slightest fear, it took my breath away. This was the kind of girl I had to find, and who would be will-ing to travel to foreign countries for no telling how long.

I had only a couple weeks left before departing for Bolivia and to make matters worse, Chang was doing very badly in the Avenida due to the public of Buenos Aires being satiated with magic. I knew he was not a man to hang around very long if things were not good and I certainly didn't want one of those cutthroat races up the west coast. I knew I had to get a good head start.

As luck would have it, I was sitting in the Yapeyu restaurant, which had formerly been the old Kessler place of Dante's time, when in walked a slender, strikingly beautiful blond, who sat down at a table near mine and was shortly joined by an elderly woman. I couldn't keep my eyes off her and thought, if only I could get a girl like that for the show. She must have noticed my staring and she bowed and smiled. That did it! I sent her a note by the waiter asking if I could talk over some business with her. She must have thought that this was a new approach as she read the note and put it in her purse without any expres-sion. "Well," I thought, "no one can say I didn't try."

I was on my coffee and almost ready to go when she came over to my table, sat down, and asked me what business I wanted to talk over. She said her name was Khelmis and the elderly lady was her mother. I introduced myself and she said she knew me by sight, having seen my show many times. If it hadn't been for that, she wouldn't have come to my table as she knew all the routines and promises to pretty girls for stage and movie careers.

I decided to play it straight and not gild the lily. I explained what the proposition was and purposely made it sound tough to get her reaction. She told me she was a tango singer in a small night spot and had no stage experience, but this was just what I wanted as there were no bad habits to break. I could train her from the beginning.

She called her mother over and after a lot of talk, she consented to give it a try. I phoned Fernandez to run out to La Plata, a city about an hour from Buenos Aires, and arrange three days at the Teatro Podesta. We were lucky that the theatre was free and after a couple of days' rehearsal, we opened.

Khelmis took to the show like a duck to water. She was born for that kind of work and I never had an assistant as fast and as good as she was—and to make it even better, she was a fairly good actress. She took a fierce pride in her work, and with her youth and beauty, she was a great asset to the show. The only stumbling block was that she was only nineteen years old, and as a woman is not an adult in Argentina until she is twenty-two, her mother made me Khelmis' legal guardian.

In June of 1952 with a small company of only eight people, we left for the Altiplano, and after a good season in La Paz, we travelled over Lake Titicaca again to Puno, where Ramiro had been killed so many years before; then to Lima my jinx town, where luckily nothing happened and we had a wonderful season and then to Guayaquil, Ecquador.

It was here that a Jibaro Indian told me about the process they used for shrinking heads. Making a vertical cut at the back of the decapitated head, they remove the skull, then sew up the cut and also sew shut the mouth, nostrils and eyelids. Through the open neck they fill the head with hot stones; then it is dipped in a liquid made from secret herbs. The hot stones are constantly changed for slightly smaller ones as the head contracts, until the stones are no larger than pebbles. By the time they get finished the contracted head is rock-hard and the skin at least a quarter-inch thick. They also showed me shrunken dogs and cats about two to three inches long. (In South America to call a person a jibaro is like calling him a blood-thirsty savage.)

I saw some remarkable Indian remedies in my tours of South America. A doctor friend of mine in Guayaquil had a small Piper airplane which he used for trips into the interior of the country in search of a certain herb which the Indians claimed would cure cancer. This doctor had large brown glass bottles of a liquid which he extracted from the herb and he claimed to have cured people in Guayaquil. He told me of a woman who had a tumor the size of a small melon and after treatment with this drug he said the cancer dissolved into liquid form and was easily removed.

I told the doctor of a similar experience I had in Mexico in 1944. Augustin Fink, the president of Films Mundiales, was dying of cancer of the kidneys and all hope was given up. One evening a Catholic priest came to my home and told me he had been cured of cancer of the kidneys by an Indian herb remedy and he gave me the formula which was handwritten on a piece of parchment paper. I rushed over with the formula to see Fink's brother and told him the story, which I found hard not to believe, due to the source from which it had come, and asked him to try it; but, unfortunately, it was too late and Augustin died the next day. I often regret that I foolishly failed to make a copy of this remedy, but I was in such a hurry that I didn't want to waste the time.

A slow change was coming over Latin America and travelling expenses were increasing day by day. In the big cities it didn't make much difference how many crates and trunks I had as I played long runs in every theatre and the transportation from one theatre to another was inexpensive. On the road tours, however, with long trips over deserts and mountains, the baggage problem became very serious. I decided to reduce bulk and weight.

During the years that I had the desire to be that mythical character, "The World's Greatest Magician," I believed, in my naive way, that the solution lay in having more props than anyone else. Over the years I had built tons of illusions and props until I found myself with an old-man-of-the-sea on my back that I couldn't dislodge.

When I built a new illusion it was mine to have and to hold until death us did part. I had no home to leave my props in and carried all I owned with me. When one entered or left a country the baggage was inspected and bonded by the customs officials, and when one left the country the exact number of trunks had to be there or else one forfeited the bond, which was usually very high.

There were times on board a ship when I cunningly schemed to chuck a few crates overboard on a foggy night, but then I realized the stuff was checked and it remained all mine. If I wanted to add a new illusion or some scenery, up went the total, and I ended up being the "world's greatest"—lost in a sea of crates.

The only practical solution I found was to put all my faith in God and grease the palm of some ambitious customs official as I left the country, happy in the knowledge that I have performed my greatest illusion: the vanishing of several tons of junk in one swoop.

Chang once told me that he carried around over 120 pieces and didn't use half of it, yet he didn't have the heart to throw anything out. Chang and I were both nomads, carrying everything we owned in the world with us, including old clothes, books, useless apparatus, and all sorts of knickknacks that we had picked up in our travels and kept with the nebulous idea of some day having a home. People with homes have attics. Our excess trunks were the attics of our shows.

I wasn't too happy about throwing out a lot of expensive illusions, but I did think that cutting down on the size and bulk of the biggest illusions would not only save a lot of weight but also make them far easier to set up and dismantle. One man could do the work of two and in half the time. It would also open up a new source of income as I could work many of the large cinemas having small stages, using the reduced illusions flat against the back wall or picture sheet.

In four months, just by working a few hours in the morning, we reduced the dead weight of the show by nearly fifty percent and the cubic feet (used on ships) by over two-thirds. At long last I wasn't paying freight on cubic feet of air.

The crates were made as light and small as possible so they could easily be handled by one or two men and not three or four as formerly. Each crate and trunk had a distinguishing trademark in one corner and the trunks were numbered from one to fifty. The crates started with number one hundred and up. This was done for a purpose. When people saw a crate carried into the theatre with, for example, "No. 148" on it, they would think the show was twice the size it was.

With my reduced show I was no longer the "world's greatest" and some years later, when the great German-Indian war broke out between Kalanag and Sorcar for the title, I mentally made them a present of it. Their feud went on for years, until it became a "Custer's last stand" between two people—with a little Sicilian throat slitting on the slide. They never learned that there were many greats in magic but never a greatest. To use this title among fellow magicians is not only bombastic and in bad taste, but downright stupid.

The crazy part of it all was that although I was cutting down, I was also adding at the same time. For many years I had been working on plans for the Indian Rope Trick. I had seen many versions in my time, including those of Thurston, Blackstone,

LeRoy, De Biere, Goldin, Chang and others. In my opinion, they were all lousy. The nearest approach to a successful, practical effect was McDonald Birch's simple but clever method. I approached this illusion with an entirely new angle, and using a new principle, it was quite successful. Then, suddenly, I did one of those madcap things that always seemed to be part of my life.

Okito and Marie Dean photographed in Chicago in 1949.

CHAPTER 43

I became nuts about color photography. It all started when I was taking advertising pictures of my show and costumes with a Speed-Graphic, using the Ectachrome color process, and doing my own developing with gorgeous results. Any amateur photographer knows how this gets to be a mania. I was at it every free moment I had and in time became quite an expert in color.

We were back in Colombia again, making that nerve wracking trek from town to town, travelling over lonely roads infested with bandits and often needing police or military protection to get from one place to another. Then came an epidemic of fires in a number of small towns that razed half the buildings. In one small town named Armonia a terrible conflagration gutted the center of the town, including the theatre, but luckily my baggage was still on the trucks waiting to be unloaded when the fire broke out.

Eventually we got to Medellin, Colombia's second largest city. If any city in the world is entitled to claim itself "air-conditioned," then Medellin is that place with a mean temperature of about 21 degrees centigrade every day and nearly all year round, except for a short rainy season. This place was a color photographer's paradise as the water was just the right temperature for perfect developing without requiring ice or heating.

An over-enthusiastic acquaintance of mine told me there was very little color photography in Colombia and a great demand for color photos for calendars the big manufacturing companies distribute to their clients. A good set of twelve color photos would be worth five to ten thousand pesos.

This seemed to be a good business and as I had been on the

road for some twenty-five years, I thought it would be nice to settle down in one place and go into a business less strenuous than show business. I made a deal with the local Kodak representative to open a color studio.

I rented a large house in the suburbs of Medellin with a large studio and a place to store the show. It cost me quite a lot of money to furnish the place and build the special color laboratory on the ground floor.

I sent the company back to their respective countries and, just with Khelmis and Fernandez, started on this new venture. We sold some good color prints of religious ceremonies in the coastal towns on northern Colombia, and were off to a good start; but I soon discovered that this sort of thing was not for me. All my life I had knocked around the world and was used to the easy going theatre crowd. I couldn't get used to the small town, narrow-minded, Peyton Place complex. I was bored stiff with their petty gripes and slowly we drifted away from the parties and fiestas until finally I had nothing else to do, between orders, but shoot a bow and arrow in the backyard. I knew it wouldn't be long before I chucked the whole deal, even though it had cost me over $11,000 to get the studio in shape and furnish the house.

One day, a theatrical impresario from Mexico, Chato Cuerra, came to town, bringing Tin-Tan and Marcelo. He couldn't believe me when I told him I had quit show business. He said he was willing to bring me to Mexico if I could put on a new show, but I told him that all I had that was new for Mexico was the Atomic Woman and a few other things. Otherwise the show was practically the same one I had done in the Arbeu in 1945. Chato said this wasn't enough as they had five TV channels in Mexico City. I would have to think up some strong gimmick to buck that kind of competition. I told him I'd think it over and let him know if I thought of anything.

For the next few weeks I hung around the studio like a lost soul, trying to figure out a new gimmick that would have audience appeal. I studied everything that had ever been done in magic since the eighteenth century and came up with nothing. I thought up a lot of half-baked ideas that looked good at midnight and awful in the next morning's light.

I can always think better with a musical background and I played all my records and slunk in a chair drinking quarts of mango juice mixed with chiramoya trying to visualize something that hadn't been done before.

One of my records was a musical comedy called "Flahooley," which, I had been told, had been a flop on Broadway yet some of the music was pretty and Yma Sumac's black magic number was thrilling. Listening to this record started the germ of an idea. What about a musical comedy based on black magic? I knew less than nothing of this branch of the theatre, but I thought if I could get good people to write the music and lyrics and stage the dances, I might be able to turn out a half-way decent libretto.

The first thing to do was figure out a plot. It had to be something about black magic or witchcraft and the illusions I already had would have to be fitted in somehow. I might have to work backwards, like a detective story, to fit the props to the plot.

A dozen ideas were outlined and thrown into the wastebasket, including a couple of pantomines like the London plays of Aladdin and Ali-Baba and the forty thieves. I even thought of an altered version of Chu-Chin-Chow but it was terrible. I was just about to give up in disgust when my brain came out of its deep freeze and I had a glimmer of what I wanted.

Looking back I can see that this story was nothing much and I wonder why it took me so long to think of it. Roughly, it was a story that starts when a magician's leading girl assistant runs off with a trumpet player the night before a new show opens, leaving the magician in the lurch. (In fact, this actually happened to Okito in London.)

The magician's apprentice Chi, a good-hearted but muddleheaded oaf, tries to help the magician by delving into forbidden black magic and invoking a girl devil as an assistant. Chi gets his ingredients mixed and invokes Satan's daughter, a fiery, red-headed princess, whose magical powers far exceed those of the magician. Much against her will she is forced, by the black magic spell, to assist the magician on the opening night, but gets her revenge by giving every illusion in the show a surprise ending that drives the magician crazy.

In the second act the magician falls in love with the redhead, but in order to marry her, he has first to reduce her to ashes from which to create a synthetic earth woman. When the devil finds out what has happened to his daughter, he comes to earth and declares war on the magician and makes his life a hell-on-earth. Again there is a series of mixed-up illusions ending with a fantastic ballet scene of the underworld; but the devil is finally beaten and the story has a happy ending.

This synopsis looked pretty good to me and I put a nice clean sheet of paper in my typewriter and wrote those magic words, "Page One; Scene One," after the title: La Hija de Satan—Satan's Daughter.

It took over six weeks (including stalling and going into tantrums) to write and rewrite the plot. I hit a lot of snags and technical difficulties, but fortunately my past experience in the theatre warned me how far I could go, so all the technical problems were solved on paper before going into expensive production. Although I worked in as many of my tricks and illusions as I could, I still had to design four or five new illusions for the continuity of the show. The show also needed six new sets of scenery and a complete new wardrobe, especially for the costuming of Satan's daughter.

The script was an entirely new departure from anything that had been done before in magic and when I reread it a few times I began to have doubts. It was a risky business treading on other people's territory and, after all, what did I know about revues and musical comedies? I had never seen a modern musical comedy and had only heard records of South Pacific and other shows of that kind. Perhaps it was just as well that I hadn't seen them or else I would never have had the courage to jump into things like this; and so, in my blissful ignorance, I waded in right up to my neck.

I sent the finished script to one of my old motion picture producers in Mexico, Pepe Luis Calderon, as I knew that no theatrical impresario would care to handle it. Pepe wrote back that he thought it was a wonderful idea but could I do it? He offered to bring me to Mexico and take over a theatre, but the cost of production would be all mine. I had expected a better offer but I figured that if the show clicked, all the property would be mine to exploit all over Latin America, so I wired back and accepted his offer.

Khelmis and Fernandez were wild with delight at the thought of getting back into show business again and, to be truthful, so was I. I was fed up with Medellin and everyone in it. I sold all the furniture for a song and practically gave my photographic equipment away.

We arranged for Fernandez to bring the baggage by boat, which would take over a month, and he started on his long voyage by taking the train down to the Magdalena port of Puerto Barrio, up the river to Barranquilla, and from there by freighter to Veracruz. As I had a deadline to meet I broke my vow and we took a plane to Mexico City. I had just over a month to get the new illusions built, scenery painted, costumes designed and made, music written, songs composed, ballet staged and all the other things that go into a debut. All my life I've hated deadlines in the theatre and this one was a lulu.

As the plane neared Mexico City and I saw Popocatepetl and the "sleeping woman," old memories came to mind. I was happy to be back in the old hunting grounds again. My first two or three days were taken up with visits and festejos with all my old friends.

My first step was to get everybody together for a big meeting. Around a long table sat Jose de la Vega, a fine composer and head of the Mexican Musician's Union; Herminio Kenny and Salvador Flores, songwriters; Ricardo Silva, a top choreographer; Magin Banda, to handle the scenery; Spreer, to build the new illusions and a few other technical men. I read the script and told them just what I wanted from each of them and they got busy making calculations. The majority agreed that the script was good. Spreer, Magin Banda and the prop men guaranteed to get their work done in time, but Jose de la Vega and the songwriters needed more time and Ricardo Silva couldn't start until Jose finished the ballet numbers. Silva claimed he would need at least a month's rehearsal. The costume designers also said that with all the trick costumes I wanted they couldn't possibly be ready. At the end of the conference I knew I had made a bad miscalculation. Not even a magician could put on that kind of a show in a month. I was forced to give them two months. I had also underestimated the costs and the show would run into about $25,000 before the curtain could go up.

There was still time to back out. I could have refunded the fares to Pepe Calderon and taken a chance with the old show. I thought it over, but perhaps the excitement of being back in the thick of show business again, and the faith I had in Mexico, influenced me. Although it might cost me my last cent, I decided to take the chance.

Spreer took the plans to his shop and began work on the illusions. He was the first one to be ready.

De la Vega wrote the three ballets first to give Ricardo more time. The first was easy as it was Gershwin's "Rhapsody in Blue" for the opening number of the show, which was supposed to represent the last night of the previous show. The setting was in blue and gold with musical motifs. My costume was also in blue and gold as were the costumes for the girls. I opened with the confetti trick using gold confetti and blue water, then produced silks in all shades of blue which the girls used for their dance. The scene ended with a girl appearing from an illusion made entirely of musical notes cut from plywood. She was dressed in a huge blue nylon gown with a golden ostrich feather headdress.

The second ballet was called the "Ballet Magique" and was based on John N. Hilliard's, "In the Beginning," from *Greater Magic*. This was a poetic story covering the earliest magicians and the superstitious people to whom everything was magic and mystery, and going through to the last man in the dying world of the future, who knows no more of the mystery of life than the first man in the beginning. During this ballet I had Satan recite Hilliard's prose as a background to the ballet. I knew I was taking a risk with this poetic business and might take a hail of criticism from the press, but I wanted something new. (And, yes, the press did take a poke at me.) This was the first time I had ever tried to write a show with a main plot and subplots with any kind of continuity; but thanks to the fantastic theme I had chosen, it had a certain crazy logic. While some of the situations were farfetched, the underlying theme justified them. This was the first time that anything like this had been attempted. The question was would the public accept it?

The third ballet was a black magic theme for the first appearance of Satan's daughter. This was suitable for the most fantastic black art and ultraviolet effects in the invocation scene. Khelmis was obliged to dye her hair a fiery red for this scene. As a publicity stunt I bought her a baby tiger which she led around town on a leash and, with her fiery hair, people in the street would stop to stare at her in amazement.

A fourth ballet was added for the finale. This spectacular dance was done in a burning "hell" scene and I managed to work in the Fire Dragon as part of it. When the two big flats painted to represent the portals of hell were opened and the blazing cave, with leaping flames of red, orange and yellow silk, was displayed, it was one of the most impressive moments of the show.

The first illusion completed by Spreer was the Synthetic Woman, in which Satanasa (Satan's daughter) was recreated by chemical means. The girls were dressed as feminine vanities such as lipstick, rouge, face powder, mascara, perfume, etc. and carried odd shaped bottles and flasks which contained the essences of love, passion, grace, purity, beauty, charm and so forth. These essences, poured into the ashes of Satan's daughter, were the ingredients to create the perfect woman and every man's ideal dream girl. Alas, one vital ingredient was forgotten, and this led to complications.

The second illusion was a magical striptease in which the girl vanished at the most interesting moment. The backstage illusion was simplified and reduced to a simple basic principle with no apparatus used except for a large cloth. It turned out to be one of the hits of the show.

The girls' wardrobe had some very interesting trick costumes. In one scene, when the devil wishes to confound the magician, he visibly transforms a witch, a vampire, a mummy, a werewolf and other monsters into pretty women and sets them loose among the assistants.

The new sets by Banda were gorgeous and one in particular, the interior of a Chinese palace, with its huge twisted and coiled dragon columns painted in Day-Glo colors, was the most beautiful stage setting I had ever had. Under the ultraviolet light it looked like a fairy palace. New travelers were made of a heavy felt-like material that hung beautifully.

The songs composed by Flores and Kenny all had magical themes, both serious and comical.

One of the sketches for the show, which proved quite successful, was based on an idea by Dariel Fitzkee. It employed the Doll House illusion in which the devil causes a skimpily clad vamp to appear in an effort to sidetrack my romance with his daughter.

The show had two acts, thirty scenes, and a prologue. The original cast consisted of over forty people on stage and took over two months getting into shape and ready for rehearsals. We worked in the Iris Theatre where we were to open.

Dona Esperanza Iris, owner of the theatre and an old hand in musical comedy, was most helpful; but her supervision ended abruptly when her husband, Paco Sierra, was jailed on the alleged charge of having hidden a time bomb on a plane loaded with Mexican workers, in order to collect their life insurance. For a time it looked as if the theatre would be closed as Dona Iris desperately needed money for Paco's defense. There was talk of turning the theatre into a picture house permanently. In spite of all her efforts, everything failed, and he was sentenced to life at hard labor.

By a curious coincidence, the very night she asked me for a loan, I had intended to ask her for one! I had invested all my money in the show and had no cash on hand. I still owed money to Magin Banda for the sets and to the costumers. Only Khelmis and Fernandez knew the true state of things, and if the word got out that I was broke, with rehearsals just starting, it would be the end of everything. Fortunately, everyone in Mexico thought I was a millionaire and I bluffed my way through. I asked Pepe Calderon to advance me $5,000 with a convincing story of not being able to get money through from Argentina, owing to the political situation. He loaned me the money without hesitation, little knowing that he had saved me. There is nothing in show business quite as bad as people knowing that one is broke. It's murder. So with a calm exterior, but with my insides trembling, I went into rehearsals.

Show business is a gamble at best, and it seems unbelievable that trained writers, directors, actors and all the rest of the experts in the business can't see the mistakes in a show before the opening night. It may be that everyone is worried about his own part, loses objectivity, and can not see the show as a whole. The test is always the opening night, when one hopes for that intangible something that spells success.

We all thought it was a great show and everyone was most enthusiastic. This idea had leaked out of the theatre and into the press, with the result that on our opening night, set for the 15th of September (the eve of Mexico's independence day), the theatre had been sold out days in advance.

I was in a terrible dither, running from hot to cold, and worrying my head off. I was really up to my neck in this thing and if it didn't click, it was over-the-hill and to the poorhouse. There were moments when I wished I'd never heard of show business. I craved that job behind the ribbon counter with a wife and ten kids living in a tenement. Anything would be better than this.

The show started promptly at eleven o'clock, following the Mexican national anthem which ends with the classical "grito" (yell) that is part of Mexico's folklore. The house was packed with the famous first-night audience and after the grito, the people cheered, blew whistles and threw confetti for a full five minutes. This charming custom has to be seen to be believed. It is thrilling to see the homage that Mexicans pay to their wonderful country.

It was under these highly favorable circumstances that the curtain rose on the prologue and the audience was in a mood to applaud and enjoy the show to the limit.

The first act finished to a good hand. One of the effects they enjoyed the most was the sudden appearance of Satan in a box in a flash of fire, from which he played his part as a spectator of the show. My spies came back with heart warming reports of the comments in the lobby and the enthusiasm of the critics. True, there had been a few slight mishaps that usually happen on an opening night, but, overall, the first act had been very good. I was walking on air when the curtain rose on the second act and I had that wonderful feeling of having the audience in the palm of my hand.

The second act started with the Synthetic Woman illusion and got more laughs than I had hoped for as the comic, Oscar Pulido, a Mexican movie star, brought the house down in this scene.

We were riding high with a hit on our hands when suddenly the show fell flat. Just like the Moon show went years before, there was a long lull with half hearted applause and a few titters once in a while. Somewhere I had gone wrong again and I was sick for the next half hour as we knocked ourselves out but to no avail.

All I had left now was the ghost routine, and maybe the hell ballet to save the show. The ghost show went over well, as it always had, and things were beginning to brighten up a little until the opening of the hell ballet. Then one of those things happened that make one a crabbed old man ahead of his time.

The seamstress' name was Luz (Light), quite a common name in Mexico. One of her duties was to wear a black-hooded cape and run behind the girls during the Fire Dragon dance, and remove the luminous capes from the girls' shoulders and carry them offstage. During the rehearsals I had given the chief electrician strict instruction not to bring up stage or houselights until he had express instructions from me, and only me, as I knew exactly at what moment he was to flood the stage with light. But on this opening night, at the moment of collecting the capes, Luz was not in her place.

Without thinking I screamed ''Luz!'' and to my dismay the stage was flooded with light, spoiling the whole scene. I yelled to the gaffer to douse the light, which he instantly did, but the damage had been done. (The next day I changed Luz' name to Gaznapia which no one could translate into light!)

The hell ballet held up well and from there on the show sailed into a smooth if unenthusiastic finish, using the Atomic Woman and the dance of the Chinese lanterns. The final applause was fairly good and so ended that memorable night. There were the bouquets and congratulations and all the rest of a debut routine, but I knew that the show wasn't what I had hoped it would be.

The trouble started after the first ten minutes of the second act. One of Dr. Bamberg's surgical operations was called for, but I didn't know where to operate. The trouble may have started earlier but I didn't know how I could find it. I knew a change was necessary in the second act, but how could I cut without changing the whole structure of the plot? This wasn't anything like the previous shows I had written where, if a sketch was poor you could throw it out, or change it, without affecting the show to any great extent. This was a continued story line where one scene depended on another and I didn't have enough experience in this kind of show to change it overnight.

The press critiques were mixed. Some went overboard in their praise and others (including the most important newspapers) stated frankly that they didn't like it. As a magical production it was excellent but as a musical comedy it was poor. I had endless sessions with the stage director, the maestro and the songwriters, but we couldn't put our finger on the weak spot; and although I speeded it up and rewrote some of the dialogue, it remained a stinker and I found no solution. It wasn't until 1960, in the Odeon Theatre in Buenos Aires, that I found the trouble and corrected it. What the show needed at that point was a sequence of pure magic, instead of dialogue and songs. The moment I worked out a sequence of two illusions and several small tricks, the show picked up and ran like a dream, with the second act beating the first. The show broke all my records in Buenos Aires by running for almost ten months.

"Satan's Daughter" ran for three months in the Iris Theatre. I earned back my investment and had a very valuable piece of stage property. I suppose I should have considered myself lucky. I tried a few of the larger Mexican cities, but the show was too cumbersome as a road show. With all those people and a fifteen piece orchestra it lost money even in good houses. Another setback came the night Khelmis plunged through the trap during the Atomic Woman illusion and the boy who was supposed to be below to break her fall wasn't in his place. She landed on her feet with full force, spraining both her ankles and was laid up for fifteen days with her legs in a cast. I returned to Mexico City and decided to store the show for a while and, not to get out of routine, I had another hernia operation. Believe it or not, a month after I left the clinic it came back again.

In the hospital I spent much of my time with Jorge Negrete, Mexico's singing cowboy, who was suffering from what he thought was dropsy. He was married to Maria Felix at the time but she was in Paris and he was alone most of the time. After he got out of the hospital he went to Los Angeles where he died. His remains were flown back to Mexico for one of the largest funerals in the history of Mexican show business. In fact, the enormous crowds got out of hand and almost wrecked the graveyard.

My old hangout the XEW radio station was now the big television center. I spent weeks studying this new technique with an idea of doing a series of shows. My pictures were still on TV and doing well and I thought of doing a series of half hour detective-magician stories. Video tape was in its infancy and had not yet come to Mexico so my shows had to be live and my tricks combined with the electronic effects of TV were hardly perfect. Another thing that I didn't like about TV was the fact that most of the programmes were directed and staged by boys from advertising agencies, who knew nothing at all about the theatre. Although I did not claim to be a know-it-all, I hated to be bossed by these snotniks who didn't know their ass from their elbow. The poor quality of the shows in general and the terrible confusion of the studios was the deciding factor to make me give up in disgust. I never did do anything on television.

I was in Mexico about a year and the time had come to either plunge into TV or get out. I chose the out and cut "Satan's Daughter" down to a small, twelve people version, including Spreer who was to be chief mechanic and stage manager.

Fernandez arranged Guatemala (Ubico was dead and artistes were admitted), and we thought that it should be a gold mine. With a fond farewell to dear old Mexico, I set forth like Don Quixote, with my trusty lance, to conquer the world with "Satan's Daughter." Unfortunately, the seven fat years had come to an end, and the seven lean years were just beginning.

CHAPTER 44

Our entrance into Guatemala was not a happy one. The trouble started on the frontier where a customs official, with a dental plate that looked like an old rubber heel fitted with shark's teeth, made us put up a bond for the show that was sufficient to balance the national budget. Luckily, Fernandez, being a Guatemalan, had friends who helped us, and after a lot of haggling and time-wasting, the bond was reduced.

We opened in one of the best theatres in town and had the unique experience of filling the theatre in the afternoons and having empty houses for the night show. This was the exact opposite of theatre conditions in any other part of the world, but was easily explained when we discovered that the political situation under the communistic Arbenz regime was at fever heat. The country was ripe for revolution at any moment. This was the reason the people were afraid to leave their homes at night.

During the third week of the season, Khelmis was suddenly taken with appendicitis and operated on in a hurry. She was still convalescing in the hospital when an amateur magician friend of mine, Senor Klein, advised me to get out of Guatemala as soon as possible as the anti-communist rebel, Castillo Armas, was getting an army ready on the Honduran frontier, ready to invade Guatemala to try to topple Jacabo Arbenz. War was expected at any moment.

After a hurried conference with Fernandez, we decided to get out at once. I decided to go with the trucks to the Salvadoran frontier, and they would follow two days later by plane, which would give Khelmis a little more time to rest after the operation. Everything went according to plan, although we cut it rather fine. Just as I crossed the frontier, Castillo Armas began his invasion. We were the last to get over the border before it was closed. I was worried that Khelmis, and especially Fernandez as a Guatemalan, wouldn't make the plane, but they were lucky and caught one of the last ones out.

As we had not time to arrange for future business, I took a few days off, which was good as Khelmis wasn't very strong and she still had to have the stitches removed. She insisted on seeing a certain doctor to have this performed, and as this man phoned the hotel several times, and Khelmis acted very mysterious, I suspected something was up. It seems the doctor in Guatemala who had performed the operation was an enemy of the Arbenz regime and had prepared a micro-message with important information for Castillo Armas. This message had been concealed, with Khelmis' consent, in the dressing covering her scar. The doctor in San Salvador who was a Guatemalan had been advised. The message was sent to Castillo Armas and whether it was of any use I will never know, but within a very short time the Arbenz government was overthrown and Don Jacabo exiled.

We were lucky to book a chain of eight large picture houses to play. Lon Chaney Jr. and Anthony Dexter were in the same situation that we were. They had been filming a picture in the Chickle jungles of Peten but had to get out of Guatemala quickly. They were now filming in El Salvador. This unit was terribly disorganized and threw money around like water, which seemed to be the norm for most movie ventures in foreign countries. This reconfirmed my belief that pictures could be made in South America for half their usual cost and this was proven some years later when Stanley Kramer produced several first class movies on a bare budget.

In El Salvador large horseshoe magnets were fastened to the crosspiece of the door frames in many of the houses. These magnets had a thin iron plate clinging to them and on the ground, directly underneath, was a large iron plate. I was told that just a few seconds before an earthquake, the upper plate would fall from the magnet and hit the lower plate with a loud clatter, which was enough warning to escape from the house. Another danger signal for an oncoming earthquake is an angry dark red sky in the evening, which is claimed to usually precede a shock.

After the Salvadoran tour we skipped Honduras and Nicaragua and jumped to Costa Rica. We played the lovely Nacional Theatre to good business, then went to Puerto Limon on the Atlantic coast where I gorged myself on fine turtle egg soup and green turtle steaks. Some of the turtles they catch there are gigantic and many of them have dates carved on their shells. If the dates are correct, they must be a couple of centuries old.

A lot of the Latin American republics were in the hands of dictators or military juntas, and visas were getting tough to obtain. We wanted to get to Caracas, Venezuela, but there was no consul in Costa Rica so we took a Dutch boat that was very expensive. They charged me over $5,000 for passages and freight to La Guaira, with a few hours stopover in Curacao where we could get our visas. The boat arrived late in Curacao and we rushed over to the Venezuelan consulate and were dismayed to find it packed with people. The porter told us that there was no chance for us to get visas that day as the consulate closed at four o'clock. The boat sailed at six that same evening. We were really in a jam if we couldn't get those visas. Suddenly I had an inspiration and I sent Fernandez down to the theatre where we had played and asked the manager for two boxes for the show that night. When he returned I put one of the invitations in my pocket and used the other to attract the attention of the clerk, who was making out some papers at a snail's pace. A few seconds later he looked up and saw me and raised his eyebrows with a puzzled look. I took the opportunity to push forward and, handing him the invitation, I said, "Please tell the vice-consul to excuse me for being late but, as I promised, here is the box he wanted for the show tonight."

The clerk said the consul wasn't in at the moment but he would give it to him later. Then he fell into my hands when he asked me if I couldn't get seats for him, too. I said nothing could give me greater pleasure, which was true, and I handed him the second invitation, for which he profusely thanked me. Just as I turned to leave, like an afterthought, I said, "By the way perhaps you can help me. I'm leaving for La Guaira on the Dutch boat tonight and I'd like you to have a look at my passport to see if everything is all right." He said it would be a pleasure, and with plenty of black looks from the people standing around, he ran through my passport and said, "You haven't a visa for Venezuela." I played the idiot role and said that I had been told that they issued the visas in La Guaira.

"No," he said. "You pay for the visa in La Guaira, but you get it here. It only takes a few minutes. Permit me." He filled out the forms which I signed and he stamped my passport and handed it to me.

"Un million de gracias," I said innocently, "I suppose the

others will have the same problem?"

"Assuredly," he said. "Who are the others?"

I waved my hand and eleven people showed up. His jaw dropped, but the free pass had done its work and he gave us all our visas. We were out in less than an hour, and if looks could kill, this would be the final chapter of my book.

We made it back to the boat with hours to spare and peacefully sailed that night for La Guaira. When we arrived at that port we took the new highway to Caracas, which takes only fifteen minutes, instead of the old road with its hairpin turns that took the better part of a day. When we hit the city limits we got into an everlasting traffic jam and it took us over two hours to inch our way to the hotel. We soon discovered that it was quicker to walk in Caracas than take a car.

The old Silencio square in the heart of town that had formerly been the red light district was torn down. A multi-million dollar skyscraper project was being built and, as a result, all traffic was detoured from the center of town. The confusion was awful. We found that the Nacional Theatre, where we were to work, was almost inaccessible. After wasting an hour or two battling his way to work and home again, the average working man was in no mood to go through it all again with his wife and kids to see a show when he had four TV channels to choose from.

The Nacional Theatre was municipal property and had been closed for months and no repairs had been made for years. The ropes and battens had been stolen and there wasn't a light bulb in the place. If you have ever tried to deal with bureaucracy in Latin America you will have a fair idea of what we went through trying to get that rat trap in working order. Fortunately, a colonel in the Venezuelan army, an amateur magician and personal friend of President Perez-Jiminez, managed to get an order to borrow the necessary material from the Municipal Theatre and in a few days we had the place in shape. I hired a local ballet for the dance numbers, and after a ten day rehearsal, we opened to half a house. From there on, with the exception of Saturdays and Sundays, business dropped off steadily until we finally had houses of fifteen to twenty people. I took a terrible beating in a theatre where I had made a fortune eight years previously.

To keep the company together and pay my debts I was forced to accept a three weeks' contract in the local Coney Island, doing the Magic Bazar on an open air stage. The owners of this attraction park were used to bringing in the most expensive foreign acts and paid them excellent salaries. By doing one fifteen minute act a day, I made far more than I had in the theatre with the full show and was able to get out of town with a fair profit. I tried a few towns near Caracas, such as Maracay, Barquesimeto and Valencia, but to poor business. We decided to get out and leave for Havana.

The boat we took to Cuba was one of those expensive $5,000 deals. I had to sell my jewelry and my 16mm movie camera equipment, including the sound projectors, to pay for the voyage. I arrived in Havana, "con una mano detras y la otra delante"— one hand in front and the other behind.

Havana hadn't changed and was the same gay, wide open city, and in spite of five TV channels, the theatres were doing good business as the Habanero loved a live show; the more women and risque material, the better. I had never used "blue material" or situations in my show as it hadn't been necessary and would have been fatal for a family show of my type. Some of the theatres in Havana, like the Shanghai, were noted for their outright pornographic revues, interspersed with French and local pornographic films. Some impresarios claimed that this was the only way to fight TV. Perhaps they had a point, for the theatres were packed. It was really funny to see some innocent American tourist, who didn't understand a word of Spanish and had no idea of what they were going to see, suddenly turn vivid red, and with a muttered "holy cow," get up and leave the theatre. During the following years things got worse instead of better and the films and novels were getting more pornographic every day. Finally it hit the TV screen as well. If this trend keeps up, it is hard to figure what the end of show business will be like.

The only concession I made was to hire a splendid ballet of twelve girls and let them wear very brief bikinis for the rhumba and cha-cha-cha numbers. The Nacional Theatre, where I had always played, was now a movie house so I took over the Marti Theatre, a popular revue house. I engaged a number of popular TV stars to play the devil and one or two other small parts. We did very well in the Marti and I was a few thousand dollars in the black at the end of the season. From there we played the Blanquita and the Radio City Theatre to good business and then played the interior of the island and returned to Havana just as the Mardi Gras was starting. In both my previous engagements in Havana I played through the Mardi Gras days and it hadn't affected my business in the least, but that was because I was at the Nacional Theatre on the main street. Unfortunately the Marti Theatre is on a side street that leads off from the Prado and that is where I made my big mistake. I took over the Marti again for this season at popular prices but the street was blocked off on the four Saturdays and Sundays of carnival and that did it. I went broke!

Even worse, Ringling Brothers Barnum and Bailey Circus came to town and opened up a few blocks from where I was playing. You can't pinch pennies in show business, so the great secret is to know when to cut your losses, close the show, and get out of town. Advertising for the big top and a magic show were very similar. The eye-catching, flashy posters Ringling plastered over the town couldn't be matched. If I pasted up a hundred lithos, they would smother them with a thousand. I was completely swamped. I dissolved the show, sending everyone home. Only Khelmis, Fernandez and a former assistant of mine, Macaco, and I were left.

With this small company I opened with a pure magic show in a Chinese Theatre in the Chinese part of Havana. Most of the audience spoke no Spanish, and as I spoke no Chinese, I had to do an almost pantomime show, using a typical Chinese orchestra. As I had practically no expenses, surprisingly, I made money in that little theatre. Near the end of this season, a Chinese newspaper man and a really good friend of mine, tipped me off that two Chinese theatrical companies had come to Havana, but both leading ladies had gotten married before the debut, and as the shows had never opened, the wardrobes were for sale. I went over to the rival Chinese theatre to have a look, and when they opened those wooden chests and displayed gorgeous Chinese stage costumes, I nearly went out of my head. I knew I couldn't afford it but this was the chance of a lifetime. Everything was so beautiful that I bought the lot for a thousand dollars which left me flat broke.

Here I was with a property worth a fortune and no cash. What was I to do now? Mexico and Central America were out. I had just come from Venezuela and the north of South America was in a bad state. Haiti was in one of their eternal revolutions and Santo Domingo was under the thumb of Trujillo; he had declared a curfew which killed night shows, and all the theatres and TV were controlled with the subtle pile-driver delicacy of "The Great Benefactor," Trujillo. There was still Puerto Rico, but where could I go from there? I could go back to Cuba or else try the United States but my friends there informed me that show business for my type of show was in a mess. As my father would have said, "My dear Watson, this is indeed a three pipe problem."

There was only one place to go. Spain! (Argentina was out for the moment as the Peron revolution was going on and no one knew how things would be after it was over.) We decided on Spain but I had to borrow money to even get out of town. The four of us took a Spanish freighter, loaded with sugar and stinking hides, and after a ghastly forty day trip, we arrived in Barcelona. Since I had been in Spain twenty years before, things had changed—as I was soon to find out.

The first thing I needed was cash, but I wasn't worried about that as all my author's rights for my 1935 season in Mexico, when Torres Belena was my impresario (and also representative for the Spanish Authors Guild), had mounted up. With my two years in Mexico and the first Cuban deal, I figured I had well over $25,000 in Madrid waiting for me. The day I arrived I paid a visit to the Barcelona branch of the Authors Guild. They telephoned Madrid to see how much I had there, hopefully enough of an advance to get me started. Madrid replied that I had exactly 14 pesetas to my credit. I owed dues for twenty years and would I please pay. Belena had not sent a penny of mine or anyone else's money to Spain. Later, when the Spanish Civil War was being fought, to be followed by World War II, no communication was possible. In the meanwhile Belena had died and that was that. A small fortune of mine went down the drain. From riches to rags—that was my story.

Barcelona was no longer the gay, carefree city it had been in 1932. Most of the cafes and bars on the Paralelo were gone. It was difficult to find a restaurant open at night after the show and the whole city was sad and gloomy. The first theatre we tried to get was the old Apolo, which had been my lucky theatre, but Senor Lluch had died and the impresario was now Senor Seret, who had no particular love for magicians. The theatre was booked until February and this meant a layoff of four months. I sent Fernandez to Madrid and he came back with the same story: all theatres booked solid until February and the Zarzuela was closed for repairs. This wasn't like the first time I was in Spain, unknown, and having to play the small towns first. This time I had to start with a splash or else!

For the first time in my life I took a partner. She was an Italian Countess who had backed Rosellini's first film, "Rome—Open City," the forerunner of the great neo-realismo school of motion pictures. I didn't know it at the time but there were rumors in Barcelona that the Countess was the head of a contraband ring which operated in France, Italy and Spain.

The Barcelona Magic Club had changed its name to the S.E.I. and there was a rival club called the C.E.A.M. This latter organization kindly stood my bond for the baggage. I engaged one of the members of this club, Reden, to play the part of the comic in the show and another old friend of mine, Senor Martinez Tudo, to rewrite the score and be the maestro.

Another friend of mine, Senor Eilio Deu, who I had financed in the printing business in 1933, returned the favor, took charge of my advertising, and had some very attractive lithos printed for me.

It was a long and expensive wait before we opened and we had plenty of vexations, principally caused by the excessive censorship which bordered on the ridiculous. The libretto of the show was condemned by the authorities as immoral and the title, "Satan's Daughter," was definitely out. No mention of the devil in any shape or form was to be used, with the result that the dialogue was cut to ribbons. Some of the motifs on my scenery had to be painted out and wishy-washy designs painted over them. When the costumes were modeled by Khelmis and the girls, the Commissioner for the Minister of Education sat open-mouthed and turned green. The entire wardrobe was condemned. We were obliged to lift the neckline up to the chin and lower the skirt from the hips to the ankles, with no bare midriffs. All this cost a lot of money and the final result was the girls looked terrible. They even forced the girls to wear knee length black bloomers!

The sad fact was that every town had its own censor and we had to give a special show for them in each town on the morning of the debut, and always some changes were demanded. They drove me frantic with their exaggerated false modesty. At first I was inclined to blame the Church as its influence in Spain is enormous, but a padre who came to see the show told me that he had enjoyed it immensely and saw nothing immoral in it. Yet he showed me letters he had received from pious old sows who protested, asking him to use his influence to have the show stopped.

On the other hand, there were certain rules for magic shows which I had unknowingly created during my first visit to Spain. I had become something of a legend over the years, and the Fu Manchu "school" of magic had sprung up, based on my old techniques. I was flattered to learn that I was known as "the father of magic" by the Spanish magicians, and one Catalan magician had even gone so far as to faithfully copy my show, programmes, photos and style to present a carbon copy of my 1933 show. They say that imitation is the sincerest form of flattery, but it can be damned irritating at times!

If I had any sense I should have set aside the "Satan's Daughter" show and gone back to my 1945 comedy show from Mexico; but I was bullheaded and tried to force it down their throats. I took my chances and opened with a hybrid show in the Apolo Theatre. Surprisingly enough, they liked it. Business was good and we immediately got contracts from the Martin Theatre in Madrid, where business was excellent.

It was my privilege, in Madrid, to become an intimate friend of Senor Arturo Ascanio, an excellent amateur magician and member of the Madrid Magic Club. Ascanio was a born magician. He did many of Fred Kaps' pet effects, and although he had never met Dai Vernon or Sam Horowitz, he did all their published tricks to perfection, in spite of the drawback of not speaking English. His original version and routine for the color changing knives was extraordinary, and he later published a book of knife routines which was a classic. I spent many happy hours with Arturo Ascanio and consider him the best magician I ever saw in Spain or in Latin America. Any lover of the art of magic would be proud to know Arturo.

We played all over Spain and things were going well and I was beginning to get on my feet again. Then the Suez crisis and the Hungarian revolt cropped up and everyone was scared stiff. I hadn't realized under what nervous tension the Europeans lived until these two events occurred. I saw lines of people buying and feverishly reading the latest reports. Attendance in the theatre dropped to a minimum and show business, always the barometer of any crisis, was the first to suffer.

My dreams of a triumphal European tour soured and I didn't want to be in Europe if hostilities broke out. I booked passages on a Spanish boat for Buenos Aires. Khelmis refused to return to Argentina and from Madrid she left for Barcelona to join up with the Countess Carla. Fernandez, Macaco and I sailed from Vigo for South America. When we arrived at Santos, Brazil, I found that Kalanag was playing in Sao Paulo on his way to Buenos Aires. Chang was already there at the National Theatre and I would be caught between them. "There's no business like show business" as the song says.

CHAPTER 45

On February 2, 1957, we docked in Buenos Aires and who was waiting on the pier to welcome me? None other than Chang and his American wife, Shirley. He had a sad story to tell. He had been contracted by the National Theatre to appear in combination with their regular revues but things had turned out badly. As in the rest of South America, the average revue in Buenos Aires was based on pornography and politics. They had tried to mix a magic show into this mess, which was like mixing whipped cream with sour herring. The people who came to see Chang were horrified with the revue part of the show and those who came to see a hot revue were bored to death with a magician. As usual, when a show flops, it is always the other guy's fault, and usually the strongest side wins. In this case it was the theatre, who embargoed Chang's baggage and a lawsuit began. By stalling around, a lawsuit in the Argentine can be stretched out for years and Chang was terribly depressed.

Fernandez and I paid a visit to the impresario of the National who was an old friend and finally an agreement was reached and Chang got his baggage free.

Chang told me that a Hungarian magician, Tihanyi, was doing a full evening's magic show in Brazil with a line of girls and variety acts, in a beautifully equipped tent. Chang had made a deal with an Argentine circus impresario to do a similar show, and in a short time he opened in a small tent in the Calle Rivadavis with surprising success. Soon he was back on his feet again.

But the National Theatre debacle had caused a bad impression among the impresarios of Buenos Aires and I couldn't get a theatre. I had no alternative but to take my show on the road. I decided to try "Satan's Daughter" and formed a small company. For the role of Satanasa I engaged a striking redhead, Zairo Nazar, a Syrian girl. With her sexy manner, she played the part of Satan's daughter as if she had been born to it.

Two days after I signed the contract for the tour I received a cable from Milbourne Christopher in New York offering me $5,000 and three round-trip plane fares to appear for a fifteen minute act on his Producer Showcase TV programme. I could have used the $5,000, but I had to refuse. I tried to swing it for Chang but they couldn't come to any agreement and finally Christopher settled for Sorcar.

When I returned to Buenos Aires, after a six month's tour, I looked around for some business that would keep me in Buenos Aires.

I made a deal with Rodolfo Literas, owner of the Bazar Yankee, the largest magic shop in town, for the construction and sale of a new line of exclusive magical apparatus but the business didn't work out as there was practically no demand for higher priced magic in that part of the world.

My second venture was a Chinese nightclub on the Calle Florida y Diagonal called The Pagoda, but as this was the banking section of town, the nights were dead, and the venture was a failure. I should have opened a place in the suburbs of Olivos or San Isidro.

I didn't want to do "Satan's Daughter" in Buenos Aires as I had never found a good solution for the weak second act and in Spain the show had been so fearfully cut that I had given up any further thought of doing it. I was offered the Astral Theatre if I could bring out something radically new, and together with an Argentine author, Raul Gurruchaga, we wrote a magical-political play provisionally titled, "The Witch Minister," the story of a magician who is prime minister of a tiny oriental kingdom a mile square and divided into twenty provinces, of which eighteen are in the possession of the minister who had won them in crooked poker games with a boneheaded king. However, the magician's insatiable craving for power leads him to misuse Aladin's lamp. In a series of comical episodes he overplays his hand and is condemned to the gallows, but his life is spared when he performs his best trick to save the kingdom.

This play was a satire on Latin American politics and read well but the cost of production was steep and the impresario was afraid to finance it alone. I had no money to sink into it so it was shelved, which was a pity as I think it would have been a hit.

Curiously, television still hadn't been a success in Buenos Aires; they still had the one channel and had sold about 50,000 sets all told in a city of over six million. The theatres and movie houses were still doing fair business, but it was the "blue" show that was packing them in.

In my time I had written a number of magician-detective stories for the screen and radio but never anything of this type for the theatre. I had seen a number of plays about magicians in my time but in nearly all of them the magic was poor and so childishly contrived that no professional magician would stoop to perform such obvious nonsense. The best of the lot was Fulton Ousler's, "Spider," but I thought the plot was far too confusing and complicated, although the gimmick was stupendous. I thought, why not do a switch on this type of story, but with better magic and more logic? My bond with Ian Fleming burst into flame and into the typewriter went a clean sheet of paper and so started the murder mystery, "La Butaca de la Muerte." (In Spanish a "butaca" is an orchestra seat. So, literally translated, it was, The Death Seat.)

In my play a spectator sitting in the darkness of the fifth row is shot to death from the stage during the dance of the luminous skeletons. A mind reading act was specially written, with the mentalist answering genuine questions by using "The Sands of Destiny," instead of a crystal ball. There were some good magic and illusions in the show, including good escapes and a combined quick-change-cum-substitution trunk switch that ended the show with a strong finish.

This show cost very little to produce as I used all my old illusions and switched them around to fit the plot. As they were stage tested, I knew they couldn't fail.

We opened the play at the Smart Theatre on the Calle Corrientes, with a cast of top Argentine actors and "Pinky" Guttenberg playing the combined role of comedian and unsuspected murderer.

Once again the second act was the weak spot of the show and only its strong finish saved it on the opening night. *La Prensa,* Argentina's number one newspaper, called it an ingenious, well-produced but over-written and confusing play. My overnight changes in the script almost drove the actors crazy, but after a week I got it right and the play caught the public's imagination and played a four month's run to packed houses, twice a night, and was even broadcast from the theatre over thirty times on one of the major radio networks. A dummy with a bullet hole in its chest, slumped over a theatre seat, was placed outside the theatre, and in a ghastly voice (through a loudspeaker in its chest) warned the public to stay away—which made them all the more anxious to get in. Finally we had to close as the theatre was booked by another company who refused a large sum to let us stay on.

We made a tour of the country with "The Death Seat" and returned to Buenos Aires to open in the Avenida Theatre with the same show. We did far better business than in the Smart due to the Avenida's larger seating capacity. By the time we closed, the play had lasted exactly one year.

Making up a long list of all the bonehead deals I had made in the past when I was in the money, I figured that this time I was going to play it safe. I bought a small house with a storage place for the baggage in Bernal, a small town in the province of Buenos Aires, just twenty minutes by train to the center of town. I fitted up a little workshop for repairs and construction of any new illusion I needed. At last I had a place to store my material without having to chase around and drag it from one place to another.

Now that I had my own little place I bought a copy of *Life's Picture Cook Book* and learned to cook Chinese and other oriental dishes. I discovered a new kind of magic in the kitchen and soon learned to cook all kinds of wonderful dishes until, to my dismay, I put on forty pounds! I had to go easy as I was outgrowing my costumes. Still I was happy building a prop with my right hand and stirring the chop suey pot with the left.

As I had never thrown anything away, I had trunkfuls of old press clippings, programmes and other material that needed sorting and pasting into scrapbooks. It was while I was going over the "Satan's Daughter" story that I suddenly got a flash that solved the weak spot in the second act.

I got to work at once and built a Leg Chopper and the Broom illusion. Combining them with Sawing a Woman and the Multum-in-Parvo glasses, I had a strong magical sequence to replace the heavy dialogue. The sketch was simple, but in its way, logical. After bringing the synthetic woman to life, we discovered that one leg was shorter than the other. To remedy this she was suspended in the air on the broom to measure her legs. The leg chopper brought them down to size. She was still a dizzy dame and undoubtedly had a short circuit somewhere, so she was placed on the sawing table and cut in half to have her ignition repaired and her wiring straightened out.

I took the finished script over to the impresario of the National and the Maipe revue theatres. After a reading, they agreed to take over the Odeon Theatre under the direction of Carlos A. Petit for my opening. I now had the resources of the two biggest revue houses in town backing me and the pick of the best chorus girls. In spite of dismal forecasts, I refused to put any "blue" material in the show. A strip tease was added but it was a very mild one. Zaira Nazar had already left the show, and to play the part of Satan's daughter I chose Gilda Rey, a stunning blonde, of the National Theatre. Gilda was another of those girls like Khelmis, who take a great professional pride in their work. She was terrific in the part.

My hunch had been right and the new sequence straightened out that weak second act. The show was a laughing success from start to finish. Why hadn't I thought of that in Mexico and Cuba? The press reported that it was the best show I had ever produced in Buenos Aires and we did over four months to full houses, then moved over to the Smart Theatre where we did another five months, running in fifth place of all the shows produced in Argentina for that year. I was really sorry when the closing night came around. I will always look back with affection on "Satan's Daughter."

The new sequence had been so effective that Daniel Tinayre, one of the leading motion picture directors, wanted to use part of it for the magical sequences of his new film, "The Ruffian," starring Carlos Estrada. I worked with Tinayre on this film which won first prize in Cannes the following year.

The following season I was back in the Avenida again with a new version of the Magic Circus, with no plot but plenty of magic, variety acts and trained animal acts. This was quite a happy venture and we had a good season.

During this run I met Chop-Chop (Al Wheatley) and his charming wife who had been engaged for the new TV channel 13, where they were very successful. Television had come in with a rush and we now had four channels going and were beginning to feel the pinch in the theatres.

I had read of Chefalo's death during the war and therefore was greatly surprised one evening, between shows in the Avenida, when the doorman brought me a visiting card that read "Chefalo the Magician." Thinking it was some imitator using the old maestro's name, I told the porter to ask the man to come backstage, with the idea of telling him off. Imagine my surprise when a chipper Chefalo walked in with his handsome wife. He was seventy-seven years old but looked fifty. After greetings he told me he was opening the next week with the Berlin Circus in Luna Park. He stayed to see the second show and the next day I received a bouquet of roses from him with a note telling me how much he enjoyed my performance.

A few weeks later I caught his act. He had worked out a number of strong illusions for a circus ring and without using twins. As usual his fake staircase for the getaway of the girl was something to warm a man's heart. He had lost none of his touch with his small magic either, and he told me that this work was far less tiring than the full night's show. He was getting a very good salary with no responsibilities. From Buenos Aires Chefalo and his wife left for Korea. There he died of a heart attack and I lost another good friend.

Just before I closed down at the Avenida I had another surprise when Khelmis came backstage after the show. She was more beautiful than ever. The years had been kind to her. She told me that the Countess Carla had been killed in an automobile accident in the Pyrenees on her way to Andorra. After this tragedy, Khelmis had combined a number of simple tricks into a small fifteen minute act and had tried her luck in the Middle East. She had been quite successful in Damascus and Bagdad and from there had toured Italy and France. Khelmis didn't stay long in Buenos Aires. She was so used to the European life that she left for Spain a few weeks later.

The Hungarian magician, Franz Tihanyi, whose tent show had so inspired Chang, tried his luck in Montevideo, Uruguay, and in Argentina with spectacular success. I saw his show when he played Buenos Aires and he had a good personality with a certain dry humor; his Brazilian accent charmed his audiences. His illusions were standard but excellent, and his sawing illusion—similar to the one presented by Virgil—was the finest version I have seen of this illusion. His tricks had been selected with care, not for originality, but for audience appeal and he had made excellent choices. A line of girls and some good variety acts topped off a well rounded show. Tihanyi's business acumen and his knowledge of the handling of the tent (which is an art in itself) made for a most successful venture.

The National Theatre had given up the revue shows for the time and produced "My Fair Lady" with outstanding success. They were so enthusiastic that they decided to continue with musical comedies. Their next selection was "Carnival," the circus musical based on the motion picture, "Lili." This show had been a hit in New York with Roy Benson in charge of the magical sequences.

I was approached by the National Theatre to be stage manager for this production and do Roy Benson's work; but he had done such an excellent job and made such a wise selection of tricks that there was nothing for me to do except follow his routine. Shepard Traube directed the play and Gene Bayliss did the choreography. Unfortunately, the principals were miscast, especially Marcos the magician, and the show, although beautifully staged, folded after a few weeks. But "Carnival" proved one thing: magic and musical comedy worked well together. This had always been a pet theory of mine, which I had proved, on a less artistic scale, in "Satan's Daughter." I strongly believe that this combination can be further improved by blending great magical effects even more subtly and effectively with modern stage design. One of the things the future magician will have to forego is the obviously tricked box-like cabinet illusion where the curse of the straight line is a clue, to a thinking audience, where a person could be concealed. The modern art design for stage props that have no definite shape or form lends itself admirably to the possibility of concealed spaces for illusionary effects. It is quite possible that the day will come when new stage illusions will be based on this principle.

After leaving Caracas, Okito spent the next seventeen years in the United States and finally settled down in Chicago where he married Marie Dean, his assistant for nearly thirty years. (Marie passed away in Chicago in 1950.) We were in constant communication and Okito frequently sent me magic books and various magical magazines and also kept me posted on the latest tricks and illusions. Even at an advanced age he never lost his keen interest in the art and he often told me in letters that his choice of living in Chicago had been a happy one as he was surrounded by many kind friends, all interested in magic. He was deeply grateful for the kindness and attentions he received over the years.

In June of 1963, at the age of eighty-eight, he died. No man had ever enjoyed a closer association with more of the masters than Okito. He was fortunate to have lived in the most interesting era in our history. He saw the birth of most of the great inventions that so changed the world. I remember him telling me what a sensation it was to play in a theatre lighted by electricity and his amazement when he saw the first primitive motion picture. He lived to see the first men orbited into space in the atomic age. From a boy of eight, as assistant to his father, he lived in a world of magic. For eighty more years he played his part well. It saddened him when his colleagues passed on. He was nearly the last of the grand old masters of the golden age of magic.

In 1964 I dusted off "The Death Seat" and gave another season at the Odeon Theatre. Shortly after that I was asked to give lectures on the psychology of magic. I wrote a dissertation combined with a series of twelve magical effects that ranged from the oldest known trick—the cups and balls from ancient Egypt—to the magic of the future, based on H.G. Wells' story, *The Time Machine*. This lecture was very well received in certain literary quarters. I really enjoyed doing it as I had never done this kind of magic and found it most fascinating.

One of the items in this lecture was a version of Charles E. Miller's Lesson in Magic, based on an arrangement of David Devant's and also featured by Alexander Herrmann under the title, Le Mouchoir Serpent. After a lengthy correspondence with Mr. Miller I changed the plot to suit my style and presented it as "The Sorcerer's Apprentice." The outstanding success of this presentation opened up a new field for me in manipulative magic.

How time changes the presentation of magical effects is very neatly described by Mr. Goodliffe, editor of England's splendid weekly *Abracadabra*, when he states, "The fascinating thing is that a half-century ago nobody thought anything of a stage magician unless he had elaborate tables and—to put it bluntly—fishy looking props. Then the wheel turned and the fashion changed to tricks done under your nose with articles which appear ordinary. Now there is a new cycle: close up magic but with obviously special apparatus... We might conclude that this is the magic of the immediate future; one hesitates to go further because in twelve months time, so rapid is the rate of change these days, some other 'art form' may have replaced this.''

My personal opinion is that it doesn't really matter one way or the other. The main thing to keep in mind is entertainment value. If the trick requires a simple brown paper sack or an African witch doctor's ju-ju box, both are equally good as long as the final effect gives the appearance of pure magic. Henry Christ's Dead Man's Hand and Arthur Monroe's Voodoo are good examples of what a dramatic or weird build up, cleverly woven about these two excellent tricks, can do to make magic good theatre. Another example is Dai Vernon's Cutting the Aces and his highly amusing story of the one armed Mexican gambler. This presentation lifts a card trick into the realm of an intriguing mystery and the spectators finally burst into appreciative laughter at the unexpected and surprising finish.

There are very few magicians who can infuse an air of mystery into a magic trick, but every so often you will meet one who has that mysterious charismatic gift called presence, a kind of animal magnetism, an ineffable extrasensory something that rivets the audience's attention on the performer. It may seem to the reader that I am contradicting myself in view of the comedy and gag shows that I produced, but I want to point out that, under this flood of humor, there was a solid base of mystifying magic; and as surprise and laughter go hand in hand, the climax of even a serious trick will be greeted with laughter. This results in high entertainment value.

I would also like to mention that in rehearsals one must be able to trust one's own theatrical judgement and discard, to a large extent, the reactions of the actors and assistants whose laughter is no judge of a play. Most actors appear to be exhibitionists, but at heart they are shy, frightened people who generally laugh at a bad line just to please the boss. Theatrical temperament is usually a mask for fear, which explains the bursts of temper, the exuberance and sometimes childlike behavior.

EPILOGUE

The curtain falls for the last time as the applause fades away and later you sit alone in the empty, darkened theatre watching the boys pack the illusions, the wardrobe mistress carrying bundles of clothes across the stage and the stagehands striking and folding the scenery. After a while there is only a bare brick-walled stage with a single pilot light picking out the crates and trunks scattered about and waiting for the trucks to take them away.

Then you are really alone in that sea of empty seats and the color, light, music and warmth of the applause are just a memory, and in spite of all the excitement, you know it's been a lonely life. John Le Carre expressed it well, "He had become a solitary, belonging to that tragic class of active men prematurely deprived of activity; swimmers barred from the water or actors banished from the stage."

Last night I went to the workshop to get a hammer and there, in the harsh light of the unshaded bulb, stood the tall crates, the travel-beaten trunks of all shapes and sizes, all standing there faithfully waiting like the old friends they are. They had served me well; but what is their worth now? I thought of Dante who, before his death, unpacked everything, leaving his illusions exposed to the elements. In time, dust, dirt and water rotted the show away until there was little left.

I think that the old props deserve a better fate than that. It is true that although they are invaluable to the magician, they are worth nothing to anyone else. Just a lot of wood, metal and glass that comprised the priceless secrets of the man who conceived them. A fantastic world of mystery and illusion are locked in those old crates. Their rusty hinges and old shipping labels, covered with dust and grime, tell a story of high adventure. This book is their story and is dedicated to those old friends of so many years, who gave pleasure and joy to hundreds of thousands. With one last nostalgic glance I switch off the light and return to my study to look back over the years—and finally come to the conclusion that I must go on. After all, it is my life.

This morning a telegram came from an impresario of a theatre in town, asking me if I was interested in a season for 1965-66, and did I have a new gimmick?

To be honest I haven't the slightest idea what to do; but the only way to find out is to put a clean sheet of paper in the typewriter and with my two-fingered technique write those magic words.

"Act One. Scene One."—and pray that I won't get stuck on that second act again.

NOTES ON CHAPTERS

Chapter 2

p. 4   **Harry Kellar** (1849-1922) was the first great American-born illusionist. He turned his show over to Howard Thurston in 1908.

p. 4   **Frederick Eugene Powell** (1856-1938), a veteran American magician, succeeded Kellar as Dean of the Society of American Magicians.

p. 4   **Bernard M.L. Ernst** (1879-1938), Harry Houdini's attorney and close friend, succeeded Houdini as president of the Society of American Magicians in 1926.

p. 4   **Samuel Leo Horowitz** (1894-1971) was an outstanding sleight of hand performer.

p. 4   **Harry Houdini** (Erich Weiss, 1874-1926), the celebrated escape artist, has been called the greatest showman of the vaudeville era.

p. 5   **William J. "Doc" Nixon** (William J. Dixon, 1884-disappeared 1939) had a long career in vaudeville.

p. 6   **Howard Thurston** (1869-1936) performed around the world before succeeding Kellar with the nation's top magic road show attraction.

p. 6   **William Nicola** (William Mozart Nicol, 1880-1946) was particularly successful in his tours of the Orient with a large illusion show.

p. 6   **Charles J. Carter** (1974-1936), an American magician, made a notable success in England in 1910 and traveled the world with a large show, often playing in opposition to Nicola.

p. 6   **Maurice Raymond** (Morris Raymond Saunders, 1877-1948) was an American who, like Nicola and Carter, toured the world with his magic show.

p. 6   **Horace Goldin** (Hyman Goldstein, 1873-1939) was born in Poland and immigrated to the United States. He became a leading variety performer with his rapid-fire illusions.

p. 6   **Buatier de Kolta** (Joseph Bautier, 1847-1903), born in France, was one of the greatest magical inventors.

p. 6   **Servais Le Roy** (1865-1953) was a Belgian who grew up in England and became an outstanding inventor and international performer.

p. 6   **Percy Selbit** (1881-1938) was the stage name of P. T. Tibbles, an English variety performer and inventor of many widely used illusions.

p. 6   **Oswald Williams** (1880-1937), an inventive English magician, succeeded David Devant as the principal conjurer for Maskelyne's Mysteries at St. George's Hall.

p. 6   **Paul Valadon** (Adolph Waber, 1869-1913), a German magician, became featured performer at Maskelyne's Egyptian Hall and subsequently joined the Kellar show in America.

p. 6   **Owen Clark** (1877-1929), another highly original English magician, appeared for many years at St. George's Hall.

p. 6   **Louis Nikola** (Walter J. Obree Smith, 1878-1936) made his debut at St. George's hall in 1908. He performed in many parts of the world and is widely know for his magical inventions.

p. 6   **John Nevil Maskelyne** (1839-1917) founded the theatrical enterprise which provided ''England's Home of Mystery'' for over sixty years.

Chapter 4

p. 14   **Eliaser Bamberg and Pinetti.** A playbill announcing the appearance of ''A. L. Bamberg'' in Berlin in 1823, reproduced in J. B. Findlay's *Eighth Collectors Annual - International Guide to Posters & Playbills* (Shanklin, Isle of Wight, 1972), states that the performer was a pupil of Pinetti.

p. 15 **Kircher.** See Erik Barnouw, *The Magician and the Cinema,* Oxford University Press, New York-Oxford, 1981, p. 16. "The magic lantern...had been discussed by the Jesuit scholar Athanasium Kircher in the 1646 edition of his book *Ars Magna Lucis et Umbrae* (The Great Art of Light and Shadow) and it was described in detail in 1659 by the Dutch scientist Christian Huygens."

p. 15 **"Servante."** This French word meaning a servant-girl or dumb-waiter has been adopted by magicians as a technical term for a hidden receptacle into which the conjurer may drop objects secretly or quietly remove them prior to their coming into view "magically."

p. 16 **Okito's deafness.** In *Okito on Magic* (page 31), Theo Bamberg ascribed his deafness to "a mishap incurred while swimming."

p. 16 **Jean Eugene Robert-Houdin** (1805-1871) was the most important French magician of the nineteenth century. His style of presentation greatly influenced Tobias and David Tobias Bamberg.

p. 16 **Johann Nepomuk Hofzinser** (1806-1875) was an outstandingly original Viennese magician, many of whose tricks were adopted, with his permission, by Compars Herrmann (1816-1887), skillful German conjurer and brother of Alexander Herrmann (1844-1896). As "Herrmann the Great," Alexander became the leading American magician of his day.

Chapter 5

p. 18 **The Mat Trick,** which Okito used to conclude his act, involved a tremendous production of silks, flowers, and livestock from a mat which was formed into a tube and suspended above the stage.

p. 19 **Aga** is a form of human levitation depending upon a supporting rod from beneath the stage.
Asrah is a levitation illusion in which the subject rises while covered by a cloth, only to vanish in thin air.

p. 19 Magical entertainments were presented at the **Egyptian hall** in Piccadilly under the direction of Maskelyne and Cook from 1873 to 1905, when the Hall was torn down. The programs continued at

St. George's Hall under the direction of Maskelyne and Devant from 1905 to 1915. Thereafter, as Maskelyne's Mysteries, the shows continued under the Maskelyne family.

p. 19   **Charles Bertram** (James Bassett, 1853-1907), a leading London society entertainer known as the "King's Conjurer," was reported to have performed before King Edward VII twenty-two times (Sidney W. Clarke in *The Sphinx,* January 1936). He appeared occasionally at the Egyptian Hall.

p. 19   **The Entranced Fakir** was the name of the sketch in which Maskelyne's remarkable levitation illusion was first presented at the Egyptian Hall on April 6, 1901. It remained a feature into the following year. David may be using poetic license in describing a 1903 visit to the show by Bertram and the two Bambergs. Their reaction to the illusion, however, is precisely that described by Theo in *Okito on Magic* (p. 21).

Chapter 6

p. 22   **Wilfred Zelka** (W. F. Clarke) served as business manager for the Servais Le Roy Company. He died in 1935.

p. 22   **B. Bretma** (Bert Brown) was an English craftsman, stage manager, and magic dealer. He died in 1936.

p. 22   **Percy Naldrett** (1888-1973) was a printer and poet in Portsmouth, England, and the author of a series of books on magic.

p. 22   **Max Sterling** (J. G. E. MacLachlan, 1870-1941) was a music hall performer, author, and editor.

p. 22   **Arnold De Biere** (Arnold Bere, 1878-1934) was an American who played the English music halls with a large illusion show, but was best known for his performance of smaller tricks such as the Egg Bag and the Vanishing Birdcage.

p. 22   **Chung Ling Soo** (William E. Robinson, 1861-1918) was an American performer who made a great success in England and Europe with an elaborate Oriental act. He died as the results of an apparent accident in the performance of the Bullet Catching Trick.

p. 22   **Carmo** (Harry Cameron, 1881-1944), an Australian, played in England for many years with a spectacular illusion show.

p. 22 **Carl Rosini** (John Rose, circa 1885-1969), born in Poland, began his magical career in England and came with Harry Lauder to America, where he became a featured vaudeville act.

p. 22 **Raffaelo Chefalo** (1885-1963) was an Italian magician who played throughout the world.

p. 22 **Rameses** (Albert Marchinski, 1876-1930), an English performer, presented illusions in an Egyptian setting.

p. 22 **Fred Culpitt,** an English music hall performer and author, invented the widely used illusion of producing a woman from a doll house. He died in 1944.

p. 26 **Moira** is defined in the Random House Dictionary (New York, 1966) as "the personification of fate." Bergen Evans' *Dictionary of Mythology* (Dell Publishing Co., Inc., New York, 1970) says that The Fates, called in Greek *Moerae*, were the controllers of individual destinies and were conceived as old women who were present at every birth. There were three of them, each with a special function.

Chapter 7

p. 29 **Guy Jarrett** (1881-1972) was an eccentric mechanic and illusion builder who joined the Thurston show for the 1910-11 season, the same year Okito became a member of the company. Jarrett worked for Thurston only one season. The comments with which David took issue are in the book, *Jarrett Magic and Stagecraft, Technical* (1936), republished in 1981 by Magic Inc., Chicago, with much additional material by Jim Steinmeyer.

Chapter 8

p. 31 **Robert Heller** (William Palmer, 1829-1878) was an English magician who was particularly successful in America. Although they were contemporaries, Alexander Herrmann, in effect, succeeded Heller as the nation's most popular wizard, and Kellar, in turn, gained preeminence in the field after the death of Herrmann.

p. 33 **The Levitation cradle** was, of course, the concealed support for the "floating lady." Although it may seem mundane, the principle of employing many wires in a configuration which rendered them invisible on a well-lighted stage was one of the great discoveries in the history of magical stagecraft.

p. 34 **Lafayette** (Siegmund Neuberger, 1872-1911) was a German-born American who toured with a spectacular show that featured quick changes, impersonations, and illusions. He died in a theatre fire in Edinburgh.

p. 34 **David Devant** (David Wighton, 1868-1941) was recognized as England's greatest magician. He became a partner of John Nevil Maskelyne.

p. 35 **Chung Ling Soo's piercing-arrow trick** was an illusion in which an arrow attached to a ribbon was apparently shot through a woman.

p. 40 **Kalanag** (Helmut Schreiber, 1903-1963) was a German film director prior to taking out a magic show after World War II.

p. 41 **Tampa** (Raymond S. Sugden, 1888-1939), who headed the Thurston Number Three Show in 1926, later became a radio broadcaster in Pittsburgh.

p. 41 **Dante** (Harry Jansen, 1883-1955), an outstanding showman, developed his "Thurston unit" into one of the world's major illusion shows.

p. 41 **Carl Rosini's Tavma,** introduced in 1926, involved the apparent dismemberment of a woman garbed as a doll. In the end, the torso proved full of gears and wheels. Was Tavma a woman or a machine? (Arthur Leroy in *The Sphinx,* March 1951.)

Chapter 9

p. 44 **Will Goldston** (1878-1948), a London magic dealer, was the author of many books, including two volumes whose covers were secured with padlocks to protect the secrets disclosed therein.

p. 44 **C. Lang Neil** was the author of a classic text on conjuring, *The Modern Conjurer and Drawing-Room Entertainer* (C. A. Person, Ltd., London, 1902).

p. 44 **Professor Hoffmann** (Angelo John Lewis, 1839-1919) was an English barrister and amateur magician whose three major works, *Modern Magic* (1876), *More Magic* (1889), and *Later Magic* (1904), are fundamental texts on conjuring.

p. 44 **Mme. Adelaide Herrmann** (1854-1932) had a long career in vaudeville following the death of her husband, Alexander Herrmann.

p. 44 **Ching Ling Foo** (Chee Ling Qua, 1854-1922) was the first Chinese magician to become a headliner in English and American variety. He was featured in the "Ziegfeld Follies of 1912" and last played in America in 1915. He died in China.

p. 44 **Dr. Samuel C. Hooker** (1864-1935) was an inventive amateur magician whose effects baffled well-informed magicians. A chemist of English birth and education, his professional career was spent in America.

p. 46 **T. Nelson Downs** (1867-1938) built his internationally successful act, "The Miser's Dream," around the manipulation of half dollars.

Chapter 10

p. 52 **Harry Sears** may not have disappeared as completely as was then believed. In *The Sphinx* for March 1929, the editor, Dr. Wilson, wrote: "Harry Sears, who 20 years ago was one of the best vaudeville magicians on the stage, is now the owner of a gold mine in California and tells me he is prospering and out of magic as a profession."

p. 54 **Ziska and King,** consisting of Paul Ziska (William Griffin) and Louis King, were a standard act in American vaudeville. Ziska died in 1926.

p. 54 **Frank Van Hoven** (1886-1929) was a vaudeville headliner with his comedy turn as "The Dippy Mad Magician" in which everything went wrong.

Chapter 11

p. 56 **Paul Rosini** (Paul Vucci, 1902-1948) was born in Trieste and immigrated to the United States. He was a superb sleight of hand performer and outstanding as a night club entertainer.

p. 60 **John Mulholland** (1898-1970) presented his magic primarily in the lecture field and through private engagements. An authority on the history of magic, he possessed one of the great collections of books related to conjuring. He edited *The Sphinx,* "An

Independent Magazine for Magicians," for twenty-three years.

p. 62 **Frank Lascelles,** lord of the manor at Sibford Gower, Oxford, where he was born, was a noted sculptor whose subjects included the Prince of Wales, the Duke of Connaught, the Aga Khan, and Earl Grey (for the Parliament buildings at Ottawa). He gained renown as a designer and director of pageants, having served as master-in-chief at the British Empire exhibition in 1924, as well as for earlier festivals held at Oxford, Quebec, and Cape Town. He died in poverty in Brighton on May 24, 1934. According to the *New York Times* obituary, friends attributed much of his financial plight to excessive generosity.

Chapter 13

p. 74 **Linga Singh** (A. N. Dutt, 1884-1937), an Englishman, performed as an Indian wonder worker.

p. 74 **Jardine Ellis** was a Scot named Duncan Lorne Campbell. His original tricks, performed without elaborate apparatus, and his individual style of misdirection mystified magicians as well as laymen. He died in 1923, "a comparatively young man," according to George Johnson, London magic publisher.

p. 75 **Allan Shaw** (1875-1953), an Australian magician, performed throughout the world with his coin act.

p. 75 **The Bangkok Bungalow** was devised by Guy Jarrett for the Thurston Show. In this illusion a man disappeared by apparently shrinking in size and sneaking into a small doll house, which was carried off the stage.

p. 75 **Gus Fowler** (1888-1960) concluded his act with a stage filled with ringing alarm clocks.

p. 75 **Arnold De Biere,** see Notes on Chapter 6.

p. 75 **Billy O'Conner** (Eugene Devot, ca. 1895-1974) played the English halls with is "52 Assistants," a pack of cards.

p. 75 **Fred Culpitt,** see Notes on Chapter 6.

p. 75 **Chris Charlton** (1887-1963), billed as "Conjurer to H. M. King George the Fifth," presented an act featuring a magic tea kettle which poured any drink called for and the evanishment of a "bathing girl" from a cabinet suspended in midair.

p. 75 **Henry Hilton** presented an act of general magic concluding with the production and disappearance of four fish bowls. He died in 1956.

p. 76 **Henry Bate,** who had experience in making tricks for toy shops, was discovered by David Devant in Brighton in 1902 and became Devant's chief mechanic.

p. 76 **The Mascot Moth** involved the disappearance of a woman garbed as a moth. Introduced at St. George's Hall in 1905, it was revived in 1983 by Doug Henning in the Broadway musical, "Merlin."

p. 76 In the **Chocolate Soldier Illusion,** an assistant dressed as a toy soldier was reduced in size to a small doll, still marking time in military manner.

p. 76 In the **Artist's Dream,** a picture on canvas became a living woman who subsequently vanished.

p. 76 In the **Birth of Flora,** petals dropped into a bowl of fire were transformed into a woman surrounded by flowers.

p. 76 **The Enchanted Hive** was a sketch in which a detective, seeking the magician who is concealed under a hive, turns out to be the magician.

p. 76 **The Window of the Haunted House** was first presented by David Devant in 1911 and was subsequently revived by Noel Maskelyne. The illusion involved the production of a series of scenes acted in the window of a "haunted house" which stood in apparent isolation on a platform. At the conclusion, a fire burst out and two firemen stepped from the window in the act of rescuing a young lady.

p. 76 **Carlton** was the stage name of Arthur Philps (1881-1942).

p. 79 **Channing Pollock** is an American magician whose manipulative act featuring the production of doves (introduced in the 1950s) was widely imitated.

Chapter 14

p. 81 **The Silks and Soup Plate** is an effect originated by Buatier de Kolta. Okito's presentation of this classic has never been surpassed. Two white silk handkerchiefs, produced from the air, magically changed color, only to disappear and reappear beneath a soup plate. Okito's barehanded production of the two handkerchiefs, which spurted suddenly from the fingertips, was breathtaking.

of the great exponents of pure sleight of hand.

p. 109 **Evelyn Nesbit** (1885-1967) who gained notoriety when her husband, Harry Thaw, killed the prominent American architect, Standford White, in 1906, had a long career as a singer and dancer.

p. 111 **Mercedes** (Joe Cohen, 1888-1966) and his wife, "Mlle. Stantone" (Nellie L. Clement), headlined in vaudeville with an act in which musical selections whispered to Mercedes by spectators were immediately played on the piano by Mlle. Stantone.

p. 111 **The Svengali Trio,** headed by Hugo Lorenzo and his wife, Ella, played in the United States and Europe from the turn of the century until around 1925 with an act in which two performers on stage impersonated individuals and sang songs in response to requests whispered to Lorenzo.

p. 111 **Alexander** (Claude Conlin, 1872-1954), billed as "The Man Who Knows," was one of the most successful of the vaudeville magician-mind readers.

p. 112 **Max Holden** (William Holden Maxwell 1884-1949) was a versatile performer who featured hand shadows in colors. He later had magic shops in New York City and Boston.

Chapter 19

p. 118 **Frank Ducrot** (T. Francis Fritz, 1872-1939) was a versatile magician and for many years a New York magic dealer.

p. 119 **Al Baker** (1874-1951), a remarkably clever magician and humorist, was the inventor of subtle methods adopted by many other magicians.

p. 119 **Dr. A. M. Wilson** (1854-1930), a Kansas City physician and amateur magician, was for twenty-six years editor of the American magic journal, *The Sphinx.*

p. 119 **Dorny** (Werner Dornfield, 1892-1982) played in vaudeville with magic and comedy and gained fame as a magical master of ceremonies.

p. 119 **Fred Keating** (1897(?)-1961) starred in vaudeville and revues with his magic and wit and acted on Broadway and in motion pictures.

Chapter 20

p. 123 **Ottokar Fischer** (1873-1940) was a notable Viennese magician, author, and authority on the magic of J. N. Hofzinser.

p. 124 **The Tarbell Course in Magic** by Harlan Tarbell (1890-1960), a Chicago magician and commercial artist, was initiated as a correspondence course in 1926 and completed in 1928. It has been republished in expanded form by Louis Tannen, New York City. The Fischer-Bamberg Packing Box Escape is described on pages 301-306 of Volume VI, published in 1954.

Chapter 21

p. 126 **Grock** (Karl Adrien Wettach, 1880-1959), a Swiss, became known as "King of Clowns." Grock, Okito, and Alfredo Codona, the brilliant Mexican-born aerialist, once starred together—three perfectionists—in the same theatre in Vienna, according to Donald Bamberg.

p. 126 **Charlie Rivels,** the great Spanish clown, was reported still to be working in 1979 at the age of 83.

Chapter 22

p. 136 **Li-Ho Chang** (Juan Jose Pablo Jesorum, 1889-1972), a Panamanian of Chinese ancestry, played throughout the world with an elaborate show. He was reported to have closed his large production in Spain in 1955 and continued thereafter with a smaller show.

Chapter 24

p. 154 **The Great George** (Grove G. George, 1887-1958) was an American magician who had considerable success in Latin America.

Chapter 25

p. 156 **Dante's Barber Shop Illusion** ("The Un-Sevilled Barber") involved a comedy sketch which culminated in Dante, as the barber, magically changing places with the man he was shaving.

p. 156 **Backstage** purported to give the audience a

Chapter 29

p. 185   **The Bridal Chamber** illusion involved the production of an appropriately garbed woman with a completely furnished boudoir from a curtained cabinet which was initially shown empty.

p. 186   **Max Malini** (Max Katz, 1873-1942) traveled about the world with great success, especially in the entertainment-hungry outposts of European colonies.

p. 188   In **Malini's Card Stabbing** routine, the performer located selected cards in a deck scattered upon a table, stabbing the correct cards with a knife while blindfolded.

p. 189   In the **Indian Sand Trick,** colored sands were mixed in a bowl of water. Sand of the separate colors was then extracted and allowed to stream in a dry condition from the magician's hand.

p. 189   **The Dizzy Limit** illusion, invented by Oswald Williams, produced the mid-air evanishment of a woman in a hammock.

p. 190   **Amac** (Robert William MacFarland, 1890-1961) built his entire vaudeville act around Find the Lady. He apparently had left the field by the time David Bamberg developed his version of the illusion.

p. 190   *Greater Magic* by John Northern Hilliard, published by Carl Waring Jones, Minneapolis, 1938, is a classic treatise on magic. Hilliard, for many years advance publicist for the Thurston Show, died before the work consisted of much more than rough notes. Jean Hugard, an Australian magician and author who retired in Brooklyn, NY, completed the book. David Bamberg contributed a chapter on stage presentation.

Chapter 34

p. 234   **Floyd Thayer** (1877-1959) was an expert wood turner who became a leading manufacturer of magical apparatus in Los Angeles.

p. 234   **Caryl Fleming** (1890-1940) a California banker and an amateur magician, played a prominent part in West Coast magical organizations.

p. 234   **Laurie Ireland,** a sleight of hand expert and

craftsman, was a Chicago magic dealer. He died in 1954.

p. 234 **Charles E. Miller** (1909-1989) was recognized since he was in his early twenties as one of America's most accomplished sleight of hand performers.

p. 234 **Dariel Fitzkee** (1898-1977) wrote numerous books on magic, including a basic text on misdirection, the technique of manipulating the attention of an audience.

p. 234 **William Larsen, Sr.** (1904-1953), a Los Angeles attorney and inventor of tricks, founded the conjuring journal, *Genii,* in 1936.

p. 234 **Harry Mendoza,** (1905-1970), a prominent California magician, provided magical sequences in various motion pictures.

p. 237 **Theodore Annemann** (Theodore John Squires, 1907-1942) was known for the invention and performance of magical effects with psychic themes and for his dramatic presentation of the Bullet Catching feat. He edited and published *The Jinx,* a periodical for magicians, from 1934 to 1942.

p. 239 **Jack Gwynne** (1895-1969) presented a vaudeville and nightclub act which featured astonishing productions culminating in the appearance of a tall stack of glass bowls filled with water and goldfish. The production box referred to by Bamberg was probably a set of hinged boards resting flat upon a tray. They were quickly pulled up to form a box from which a very large rabbit was produced.

Chapter 36

p. 250 **Dorothy Wolf** was secretary to John Mulholland, editor of *The Sphinx,* and served as business manager of the magazine. She died in 1965.

p. 251 **U. F. Grant** (Ulysses Frederick Simpson Grant, 1901-1978) was a magic dealer and inventor of tricks.

p. 252 **Al Baker,** see Notes on Chapter 19.

p. 252 **Richard Cardini** (Richard Valentine Pitchford, 1896-1973) created one of the great variety acts of all time in the character of a bemused Englishman manipulating cards, billiard balls, and lighted cigarettes.

p. 252 **Arthur Finlay** was a member of the inner circle of New York card experts.

p. 252 **Paul Fox,** an inventor of conjuring methods, died in 1976.

p. 252 **S. Leo Horowitz,** see Notes on Chapter 2.

p. 252 **J. Warren Keene** a vaudeville performer who featured card tricks, died in 1945.

p. 252 **Nate Leipsig** (1873-1939) was highly successful in vaudeville with an act of pure sleight of hand.

p. 252 **Max Malini,** see Notes on Chapter 29.

p. 252 **Charles E. Miller,** see Notes on Chapter 34.

p. 252 **Garrick M. Spencer** was a close friend of the adepts of pure sleight of hand in an around New York City. He died in 1942.

p. 252 **D. W. Vernon,** see notes on Chapter 18.

p. 252 **"Do as I Do"** is a trick in which cards selected by the magician and a spectator match.

p. 252 **The Brain Wave Trick,** developed by Dai Vernon, provides a means of apparently predicting the card that a spectator will name.

p. 252 **The French Drop** is a standard sleight for the evanishment of a small object.

p. 254 **Departure from the United States.** In *The Sphinx* for July 1937. John Mulholland wrote: "On Friday evening, June 11th, S. Leo Horowitz, Dai Vernon, Chang [and I] and our wives spent the evening with Mr. and Mrs. David Bamberg and their son, Robert. It was a nice party but all evening there was an undercurrent of sadness because it was the eve before the sailing of David Bamberg back to the Latin American countries. Fu Manchu with his beautiful show was an artistic and financial success during his stay in America, but the conditions under which he had to work, the almost continuous performances, the Union rules, and this, that and the other, were so different from his work in South America that he decided work in America was not worth the gruelling effort. David Bamberg will be missed in America."

Chapter 37

p. 260 **The Million Dollar Mystery** was an illusion developed by P. T. Selbit (see Notes on Chapter 2) based on a principle devised by an English showman, Walter Cerretta Jeans (Walter Janes, 1877-1942). A series of curious happenings occurred in relation to a small, cubical cabinet. These included the production of water from an empty bucket placed within the cabinet, the production of great numbers of ping pong balls and balloons, the pushing of a rectangular box through a side door of the cabinet, compressing it into space much too small to contain it, the withdrawal of the rectangular box through the front door of the cabinet and the production of a man from the box, and, finally, the transformation of the man into a woman.

Chapter 38

p. 276   *The Life and Mysteries of the Celebrated Dr. "Q".* (Alexander, Los Angeles 1921, reprinted 1946 by Nelson Enterprises, Columbus, Ohio) was an expose of the methods of fraudulent mindreaders and mediums. The author, C. Alexander (see Notes on Chapter 18), attributed the information to a Dr. "Q" whom he encountered while performing in Tegucigalpa, Honduras. The magic dealer, Floyd Thayer, used the Dr. "Q" name to identify some of his products.

Chapter 39

p. 280   **The Vampire** illusion, also known as Creo, was associated with Richard Boehlke (1874-1923), who performed under the name of Herr Bolke. Frazee (William Meyenberg) writes in the November 1945 issue of *The Sphinx* that the illusion actually was invented by the Todd brothers of Philadelphia, who worked it until one of the brothers died and the other gave up the act. It involved the construction of a clothes dummy which changed into a living woman. In the illusion sketch, Battle of the Toy Soldiers, a dummy soldier's head was placed on a tripod formed by three rifles and a cloak was wrapped around the structure. The dummy came to life, while the magician disappeared at the shot of a cannon. When the soldier removed his false head, he turned out to be the magician.

Chapter 40

p. 306   **The Banknote and Orange** sketch was performed with the assistance of a small boy and girl from the audience. All of the actions were performed by the girl as instructed by the "movie director." In the course of events, a borrowed banknote which had been sealed in an envelope and burned was found in an orange held by someone in the audience. The girl was promised an "Oscar" for her performance.

p. 307   In the **card manipulation and sling-shot bit,** David appeared to have difficulty getting the spotlight to follow him while he manipulated playing cards. Finally he abandoned the cards and appeared to fire at the spotlight with a sling-shot, resulting in a loud crash and a blackout.

p. 306   **The Thief of Bagdad** was a trick using a large sheet of glass with a small hole in the center. The glass was placed in a stand and secured by a long ribbon threaded through the front and the back doors of the stand as well as through the hole in the glass. When David was about to steal the glass magically from the frame, the argument in the theatre box ensued, followed by the dummy being thrown to the stage. When the audience recovered they saw David holding the glass in his hand, while the ribbon remained threaded through the stand.

Chapter 41

p. 322   **Weller beer bottles** were collapsible latex bottles expertly crafted by Charles S. Weller (1878-1953), an American manufacturer of magician's supplies.

p. 322   **Robert Bamberg** became Professor and Chairman of the Department of English at Kent State University, Kent, Ohio.

p. 322   **The Brunel White Hat,** named for its English inventor, was a derby hat which appeared empty although it contained a "load" (concealed objects for subsequent production).

Chapter 42

p. 324   **Francis Carlyle** (Francis Finneran, 1911-1975) was an entertaining performer and an expert with cards.

p. 324   **Dr. Stanley Jaks** (Siegmund Jaks-Stanley, 1903-1960) was born in Germany and spent much of his life in Switzerland before coming to the United States in 1946. He specialized in close-up magic and mental mysteries.

p. 324   **Milbourne Christopher,** (1914-1984) was a performer, author, and authority on the history of magic.

p. 328   **Eva Peron** (Maria Eva Ibarguren Duarte, 1919-1952) had more than a peripheral effect on the life and times of David Bamberg. In a letter (slightly edited) to Robert Lund, David wrote: ''In 1937 I was playing the old Boedo Theatre in Buenos Aires and one of my girls left the show for some reason and I phoned a girl friend of mine to take her place as a dancer and assistant. This girl showed up with a blonde friend whom she introduced as Eva Duarte and asked me to take her, too, as she needed the work. For some unholy reason, I refused as I only needed one girl. (Where my crystal ball was I'll never know.) So this blonde gives me an ugly look and that was that. I left the Argentine...and made a tour of Latin American....

''When I came back in 1950 the Peron government was turning into a dictatorship. There was a lot of talk about Peron's wife and the control she had, together with her brother, Juan Duarte. One day I met my girl friend again and she reminded me of her pal back in 1937. I nearly died. The blonde was now the controlling power in this country. I had forgotten the whole thing. But Eva didn't. She had a long memory. Once she was in a small bar with a girl friend, Libertad Lemarque, an actress. They got into an argument and Libertad slapped her face and walked out. An Argentine tango singer named Hugo Del Carril came in and found her crying and bought her a cup of cafe. That cafe was his passport to the control of the movie industry years later.'' [According to John Barnes' biography, *Evita - First Lady* (Grove Press, New York 1978), Libertad Lemarque introduced Eva to Colonel Juan Domingo Peron in

1944. The slapping incident was said to have occurred on a movie set when Eva took over the chair bearing Libertad's name. Libertad was subsequently forced into exile and her films banned in Argentina.]

"Eva didn't forget. She didn't forget me, either. In 1951, I was at the Smart Theatre and a phone call came thru from the Presidential Palace in Olivos. Would Mr. Fu be so good as to give a show for the First Lady there and what would he charge.

"Mr. Fu would be delighted and there was no question of a charge. So Mr. Fu hikes it out to Olivos and gives the show. Peron watched with interest, but his wife turned her back and talked constantly to Mercante, the Governor of the Province of Buenos Aires.

"A few days later, another phone call. Would Mr. Fu be so good as to give a show for the children in the Alvear Theatre in the morning? Fu did the show in the morning. So it went until the payoff. At the close of the season in the Smart Theater, the show was suddenly interrupted by some men walking up onto the stage and presenting Mr. Fu with the Eva Peron Gold Medal, thus indicating his affiliation with the party. If you know anything of Latin American politics, you will realize what a tough spot I was in. Half the audience were contra and half were Peronistas. I had to make a speech of thanks. I had to think quickly, too. So I said, in brief, that I was grateful for another attention from the Gran Nacion Argentina (the Great Argentine Nation). This satisfied the audience but not the secretary of the party. After the show, he asked me why I hadn't specifically mentioned the President's name or his wife's. I told him I had specifically mentioned the Gran Nacion Argentina and that I believed that this included both of them. He studied me for a while. 'You are English, I believe. A nation of diplomats.' I thanked him and we parted with mutual assurances of esteem. But I got the hell out of B.A. and went on tour."

p. 329   **Khelmis** may have been David's most remarkable

female assistant. In a letter to Robert Lund dated December 1, 1963, he told a slightly different story of their initial encounter, along with the wildly romantic sequel. "One summer night in 1951 I was eating after the show in a restaurant on the Calle Corrientes when Khelmis walked in. She wore a long white badly made evening dress with some awful artificial flowers, they had ruined her hair trying to make her an ash blonde and it had a strawlike texture, her nails were extremely long and painted gold, but she was so goddam beautiful that everyone stared at her. I asked my waiter who she was. . . . It seems she was. . .a special protege of Alaria who made such a sensation in Paris years later. I sent her a note via the waiter and she came to my table and I asked her if she would be interested in assisting me in my show. So she became my assistant. . .I found in her a strange mixture. Extremely valorous, intelligent and stupid at the same time, a tremendous interest in the show and a remarkable personality. By this time she had her natural hair back again, a soft and silky dark blonde, out were the trick nails and the paint job and she looked what she was—just a kid of 19 with a grudge against the world. But anyway she wasn't the gilded lily anymore. And so we went up the west coast and in Medellin, Colombia, I disbanded the show and opened that goddam color studio for the Eastman Color Process. I am no business man and I lost money again. I had bought a house on a hill overlooking the city and we were all alone in the Colombia hill country. One evening after one of our horrible arguments I asked her what made her such a little bastard and she answered, 'I'm satan's daughter.' I loved that and was inspired to write the play 'Satan's Daughter' which was written for her. I sent the manuscripts to Mexico and they sent me fares and expenses to open in Mexico City. The show cost me $14,000 to produce and it was a smash hit in Mexico. She was wonderful in it. . . .

"So we went to Costa Rica and Venezuala where she got mixed up in a goddam plot against

Perez-Jimeniz and some lousy bullfighters. From there we went to Havana and she paraded around town with a cub tiger they had given her in Caracas. From there I went to North Africa and then came Barcelona. It was there that an Italian Countess fell in love with her. Countess Carla (an ex flame of Humberto of Italia) followed us all over Spain and in Madrid I saw Khelmis for the last time. I left for the Argentine and met Zaira, a Syrian-Lebanese woman and she became the second Satan's Daughter. Zaira died of cancer and I was pretty cut up. Then one night a little over a year ago, Chefalo arrived in B.A. He came to see the show at the Avenida Theatre and I was looking into the audience trying to find him and nearly dropped dead when I saw Khelmis sitting in the first row. This is the story she told me. The Countess Carla was the head of a smuggling ring that worked in Italy, the south of France and the Andorran Republic. They brought in their goods thru Andorra into Cataluna. (I had known that Carla was a contrabandista previously in Spain.) Khelmis joined the ring and had a high time for a couple of years. However, the Countess was murdered on a high road in Andorra when they shoved her car over a cliff with her in it. Khelmis returned to Barcelona without a dime. She got in touch with Cuchelli who has that magic store in the Calle Princessa and got him to teach her a few tricks and put on a nightclub act and went to Damascus. She also sang tangos and had a marvellous voice for that type of song. (I had seen rough miners in Asturias cry when she sang 'Nostalgia' and other Argentine tangos.) She floated around the Middle East for some time and married a Cypriot baron. But it didn't last and she went to Rome. She wouldn't talk about that episode but she returned to Buenos Aires. She had a little girl (Carla), a beautiful child. Khelmis returned a woman of the world—beautifully dressed, well mannered, marvelous taste, she had learned to speak Italian, Arabic and some French. She is far more beautiful now at 30 than when she was 19. But we couldn't make it a go. Something had snapped.''

p. 332 **P. C. Sorcar** (Pratul Chandra Sarcar, 1913-1971) of Calcutta and the German showman, Kalanag (see Notes on Chapter 8), carried on a feud in the magic journals concerning their stature in the field. They headed major illusion shows and were fervent publicists.

p. 332 **George McDonald Birch,** who was born in 1902 played throughout the United States for many years with a full-evening show. His version of the Hindu Rope Trick was published in the March 1951 issue of *The Sphinx.*

Chapter 44

p. 353 **Fred Kaps** (P. A. Bongers, 1926-1980), born in Holland, was one of the most original and accomplished of all sleight of hand performers.

Chapter 45

p. 354 **Tihanyi** (Franz Czeiler) was born in Hungary in 1916 and went to Brazil in 1953, where he created the Circo Magico Tihanyi.

p. 357 In the **Broom Illusion,** two brooms are placed beneath the armpits of an assistant who stands on a low stool. The stool is removed; so is one of the brooms. The assistant is then raised to a horizontal position and remains suspended with only an elbow or shoulder touching the broomstraws. The suspension in this form (but performed with canes rather than brooms) was introduced by Robert-Houdin in 1847.

p. 357 **Multum-In-Parvo** involves the pouring of a glass of liquid into successively smaller glasses without loss of fluid. The trick was invented by Benson Dulay of England and Tan Hock Chuan of Singapore.

p. 358 **Chop-Chop** (Albert H. Wheatley) was born in Australia and came to the United States in 1906. He also worked under the name of Tung Pin Soo, presenting a colorful magic act in Chinese costume. He died in 1964.

p. 359 **Virgil** (Virgil Harris Mulkey), born in 1900 in Eugene, Oregon, played throughout the United States with a full-evening show and made a world tour in 1952. He died in 1989.

p. 360 **Roy Benson** (1915-1978) was a superb magician and monologist who performed in vaudeville and night clubs.

p. 360 **Death of Okito.** As Conan Doyle fans, David and his father frequently addressed each other as Holmes and Watson. Shortly before Okito's death, David wrote, "Holmes, I have a confession to make. I don't know who the hell I'm going to write to when you are gone. We think so much alike in things magical that it's going to be hard. Our kind of magic seems to be going out of existence. There were very few men I could really talk magic to. I remember Raymond, Chang and a few others that didn't like magic. They wouldn't talk about it. Real enthusiasts I very rarely found. . . . Outside of yourself there were very few professional magicians who could solve a problem on the drawing board."

p. 361 **The Lesson in Magic** is a series of magical surprises which begins with the mutilation of a gentleman's handkerchief and continues with the transformation of the handkerchief into a long strip of cloth and then into a lemon. The lemon is cut open and the handkerchief found inside, but in the process the center is cut out of the handkerchief. In an attempt to resolve matters, the center of the spectator's handkerchief and that of the performer's handkerchief become transposed. Ultimately the handkerchiefs are restored.

p. 361 **Goodliffe** (Charles Goodliffe Neale, 1912-1980) edited and published *Abracadabra,* the world's only magical weekly, founded in 1946. Publication of the journal continues under the editorship of Donald Bevan.

p. 361 **Henry Christ's Dead Man's Hand** (published in Annemann's *The Jinx* for June 1937) is a card trick which recreates the shooting of "Wild Bill" Hickock while playing poker with his back to the door.

p. 361 **Arthur Monroe's Voodo** (*The Jinx,* May 1937) takes place in a seance setting. In the glow of a dim green light, a box which was previously hidden by a spectator materializes in the magician's hands and its contents—a marked Chinese coin tied on a cord—is magically disengaged from the cord and dropped on the table. The box then disappears. The marked coin is identified and the box is subsequently found where it was hidden, but it now contains only the string which was tied around the coin.

p. 362 **Dai Vernon's Cutting the Aces** is explained along with its patter story, in the publication, *Stars of Magic,* Louis Tannen, New York 1961.

BIBLIOGRAPHY

Albo, Robert, Eric Lewis and David Bamberg, *Oriental Magic of the Bambergs.* San Francisco, House of Magic, 1973.

Albo, Robert, *Classic Magic Supplement II.* San Francisco, 1989. "The Illusion Show Completed," pp. 65-153.

Bamberg, David T., Letter from New York City. *The Sphinx* (April 1924), p. 50.

———, Letter from Vienna. *The Sphinx* (November 1924), p. 295.

———, Letter from Graz, Austria. *The Sphinx* (December 1924), pp. 322-323.

———, Letter from Nuremberg. *The Sphinx* (March 1925), p. 13.

———, Letter from Budapest. *The Sphinx* (May 1925), p. 95.

———, Letter from Paris. *The Sphinx* (October 1925), p. 238.

———, Letter from Buenos Aires. *The Sphinx* (February 1928), p. 471.

———, Letter from Buenos Aires. *The Sphinx* (August 1928) pp. 276-278.

———, "Magic's Deadly Enemy." *The Sphinx* (February 1929), p. 570.

———, "Great Artist—Okito." *The Sphinx* (April 1937), p. 44.

———, "The Growth of Flowers." *The Sphinx* (June 1937), p. 101.

———, "El Buen Companero." *The Sphinx* (December 1937), p. 295.

———, "The History of Magic and Magicians in Mexico." *The Sphinx* (May 1938), pp. 71-72.

———, "The Oracle." *The Sphinx* (June 1939), p. 98.

———, "The Weird Adventure of Dr. 'Q'." *The Sphinx* (December 1940), pp. 250-253.

_____, and Okito (Theo. Bamberg), "Hi-Strung." *The Sphinx* (March 1941), pp. 16-17.

_____, Carlos H. Colombi, and Graciela N. Avendana, "Variations on The Flower Cone." *The Sphinx* (March 1948), p. 6.

_____, "The Metiche." *The Sphinx* (May 1948), pp. 66, 80.

_____, "I Learn a Card Trick." *The Sphinx* (May 1949), pp. 76-77.

_____, "Fu's Rising Card." *The Sphinx* (October 1949), p. 192.

_____, "Letter to Harold" (Tribute to Al Baker). *The Sphinx* (January 1951), p. 255.

_____, "...For the Angels." *The Sphinx* (March 1951), pp. 30-34.

_____, "Don't Blame Magic." *The Sphinx* (March 1953), pp. 19-25.

Bamberg, Theodore, "One of the Bamberg Dynasty." *The Sphinx* (October 1945), pp. 214-217.

_____, with Robert Parrish, *Okito on Magic, Reminiscences and Selected Tricks.* Chicago, Edward O. Drane and Company, 1952; 2nd edition, Chicago, Magic Inc., 1973.

Blackstone, Harry, with Charles and Regina Reynolds, *The Blackstone Book of Magic and Illusion,* New York, Newmarket Press, 1985.

Briant, E. Leslie, "Fu Manchu's Crazimagicana." *The Sphinx* (April 1947), p. 55.

_____, "Behind the Scenes with Fu Manchu." *The Sphinx* (December 1947), pp. 316 and 326.

Christopher, Milbourne, *The Illustrated History of Magic,* New York. Thomas Y. Crowell Company, 1973.

Clark, A. Ren, "Fu Man Chu." *The Linking Ring* (February 1946), pp. 15-18, 74.

Columbi, Carlos H., "Fu Manchu—The Man and the Magician." *The New Tops* (February 1966), pp. 4-7.

Dawes, Edwin A., *The Great Illusionists.* Secaucus, New Jersey, Chartwell Books, Inc. 1979.

Devant, David, *My Magic Life.* London, Hutchinson & Co., Ltd., 1931.

_____, *Secrets of My Magic.* London, Hutchinson & Co., Ltd., 1936. These two Devant books are available in reprints published by The Supreme Magic Company, Bideford, Devon, England.

Findlay, J. B., *International Guide to Posters & Playbills* (Eighth Collectors Annual). Shanklin, Isle of Wight, published by the author, 1972.

Foster, Neil, "My Friend Fu Manchu." *The New Tops* (October 1974), pp. 11-12.

Furst, Arnold, *Famous Magicians of the World*. Los Angeles, The Genii Publishing Company, 1957.

Hilliard, John Northern, *Greater Magic, A Practical Treatise on Modern Magic*. Minneapolis, Carl Waring Jones, 1938.

Horowitz, S. Leo, "Fu Manchu." *The Sphinx* (June 1952), pp. 96-99.

Jarret, Guy, *Jarrett*. Guy Jarrett's 1936 *Jarrett Magic and Stagecraft, Technical* with additional material by Jim Steinmeyer, Chicago, Magic Inc., 1981.

Martinez, Enrique Jimenez, "Films of Fu Manchu." *The Linking Ring* (September 1977), pp. 46-49.

Mulholland, John, *Story of Magic*. New York, Loring & Mussey, 1935.

_____, "The Chuang Chin." *The Sphinx* (May 1948), p. 67.

Nelson, Robert (editor), *Sensational Mentalism*. Columbus, Ohio, Nelson Enterprises, 1965. ("Fu-TURE-Prediction," by David Bamberg).

Olson, Robert E., *Illusion Builder to Fu Manchu. A Tribute to Edmund Spreer*. Charlotte, N.C., Morris Costumes, 1986.

Pelaez, Cesareo and members of "Le Grand David and his own Spectacular Magic Company," *Lecture Notes*. Beverly, Massachusetts, White Horse Productions, Inc., 1987.

Price, David, *Magic, A Pictorial History of Conjurers in the Theater*. New York, London, Toronto, Cornwall Books, 1985.

Ransom, Elmer P., "David Bamberg (Fu Manchu)." *The Sphinx* (April 1937), p. 44.

Reynolds, Charles and Regina, *100 Years of Magic Posters*. New York, Grosset & Dunlap, 1976.

Robert-Houdin, Jean Eugene, *Confidences d'un prestidigitateur*. Blois, Lecesne, 1858.

_____, *Memoirs of Robert-Houdin* (translated by Dr. R. Shelton Mackenzie), Philadelphia, 1859. Recent edition: New York, Dover Publications, Inc., 1964.

Shevlin, Clay Hamilton, *Historian's Guide to Conjuring*, San Leandro, California, The Conjuring Historical Society, 1981.

Snader, Craige M., "Edmund Spreer: Master Show Mechanic and Creator of Illusions." *Magicol* (February 1977), pp. 2-5.

Tarbell, Harlan, *The Tarbell Course in Magic,* Volume IV. New York, Louis Tannen, 1945. (David Bamberg's "The Girl from the Light".)

———, *The Tarbell Course in Magic,* Volume V. New York, Louis Tannen, 1948. ("Magic of the Bambergs.")

———, *The Tarbell Course in Magic,* Volume VI. New York, Louis Tannen, 1954. ("Fu Manchu's Utility Bag," "Fischer-Bamberg Packing Box Escape," and "Fu Manchu's Magic Microphone.")

Vergonjeanne, Alberto, "The Last Year of Fu Manchu." *The New Tops* (December 1974), pp. 34-37.

Whaley, Bart, *Who's Who in Magic.* Oakland, California, Jeff Busby Magic, Inc., 1990.

INDEX

Page numbers in italics refer to "Notes On Chapters"